# AUTHORITY AND AUTHORITATIVE TEXTS IN THE PLATONIST TRADITION

All disciplines can count on a noble founder, and the representation of this founder as an authority is key in order to construe a discipline's identity. This book sheds light on how Plato and other authorities were represented in one of the most long-lasting traditions of all time. It leads the reader through exegesis and polemics, recovery of the past and construction of a philosophical identity. From Xenocrates to Proclus, from the sceptical shift to the re-establishment of dogmatism, from the Mosaic of the Philosophers to the Neoplatonist Commentaries, the construction of authority emerges as a way of access to the core of the Platonist tradition.

MICHAEL ERLER is Professor Ordinarius of Classical Philology at the Julius-Maximilians-Universität Würzburg. He is the author of several books and articles on Plato, Platonism, Epicurus and the Epicurean tradition, drama, and Hellenistic and Imperial literature.

JAN ERIK HEßLER is a Lecturer in the Department of Classics at the Julius-Maximilians-Universität Würzburg. He has published an edition of Epicurus' Letter to Menoeceus (2014), and co-edited *Argument und literarische Form in antiker Philosophie* (2013), as well as publishing numerous articles on the Platonic and Epicurean tradition.

FEDERICO M. PETRUCCI is Professor of Ancient Philosophy in Turin. His main research areas are Plato and the Platonist tradition, and his publications include the first English translation of the texts of the Platonist Taurus, in *Taurus of Beirut: The Other Side of Middle Platonism* (2018).

# AUTHORITY AND AUTHORITATIVE TEXTS IN THE PLATONIST TRADITION

EDITED BY

MICHAEL ERLER

*Julius-Maximilians-Universität Würzburg, Germany*

JAN ERIK HEẞLER

*Julius-Maximilians-Universität Würzburg, Germany*

FEDERICO M. PETRUCCI

*Università degli Studi di Torino, Italy*

WITH THE COLLABORATION OF

MICHAEL McOSKER

*Ohio Wesleyan University*

# CAMBRIDGE
## UNIVERSITY PRESS

University Printing House, Cambridge CB2 8BS, United Kingdom

One Liberty Plaza, 20th Floor, New York, NY 10006, USA

477 Williamstown Road, Port Melbourne, VIC 3207, Australia

314–321, 3rd Floor, Plot 3, Splendor Forum, Jasola District Centre, New Delhi – 110025, India

79 Anson Road, #06–04/06, Singapore 079906

Cambridge University Press is part of the University of Cambridge.

It furthers the University's mission by disseminating knowledge in the pursuit of education, learning, and research at the highest international levels of excellence.

www.cambridge.org
Information on this title: www.cambridge.org/9781108844000
DOI: 10.1017/9781108921596

© Cambridge University Press 2021

This publication is in copyright. Subject to statutory exception and to the provisions of relevant collective licensing agreements, no reproduction of any part may take place without the written permission of Cambridge University Press.

First published 2021

*A catalogue record for this publication is available from the British Library.*

ISBN 978-1-108-84400-0 Hardback

Cambridge University Press has no responsibility for the persistence or accuracy of URLs for external or third-party internet websites referred to in this publication and does not guarantee that any content on such websites is, or will remain, accurate or appropriate.

# *Contents*

| | |
|---|---|
| *List of Figures* | *page* vii |
| *List of Contributors* | viii |
| *Acknowledgements* | ix |
| *List of Abbreviations* | x |

Introduction     1
*Michael Erler, Jan Erik Heßler and Federico M. Petrucci*

1   Xenocrates' Invention of Platonism     12
    *David Sedley*

2   An Iconography of Xenocrates' Platonism     38
    *David Sedley*

3   Arcesilaus' Appeal to Heraclitus as a Philosophical Authority
    for His Sceptical Stance     64
    *Anna Maria Ioppolo*

4   Authority beyond Doctrines in the First Century BC: Antiochus'
    Model for Plato's Authority     89
    *Federico M. Petrucci*

5   Authority and Doctrine in the Pseudo-Pythagorean Writings     115
    *Bruno Centrone*

6   Constructing Authority: A Re-examination of Some
    Controversial Issues in the Theology of Numenius     130
    *Alexandra Michalewski*

7   Plutarch's *E at Delphi*: The Hypothesis of Platonic Authority     149
    *George Boys-Stones*

vi Contents

8 Aristotle's *Physics* as an Authoritative Work in Early
Neoplatonism: Plotinus and Porphyry 163
*Riccardo Chiaradonna*

9 Conflicting Authorities? Hermias and Simplicius on the Self-
Moving Soul 178
*Saskia Aerts*

10 *Kathēgemōn*: The Importance of the Personal Teacher
in Proclus and Later Neoplatonism 201
*Christian Tornau*

11 'In Plato we can see the bad characters being changed
by the good and instructed and purified.' Attitudes
to Platonic Dialogue in Later Neoplatonism 227
*Anne Sheppard*

*References* 245
*Index Locorum* 264
*General Index* 279

# *Figures*

1.1 Gaiser's reconstruction of the celestial sphere, adjusted for perspective. From K. Gaiser (1980), *Das Philosophenmosaik in Neapel. Eine Darstellung der platonischen Akademie*, Abhandlungen der Heidelberger Akademie der Wissenschaften, Phil.-hist. Klasse, Heidelberg. Reproduced courtesy of Winter Verlag.    *page* 35

2.1 *The Mosaic of the Philosophers*. Museo Archeologico Nazionale di Napoli 124545. Photo by Giorgio Albana. Reproduced by permission of Ministero per i Beni e le Attività Culturali – Museo Archeologico di Napoli.    40

2.2 *From the Academy to the Lyceum*, drawing by Candace H. Smith. From A.A. Long & D.N. Sedley (1987), *The Hellenistic Philosophers, Vol. 1: Translations of the Principal Sources with Philosophical Commentary*, Cambridge. Reproduced, with slight modification, courtesy of Candace H. Smith.    46

2.3 *The Sarsina Mosaic*. Rome, Villa Albani Torlonia. © Fondazione Torlonia. Reproduced with permission.    53

2.4 *Aratus and Urania*, mosaic. Rheinisches Landesmuseum Trier. Photo by Th. Zühmer. Reproduced courtesy of Die Generaldirektion Kulturelles Erbe Rheinland-Pfalz, Direktion Rheinisches Landesmuseum Trier.    57

# Contributors

SASKIA AERTS is a PhD student in Ancient Philosophy at KU Leuven.

GEORGE BOYS-STONES is Professor of Classics and Philosophy at the University of Toronto.

BRUNO CENTRONE is Professor of Ancient Philosophy at the University of Pisa.

RICCARDO CHIARADONNA is Professor of Ancient Philosophy at the Roma Tre University.

ANNA MARIA IOPPOLO is Professor Emerita of Ancient Philosophy at the Sapienza University of Rome.

ALEXANDRA MICHALEWSKI is a Research Fellow at the CNRS – Centre Léon Robin, Paris-Sorbonne.

FEDERICO M. PETRUCCI is Professor of Ancient Philosophy at the University of Turin.

DAVID SEDLEY is Emeritus Laurence Professor of Ancient Philosophy at the University of Cambridge.

ANNE SHEPPARD is Professor Emerita of Ancient Philosophy at Royal Holloway, University of London.

CHRISTIAN TORNAU is Professor of Classical Philology at the University of Würzburg.

# *Acknowledgements*

This volume has its roots in a conference held at the Institut für Klassische Philologie of the University of Würzburg in February 2017 and generously funded by the Thyssen Stiftung and the Faculty of Philosophy of the University of Würzburg. Some of the papers given at that conference were selected as the core of the present volume, while others were added upon invitation. A twin volume, *Authority and Authoritative Texts in the Epicurean Tradition*, with the same editors and stemming from the same conference, is now in preparation. As editors, we wanted different areas of scholarship to be represented, and we especially sought to combine papers by younger researchers with ones by more experienced scholars. For his expert proofreading, we would like to warmly thank Michael McOsker. The support of the Department of Classics and Ancient History of Durham University, of the Institute of Advanced Study at Durham University, and of the Department of Philosophy and Educational Sciences of the University of Turin has been fundamental for the realisation of this volume.

This volume is dedicated to the memory of
Anna Maria Ioppolo (1943-2020)

# *Abbreviations*

BS    Boys-Stones, G. (2018). *Platonist Philosophy 80 BC to AD 250. An Introduction and Collection of Sources in Translation.* Cambridge.

IP    Isnardi Parente, M. (1980). *Speusippo. Frammenti.* Naples.

IP²    Isnardi Parente, M. (2012). *Senocrate e Ermodoro. Testimonianze e frammenti.* 2nd ed., ed. T. Dorandi. Pisa.

L&S    Long, A.A. & Sedley, D. (1987). *The Hellenistic Philosophers.* Cambridge.

As a rule, references to ancient authors and works follow the *Oxford Classical Dictionary.*

# Introduction

## Michael Erler, Jan Erik Heßler and Federico M. Petrucci

> Plato came after all these: sent to us from the gods so that
> philosophy could through him be seen in its organic integrity.
> He left nothing out and perfected everything,
> neither falling short in what was necessary,
> nor carried away into anything useless
> (Atticus, fr. 1, trans. 1A BS)

If one had to provide a formal account of what 'being a Platonist' means, it would be tempting to refer to the broad idea that a Platonist is, in general, a follower of Plato, which implies a commitment to Plato's authority. After all, this would be a reasonable description for all heirs of Plato, from the Academics – the scholarchs of the Academy were in any case the successors of Plato, and claimed for themselves the privilege of this relationship – to late-antique Platonists, who regarded themselves as exegetes and interpreters of Plato's thought. Things are not that easy, however, for once one examines such a general account in detail a series of serious questions emerge. A first – and clearer – puzzle is related to the discontinuity of the tradition: while on the one hand one can say that there is a continuous stream of heirs of Plato from the Early Academy to late Neoplatonism, on the other it is quite obvious that, even admitting a strong continuity between Middle Platonism and Neoplatonism, the philosophical history of the 'Platonist tradition' from the Early Academy to the early Imperial Age hardly constitutes a unified whole. As a consequence, just stating that all followers of Plato were committed to his authority would amount to an empty and uninformative statement: the more one generalises the notion in order to make it comprehensive, the less it is specific and able to really include the distinguishing features of each stage of the tradition. So, the only way to make sense of this description is to systematically specify it on a case-by-case basis by asking when and in what form the idea of Plato's authority was produced, and what transformations it underwent throughout the tradition. Furthermore, notwithstanding the fact that all those who regarded themselves as Plato's heirs were committed to Plato's authority to some extent, this authority could either leave room for other important authorities or not, which in turn was crucial in order to shape specific conceptions of Plato's authority. In other words, the fact that Plato is an authority does not imply that, at each stage of the tradition, there is a single conception of authority, or that just one thinker – namely, Plato – is regarded as an authority. Finally, and most importantly, the fact that a thinker commits himself to the authority of Plato tells us nothing about the reasons why he did so, the function of this commitment, and the arguments (if any) he employed to sustain this claim. All in all, therefore, it emerges that if one wishes to really exploit the notion of authority as a way to access different stages of the Platonist tradition, specificity must be preferred to sensitivity, discontinuity to continuity, anomaly to homogeneity, debate to agreement. Such an enquiry into the notion of authority in the Platonist tradition has never been carried out, and the present volume fills this gap: it takes the aforementioned points as methodological boundaries and aims to produce a new narrative of the Platonist tradition by observing the different notions of authority and the different uses of authoritative texts which shaped it.

The narrative which this book develops is located within a well-established stream of studies. On the one hand, the Platonist tradition has been progressively made the object of extensive research concerning all periods of its development, from the Early Academy to late Neoplatonism, both in wide-ranging collections of papers (see, most recently, Tarrant et al. 2018) and editorial projects (especially the German *Der Platonismus in der Antike*), as well as in more focused, but still extensive, monographs. Indeed, studies on the philosophy of the Early Academy (e.g. Dillon 2003), the Hellenistic Academy (e.g. Brittain 2001 and Bonazzi 2003), Middle Platonism (Dillon 1977, and now Boys-Stones 2018a), and Neoplatonism (e.g. most recently, Gerson 2013 and d'Hoine & Martijn 2016) have highlighted specific, fundamental aspects of these philosophical movements. To put it briefly, the history of Platonism is currently a field of study in continuous expansion. On the other hand, scholarship has been progressively taking authority as a notion deserving a specific enquiry, both for its historical significance and its potentialities in revealing the commitments of intellectual movements or important authors. In this sense, authority proves a boundary-crossing notion, which can be examined both in itself, as an epistemological issue, or in relation to different fields of thought (see, most recently, Graßhoff & Meyer 2016 and König & Woolf 2017). In the latter case, it has proven particularly important in the

*Introduction* 3

consideration of ancient philosophical movements (see the papers collected in Bryan et al. 2018).

All this, however, represents more of a starting point for new research than a stable foundation. The point is *not only* that a comprehensive enquiry into the notion of authority in the Platonist tradition is still lacking, but that the notion of authority and its relation with those texts playing an important role in the Platonist tradition can shed light on the nature both of each stage in the tradition and of the tradition as a whole (only quite focused, yet fundamental, enquiries have appeared on specific stages of the tradition: see e.g. Sedley 1997, Ferrari 2001, Petrucci 2018: 146–97, Erler 2018, Boys-Stones 2018b; Opsomer & Ulacco 2016 represents a very intriguing attempt at defining epistemic authority with respect to social and historical dimensions, within the framework of a research project on the theme based at KU Leuven). More specifically, the assumption that a follower of Plato regards Plato as an authority potentially has the (much more promising) implication that, by discovering each follower's conception of Plato's authority, his or her strategies in relating Plato's authority to that of other thinkers, and the way in which these very conceptions and relations play an argumentative and constructive role in his or her thought, one is in a position to really understand crucial aspects of discontinuity and specificity within the Platonist tradition. In other words, if the focus is not on whether a follower of Plato is committed to Plato's authority, but rather on the real import of this commitment, its grounds and function, and the potential room left to other authorities, then it is possible to answer the following questions: What is the relationship between the representation of Plato's authority at a certain stage of the tradition and the philosophy characterising this particular stage? How is Plato's authority affected and reshaped by debates between the followers of Plato and other philosophies? Or, again, to what extent does the treatment of Plato's texts mirror a specific conception of the master's authority? The papers collected in this volume will answer these and related questions, thereby unravelling a new 'discontinuous' narrative of the Platonist tradition: paradoxically, the very fact of appealing to Plato's authority will prove a crucial and substantial element highlighting the philosophical peculiarities of different stages in the Platonist tradition.

\* \* \*

It is often assumed that a 'Platonist tradition' – as opposed, or at least contrasted, to the Academy – only really emerged in the early Imperial

Age. This might be correct from the point of view either of doctrines (i.e. the doctrines we usually identify as 'Platonist') or of self-representation (as is widely known, Plato's heirs usually called themselves 'Academics' until the first century BC, and even beyond). If, however, one rather refers to the idea that followers of Plato regarded *Plato himself* as philosophical authority, then it can be argued that Platonism was founded within the Early Academy. Indeed, David Sedley's twin papers on the Early Academy establish that a clear and well-defined notion of Plato's authority had already emerged in the Early Academy, namely under Xenocrates (Chapters 1–2). Yet this cannot be taken just as an unqualified notion, or a generic statement. Rather, Plato's authority was first established by Xenocrates in the specific sense that the second scholarch, going far beyond Plato's intentions and at the same time addressing some of Speusippus' views, reshaped Plato's philosophy around a highly selective canon of dialogues, representing the core of Plato's thought: these key texts are the *Phaedrus* and the *Timaeus*. Sedley shows that, in spite of its high degree of selectivity and partiality, such a choice ensures at least two fundamental pay-offs: first, Xenocrates was able to reduce Plato's dialogical thought to a system of doctrines with strong textual bases in these dialogues, once their reciprocal consistency was shown; second, by appealing to these dialogues, Xenocrates was able to challenge and dismiss some of Speusippus' views, or to incorporate them in his version of dogmatic Platonism. All this leads Sedley to regard Xenocrates as the founder of Plato's authority, in the sense that he was the first to conceive Plato's authority as the result of a dogmatic organisation of Plato's thought through the establishment of a way of organising his writings; but he was also the first to address the issue of Plato's authority by taking into account the contributions of other thinkers (namely, Speusippus) as well. To put it briefly, Xenocrates sought to be the first *true* faithful heir of Plato, the one deserving philosophical supremacy even within the school of Plato's heirs. Moreover, it is likely that Xenocrates succeeded in this attempt, as Sedley's iconographic interpretation of the 'Mosaic of the Philosophers' shows. By strongly supplementing recent interpretations and by discovering a subtle and elegant interplay of symbols and allusions, Sedley makes a scenario of investiture emerge out of the Mosaic: while Speusippus and Aristotle are represented as deviating from Plato's teaching – and in turn as being ignored by Plato – Plato himself symbolically ensured Xenocrates' authoritative legacy by teaching the latter's cosmological doctrine, and in such a way Xenocrates himself gained the role of an authority as Plato's heir. The Mosaic, then, represents a vivid picture of the

## Introduction

emergence of Plato's authority, and in turn highlights the fact that Platonism was born with Xenocrates *because* a very specific notion of Plato's legacy arose with him.

This representation brings out some crucial aspects grounding the emergence of the notion of Plato's authority, such as the attempt to reconstruct a dogmatic doctrine based, on the one hand, on the selection of a canon of Platonic texts and, on the other, on the use of such texts in order to claim a specific relation with the master, one which is stricter than that ascribable to other heirs of his. A continuous and flattening idea of authority might be taken to exclude that the very notion of authority played any significant role after Arcesilaus' sceptical shift. Anna Maria Ioppolo's paper (Chapter 3) shows that this is not the case, and sheds light on the way in which authority was used as an argument by Arcesilaus. As a matter of fact, it is recognised nowadays that Arcesilaus made a significant effort to lay claim to Plato and Socrates' legacy: albeit within the new framework of Arcesilaus' sceptical stance, the founder of the school was still regarded as an eminent authoritative figure. As Ioppolo argues, however, this is only a part of the story, for Arcesilaus' polemic against the Stoics was also based on the appeal to other philosophical authorities and their connection with Plato. Rather than merely establishing Socrates and Plato as the founders of a sceptical tradition, Arcesilaus also appropriated the authority of Heraclitus, which the Stoics claimed for themselves. This move had a crucial pay-off: on the one hand, it undermined the Stoic appeal to Heraclitus as an authoritative ancestor for their psychological doctrine; on the other, given the role Heraclitean doctrines play in Plato's *Theaetetus*, Arcesilaus' affirmation of Heraclitus' authority is in any case strictly bound to Plato's. All this means that affirming the authority of certain philosophical ancestors is a strategic move which in itself transcends the commitment to a system, and can rather be conceived of as an argument aimed at undermining rival positions and establishing a sceptical philosophical identity.

Also in this case, one might wonder whether there is any substantial link between Arcesilaus' scepticism and this 'formal' use of authority as an argument: the chapters on the first century BC show that this is not the case. As Federico M. Petrucci shows (Chapter 4), one can really place Antiochus in the Platonist tradition and understand his role therein by avoiding any commitment to the fact that his doctrines are either Platonist or Stoic. Rather, Antiochus' contribution to the history of Platonism relies on the (re-)discovery of a notion of dogmatic authority which is substantially anterior and primary with respect to the content of the system which this notion frames: Antiochus wanted to build up a *formal* argument for Plato's authority ensuring both the possibility that the latter may have construed a positive system and his supremacy over other Hellenistic thinkers. This construction also serves a crucial function against specific adversaries, namely the Academic sceptics: paradoxically, Antiochus turned against the sceptics an argument, that of the authority of eminent ancestors, which – as we have seen – they used against the Stoics. At the same time, however, there is one aspect of Antiochus' conception of Plato's authority which is key and peculiar: by implicitly recovering and rethinking a nuance in Xenocrates' operation – as described by David Sedley in Chapters 1–2 – Antiochus stressed the fact that, in order to establish the authority of the master, one should also be able to effectively account for a *specific* relationship between the master himself and his heirs. Antiochus' solution is based in the possibility of drawing a continuous stream of positive teaching stemming from Plato. This pattern can also be exploited in a different way, as emerges from Eudorus' Pythagorising view of Plato: Plato was not only the founder of the Academy and the one who taught a positive system of doctrines to his students, but also a privileged heir of the Pythagoreans. To put it briefly, authority in first-century Platonism is strictly bound to the existence of a *diadochē*. Interestingly, this is also the intellectual strategy at the basis of the production of a peculiar *corpus* of writings related to the Platonist tradition, namely the *Pseudopythagorica*. As Bruno Centrone shows (Chapter 5), although the logic according to which the fictional authors were selected seems obscure, it is possible to discover very precise reasons why the forgers wanted both Archytas and minor Pythagoreans to be credited with such writings. By reconsidering extant testimonies on Pythagoras and the Pythagorean *diadochē*, Centrone demonstrates that the forgers wanted to ascribe a particular authority to – or, conversely, regarded as authoritative – those Pythagoreans who were directly linked to Pythagoras as *diadochoi* of the 'school' in Iamblichus' *The Pythagorean Life* (265–6). In other words, just as in the case of Antiochus' argument for Plato's authority, the very possibility of establishing a continuous teaching tradition within a school preserves its dogmatic unity, and singles out the founder's authority, but also ensures the transmission of this authority throughout the succession. And it is telling for our narrative that the last name in the Pythagorean *diadochē* – and the fictional author of most of the *Pseudopythagorica* – was Archytas of Tarentum, who was in turn usually associated with Plato. All in all, therefore, a substantial reshaping and argumentative use of the notion of authority was key to the attempt of ensuring the possibility of a positive

*Introduction* 7

Platonist philosophy at the dawn of the Imperial Age: far from being a somewhat superficial commitment, developing an effective notion of authority, along with a set of specific relevant assumptions, was a fundamental strategic move in the revival of dogmatic philosophy.

It is very telling that, while from the point of view of doctrines the first century BC could hardly be regarded as having set the standards for post-Hellenistic Platonism, the chapters on the Middle Platonists Numenius and Plutarch show that its notion of authority proved seminal. This emerges clearly in Alexandra Michalewski's paper on Numenius (Chapter 6). Numenius' attempt to challenge the Academic interpretation of Plato is closely intertwined with the search for a specific doctrinal identity for post-Hellenistic Platonism: in both respects, as Michalewski shows by focusing on Numenius' theology, the affirmation of an ancestor's authority plays a crucial role in Numenius' strategy. Indeed, on the one hand he identified Pythagoras as the holder of ancestral and pure wisdom, whose core had been inherited by Plato; on the other, and unexpectedly, he also wanted Socrates to be the coiner of Plato's theology. In this way Numenius was able to *create* a unique pedigree for Plato's philosophy, at once rejecting all possible sceptical interpretations of his thought based on Socrates' teaching and placing Plato within a tradition of ancient lore. Rather than merely representing a superficial fiction, then, Numenius' construction of the authority of Plato's 'masters' was a way to secure, in turn, the authority of a specific version of Plato's philosophy, namely a dogmatic and Pythagorising one. It is not by chance that, as Michalewski shows, when Proclus came to attack Numenius' demiurgy he also – and first – had to dismiss Numenius' specific narrative of Plato's authority. All this led Numenius to regard Plato's authority not as a fideistic commitment, but as an argumentative weapon, or a notion to be shaped on the basis of specific exigencies – the intriguing implication being that the very idea of Plato's authority could not be regarded as a blind dogma. But could one go so far as to claim that Plato's authority was provisional, or hypothetic? This is the challenging view which George Boys-Stones discusses in his paper on Plutarch (Chapter 7). By taking the overall structure of the *De E apud Delphos* as a manifesto of Plutarch's Platonism, Boys-Stones reveals that Plato's primacy is not taken for granted as such by Plutarch, but is rather bound to the fact that Plato is an authority inasmuch as he was acquainted with the truth. Accordingly, a scenario in which people other than Plato reach the truth, and hence are as authoritative as Plato, is entirely possible to envisage. This view has two crucial consequences. First, within a framework in which authority is a topic of debate and may involve several philosophers, Plutarch makes a further actor enter the stage, namely each person who practises philosophy: Plato's authority is a sort of working hypothesis, which is fundamental until one becomes oneself a philosopher, who is able to grasp the truth autonomously. Second, while admitting the priority of Plato as a teacher, Plutarch's view of philosophical authority represents a theoretical model justifying the possibility of *multiple* epistemic authorities.

At this point, the Platonist debate has reached the boundary between Middle Platonism and Neoplatonism, and post-Hellenistic Platonism can be regarded as contributing at least two key ideas related to the notion of authority. First, and more generally, Plato's authority is an argumentative tool, or a working hypothesis, rather than a blind commitment. Second, Plato's role as an authority is not isolated, but dialectical: the establishment of Plato's authority must be framed within a wider scenario, in which other thinkers can play important roles for specific exigencies. These ideas will still prove fundamental in later Platonism, which however, as it emerges in Chapters 8–11, develops them in a very different way, and on the basis of profoundly different philosophical needs. This is of particular importance, for the issue of the continuity of the Platonist tradition from the post-Hellenistic Age to Late Antiquity is a much-debated one, and some scholars have proposed to simply abolish it (see, most recently, Catana 2013). By contrast, the papers concerning Neoplatonism testify to an actual shift, starting from Riccardo Chiaradonna's contribution on the authority of Aristotle in Plotinus and Porphyry (Chapter 8). By studying the reception of Aristotle's *Physics* as a test-case, Chiaradonna argues that this text has a pivotal position in Plotinus' metaphysics and physics, but also that Plotinus' attitude towards it was generally critical. In this sense, Porphyry takes Plotinus' attitude one step further, since he not only regards Aristotle's *Physics* as a fundamental text, but also makes it *authoritative for his Platonist physics* by establishing a close interaction between it and Plato's *Timaeus*. The point is that we are far from any vague appeal to Peripatetic notions (see already Petrucci 2018: 104–27, for the Middle Platonist background). Indeed, from Plotinus onwards, *Aristotle's authority* and the use of some of his writings *as authoritative texts* become central, albeit with significant nuances: while Plotinus is ready to acknowledge Aristotle's role as an 'authoritative' polemical target by specifically dealing with his texts and carefully appropriating some of his philosophical claims, Porphyry starts regarding Aristotle's philosophy and texts as unavoidable Platonist devices. In other words, the attempt to conceptualise Aristotle's authority and to adapt it to a Platonist perspective is the framework within

*Introduction*

9

which the well-known Neoplatonist harmonisation of Plato and Aristotle must be set. This does not imply, however, that after Porphyry one must envisage a flat and homogeneous scenario: rather, the specific issue of how to appropriate Aristotle's doctrine and, consequently, of how to square Plato's and Aristotle's authority, becomes crucial in itself in later Neoplatonism, as Saskia Aerts shows (Chapter 9). As a matter of fact, the project of harmonising Aristotle and Plato and of regarding them *both* as authorities – albeit to different extents – also implies dealing with all those texts and doctrines which seem to sharply contradict one another, and this requires the production of exegetical strategies and ways to balance them. This clearly emerges from Hermias' and Simplicius' treatment of the doctrine of the self-moving soul, a core Platonic doctrine which was severely criticised by Aristotle. Aerts shows to what extent the commitment to the joint authority of both Plato and Aristotle can lead Platonists to exegetical twists and extreme harmonising strategies: moving along the broad lines of the Middle Platonist opening to several authoritative figures, by focusing on Aristotle's role and elevating him to a very high status these authors had to produce a new ideological framework for the management of the issue of multiple authorities.

This is only a part of the story, however, for the Neoplatonists also felt the need to develop and discuss an issue which had already emerged at the dawn of the tradition, with Xenocrates, and had proved important in Middle Platonism, namely the sense in which everyone doing philosophy should conceive his or her own relationship with Plato as an authority. Interestingly, as Christian Tornau shows by focusing on Proclus and Simplicius (Chapter 10), Plato's authority in Neoplatonist schools is not experienced as a direct relationship, but requires mediator-teachers, or *kathēgemones*, ensuring access to Plato's authoritative texts and doctrines and hence becoming, because of this role, authorities themselves, although at a remarkably lower level than Plato. This is not just an extrinsic construction, for the triadic pattern which emerges from this conception (Plato, teacher, student of philosophy) is in turn grounded in Neoplatonist metaphysics, and hence in Plato's dialogues. In other words, the Neoplatonists provided their school activity and learning of Platonism with a formal conception of philosophical teaching based on Plato's texts: the Neoplatonist theory of the *kathēgemōn* as a mediator highlights the importance of oral guidance for anyone seeking to become acquainted with Plato's texts, each level entailing a specific kind of authority. Of course, this also meant exploiting to some extent the way in which doing philosophy is presented in Plato's dialogues: this is a very intriguing issue, for apparently the dialogue form could discourage the formation of any system, and any insistence on this literary aspect could be regarded as dangerous for Neoplatonists. But, as Anne Sheppard shows (Chapter 11), the opposite is the case. By focusing her enquiry on Proclus, Olympiodorus, and the *Anonymous Prolegomena to Plato's Philosophy*, Sheppard highlights the way in which later Neoplatonists of the fifth and sixth centuries AD conceived of Plato's dialogues as a very specific form of *drama*, namely one that turned the lively personalities found in the pages of Plato into metaphysical abstractions. In this sense, Plato's dialogues became authoritative not only as bearers of doctrines, but also as metaphysically unique pieces of philosophical literature, and in turn the very literary analysis of the dialogues became a way to *demonstrate* Plato's authority.

\* \* \*

This volume narrates the emergence and metamorphoses of the notion of authority from the very beginning of the Platonist tradition to Late Antiquity, with no significant gaps: highlighting the complex discontinuity, multiple shifts, and several reformulations and applications which the notion of authority progressively underwent is one of the pay-offs of the diachronic structure we have opted for. This does not imply, however, that the Platonist tradition developed views about Plato's authority in a radically episodic way. On the contrary, there are other hidden paths within this volume which point to the persistence of issues throughout the tradition and which, more generally, reveal a synchronic dialogue within it. For instance, a fundamental point related to Plato's authority is the treatment of thinkers other than Plato, who can be challenged through specific conceptions of authority or, on the opposite side of the spectrum, can in turn be viewed as authorities: the very beginning of the Platonist tradition coincides with Xenocrates' response to his predecessor Speusippus; the combination of Plato's authority with that of other thinkers plays a fundamental role both in Arcesilaus' polemics against the Stoics and in the Middle Platonist polemic against Arcesilaus himself; and the squaring of Plato's authority with Aristotle's is a crucial issue in Neoplatonism. Similarly, the issue of the correct way to appeal to, and use, Plato's dialogues as authoritative texts is constantly at stake. As a matter of fact, the birth of Plato's authority is bound to the selective use of some dialogues by Xenocrates, namely the *Timaeus* and the *Phaedrus*, while Arcesilaus construed his narrative of the authority of Plato and

*Introduction*

Heraclitus by building on the *Theaetetus*; fundamental passages of the dialogues (especially the *Parmenides*) are key to the Neoplatonist representation of the mediator-teacher as an authoritative *kathēgemōn*; and, more generally, producing an overall theory of the dialogues as philosophical dramas ultimately proved fundamental for Neoplatonists wishing to represent Plato as a dogmatic authority. Furthermore, a constant issue addressed in the Platonist tradition is the correct way to gain access to the philosophy of an authority – as embodied in Plato's dialogues and in the kernel of truth they contain. In turn, this implies ascribing special authority also to some mediators: this is an exigency implicit in the role Xenocrates claimed for himself as the only suitable successor of Plato in the Academy; this is the horizon within which Plutarch's idea of potential multiple authorities can be read; and, ultimately, this is the reason why Neoplatonists conceived of the *kathēgemones* as authoritative figures along with Plato. Finally – and most importantly – given the plurality and complexity of Platonist approaches to the issue of authority, at no stage of the tradition could Plato's authority be regarded as a mere given, or a fideistic assumption: at the very least, it was a notion to be justified by looking into the dialogues, a notion to be defined in very philosophical terms; but it could also become a *demonstrandum*, a working hypothesis, an argumentative tool, a strategic key. At no stage of the tradition was entering a school of Platonism like joining a religious order; and regarding certain philosophical texts as authoritative never amounted to merely acknowledging a set of decrees. If nothing else, what this enquiry into the notion of authority shows is that Platonist thought never ceased to be properly *philosophical*.

CHAPTER I

# Xenocrates' Invention of Platonism[*]

## David Sedley

### 1.1 Plato's Authority

From Plato's generation onwards it became the practice among leading philosophers to set up a school within one's own lifetime, and upon one's own death either to bequeath its headship to one's own chosen successor, or to entrust to the school's members the task of electing the next head. It was only with that succession, when the school's intellectual legacy needed to be defined and secured, that the founder's authoritative status was likely to come to the fore. The process is nowhere better illustrated than in the Early Academy.

Whatever its institutional status may have been, there is little doubt that the Academy became in Plato's own lifetime a celebrated centre of learning, of which he himself was the acknowledged leader. A well-known fragment from a contemporary comedy by Epicrates describes a lesson in botanical taxonomy given by Plato in the Academy grove, in which he set his pupils a task in the method of division: classify the pumpkin.[1] Whether or not we somewhat implausibly infer from this comic scene that botany was on the school's curriculum, the passage is strong confirmation that Plato's school was a publicly visible institution, and that his leadership of it was an equally visible fact.

Around Plato, moreover, there gathered a penumbra of talented individuals, most of whom either were or became prolific authors in their own right. These included the young Aristotle, later to found his own school in

---

[*] For fruitful discussion and suggestions at various stages, my thanks to audiences at Würzburg, Harvard, Durham and Athens, and to Stephen Menn, Marwan Rashed, Francesco Verde, Federico Petrucci, Dimitri El Murr, Gábor Betegh, Phillip Horky, Roberto Granieri, Carl Huffman, Victor Gysembergh, Voula Tsouna, Richard McKirahan, Harold Tarrant, Paul Kalligas and Vassilis Karasmanis, and the anonymous readers at Cambridge University Press. No one listed here should be assumed to agree with all my conclusions.

[1] Epicrates fr. 10 Kassel-Austin. For an especially nuanced picture of the Academy under Plato's headship, see Frede 2018.

the Lyceum; probably Theophrastus, later to succeed Aristotle as head of the Lyceum; Plato's nephew and eventual successor Speusippus; Xenocrates, who would in turn succeed Speusippus as school-head; and leading mathematicians of the day, including notably the astronomer Eudoxus, also well known, however incongruously, as an advocate of hedonism. What held this intellectually diverse group together? Undoubtedly, it was something more like Socratic joint inquiry and mutual interrogation than the transmission of doctrine from master to pupils.

If nevertheless, as most scholars in the field rightly believe, Plato did have a body of doctrines,[2] these will have emerged from discussions within the school, rather than as a comprehensive system that could be taught in its entirety from the outset. But his trademark doctrine, above all others, was his theory of transcendent Forms. And the open dissent of Aristotle, Eudoxus and Speusippus testifies that even this theory was not one that members of the Academy were required to adopt as their own. Nor should we forget that Plato himself joined them in this enterprise when, in the opening part of his *Parmenides*, he presented arguments which appeared intended to undermine the theory of Forms, albeit hinting that the objections could somehow be answered.

In short, under Plato's headship, and probably in its immediate aftermath, the Academy had a degree of doctrinal identity and no doubt enough community of thought to make constructive debate possible, but not so much consensus as to stifle independent reasoning and the undogmatic exploration of competing alternatives.

It was after Plato's death that the picture changed. From then on, or at any rate after a transitional period which I shall go on to discuss, a primarily written legacy bequeathed by Plato was destined to be the school's special link to him. The Platonic corpus can, after all, compete for recognition as the finest coordinated body of philosophical writing ever produced. Plato had himself warned that fixed written texts could not adapt so as to become participants in developing debates, but his Platonist heirs nevertheless took the view that his writings already contained the key to his philosophy, and thereby to the truth, if only the texts were properly interrogated and deciphered. Along with this reverence came the story of Plato's divine birth, divulged as a piece of family lore by his own nephew Speusippus.[3]

---

[2] See n. 17.     [3] DL 3.2 > 147 IP = F1a Tarán.

## 1.2  Aristotle

Contrast the Peripatos. Aristotle never became 'divine' (*theios*), even to his most devoted followers. Nor did those followers normally call themselves Aristotelians: like the Stoics, they named themselves after their original place of meeting, 'Peripatetics'. Finally, although the close study of Aristotle's text became their fundamental educational practice, it is hard to identify, between Aristotle's death in 322 BC and the *floruit* of Alexander of Aphrodisias five centuries later, any Peripatetic who treated Aristotle as altogether infallible.[4] Even Alexander, despite his almost unlimited respect for Aristotle, and despite his authorship of numerous commentaries on the school treatises, is prepared on occasion to say that Aristotle has got something wrong.

I am not sure that it has ever been explained why the Peripatetics, devoted Aristotelians though they were, never conferred infallibility on their founder. But I find it easy to imagine that Aristotle himself in his last years, watching with horror the virtual deification and (dare one say?) fossilization of Plato in the Academy under the headship of Xenocrates, might have given instructions that on no account was he himself to be uncritically revered after his death.

## 1.3  Plato, Speusippus and Xenocrates

Plato, in choosing as his successor his nephew, the non-Platonist Speusippus, may well have intended similarly to ensure the continuation of open debate in the school, unobstructed by doctrinal allegiance to his own views. Speusippus' metaphysics, for example, posited for each domain its own pair of ultimate principles: for arithmetic these were one and plurality, from which numbers were generated; for geometry point and extension, from which came lines and figures; and so on. Although arithmetic was necessarily prior to geometry (the study of figures requires numbers, but not vice versa), that did not mean that geometry and the other sciences could be derived purely from arithmetic. Rather, to repeat, each science flowed from its own first principles. This piecemeal derivation of reality from a series of independent pairs of principles, without any ultimate higher principles to unite them, could not easily be dressed up as

---

[4] I discount Theophrastus, because in general we have no way of distinguishing which parts of his work were done after Aristotle's death, when the founder's (in)fallibility first became a potential issue.

## Xenocrates' Invention Of Platonism

corresponding to Plato's committed position, and it no doubt owed more to Pythagoreans like Philolaus.[5]

Nevertheless, during Speusippus' eight years at its head the school worked towards narrowing the gap between him and Plato. If nothing else, by heading the school Speusippus could, as Plato's hagiographer, nephew and heir, be custodian of its heritage from the now divinized founder, and serve as a bridge to its new era. And it was Xenocrates, soon to succeed Speusippus and become the unifying third school-head, who played the key role in the forging of Platonism.[6] How was this achieved?

One part of Xenocrates' solution, it seems, lay in emphasizing a pair of universal principles, the One and the Indefinite Dyad, the latter also known as the large-and-small. This pair of principles could be viewed as unifying the three ontologies, that of Plato, that of Speusippus, and that of Xenocrates himself, in so far as it went beyond anything that Plato had made explicit. The One and the Dyad could serve as the ultimate principles from which to derive Speusippus' various pairs of subject-specific principles.[7] But they were also principles which Plato himself was reported to have favoured in his famous public lecture on the Good,[8] and probably elsewhere, even if they never made an explicit appearance in his dialogues. According to what became a widely endorsed reading of Plato, supported by Xenocrates,[9] the One and the Dyad were the principles from which he derived absolutely everything, including the Forms themselves.

Xenocrates' own constructive use of these same principles seems to have lain partly in his cosmology, where he analysed the universe as composed by the One – also named the 'monad', 'Zeus' and 'intelligence' (νοῦς) – acting directly on what he called the 'Dyad' and 'the ever-flowing' (τὸ ἀέναον), meaning

---

[5] There is a considerable body of evidence linking Speusippus to Pythagoreanism, especially to that of Philolaus, e.g. [Iambl.] *Theol. Arithm.* 82.12–15 De Falco (<122 IP = F28 Tarán: ἐκ τῶν ἐξαιρέτως σπουδασθεισῶν ἀεὶ Πυθαγορικῶν ἀκροάσεων, μάλιστα δὲ τῶν Φιλολάου συγγραμμάτων, βιβλίδιόν τι συντάξας γλαφυρὸν ἐπέγραψε [*sc.* Σπεύσιππος] μὲν αὐτὸ Περὶ Πυθαγορικῶν ἀριθμῶν). In the following chapter I shall point to evidence, hitherto in short supply, of a contemporary Pythagorean influence on Speusippus, namely that of Archytas. (In references to Speusippus the simple 'IP' refers to Isnardi Parente 1980; in references to Xenocrates, 'IP²' refers to Isnardi Parente 2012.)

[6] See esp. [Galen], *Hist. phil.* 3 (=19 IP = T12 Tarán): 'Speusippus remained head of his school for a short time, and having succumbed to arthritis he appointed Xenocrates, instead of himself, as interpreter of the Platonic doctrines.'

[7] This proposal has the attraction of accounting for the otherwise inexplicable statement at DL 4.1 that Speusippus maintained the same doctrines as Plato. See also the following chapter, p. 60.

[8] Simplicius, *in Phys.* 151.6–11 (=F18 IP²).      [9] F37 IP².

16 DAVID SEDLEY

matter.[10] One particularly rich example of this dualism applies it to the internal metaphysical analysis of the world soul itself:[11]

|  | **θεούς** | |
| --- | --- | --- |
| τὴν μονάδα | 1 | τὴν δυάδα |
| τὴν μὲν ὡς ἄρρενα | 2 | τὴν δ' ὡς θήλειαν |
| πατρὸς ἔχουσαν τάξιν | 3 | μητρὸς θεῶν δίκην |
| ἐν οὐρανῷ βασιλεύουσαν | 4 | τῆς ὑπὸ τὸν οὐρανὸν λήξεως ἡγουμένην |
| ἥντινα προσαγορεύει καὶ Ζῆνα καὶ περιττὸν καὶ νοῦν | 5 | <ἥντινα προσαγορεύει καὶ "Ηραν καὶ ἄρτιον καὶ ψυχήν> |
| ὅστις ἐστὶν αὐτῷ πρῶτος θεός | 6 | ἥτις ἐστὶν αὐτῷ ψυχὴ τοῦ παντός |

|  | **gods** | |
| --- | --- | --- |
| the monad | 1 | the dyad |
| corresponding to male | 2 | corresponding to female |
| holding the rank of father | 3 | in the role of mother of the gods |
| reigning in heaven | 4 | leading the zone beneath the heaven |
| named by him both 'Zeus' and 'odd' and 'intellect' | 5 | <named by him both 'Hera' and 'even' and 'soul'> |
| who is his first god | 6 | who is his soul-of-the-universe |

This schema reflects in particular Xenocrates' attempt to map Plato's pair of oral principles onto the metaphysical structure of the world soul according to the *Timaeus*. The items in the left column evidently correspond to the cosmic intellect, those in the right column to the cosmic soul in which the cosmic intellect resides. The idea underlying the full oral theory of principles was that this same dualistic mode of analysis could be repeated at all metaphysical levels, typically in mathematical terms, and could include the definitions of the Forms themselves.

[10] F21–2, F133 IP².
[11] Aetius 1.7.30 < F133 IP²: 'Xenocrates of Chalcedon, son of Agathenor, identifies the Monad and the Dyad as gods, the one as male, having the role of Father, reigning in the heavens, whom he calls Zeus, odd and intellect, which is for him the primary god; the other as female, in the manner of mother of the Gods, leading the realm below the heavens, who is for him the soul of the universe' (Ξενοκράτης Ἀγαθήνορος Καλχηδόνιος τὴν μονάδα καὶ τὴν δυάδα θεούς, τὴν μὲν ὡς ἄρρενα πατρὸς ἔχουσαν τάξιν ἐν οὐρανῷ βασιλεύουσαν, ἥντινα προσαγορεύει καὶ Ζῆνα καὶ περιττὸν καὶ νοῦν, ὅστις ἐστὶν αὐτῷ πρῶτος θεός· τὴν δ' ὡς θήλειαν, μητρὸς θεῶν δίκην, τῆς ὑπὸ τὸν οὐρανὸν λήξεως ἡγουμένην, ἥτις ἐστὶν αὐτῷ ψυχὴ τοῦ παντός). Evidently we are being asked by Xenocrates to recognize the complex set of dualities I have set out in the main text. That the Aetius passage contains a corruption is well recognized (e.g. Dillon 2003: 102–4), and I propose as a sufficient remedy the completion shown in line 5. Despite the absence of other evidence for Hera being assigned this role by Xenocrates, the missing sense, even if not the precise wording, is virtually guaranteed by the carefully contrived symmetry between the two columns.

Even Speusippus, although there is no evidence that he gave Plato's theory of the One and the Dyad his blessing,[12] acknowledged that it had an ancient pedigree.[13] Some may remain sceptical whether Plato himself had ever, even orally, adopted these ultimate principles.[14] The fact remains that during the decades immediately following his death the doctrine of the One and the Dyad was to be strongly associated with Plato's philosophy, and plentiful attestations by Aristotle confirm the probability that it really had been endorsed by his teacher.

It seems to have been above all an at least superficial consensus on the twin principles that helped secure the early school's continuity and cohesion, creating as it did a smooth transition from Plato, via Speusippus, to Xenocrates. Xenocrates as a result became the first committed Platonist head of the Academy, and indeed the very first Platonist.[15]

The reconstruction of Xenocrates' Platonist metaphysics is a delicate and risky enterprise which involves inter alia hypothesizing that he is the unnamed subject or target of a number of Aristotelian and other passages. I shall not be attempting that here, nor will I be assuming that, like Speusippus, he had significant Pythagorean leanings.[16] The evidence for

---

[12] Procl. *in Prm.* 501.4–11 Steel = Speusippus 62 IP = F48 Tarán. Moerbeke's medieval translation has Speusippus *narrans tamquam placentia antiquis*, well back-translated by C. Steel as ἱστορῶν ὡς ἀρέσκοντα τοῖς παλαιοῖς. My thanks to Stephen Menn for bringing this to my attention, and for showing me that there is no reference here to the doctrine being claimed by Speusippus as his own, as some (not including Isnardi Parente herself) have assumed, e.g. Dillon 2003: 56–7, who translates 'presenting his views as the doctrines of the ancients'. I am taking it (a little controversially) that 'ancients' is Speusippus' term, not Proclus'.

[13] When Speusippus traced the One and the Indefinite Dyad back to the 'ancients', he is often taken to have meant the Pythagoreans. Although this might be suggested by his own Pythagorean leanings, an attractive alternative is that he meant Parmenides. The first half of Parmenides' poem is about a determinate one, the second half about a variable dyad. In Plato's *Parmenides*, the august Parmenides' prolonged demonstration of inferential gymnastics to the young Socrates might be read as preparatory for the use of these tools in metaphysical analysis. Dillon 2003: 56–9 makes helpful suggestions for connecting the theory outlined by Speusippus to the *Parmenides*, even if (see previous note) he goes beyond the evidence in representing it as one endorsed by Speusippus himself. Some have connected the One and the Dyad instead, via the *Philebus*, to Philolaus' Pythagoreanism. This is not implausible, but we should remember that the Phileban ontology is triadic (limit, unlimited, intellect), not dyadic.

[14] Cherniss 1945, in seeking to delegitimize the tradition of the unwritten doctrines, has had a lasting effect, especially on Anglophone Plato scholarship, where they are rarely even mentioned.

[15] There is no reasonable ground for denying Xenocrates the label 'Platonist', and indeed the earliest surviving reference to anyone as a 'Platonist' (*Platonicus*) is to Epicurus' teacher Pamphilus, a member of the Academy in this period: Cic. *ND* 1.73, aptly cited by Brittain (2001: 223–4 n. 8) to modify the assertion of Glucker (1978: 206–25), that Πλατωνικός is unattested before the second century AD.

[16] The case, such as it is, for Xenocrates' Pythagorean tendency is succinctly made by Dillon 2014: 254–7. In the following chapter I shall be presenting iconographic evidence in which the pro-Xenocratean lobby strongly dissociates him from the contemporary Pythagoreanism of Archytas.

that characterization seems to lie largely in the basic ontological role that numbers played in his system, a feature likely to flow as much from his emphasis on the One as first principle as from anything more narrowly Pythagorean. Instead of following such paths as these, legitimate though they are, I shall concentrate on picking out some main threads which have I think escaped scholarly attention.

As I have already hinted, for Xenocrates, as for most Platonists, the key text for Platonic doctrine was the *Timaeus*. The speech of Timaeus in it is after all unrivalled as *the* passage that seems to set out Plato's philosophical system in detail. True, Timaeus' speech is devoted to physics, with the result that the system it contains is itself presented mainly from the perspective of physical theory, even when dealing with ethics, psychology and metaphysics. But there is a huge doctrinal overlap with theses defended piecemeal elsewhere in the corpus, including the tripartite soul and the theory of Forms.[17] The preference for treating the fictional or semi-historical speaker Timaeus as Plato's virtual alter ego, and his speech as the basis of any authentic Platonist system, was entirely reasonable.

One probable consequence of this policy was that Xenocrates, reportedly the first to adopt explicitly what thereafter became the standard tripartition of philosophy into physics, ethics and logic, apparently placed the parts in precisely that order, with physics first.[18] As likely as not, this choice itself reflects his understandable conviction that the cosmological discourse of Timaeus is the proper entry route into Platonism.

## 1.4   The Sempiternalist Reinterpretation

Indeed, *the* major talking point among early Platonists seems to have been the very first question addressed by Timaeus, and therefore in Xenocrates' eyes presumably the one with which philosophy itself properly begins: is the world sempiternal – with an infinitely extended past as well as an infinitely extended future – or did it have a temporally defined beginning? The primacy of this question is reflected by Xenocrates' own place at the very start of the long-running debate, still unresolved today, between

---

[17] That Timaeus' speech systematically voices Plato's own doctrines is a claim I argue in Sedley 2017, and more fully in Sedley 2019.

[18] SE *M* 7.16 = F1 IP². It has been suggested (IP² *ad loc.*; Dillon 2003: 98–9) that Xenocrates' favoured order was ethics–physics–logic, as listed by the Antiochean Varro at Cic. *Acad. post.* 19. But that order is adopted primarily to prepare us for the sequence of exposition in the ensuing chapters. The primacy awarded to ethics there thus reflects Antiochus' own priorities, and no evidence suggests that it was of Xenocratean origin.

literalist and sempiternalist interpreters of the *Timaeus*. For it was Xenocrates who first set out to argue that the *Timaeus*, appearances to the contrary notwithstanding, presents the world not as the product of a past act of creation, contingently everlasting into the future only thanks to divine benevolence, in accordance with a literal reading, but as temporally altogether unbounded.[19] Famously, he explained that Plato's narrative account of the world's creation was adopted only for expository purposes (*didaskalias charin*), analogously to the way that geometers construct a figure line by line even though the actual figure represented, being an unchanging entity, never came into being that way.

Although the defence of this sempiternalist interpretation is securely attributed to Xenocrates, it is reported to have had Speusippus' backing.[20] This seems to show that Xenocrates' distinctive contribution to the development of a Platonic canon, which I shall be charting in what follows, did not have to wait until he succeeded Speusippus as school-head, but was already under way during the latter's headship. We need not suppose that Speusippus endorsed all of Xenocrates' doctrinal choices, but there is no reason to doubt that the broad project of unifying the Platonic heritage, if only for the sake of the school's present and future cohesion, had his blessing.

Xenocrates' sempiternalist reading of Plato's cosmology is likely to have helped shape other doctrines for him. He was, for example, especially well known for his theory of indivisible lines,[21] a doctrine with no actual antecedents in Plato's writings, but which Xenocrates nevertheless succeeded in linking to Plato.[22] Presumably his idea was that these indivisible lines are presupposed by the *Timaeus*, where Plato's god constructs the physical world out of primary triangles, with an allusion (53d6–7) to certain further principles from which those triangles themselves are derived – principles, Timaeus adds darkly, that 'are known to god and, among men, to any he loves'. This privileged group could hardly fail to include Plato himself. Hence Xenocrates, as one of the master's most intimate associates, appeared well placed to disclose the true nature of the ultimate physical principles. His motive for identifying them as indivisible lines was, I believe, to support his own sempiternalist interpretation of the *Timaeus*. For only by positing ultimate constituents altogether incapable of further subdivision could he

---

[19] F73–7 IP².

[20] I put it this way because the actual argument is mainly attributed to Xenocrates in the sources (see previous note).

[21] F44–71 IP².

[22] Since Aristotle attributes this doctrine to Plato (*Metaph.* A9.992a20–2), it is possible that Xenocrates was able to claim support for it in his master's oral teaching.

ensure that, whatever transformations the world might undergo, there would be for all eternity a mathematically fixed lower limit to its potential dissolution.[23] This in turn helps make the world's indestructibility an intrinsic feature, rather than one relying on divine protection.

The link I have suggested between Xenocrates' cosmic sempiternalism and his thesis of indivisible lines is not, as far as I know, directly confirmed by our sources. But their interconnection gets some support from the fact that, in the next generation of the school, under the headship of Polemo (from 314 BC), the physical system reported by Cicero as being representative of the school simultaneously rejects both (*Acad. post.* 26–8):[24] (a) it reverts to the literalist reading of cosmic creation and (b) it very emphatically upholds the infinite divisibility of both matter and space (27–8). With Aristotle no longer on the scene, it seems, the original motives for rereading the Timaean creation non-temporally had receded, and a reaction against Xenocrates' modifications taken place.[25] This should serve us as a salutary reminder that even the founder's leading exegete, for all his impact on the subsequent tradition, could never acquire the absolute authority that the founder himself was guaranteed.

The theory of indivisible lines is a small foretaste of how under Xenocrates' headship, although the *Timaeus* was unchallenged as the primary handbook to Plato's doctrines, its interpretation underwent significant development. The most prominent aspect of that same modification seems to me to have been a systematic rereading of the *Timaeus* through the lens of a second Platonic dialogue that Xenocrates especially favoured. In taking this step, Xenocrates will have been inaugurating the long history of Platonist reinterpretation. Starting from the *Timaeus*, the process of identifying a web of other key passages from the Platonic corpus and integrating them doctrinally with the *Timaeus*, a process whose fruits are an unmistakable feature of the later history of ancient Platonism, evidently started here. Which Platonic dialogues and passages made up Xenocrates' Platonist canon, and which were excluded from it, is I think

---

[23] I have argued this previously in Sedley 2002a: 67–9.

[24] In Sedley 2002a I argued at length against the universal assumption that this report of the Early Academy is a mere retrojection of Stoic physics by Antiochus. That it represents the generation of Polemo (not necessarily the work of Polemo himself) I infer from Antiochus' usual practice of relying on the final summative voices of the Early Academy for the best statement of its views. I am aware that this issue remains controversial: see most recently Algra 2017 (who, however, does not take into account my supplementary argument at Sedley 2012b: 101–3).

[25] I say this despite the fact that in that same generation at least one leading figure of the school, Crantor (10 (3) Mette), celebrated as the first author of a commentary on the *Timaeus*, had retained Xenocrates' deliteralization.

# Xenocrates' Invention Of Platonism

*the* big unasked question regarding the school's history in this formative phase, and I now turn to it.

Alongside the *Timaeus*, Xenocrates' second guide to Plato's authoritative views was, I shall argue, the myth in Plato's *Phaedrus*. I have in mind a variety of clues, which will be set out in Sections 1.4–1.7 and 1.9–1.10, and should be taken cumulatively. His assignment of canonical status to the *Phaedrus*, if confirmed, is important not just as evidence of his working methods, but also, as I hope to show, because it enables us to discover and interpret vital aspects of his Platonism that have hitherto gone unnoticed.

I have already emphasized Xenocrates' sempiternalist interpretation of Timaeus' cosmogony. But why did this issue matter so much? Probably because of the need to resist the criticisms of Aristotle. In *De caelo* 1.10, and no doubt in his own teaching, Aristotle denounced as seriously incoherent Plato's idea of a temporally asymmetric world with a finite past existence but an infinitely extended future existence. What better way for Xenocrates to protect Plato from Aristotle's charge than by producing evidence that the author of the *Timaeus* had himself in fact been, for anyone with the wit to read below the surface of the text, a sempiternalist? And what better way to achieve *that* than by invoking the doctrine, defended at the start of the *Phaedrus* myth,[26] that all soul, including the world soul,[27] is in fact eternal and uncreated?[28]

---

[26] *Phdr.* 245c–246a, which can be paraphrased as follows:
  (1) 245c5: All soul, being always in motion, is immortal. <The reasons are as follows.>
  (2) 245c5–8: That which provides a mere link in the chain of motion can cease moving, and hence die; only that which moves itself, since it is never separated from itself, never ceases moving.
  (3) 245c8–9: That which moves itself <therefore> serves as a source of motion for other things.
  (4) 245d1–3: Anything that is a source must be ungenerated, since if it were generated it would *have* a source, instead of *being* one.
  (5) <Therefore that which moves itself is ungenerated.>
  (6) 245d3–6: Therefore that which moves itself must also be imperishable, since if it could cease it could not restart motion in itself or anything else.
  (7) 245d6–e2: Thus that which moves itself is the source of motion, and it cannot perish, or the whole world would collapse, stand still, and never restart.
  (8) 245e2–6: That which moves itself can be identified specifically with soul, because soul is by its nature not an external but an internal mover of whatever it animates.
  (9) 245e6–246a2: Therefore soul is both ungenerated and indestructible.

[27] Cf. *Phdr.* 246b6–c2: 'All soul takes care of all that is soulless, and circles round the whole heaven, coming to be in different forms at different times. Thus when it is perfected and winged it both travels aloft and regulates the whole world' (ψυχὴ πᾶσα παντὸς ἐπιμελεῖται τοῦ ἀψύχου, πάντα δὲ οὐρανὸν περιπολεῖ, ἄλλοτ' ἐν ἄλλοις εἴδεσι γιγνομένη. τελέα μὲν οὖν οὖσα καὶ ἐπτερωμένη μετεωροπορεῖ τε καὶ πάντα τὸν κόσμον διοικεῖ).

[28] Plutarch (*De procr. an.* 1016A) speaks of the *Phaedrus* passage as being cited by 'virtually all' participants in this debate, and it is hard to imagine that the debate's co-founder Xenocrates was among the rare exceptions.

## 22    DAVID SEDLEY

If it was for the purpose of defending Plato against attacks emanating from Aristotle that Xenocrates turned to the *Phaedrus* myth as a canonical source of Platonic doctrine, that has every chance of being his initial motivation for highlighting the passage. Once the process of synthesis had begun, however, it spread much further – if not to the whole *Phaedrus*, at least to the remainder of the *Phaedrus* myth, a self-contained passage which we may infer Xenocrates felt obliged to canonize, if at all, in its entirety.[29]

### 1.5    Cosmic Epistemology

Consider, then, Xenocrates' epistemology. The *Timaeus* has to all appearances a two-world epistemology and a matching dual ontology:[30] knowledge is focused on being, equated with the Forms; opinion (*doxa*) on becoming. But another part of the oral tradition about Plato, well attested by Aristotle, attributed to him a third, 'intermediate' class, the 'mathematicals'. And Xenocrates found a way to incorporate them.

According to the explicit testimony of Theophrastus, Xenocrates alone of recent and contemporary thinkers had managed to amalgamate all the major components of Platonic ontology, and moreover had incorporated them all into a single *cosmological* structure. These items, combined in Xenocrates' ontology, are reported by Theophrastus as fourfold:

> Concerning the heaven and the other entities they do not go on to make any further mention. Nor does the circle of Speusippus, nor any of the others, apart from Xenocrates. For Xenocrates has a way of distributing everything around the cosmos – perceptibles, intelligibles and mathematicals alike, and also the divine beings. (Thphr. *Metaph.* 6b6–9)[31]

As for how these four entities are combined, we get important details in a passage of Sextus Empiricus almost certainly derived from Antiochus' *Canonica*:

---

[29] If my contention is right, Xenocrates becomes the likely originator of the tradition (DL 3.38) that the *Phaedrus* was Plato's first dialogue. This supposed chronological primacy (not to be confused with its place in the teaching order) could be invoked when maintaining that all other dialogues, even the *Timaeus*, were intended to be read in the light of it.

[30] *Ti.* 27d–28c, 51b–52a.

[31] τοῦ δ' οὐρανοῦ πέρι καὶ τῶν λοιπῶν οὐδεμίαν ἔτι ποιοῦνται μνείαν· ὡσαύτως δ' οἱ περὶ Σπεύσιππον, οὐδὲ τῶν ἄλλων οὐθεὶς πλὴν Ξενοκράτης· οὗτος γὰρ ἅπαντά πως περιτίθησιν περὶ τὸν κόσμον, ὁμοίως αἰσθητὰ καὶ νοητὰ καὶ μαθηματικὰ καὶ ἔτι δὴ τὰ θεῖα. For discussion of this passage in its Theophrastean context see Horky 2013. Cf. also Arist. *Metaph.* Z 2.1028b24–7.

Xenocrates says that there are three substances: one of them perceptible, one intelligible, and one that is combined and opinable (*syntheton kai doxastēn*). Of these, the one inside the heaven is perceptible, the one consisting of everything outside the heaven is intelligible, and the one belonging to the heaven itself is opinable and combined, since by perception it is visible, while by astronomy it is intelligible. These being thus, he declared knowledge to be the criterion of the intelligible substance outside the heaven, perception the criterion of the perceptible substance inside the heaven, and opinion (*doxa*) the criterion of the mixed substance. And of these quite generally, the criterion that operates through scientific reason he said to be both dependable and true; the one that operates through perception to be true, but not in the same way as the one that operates through scientific reason; and the combined one to be common to true and false, because of opinion some is true, some false. (SE *M* 7.147–9 = F2 IP²)[32]

The use here of 'criterion' is certainly unhistorical, in all probability representing one stage in Antiochus' extended attempt in his *Canonica* to discern a basic inter-school consensus regarding what in his own day, though not in Xenocrates', was called the 'criterion of truth'. But there is no similar reason to doubt the other main details reported,[33] chiming in as they do with the strong contemporary evidence of Theophrastus. In Xenocrates' cosmos, it emerges, the perceptible realm is below the heaven, the noetic realm lies beyond the heaven, and between them the heaven itself is a 'doxastic' realm. As far as I know it has gone virtually unnoticed that this is the world uniquely as described in the *Phaedrus* myth (245c–249d).[34] Consider the following correspondences.

Within the Platonic corpus, placing the intelligible realm beyond the heaven is a piece of imagery unique to the *Phaedrus* myth, in which the gods, each followed by a parade of disembodied souls, process around the

---

[32] Ξενοκράτης δὲ τρεῖς φησιν οὐσίας εἶναι, τὴν μὲν αἰσθητὴν τὴν δὲ νοητὴν τὴν δὲ σύνθετον καὶ δοξαστήν, ὧν αἰσθητὴν μὲν εἶναι τὴν ἐντὸς οὐρανοῦ, νοητὴν δὲ <τὴν> πάντων τῶν ἐκτὸς οὐρανοῦ, δοξαστὴν δὲ καὶ σύνθετον τὴν αὐτοῦ τοῦ οὐρανοῦ· ὁρατὴ μὲν γάρ ἐστι τῇ αἰσθήσει, νοητὴ δὲ δι' ἀστρολογίας. τούτων μέντοι τοῦτον ἐχόντων τὸν τρόπον, τῆς μὲν ἐκτὸς οὐρανοῦ καὶ νοητῆς οὐσίας κριτήριον ἀπεφαίνετο τὴν ἐπιστήμην, τῆς δὲ ἐντὸς οὐρανοῦ καὶ αἰσθητῆς αἴσθησιν, τῆς δὲ μικτῆς τὴν δόξαν· καὶ τούτων κοινῶς τὸ μὲν διὰ τοῦ ἐπιστημονικοῦ λόγου κριτήριον βέβαιόν τε ὑπάρχειν καὶ ἀληθές, τὸ δὲ διὰ τῆς αἰσθήσεως ἀληθὲς μέν, οὐχ οὕτω δὲ ὡς τὸ διὰ τοῦ ἐπιστημονικοῦ λόγου, τὸ δὲ σύνθετον κοινὸν ἀληθοῦς τε καὶ ψευδοῦς ὑπάρχειν· τῆς γὰρ δόξης τὴν μέν τινα ἀληθῆ εἶναι τὴν δὲ ψευδῆ. For the continuation see n. 59.

[33] For Antiochus as source, see Sedley 1992. On the use of οὐσίαι, see Asclepius, *in Metaph.* 377.22–4 = F16 IP², who reports that, although in strict Platonist doctrine 'being' is limited to intelligibles, a broader use of the term is found in Plato, Speusippus and Xenocrates – a list to which we might add Aristotle, in that his own distinctive notion of substance (οὐσία) appears to have emanated from this same background of debate in the Academy.

[34] Two notable exceptions are Dillon 1977: 25–6, and Schibli 1993: esp. 145–7.

# DAVID SEDLEY

heaven. The soul-charioteers driving the individual soul-chariots crane their necks in a bid to feast on the sight of the Forms, which lie outside the heaven, but in the struggle their horses' wings break and they are sooner or later dragged back down into the heaven. This image – interpreted rather literally,[35] it seems – is being used by Xenocrates to elaborate what is in most other respects the Timaean cosmology. Let me amplify.

Timaeus (46e6–47c4) builds on the account of astronomy already presented in *Republic* 7, according to which observation of the heaven is cognitively transitional, a mixture of the empirical and the intellectual, facilitating an educational progression from the perceptible to the intelligible realm. In Xenocrates' ontology, it seems from Theophrastus' report, this account of astronomy as mixing the empirical with the intellectual had been further developed, by identifying astronomy's domain as one of mathematical intermediates. The Forms lie beyond the heaven, the sensibles below the heaven, and the heaven itself is a realm of mathematical intermediates,[36] where the visible and the intelligible are interwoven.

The obvious puzzle is why, in Sextus' report, the heavenly realm is 'opinable' (*doxastē*), that is, an object of mere *doxa*. If Xenocrates were using the *Republic* as an interpretative key here, he could hardly have failed to notice that, in *Republic* 6's Divided Line, advanced mathematical disciplines, astronomy included, are the domain of *dianoia*, which belongs not to the doxastic but to the epistemonic section of the Line.

But now, instead of the *Republic*, consider the epistemology of the *Phaedrus* myth. The souls parading round the heaven, in jostling to feast on the sight of Forms beyond the heaven, eventually break their wings and

---

[35] This tends to confirm the suspicion that Xenocrates' 'anti-literalism' regarding the world's creation was assumed for a specific purpose, rather than being reflective of any general resistance to literal readings of Platonic myths. The Aristotelian parallel at *DC* 1.9 (see n. 38) confirms that we cannot safely, with IP²: 240, explain away Xenocrates' talk of an extra-celestial zone as simply signifying transcendence. But wasn't he in that case going too far in assigning a spatial location even to the intelligibles, in defiance of *Ti.* 52a8–d1, where Timaeus exposes the error of thinking that all Being must be in a place, 'and that what is neither on the earth nor somewhere about the heaven is nothing' (τὸ δὲ μήτ᾽ ἐν γῇ μήτε που κατ᾽ οὐρανὸν οὐδὲν εἶναι, *Ti.* 52b5)? No, because he can take 'neither on the earth nor somewhere about the heaven' to point, not to altogether non-spatial Being, but to Being that as described in the *Phaedrus* lies beyond the sub-celestial and celestial zones, which would thereby be beyond the material 'receptacle' as well, but would nevertheless be 'somewhere'.

[36] One might think that the heaven cannot be the location of *all* mathematicals. Certainly Xenocrates' cosmography, following the *Timaeus*, is prioritizing astronomy (and no doubt, if to a lesser extent, harmonics) over other branches of mathematics, thereby achieving a proper focus on the mathematical structure of the Timaean world soul. As for the intermediates studied by arithmetic and geometry, these might be thought not necessarily to have any location at all. On the other hand, that would go against Theophrastus' testimony that Xenocrates' ontology gave *everything* a cosmic location. And if even Plato's ideal city, an intermediate of sorts, can be a model 'laid up in heaven' (*Republic* 9.592b1), the same might be true of all mathematical intermediates too.

## Xenocrates' Invention Of Platonism

fall back, whereupon they lose their 'vision of Being', and instead have to make do with 'opinable nourishment' (τροφῇ δοξαστῇ, 248b5).[37] Since the fallen souls have at this stage returned to the parade round the heaven, not yet descending into reincarnation, Xenocrates seems to be justified in inferring that *doxa* has been picked out by Plato as the cognitive faculty specially correlated to mathematical objects such as stellar motion, accessible through a combination of thought and perception.

The precise notion of *doxa* intended by Plato will surely be one that Xenocrates found explicated, not in the *Republic*, but at *Timaeus* 37b3–8. There we are told that even the world soul, whose structure the human rational soul mimics, is in a state of true *doxa* whenever it engages in internal silent discourse about perceptibles. Xenocrates is likely to be right in concluding, with the help of the *Phaedrus* myth, that astronomical thought is a paradigmatic case of such *doxa*, with the qualification, of course, that the human soul's *doxa* about the stars, unlike that of the world soul, is capable of falsity.

### 1.6  Gods and Daimons

Theophrastus, as we saw in the previous section, reports that the divine beings too were incorporated by Xenocrates into the same cosmic structure. But we are left to conjecture where they are located. The answer is almost certainly: in the heaven. This is suggested by the parade of souls, led by gods, graphically described in the *Phaedrus* myth. True, the gods of the *Phaedrus* do travel unimpededly into the supracelestial region to feast on the sight of the intelligibles, but having sated themselves they are said to descend back into the heaven, a descent which, significantly, is described as their return 'home' (οἴκαδε, 247e4).[38]

It remains unclear whether or not this class of divine beings includes daimons as well as gods. Xenocrates is reported to have upheld a three-level

---

[37] *Phdr.* 248b1–5: 'Hence there arise a mêlée, a struggle and extreme sweating, in which bad steering causes many souls to become lame, and many others to suffer multiple wing-breakages. All of them depart in dire straits from the vision of Being without completing it, and following this departure feed upon opinable nourishment' (θόρυβος οὖν καὶ ἄμιλλα καὶ ἱδρὼς ἔσχατος γίγνεται, οὗ δὴ κακίᾳ ἡνιόχων πολλαὶ μὲν χωλεύονται, πολλαὶ δὲ πολλὰ πτερὰ θραύονται· πᾶσαι δὲ πολὺν ἔχουσαι πόνον ἀτελεῖς τῆς τοῦ ὄντος θέας ἀπέρχονται, καὶ ἀπελθοῦσαι τροφῇ δοξαστῇ χρῶνται).

[38] Aristotle, *De caelo* 1.9.279a17–30 speaks of a non-spatial and non-temporal domain beyond the heaven, inhabited by (it seems) gods, but this, as Stephen Menn has pointed out to me, appears to be a critical adaptation of the *Phaedrus* myth, in which case the difference regarding the gods' location is unsurprising.

26                          DAVID SEDLEY

schema, with daimons intermediate between gods and humans,[39] and to have ascribed the intermediate status of daimons to the fact that their nature is a mixed one: they have divine powers but mortal passions. As scholars have well brought out,[40] Xenocrates had a particular penchant for such triple taxonomies, where an initial duality was enlarged by adding an intermediate mixed class, a tendency well exemplified by his three-level epistemology in the previous section.

In the case of daimons, their intermediate status could in principle owe something to *Symposium* 202d–204b, where Diotima explains their role as intermediaries between gods and humans.[41] But is that enough? It will not help us much towards understanding what warranted Xenocrates' specific reason for their intermediate status, namely a nature which makes them, despite their divine powers, subject to mortal passions. To make the best sense of this we must once again recognize the *Phaedrus* myth as Xenocrates' guiding text. There Zeus is followed around the heaven by 'an army of both gods and daimons'.[42] Yet when we read on we find that, of these, it is only the 'race of happy gods' (*Phdr.* 247a5, θεῶν γένος εὐδαιμόνων) that is compared to charioteers completely unconstrained by the resistance of a bad horse (247a2–c2, cf. 246a7–9) – that is, by passions. In this reference to 'happy gods' some may suspect Plato to have been speaking generically of gods and daimons, and not to have intended the term to exclude these latter. But Xenocrates, attuned as he was to threefold taxonomies, was justified by the letter of the text in reading this passage as accounting for the intermediate status of daimons: although superior to human souls in their powers, they are inferior to the gods in virtue of being, like human souls, subject to passions.[43]

On the gods, there will be more to say in Section 1.10.


## 1.7  Soul

In the *Timaeus*, the soul is tripartite, but only the intellect, housed in the head, is immortal. The highest form of incarnate happiness lies in the well-

---

[39]  F142 IP² = Plut. *De def. or.* 416C-D; cf. F143–6 IP².        [40]  E.g. Dillon 2003: 123–9.

[41]  Thus Dillon 2003: 129. At *Smp.* 203d8–e5 Eros, a *daimōn*, is intermediate between immortality and mortality, and between wisdom and folly. It seems likely that Xenocrates has interpreted these intermediacies to fit the *Phaedrus* account even better than Diotima's own: a *daimōn* is immortal but has the passions characteristic of mortals, and is intellectually wise but not unaffected by the folly of the lower soul-parts.

[42]  *Phdr.* 246e6: τῷ δ' ἔπεται στρατιὰ θεῶν τε καὶ δαιμόνων.

[43]  At [Plato] *Epinomis* 985a3–6, daimons are said to experience pleasure and pain. It is conceivable that this already reflects Xenocrates' influence.

## Xenocrates' Invention Of Platonism

being of this one immortal part, as captured by the etymology of *eudaimonia*: happiness consists in the *well*-being (*eu*) of your intellect – of the *daimōn* that dwells in your head (90b6–c6). Thus, incarnate happiness is closely associated with the exercise of *intellectual* virtue, which is the nearest a human being can come to immortality.

Xenocrates, in contrast, held that the *entire* soul, rational and irrational alike, is immortal, presumably deferring to the explicit statement at *Phaedrus* 245c5, 'All soul is immortal' (ψυχὴ πᾶσα ἀθάνατος).[44] He correspondingly identified *eudaimonia* with the soul's overall good state, moral as well as intellectual, saying that the *eudaimōn* person is one whose *daimōn*, now equated with their entire soul, fares well in the sense of being virtuous (*spoudaios*, a term which centrally includes moral virtue).[45] All this suggests yet again the use of the *Phaedrus* to modify the *Timaeus*. For the *Phaedrus* myth is the sole Platonic passage to bestow an indissoluble unity and joint immortality on the entire complex soul.[46]

Besides, as we have seen in Section 1.6, the same *Phaedrus* passage was read by Xenocrates as ascribing not only to human souls but even to daimons an irrational component, one which they would have to bring into harmony with the rest of the soul before they could aspire to the *eudaimonia* already effortlessly enjoyed by the gods. Although this theory is at least primarily one about daimons which are active in the external world, it establishes a very close isomorphism between those cosmically powerful daimons on the one hand and the human being's internal 'daimon', or soul, on the other. Both alike are rendered inferior to the gods by their possession of natures which include irrational drives.

In this context, consider too Xenocrates' notorious definition of soul as 'self-moving number',[47] which neatly exemplifies his way of combining

---

[44] I have not found explicit evidence that Xenocrates retained Plato's tripartition of the soul, but at F126 IP² we learn that he at least divided soul into an *aisthētikon* and a *logistikon* part, the former seemingly corresponding to the entire irrational soul as described at *Ti.* 69c5–71a3. The motive for this bipartite description was no doubt to account for the discarnate soul's capacity for astronomy, which requires a mixture of intellection and perception: see text in n. 32.

[45] Immortality of whole soul: F131 IP²; happiness as moral state of soul: F154–8 IP².

[46] Compare IP², commentary p. 311: 'Tarrant, *Plato's Interpr.*, 52, parla di una prevalenza del *Fedro* sul *Timeo* nel pensiero di Speusippo e Senocrate riguardo alla questione dell'immortalità dell'anima; ma questo sarebbe un caso unico e singolare.' If my contentions are right, it would be, on the contrary, an entirely typical case. Her reference is to Tarrant 2000, and the sentence cited is indeed virtually the only link between Xenocrates and the *Phaedrus* that I have so far found suggested in the modern literature, with the exception of Dancy 2003: §1, who observes the echo of *Phdr.* 254b7, ἐν ἁγνῷ βάθρῳ βεβῶσαν, in F14 IP²; and of Dillon as cited in n. 69. Dillon 2003: 123 also echoes Tarrant's point about the whole soul's immortality.

[47] F85–119 IP².

28                      DAVID SEDLEY

elements from the unwritten doctrines, the *Phaedrus* myth and the *Timaeus*. The differentia of soul as 'self-moving' is once again drawn primarily from the *Phaedrus* myth (245c).[48] That soul is by genus 'number' follows from the status of the One or Monad as the supreme principle. Speusippus had insisted, and Xenocrates apparently conceded the point, that the One was a principle from which nothing but number could be directly derived. Speusippus (cf. Section 1.3) inferred that other domains must be populated in parallel fashion by derivation from analogous principles,[49] earning Aristotle's derision for advocating an 'episodic' ontology with no unifying supreme principle.[50] Xenocrates, committed to Plato's oral doctrine of the One as the unifying first principle, preferred the solution of saying that not just arithmetic but *all* domains must be populated primarily by number. Typically he identified the generated numbers with the Platonic Forms germane to each discipline. But the status of soul as itself a special kind of number is another outcome of that same reasoning. And it seemed to him to have the direct backing of the *Timaeus*: when Plato there analysed rational soul as mixed out of indivisible and divisible Being (34b10–36b3), Xenocrates identified this indivisible Being with the One, and divisible Being with the Indefinite Dyad.[51] On such an understanding, the soul had been acknowledged by Plato himself to be numerical in essence.[52]

## 1.8    Categories

At this stage I shall risk going so far as to predict that the greater part of Xenocrates' attested system can be explained as warranted by an amalgamation of just three Platonic sources. The first was the supremely canonical *Timaeus*, the one dialogue that seemed to set out Plato's whole system, at least in outline. Second was the *Phaedrus* myth, initially no doubt invoked just for its opening words, in order to reinterpret the Timaean cosmology as sempiternalist, but as a consequence treated as canonical in its entirety. In this way, strikingly, Xenocrates chose to interpret the *Timaeus*' crea-

---

[48] The identification of soul in terms of self-movement does recur elsewhere (*Ti.* 37b5, *Laws* 10), but its prominence in the *Phaedrus* myth and direct association there with the soul's uncreatedness make this passage Xenocrates' obvious source text.

[49] See p. 14.    [50] Arist. *Metaph.* Λ 10.1075b37–1076a4, cf. Z 2.1028b21–4.    [51] F108 IP².

[52] That Xenocrates should really have meant that the soul is some specific cardinal number, e.g. 17, endowed with the power of self-motion, stretches credulity. I prefer, however speculatively, to think of a Xenocratean soul as more akin to an arithmetical formula, or even algorithm.

# Xenocrates' Invention Of Platonism

tionist myth by conjoining it with the *Phaedrus'* sempiternalist myth, and using the latter to constrain and supplement his reading of the former. Finally there were Plato's orally transmitted doctrines – above all, the posited first principles the One and the Dyad, valuable in that early formative phase as a basis for harmonizing the thought of Plato, that of Speusippus, and that of Xenocrates himself where he had gone beyond the letter of Plato's text. Thus here, in the very birth pangs of Platonism as a philosophical movement, we have a small but significant foretaste of the numerous other ways in which subsequent Platonists, down to the end of antiquity, would further reshape Plato's legacy by spotlighting, reinterpreting and supplementing specific portions of text from the corpus, sometimes with input from authorized sources external to it.

Although the *Timaeus* and *Phaedrus* are proving to be Xenocrates' canonical texts, I do not want to deny that other, very different dialogues may have played a part too. One example is the challenge to Platonists represented by the Aristotelian theory of ten categories, almost certainly developed by Aristotle while still working in the Academy. Many later Platonists, especially from Porphyry on, subscribed to the harmony of Plato and Aristotle,[53] and were thus ready to incorporate the Aristotelian category theory into Platonism. But Xenocrates, working at a date when Aristotle was becoming a competitor to Platonism and harmonization was not yet an option, chose the alternative strategy of rejecting the ten categories in favour of a simpler two-category scheme, absolute and relative, of which the latter category was taken to subsume all the Aristotelian non-substance categories.[54] What was his warrant for attributing this to Plato? Neither the *Timaeus* nor the *Phaedrus* could have provided adequate support. If he felt the need for a textual basis, he will have started from *Sophist* 255c, where the speaker divides kinds of being, to all appearances exhaustively, into absolutes and relatives.

Does this mean that the *Sophist* must be added to the Xenocratean canon? It is hard to be sure. Xenocrates' colleague Hermodorus, as reported by Simplicius, seems to have invoked the *Sophist's* categorial duality as an analytic tool for working out what range of properties fell under the One and what under the Indefinite Dyad.[55] Thus the dual categorial scheme's authoritative status could have initially been inferred from its being integral

---

[53] See in general, Karamanolis 2006.     [54] F15 IP². Cf. the rich discussion in Dancy 1999.
[55] See Hermodorus F5 IP². The relevant point is that the Indefinite Dyad, especially under its alternative name the 'large-and-small', could be treated as itself a type of relativity. In consequence, the absolute/relative distinction apparently served Hermodorus as an analytic tool for establishing which items were to be included in the Indefinite Dyad. For Xenocrates' use of

30 DAVID SEDLEY

to the oral doctrines, rather than from any sort of canonical status that might have been assigned to the *Sophist* in its own right.

On the other hand, once this two-category scheme had been identified as Platonic, by whatever means, Xenocrates could no doubt go on to point out traces of it in his canonical texts, citing for example Timaeus' apparent references to relativity in the account of the world soul's thinking (*Ti.* 37b1–3), even if neither that nor any other passage in either the *Timaeus* or the *Phaedrus* myth would have sufficed to show that Plato recognized *precisely* two categories.

## 1.9   Not Even the *Republic*?

If signs of ventures into sources beyond *Timaeus*, *Phaedrus* and the unwritten doctrines are rare in our evidence for Xenocrates, that is in itself a valuable reminder that *no* Platonist ever managed to treat the whole heterogeneous corpus as uniformly canonical, and that, even in its most advanced form, ancient Platonism was to be built around a comparatively small number of key passages. Xenocrates undoubtedly knew his way round much if not all of the corpus, but it by no means follows that he regarded those numerous other dialogues, or even parts of them, as authorized guides to Plato's own doctrines.[56] For example, I see little sign that any part of the *Republic, Symposium* or *Theaetetus*[57] had yet been selected for inclusion in the canon.[58]

In some cases we can do no more than guess at the reasons for Xenocrates' particular selectivity about canonical texts. But especially

---

similar analytic tools, albeit without explicit reference to the *Sophist*, cf. F143 IP², where he correlates equality to the One.

[56] Arguably this strong preference for just two dialogues weakens the case for the hypothesis of Alline 1915: 46–50, that Xenocrates produced or oversaw the first full edition of Plato's works. Cf. the prudent doubts of Carlini 1972: 6–8.

[57] Note in particular that the *Theaetetus* Digression, later a Platonist *locus classicus*, situates astronomy *above* the heaven (173e6), in contrast to Xenocrates' own *Phaedrus*-based cosmic epistemology as we have seen it reported by Sextus.

[58] How about the *Phaedo*? The question is too complicated to discuss here. According to F138–9 IP² Xenocrates' explained *Phd.* 62b3–4, ὡς ἔν τινι φρουρᾷ ἐσμεν, in terms of our 'Titanic' or earthly, as opposed to 'Olympian' or heavenly, pedigree (see further, Dillon 2003: 133–4). This is hard to tie to any specific part of his Platonist system. I do, however, plan to argue, on a future occasion, that the Platonist 'Argument from Relatives' quoted in the remains of Aristotle's *On Ideas* (ap. Alexander, *in Metaph.* 82.11–83.26) is based on a recognizably Xenocratean reading of *Phaedo* 78d10–e4. The *Phaedo*, if considered canonical, could provide the new Platonist canon with arguments for the separation of Forms and at the same time be read, especially by – once again – concentrating on its myth, as compatible with such theses of Xenocratean Platonism as the whole soul's immortality and the triple cosmic stratification.

striking – we have already seen examples of it – is his apparent avoidance of the *Republic*, despite Plato's own emphasis on the continuity between that dialogue and the canonical *Timaeus*. This demands further consideration, especially as some scholars actually *have* detected a reference to the *Republic* in the continuation of Sextus' report (p. 23) on Xenocrates' cosmic epistemology:

> Hence too the tradition of three Fates: Atropos, whose domain is the intelligibles, since she is unalterable; Clotho, whose domain is the perceptibles; and Lachesis, whose domain is the opinables.[59]

This, it has sometimes been suggested, alludes to the Myth of Er in *Republic* 10, where (617c1–d1, cf. 620d6–e6) the three Fates (*Moirai*) are likewise named. But the symbolism in the *Republic* is palpably different: there the three of them turn the spindle of their mother Necessity, while Lachesis sings of past events, Clotho of present ones, and Atropos of future ones. Thus in the *Republic* myth the three 'Fates' are interpreted, easily enough, as the agents of an omnitemporal destiny. Xenocrates has entirely replaced this symbolism, instead correlating the three deities to three cosmic zones distinguished in his epistemology.

What, in his eyes, can have justified that radical reinterpretation of the three Fates? The answer, I suggest, lies in the *Phaedrus* myth itself, where the rules for reincarnation are set up to ensure that 'whoever lives justly shares a better fate (*moira*), and whoever lives unjustly, a worse one' (248e3–5). This is partially explicated a few lines later, when we learn how the newly departed souls are, after judgement, sent below ground for punishment, or rewarded with assignment to 'some place' in the heaven (249a5–b1). To Xenocrates these locations will have seemed to connect the three *Moirai* with his three cognitively differentiated domains: the perceptible realm below the heaven, of which the underworld is the nadir; the intelligible realm beyond the heaven, into which the most enlightened souls can venture; and between those, the heavenly realm itself, in which the cognitively mixed discipline of astronomy is practised. In the Platonic world as understood by Xenocrates, the fitting punishment or reward for a soul would be demotion or promotion to one of those cognitive domains.

I submit then that Xenocrates, far from welcoming the Myth of Er into his canon, can be seen consciously downplaying its allegorical

---

[59] SE *M* 7.149: καὶ τρεῖς Μοίρας παραδεδόσθαι, Ἄτροπον μὲν τὴν τῶν νοητῶν, ἀμετάθετον οὖσαν, Κλωθὼ δὲ τὴν τῶν αἰσθητῶν, Λάχεσιν δὲ τὴν τῶν δοξαστῶν. For the immediately preceding text see n. 32.

interpretation of the three Fates and giving priority to an alternative decoding of these divinities, one that prioritizes the *Phaedrus* myth over that in the *Republic*.

It thus seems that, if Xenocrates excluded the *Republic* from his Platonist canon, his doing so was not a mere oversight, but reflective of a policy.[60] What might have been his motive? Here is one suggestion. Speusippus is reported to have excluded the good from any role at the level of his first principles: goodness enters only at the later and hence lower stages of generation.[61] This doctrine is in manifest conflict with *Republic* 6–7, where the Good is *the* supreme explanatory principle, so supreme indeed as to be ranked 'beyond Being'. Many modern interpreters have shared Speusippus' difficulty in seeing how an evaluative principle like Good could stand even above such disciplines as mathematics, so the disagreement between Plato and Speusippus on the primacy or derivativeness of good should cause no surprise. Let us assume that this was already an openly aired issue during Plato's lifetime. Assume too, as I have already suggested, that after Plato's death Xenocrates' task was to develop a version of Platonism that consolidated and unified the school tradition. Just as this meant playing up the twin principles of the One and the Dyad, which could be linked in one way or another to Plato, to Speusippus and to Xenocrates himself, so too it meant playing down the *Republic*, which could have been included in the canon only at the cost of virtually excluding Speusippus from it. There is no reason to infer that Xenocrates himself endorsed any such objection to the *Republic*'s metaphysics: it is enough to postulate that Speusippus did.

Additionally, consider Xenocrates' reported explanation of what a Platonic Form is: it is a 'paradigmatic cause of those things which are by nature constituted at all times' (αἰτία παραδειγματικὴ τῶν κατὰ φύσιν ἀεὶ συνεστώτων).[62] This seems designed to confirm that at *Timaeus* 28a–29b the description of the Demiurge as a craftsman looking to the relevant Form, and using it as an eternal paradigm on which to model the world, is not a sign that any such act of divine craftsmanship ever took place: rather, Xenocrates is telling us, in support of his sempiternalist interpretation, the Forms are the eternal paradigms of things – animal, fire, etc. – that themselves are always present in nature and therefore never needed to be

---

[60] This latter alternative gets some support from test.4 IP², an entry in the Suda according to which Xenocrates wrote a work *On Plato's Republic* (Περὶ τῆς Πλάτωνος Πολιτείας). Whether or not (see IP² *ad loc.*) this was identical to the work entitled simply Περὶ πολιτείας recorded at DL 4.12, it is likely to have presented Xenocrates' views on the *Republic*'s relation to the canon.

[61] Arist. *Metaph.* Λ7.1072b30–1073a1 = 53 IP = 42a Tarán.     [62] F14 IP².

created. Yet, according to *Republic* 10 (596a–597b), human craftsmen not only look to Forms as paradigms, much as the Demiurge does in the *Timaeus*, but do so precisely in the process of creating new artefacts. The *Republic* 10 passage could thus easily be invoked in favour of the literalist interpretation of divine craftmanship. On that ground too it should be unsurprising to us that Xenocrates opted not to privilege the *Republic* as a canonical text for his own construction of Platonism.

His definition of a Form as 'paradigmatic cause of those things which are *by nature constituted at all times*' is often taken to have its emphasis on 'by nature', and thus to be his way of excluding Forms of artefacts from Platonic ontology. If I am right about his motivation, the emphasis is rather on 'at all times' (ἀεί): natural entities stand in an *eternal* causal relationship to the Forms on which they are modelled. If so, the exclusion of Forms of artefacts was not in itself his aim,[63] so much as a piece of collateral damage in the war against the literalist reading of Timaean creation.[64]

There turn out, then, to be multiple indications that Xenocrates was motivated to exclude the *Republic* from contributing authoritatively to the Platonist metaphysics he was constructing. If it is asked how such an exclusion could have been found credible by his circle, we should recall that the canonical *Timaeus* opens with Socrates delivering what is emphatically claimed to be a complete summary of (what readers can recognize as) the *Republic*, yet with the metaphysics entirely left out. Xenocrates was well placed to explain this surprising omission. Plato, he could say, was thereby signalling his formal exclusion of the *Republic*'s metaphysics from the canon, and marking the *Republic* as a purely ethical and political investigation.

## 1.10 Celestial Movers

The following chapter will examine a mosaic image (Museo Archeologico Nazionale di Napoli 124545) whose archetype was a painting designed to

---

[63] Cf. however Broadie 2007 for a philosophically more sensitive explanation than I have attempted here of Xenocrates' denial of artefact Forms. That artefact Forms were indeed denied by the Xenocratean Academy is confirmed by Aristotle's words at *Metaph.* A 9.991b6–7, οἷον οἰκία καὶ δακτύλιος, ὧν οὔ φαμεν εἴδη εἶναι, where the first person plural, meaning 'we Academics', locates the passage in his last years as a member of the Xenocratean Academy before leaving to found the Lyceum in 335 BC.

[64] My proposal must also assume a non-canonical status for the *Cratylus*, the only other dialogue to introduce Forms of human artefacts (389a–390b).

advertise Xenocrates' uniquely authoritative access to Plato's fundamental beliefs. In it we see Plato giving the young Xenocrates an astronomy lesson, reflectively watched over by the great astronomer Eudoxus, and by Timaeus, Plato's spokesman in the eponymous dialogue. In the dialogue itself (40d2–5), Timaeus remarks that his own oral account of celestial motion is necessarily limited: he could not, he explains, take it further without the aid of a visible model. The mosaic image shows Plato doing precisely that – using a visible model in order to explicate for Xenocrates' benefit a system of celestial movers alluded to only obliquely in his *Phaedrus* myth. It thereby insinuates that the astronomical theory of the *Phaedrus* points beyond the *Timaeus* towards a deeper or more precise celestial mathematics, one into which Plato has granted Xenocrates alone a privileged insight.

In this image, the design of the celestial sphere to which Plato is pointing with a rod has caused puzzlement. As is clear from the excellent reconstructive diagram of Gaiser 1980 (Figure 1.1), it is in no obvious way reminiscent of the heavenly sphere whose construction by the Demiurge is described in the *Timaeus* (33b10–40d5). Nor, according to Gaiser's meticulous analysis, does it appear compatible with *any* known celestial map that might have been constructed in the era of the Early Academy.[65] But we need not suspect either (with Gaiser) anachronism or simple error, because an alternative and, I hope, more satisfying explanation is available.

It can be quickly confirmed from Gaiser's diagram that the sphere has a set of six parallel bands set on one axis (A1–6) and, intersecting them, five further parallel bands set on another axis (B1–5). That makes eleven bands in all. Recall next that in the *Phaedrus* myth 'an army of gods and daimons, ordered in eleven parts' (246e6–247a1), parades around the heaven – eleven, because within it each troupe is led by one of the twelve Olympians, with the exception of Hestia, who appropriately stays at home.

We must bear in mind too the following three points about Xenocrates. (i) He considered arithmetic a fundamental tool of metaphysical analysis. (ii) He developed a theory according to which the heaven is the location of the mathematical intermediates. (iii) He treated the *Phaedrus* myth as a canonical text about the heaven, sufficiently authoritative to elaborate or modify the doctrinal content even of the *Timaeus*. In view of all this, it would be most surprising if he had *not* advanced a theoretical

---

[65] Gaiser 1980: ch. 7.

# Xenocrates' Invention Of Platonism

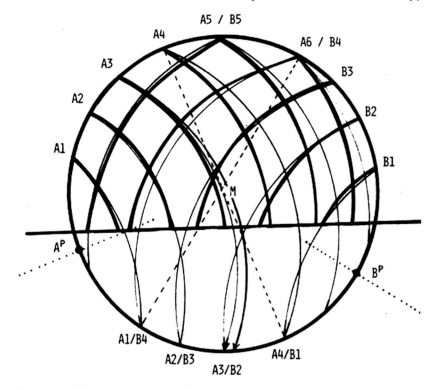

Figure 1.1 Gaiser's reconstruction of the celestial sphere, adjusted for perspective. Thick bands are as shown in the mosaic, thin ones their corrected equivalents.

From K. Gaiser (1980), *Das Philosophenmosaik in Neapel. Eine Darstellung der platonischen Akademie*, Abhandlungen der Heidelberger Akademie der Wissenschaften, Phil.-hist. Klasse, Heidelberg. Reproduced courtesy of Winter Verlag

interpretation of the *Phaedrus*' eleven circuits.[66] I have found little textual evidence for what that interpretation might have been, if indeed Xenocrates ever finalized it, but the following speculations commend themselves.[67]

---

[66] For the question what may, in other ancient contexts, have made eleven a significant number, cf. Rashed forthcoming: ch. 7.

[67] For reports of some similar speculations about the *Phaedrus* passage in its own right, cf. Hermias, *in Phdr.* 141.25–30: ζητητέον δὲ ἐν τούτοις τίς ὁ Ζεὺς καὶ τίνες οἱ δώδεκα θεοί. τινὲς μὲν οὖν τὰς δώδεκα σφαίρας τοῦ κόσμου ἤκουσαν, τὴν ἀπλανῆ, τὰς ἑπτὰ πλανωμένας καὶ τὰ τέσσαρα στοιχεῖα· καὶ τὸν μὲν Δία ἔταξαν κατὰ τὴν ἀπλανῆ ἐπειδὴ πάντα ἄγει, τὴν δὲ Ἑστίαν κατὰ τὴν γῆν διὰ τὸ ἀκίνητον. οἱ δὲ τὰς τῶν σφαιρῶν τούτων ψυχάς. οἱ δὲ ἔτι τούτων καθαρωτέρους τοὺς νοῦς τοὺς ἐπιβεβηκότας ταύταις ταῖς ψυχαῖς.

36                          DAVID SEDLEY

First of all, Hestia will correspond to the stationary earth, perhaps as its principle of stability. As for the six bands A1–6, they surely correspond to the six male gods, while the five bands B1–5 will represent the five goddesses who remain once Hestia is excluded.

These bands, given their positions on the celestial globe, can hardly be visible stellar orbits, but may nevertheless represent the circular self-motions of the divine souls jointly responsible for celestial motion. Where a male and a female band intersect, that is likely to represent a further, combined source of motion, analogous to a sexual union. With eleven simple movers, and perhaps in addition these thirty ($5 \times 6$) combined sources of motion, there are potentially forty-one different sources of motion.[68] Of these forty-one, the simple self-motion of Zeus (whom Xenocrates equated with the monad),[69] is likely to be the mover of the fixed stars, corresponding functionally to the Circle of the Same in the *Timaeus*.[70] The forty remaining motions would then somehow jointly provide the motions of the Sun, the Moon and the five planets, corresponding functionally to the Circle of the Different in the *Timaeus*.

The mosaic image, as already mentioned, shows Eudoxus reflectively watching over Plato's lesson to Xenocrates. That invites a comparison between Xenocrates' astronomical calculations, portrayed here as enjoying the blessing of Eudoxus, and Aristotle's roughly contemporary efforts in *Metaphysics* Λ 8 to count the number of (in his case *un*moved) movers required by – once again – the Eudoxan system, arriving at his own final figure of forty-seven. All this counting of movers suggests that Aristotle's calculation was developed in rivalry with Xenocrates'. It is in fact far from obvious why Aristotle ever felt the need to postulate a plurality of unmoved movers, one per sphere, rather than a single divine prime mover inspiring the movements of all the concentric spheres, as *Metaphysics* Λ 7 might have led us to expect. Xenocrates, by contrast, is counting not divine unmoved movers but divine *self*-movers, of which there would indeed have to be one per sphere. These considerations may suggest that the counting of prime movers started with Xenocrates, seeking with the help of Eudoxan theory to extract all the mathematical content of

---

[68] These complex motions were probably identified by Xenocrates with the 'many ... paths (*diexodoi*) inside the heaven along which the blessed family of gods turns (*epistrephetai*)', *Phdr.* 247a4–5.

[69] Dillon 2003: 102 n. 44, and 2007: 32–3, rightly sees an allusion to *Phdr.* 246e4, ὁ μὲν δὴ μέγας ἡγεμὼν ἐν οὐρανῷ Ζεύς, in Aetius' report (1.7.30 = F133 IP², p. 16) that Xenocrates described the monad both as ἐν οὐρανῷ βασιλεύουσαν and as Zeus.

[70] For the same suggestion see Hermias' report in n. 67.

the *Phaedrus* myth, and that Aristotle's competing Eudoxan calculation arose in response to him.

Did Xenocrates or Aristotle have the last word in this counting match? I shall address that question briefly at the end of my chapter on the mosaic, which now follows.

CHAPTER 2

# An Iconography of Xenocrates' Platonism[*]

### David Sedley

## 2.1 The Mosaic

In the preceding chapter I traced the basis on which Xenocrates, Plato's second successor as head of the Academy, created the original textual canon for building a Platonic system. It emerged that his authoritative Platonic texts were two myths – the creation myth of the *Timaeus*, and the *Phaedrus*' mythical travelogue about the destiny of eternal souls. The latter passage, I argued, was so canonical as to determine, on occasion, how even the former should be interpreted.

In this second in my pair of chapters I turn to an iconographic snapshot of the process by which Xenocrates' Platonic canon purportedly obtained its authority. The presumed original painting is preserved for us in a mosaic copy, the 'mosaic of the philosophers' from a suburban villa thought to be that of T. Siminius Stephanus, located a little north of the Vesuvian gate of Pompeii. Buried by the AD 79 eruption of Vesuvius, and rediscovered in 1897, the mosaic is today on display in the National Archaeological Museum of Naples (Museo Archeologico Nazionale di Napoli 124545). A later, inferior copy of the same original painting survives in a third-century mosaic from Sarsina in Umbria, now kept in the Villa Albani at Rome,[1] which we will have occasion to visit at a later point in this chapter. The Pompeian image, which excluding the frame

---

[*] For fruitful discussion and suggestions, my thanks to audiences at Harvard, Durham, St Louis, Cambridge, Athens, Toronto and Florence; and to Caroline Vout, Andrew Stewart, Marwan Rashed, Federico Petrucci, Ilaria Romeo, Glenn Most, Francesco Verde, Victor Gysembergh, James Allen, Francesco Ademollo, Nigel Spivey, Richard McKirahan, Caterina Pellò, Bev Sedley, Gábor Betegh, Michele Alessandrelli, Reviel Netz, Malcolm Schofield, Phillip Horky, Voula Tsouna, Carl Huffman, and the anonymous readers from Cambridge University Press. As in the preceding chapter, no one listed here should be assumed to agree with my conclusions.

[1] Richter 1965: fig. 319.

*An Iconography Of Xenocrates' Platonism*                    39

measures a mere 80 cm by 80 cm, was found by the excavators not cemented into place but propped up in a bronzesmith's workshop. Whether it was in the process of being bought or sold, or simply awaiting repairs to its regular location in the villa following damage in the earthquake of AD 62, is a matter for conjecture. The mosaic itself is in pristine condition.

The image shown is a tableau of seven philosophers, one of them pointing at a globe with a rod. The group of seven and the astronomical lesson with the globe are both recurrent motifs in Greek art, and it is very likely that they stemmed ultimately from a depiction of the Seven Sages in which Thales was showing the other six his celestial sphere. At times, the Pompeian mosaic has itself been interpreted as depicting a meeting of the Seven Sages.[2] But the overwhelming consensus, whose earliest adherents included Hermann Diels, and which has since been skilfully defended at length by Gaiser (1980) and Rashed (2013a),[3] is that the scene in fact shows Plato and certain of his associates in the Academy. If, as remains likely, it is a descendant of an older Seven Sages motif, the detailed content has been transformed.

That conclusion, that the image depicts Plato in the Academy, will serve as my own starting point, but will also be amply confirmed in what follows. In the majority of cases I also endorse Gaiser's and Rashed's identifications of the seven figures, for reasons which will be documented below. Figure 2.1 shows the mosaic along with the seven conjectural identifications. Only one of these, Timaeus, is an altogether new proposal.[4] My interpretation of the scene's meaning, on the other hand, will be an entirely new one.[5]

Third from the left is the scene's dominant figure. That this figure is Plato, and the location the Academy, is very widely accepted, and is confirmed in particular by the exedra, with its elegant semi-circular lion-footed stone bench,[6] from whose central position the figure is teaching,

---

[2] Most recently by Griffiths 2016.    [3] See e.g. Berti 2012: 31–4, who largely follows Gaiser.

[4] The figure is Heraclides Ponticus according to Gaiser, Solon according to Rashed, Philip of Opus according to Berti 2012.

[5] For reasons of space the image's decorative mosaic border is not included in the illustration (fig. 2.1). Whatever its date, it is thematically unrelated to the main image. The complete mosaic is readily available online, e.g. in the Wikipedia article 'Plato''s Academy Mosaic'.

[6] The easiest way for the eye to pick out the shape of the exedra is to start from the lion foot above which Speusippus is sitting and follow the curved bench round to the other lion foot, below Xenocrates' left leg.

```
                    Timaeus
                         Eudoxus
              Plato              Xenocrates
  Archytas  Speusippus                    Aristotle
```

Figure 2.1   *The Mosaic of the Philosophers*, Museo Archeologico Nazionale di Napoli 124545, with conjectural identifications.
Photo by Giorgio Albana. Reproduced by permission of Ministero per i Beni e le Attività Culturali – Museo Archeologico di Napoli.

that being the prized prerogative of the head of the Academy.[7] In addition to a strong general resemblance to many surviving portraits of Plato,[8]

---

[7] The same exedra/seat as was used by Xenocrates' successor Polemo was passed from scholarch to scholarch at least until the time of Carneades, and probably longer, since it was still to be seen as late as 79 BC (DL 4.19, Cic. *Fin.* 5.2, 4). I see no reason to doubt that its predecessor was already serving that function in Plato's own day, since such structures are well attested in the fourth century BC: see further Caruso 2013: 102–4, and for later developments of the teaching exedra, Sorabji 2014.
[8] Richter 1965: vol. 2, figs. 903–75.

*An Iconography Of Xenocrates' Platonism* 41

the artist has in particular caught Plato's reportedly characteristic posture with hunched shoulders,[9] in contrast to the more upright or open postures of the other six figures. In view of all this it is hard to resist Marwan Rashed's acute further observation that the person depicted is sitting directly under what is almost certainly one of the plane trees for which the Academy grove was famous, with the Greek for 'plane', *platanos*, punningly alluding to Plato's own name.[10] Some have instead identified it as an olive, the Academy being well known for these too, and the foliage and fruit of the two species are admittedly hard to tell apart in a mosaic; but what seems to me decisive are the lighter patches on the tree's trunk, representing the stripped bark characteristic of the plane.

Before proceeding to the image's detailed exegesis, let me set down three interpretative principles that have increasingly impressed themselves on me as fundamental to the image's decoding.

(1)   The artist is constantly testing our knowledge of the Platonic corpus.
(2)   Individuals are regularly identified and characterized by symbols in the space above their heads, scrupulously linked to them by a vertical connector. Plato's symbol, we have seen, is the tree directly behind him: the eye follows its trunk upwards and at the top recognizes a *platanos*. To take a second example, Eudoxus is identified when the eye follows the line of the pillar behind him up to the sundial that tops it: for the invention of a sundial known as the *arachnē* was credited to Eudoxus.[11] By my count, four more of these links still await recognition.
(3)   Nothing should be expected to have been included for merely decorative reasons. Every item depicted will prove to carry at least one allusive or symbolic meaning.

## 2.2   The Occasion

In *Laws* 6.769b7–770b8, Plato's three discussants recognize the fact that they are, as the Athenian stranger puts it, 'in the sunset of life' (ἐν δυσμαῖς τοῦ βίου, 770a6). In that situation, they agree, it is vital for the legislator to train a successor (*diadochos*, 769c4) who will maintain and further improve his initial written outline of the laws. I submit that the image shows Plato

---

[9]  Plut. *Adul.* 53C.
[10]  Plin. *NH* 12.1.5. Rashed 2013a: 36 favours a plane; Gaiser 1980: 65, followed in this by Mattusch 2008: 214, an olive (attested for the Academy at e.g. Aristoph. *Nu.* 1005, Paus. 1.30.2).
[11]  Vitruvius 9.8.1.

himself in the exactly equivalent situation – that is, in the sunset of life, and preparing a successor to carry on and perfect the work outlined in his own writings.

Here is the reason. Plato's bare feet both cast shadows. His right foot rests on the horizontal sitting-area of the exedra, and its shadow is minimal. But his left leg is extended forwards, and its foot casts a long and very prominent shadow along the vertical front-edge of the exedra.[12] Since the sundial above Eudoxus must face south, the viewer is looking north, and the elongated shadow of Plato's foot points almost east. This shows that the sun is very close to setting. At first sight that detail might seem merely to tell us the time of day – until, that is, we notice that Plato is entirely alone in casting a shadow. No other person or object present in the Academy has a shadow – not even the gnomon of the sundial, whose very raison d'être is to cast a shadow. There are some patterns in the foreground which could represent the varying play of light and shade, but nothing remotely comparable to the eye-catching shadow of Plato's foot. It follows that the sunset depicted is not a chronological marker, but *the symbolic setting of Plato's own sun*. We have here, it seems, an artfully contrived echo of the *Laws* passage.

In short, the year is 347 BC, and Plato is in the sunset of his life. Given the allusion to *Laws* 6, we must expect this to be a scene in the Academy in which Plato is instructing his *diadochos* – a successor whose task will be the one described in the *Laws*, both to maintain and to perfect the principles he has himself committed to writing. And in fact all three potential heirs to Plato's headship of the school are present: his nephew Speusippus, to whom he will in the event award the succession, and who will serve as school-head for eight years; Xenocrates, who will in turn succeed Speusippus and remain school-head for a quarter of a century; and Aristotle, destined to be head not of the Academy but of his own rival school, the Lyceum. Each of the three candidates carries a scroll.[13]

---

[12] This detail has usually been ignored, although Mattusch 2008 explains that Plato 'has slipped off his sandals', and the Museo Archeologico Nazionale di Napoli website (http://cir.campania .beniculturali.it/museoarcheologiconazionale > search 'mosaico filosofi': the URL for the actual page is too long to print here) refers to it as a geometrical figure.

[13] The roll Aristotle is carrying could (as Francesco Verde ingeniously suggests to me) be book 1 of the *De caelo*. If so, Xenocrates is probably holding the *Phaedrus* (cf. Chapter 1, Section 1.4 for the dispute about the *Timaeus* that would underlie this). If, unlike the other two candidates, Xenocrates holds his scroll with a relatively casual one-handed grip (cf. Birt 1907 for the range of typical holds), that is perhaps because he appreciates the limitations of the written word, as famously expounded in the *Phaedrus* itself, and is entirely absorbed in listening to Plato's spoken word. On this theme, see further p. 60–1.

## 2.3  Speusippus

As Plato's nephew and legal heir, Speusippus quite correctly sits to his uncle's right.[14] But he is paying no attention to Plato's lecture, being instead seduced by the blandishments of the exotically dressed figure who will turn out to be the Pythagorean Archytas. He has edged away from Plato, and is intent on Archytas' words alone. Part of the artist's message is evidently that Speusippus was so absorbed in Pythagoreanism as to be philosophically deaf to Plato,[15] and not his real intellectual heir.

The same negative portrayal finds symbolic confirmation, I suggest, in a series of further, relentlessly pejorative details. The most important of these is the dead or withered branch of Plato's tree stretching above Speusippus' head. It confirms that he will not be carrying forward his uncle's legacy. Notice too how meticulously the artist has ensured that the branch symbol refers to Speusippus alone, connected to him via the nearer (right-hand) pillar of the gateway: if the dead branch had extended so much as a millimetre further to the left, it would have had to refer to Archytas too, via the other pillar, and obscured the strictly familial point being made.

If any doubt remains that this figure is Speusippus, note how, alongside the negative philosophical innuendo, the artist has inserted subtle allusions to Speusippus' three notorious character flaws:

(a)  A hot temper.[16]
(b)  A weakness for pleasures, gastronomic as well as sexual.[17]
(c)  Breaching confidentiality: according to an obscurely reported story, he gave away secrets that Isocrates had entrusted to him.[18]

---

[14]  Gaiser 1980: 60–1 points out that, provided that Plato is assumed to be in his last years (a conjecture now confirmed by the sunset motif), the relative ages of the other characters are correctly depicted, including Speusippus, who would be around 60 at the time.

[15]  Cf. Chapter 1, Section 1.3.

[16]  Philodemus, *Ind. Ac.* col. 7 = 1 IP = T2 Tarán; DL 4.1, < 2 IP, <T1 Tarán; Suidas *s.v.* Σπεύσιππος = T3 Tarán = 3 IP.

[17]  1 IP = T2 Tarán; DL 4.1, < 2 IP, <T1 Tarán; Suidas *s.v.* Σπεύσιππος = T3 Tarán = 3 IP. Allegedly, Speusippus travelled as far as Macedonia for a wedding feast (DL 4.1), and his 'love of pleasure' (φιληδονία) also extended to the pursuit of sex and money (Athenaeus 279E–F = T39a Tarán = 7 IP; 546D = T39b Tarán).

[18]  DL 4.2: 'And he [Speusippus] was the first to bring to light, from Isocrates, what were called secrets, as Caeneus says' (καὶ πρῶτος παρὰ Ἰσοκράτους τὰ καλούμενα ἀπόρρητα ἐξήνεγκεν, ὥς φησι Καινεύς). The details are obscure, but the word order prohibits the frequent translation 'what were called secrets by Isocrates', and thereby excludes the secrets' having been, as one might otherwise have expected and as Huffman 2005: 135–6 proposes, Pythagorean ones. More probably there is a link to Isocrates' emphatic advice against revealing secrets at *Ad Demonicum* 22, cf. 25, which may have been, or been interpreted as, a rebuke to Speusippus. But the actual story of his giving away Isocrates' secrets seems to be beyond recovery. See also Tarán 1981: 181–2.

# DAVID SEDLEY

The hot temper and gluttony are captured by a bronze cooking vessel which sits on top of the gateway, linked to Speusippus by the right-hand (nearer) pillar. A cooking pot, we may reflect, on the one hand is liable to boil over,[19] but on the other is the glutton's best friend.

In addition, although the scroll Speusippus holds may formally be the mark of his candidacy, as those held by Xenocrates and Aristotle presumably are, there is a difference to notice: the scroll he holds is a *sealed* one, which he has just taken out of a box and brought into the daylight. We thus have here an allusion to Speusippus' notoriety for giving away secrets.[20] The opened box is shown facing away from us, because what matters is not what is in it (maybe nothing now), but the secret text Speusippus has already taken out of it and is about to display.

## 2.4 Aristotle

Meanwhile, symmetrically to our right, another desertion is looming: the easily recognized figure of Aristotle looks poised to leave the Academy altogether.[21] By his departure he will relinquish any claim to Plato's philosophical legacy.

I am convinced that the area visible in the right background is not, as has been very widely assumed, the Athenian acropolis, but the grove of the Lyceum, which thanks to a telescoping of its actual geographical distance is enabled to loom above Aristotle as his own identity icon, foreshadowing his ultimate destination as founder of a breakaway school located there. Aristotle is linked to his symbol, not this time by a pillar, tree or other vertical object, but by the reddish patch of ground which starts just above

---

[19] Plato often uses ζέω, 'boil', for anger, notably at *Ti.* 70a7–c1. Thus interpreted, the allusion might have an apologetic function with regard to Speusippus' irascibility, since the anger (θυμός) described by Plato is righteous indignation, acting on behalf of reason. However, according to the anecdotal tradition Speusippus' irascibility made him worse than Archytas in that, whereas Archytas' conduct was considered a paradigm of the Pythagorean injunction never to inflict punishment while still angry (Archytas A7 DK, see Huffman 2005: 283–92), Speusippus was said to have done just that, in throwing his puppy down a well (DL 4.1). So far as concerns the truth of the allegations, the three highlighted vices might seem to correspond a little too conveniently to the three Platonic soul parts: breaking confidentiality, a failure of reason; anger, an excessive reaction by the θυμοειδές; gluttony, a vice of the ἐπιθυμητικόν. On the other hand, allegations (a) and (b), if true, would lend a credible psychological motivation to his postulation of ἀοχλησία, 'freedom from disturbance', as the ethical goal (Clem. *Strom.* 2.22.133 = 101 IP = 77 Tarán), and to his denial that pleasure is even a good (Arist. *EN* 7.13.1153b1–7 = 108 IP = 80a Tarán).

[20] Cf. DL 4.2 ἐξήνεγκεν (note 18).

[21] Compare numerous portraits in Richter 1965: vol. 2, figs. 986–1013, and on his short-cut beard see also Aelian *VH* 3.19.

his head, skirts the white mound in the immediate background,[22] and then merges into a darker-coloured path. The barely noticeable white mound, located inside the Academy, has no obvious geographical reference, but it does serve to ensure by its interposition that Xenocrates is not included in the allusion to the Lyceum.

The path itself runs immediately along the outside of the city wall, passing a major gate which may well be the Dipylon, and finally, in the distance, appearing to provide access to the gymnasium. This is surely meant to be recognized as the route taken by Socrates from the Academy to the Lyceum as described in the opening lines of Plato's *Lysis*:

> I was on my way from the Academy and heading directly for the Lyceum, along the path that runs outside the wall, under the wall itself. But when I reached the small gate (θυρίς) where the spring of Panops is, I met Hippothales ... 'Socrates,' said Hippothales, seeing me, 'where are you heading for, and from where?' 'From the Academy,' I replied, 'and heading directly for the Lyceum.' (*Lysis* 203a1–b2)

Rather than take the southern route from the Academy to the Lyceum by the main road, which would have brought him into the city through the Dipylon Gate and the agora, before finally reaching the Lyceum itself, Socrates chose a route via a smaller gate further along the city wall, thereafter leading to the Lyceum 'directly' (εὐθύ) – that is, without passing through the agora,[23] where he would inevitably have fallen into conversation and had little chance of ever reaching the Lyceum. Unfortunately he failed to reach it in any case, owing to his unexpected encounter with Hippothales, but that is another story.

The details of Socrates' journey, down to the point where he was intercepted by Hippothales, are replicated perfectly in the mosaic. Not only has the artist depicted the path which he joined, running immediately under the city wall, but we can even make out at its far end a small gateway in the wall, facing out onto what must be the luxuriant patch of greenery around a spring,[24] the very spot where Socrates met Hippothales. In the mosaic, then, the precise journey from the Academy towards the Lyceum

---

[22] Its being a hill is conveyed by (a) the way it obscures the left tip of the Lyceum, and (b) its appropriately curved pattern of tesserae. The latter, less than obvious in the photograph, became very clear to me when I examined the mosaic itself.

[23] I assume that this is what Socrates means by εὐθύ, rather than that he was taking a shortcut, which the route described would not in fact have been, see Planeaux 2001. In maintaining that Socrates' words are simply false, Planeaux considers but too quickly rejects the interpretation of εὐθύ + gen. that I adopt here, as well as overlooking the alternative proposal (Richards 1901) that it had come to mean simply 'to'.

[24] For the difficulty of identifying these last two items archaeologically, cf. Caruso 2014: 203.

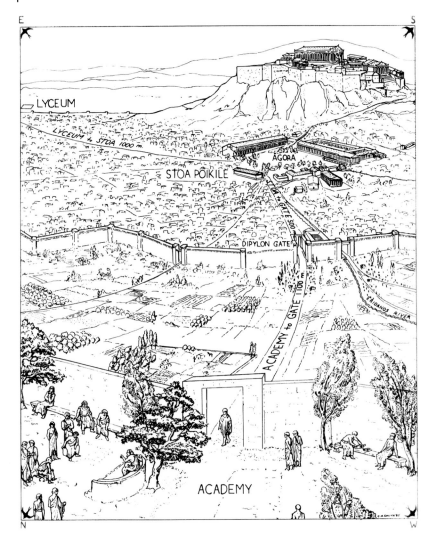

Figure 2.2 From the Academy to the Lyceum.
Drawing by Candace H. Smith. From L&S, Vol. 1, 4. Reproduced, with slight modification, courtesy of Candace H. Smith.

formerly travelled by Plato's teacher, as immortalized in the *Lysis*, is about to be travelled again, this time symbolically, by Plato's own leading pupil, in the more sinister form of a philosophical desertion.

This meticulous textual allusion fully confirms the identification of the background area as the Lyceum. Those who locate the scene in Athens normally

## An Iconography Of Xenocrates' Platonism                    47

take the row of columns at the very top to represent instead the Parthenon,[25] but the structure's apparently having no roof, while it may momentarily bring to mind today's ruined Parthenon, would have virtually excluded any such identification by ancient viewers. A roofless temple is an uncompleted temple. And these columns are in any case too broad and low to represent a completed temple. Rather, they seem to be the limestone Doric column bases of the monumental Olympeion (or Temple of Olympian Zeus), started by the Peisistratids, abandoned with their overthrow in 510 BC, resumed in 174–164 BC, and not finally completed until the principate of Hadrian. The rudiments of this monumental temple, it seems, served our artist as a familiar landmark for the adjacent Lyceum. On the assumption that the landmark was recognizable to the image's original Athenian viewers, we may with moderate confidence date the painting between 335 BC, when Aristotle founded the Lyceum, and 174 BC, when building of the Olympeion resumed, now with Pentelic marble instead of the much darker limestone shown in the mosaic.[26]

Also visible in the Lyceum are one or more areas of water, represented by the patches of blue in particular, though not necessarily limited to them. This is explained by the known fact that the Lyceum's trees, just like those in the Academy, were irrigated.[27] That the water was at times sufficient to form an extensive pool or reservoir in the grove is strongly implied by a detail of the mosaic that seems to have gone unnoticed: the uncompleted columns at the Olympeion are casting their reflection in water.[28]

Within the Lyceum itself, one further item is shown. There is a somewhat rambling colonnade on the left, casting shadows to the right. It is too irregular to be the façade of a building. I suggest that it is one of the shaded walkways – *dromoi* or *peripatoi* – that made groves like the Academy and Lyceum favoured centres of philosophical activity. Indeed,

---

[25] See esp. Gaiser 1980: ch. VI.

[26] This recognition of the rudimentary Olympeion, and its topological and chronological implications, I owe entirely to Andrew Stewart.

[27] For the irrigation of the Academy trees, cf. Plut. *Cimon* 13.7: 'turning the previously waterless and parched Academy into an irrigated grove, which he equipped with unobstructed paths and shady walkways' (τὴν δ' Ἀκαδήμειαν ἐξ ἀνύδρου καὶ αὐχμηρᾶς κατάρρυτον ἀποδείξας ἄλσος ἠσκημένον ὑπ' αὐτοῦ δρόμοις καθαροῖς καὶ συσκίοις περιπάτοις). For the aqueducts of Pisistratus and of Cimon that brought water to the Lyceum, see Caruso 2014: esp. p. 205, where she appositely cites Theophrastus' reference to the huge plane tree growing beside the Lyceum aqueduct (ὀχετός), quoted in n. 56.

[28] The Olympeion is shown separated from the Lyceum yet close enough to be reflected in its waters. This evidence of their proximity could in principle help resolve the remaining uncertainty about the precise site of the Lyceum. My thanks to Michele Alessandrelli for pointing out that what is shown is a reflection and not, as I first thought, an additional colonnade. Naturally, those who have assumed the columns above it to belong to the Parthenon were even less likely to expect water alongside it.

48                                    DAVID SEDLEY

this will not be any chance walkway, but of course *the* walkway, the celebrated one in the Lyceum after which Aristotle's school came to be known as 'the Peripatos'.[29]

Back in the Academy, Aristotle has already vacated his seat on the exedra immediately to Plato's own left, in front of the standing Timaeus. The seat for the present remains empty, but with Aristotle's departure Plato finds himself directly instructing Xenocrates, and seemingly him alone, about the celestial sphere mounted on a box. The narrowness of the vacated space, especially when contrasted with the wider gap on the other side that Speusippus has opened up between himself and his uncle, emphasizes how close Aristotle had been to Plato. The artist, although undoubtedly pro-Xenocratean, is in effect granting that Aristotle would have been Plato's eventual philosophical heir, were it not for his apostasy.

## 2.5    Textual Support

Although the identifications of Speusippus and Aristotle, two of Plato's three potential successors, seem secure, that of Xenocrates has so far found no clear confirmation. I believe that a key item of evidence can be added in its favour.[30] The fifth-century AD Christian writer Apollinaris Sidonius, in a letter (9.9) to the bishop Faustus, congratulates his friend on bringing the resources of philosophy, here represented by 'Plato's Academy', into alliance with Christianity (9.9.13). No critic, he continues (9.9.14–15), will be able to accuse Faustus of a lingering fondness for the clothing, hairstyles and other outward trappings of pagan philosophers. This last point about outward display is then continued with an elaborately constructed list of philosophers' images,[31] familiar, Sidonius says, from paintings displayed in the gymnasia of Athens and perhaps other cities.[32]

---

[29] DL 5.2, cf. 5.52, 54, 68. Cf. also Plut. *Alex.* 7 on purported relics in Macedonia of Aristotle's 'stone seats and shaded *peripatoi*'. See also, more generally, Wycherley 1962.

[30] This passage has previously been cited for its description of Xenocrates' posture (Gaiser 1980: 64, Rashed 2013a: 31 n. 2), but its broader significance has yet to be exploited.

[31] ... *neque te satis hoc aemulari, quod per gymnasia pingantur Areopagitica vel prytanea: curva cervice Speusippus, Aratus panda; Zenon fronte contracta, Epicurus cute distenta; Diogenes barba comante Socrates coma cadente; Aristoteles brachio exerto, Xenocrates crure collecto; Heraclitus fletu oculis clausis, Democritus risu labris apertis; Chrysippus digitis propter numerorum indicia constrictis, Euclides propter mensurarum spatia laxatis, Cleanthes propter utrumque corrosis.* I take the present tense *pingantur* as indicating that in Sidonius' day public copies of these paintings continued to be made.

[32] '... that they are depicted throughout the gymnasia of the Areopagus, or public buildings' (see previous note) leaves it unclear whether *Areopagitica* qualifies *prytanea* as well as *gymnasia*, and hence whether the description is confined to Athens.

## An Iconography Of Xenocrates' Platonism

The philosophers are listed in groups of two or three, each group linked by some antithesis or other. Thus the second pairing is 'Zeno with brow furrowed, Epicurus with smooth skin' (*Zenon fronte contracta, Epicurus cute distenta*); later in the same list we meet that classic contrariety, Heraclitus the weeping philosopher and Democritus the laughing philosopher; and the final group will be a trio (Chrysippus, Euclides, Cleanthes) differentiated by the appearance of their fingers (respectively contracted, spread, gnawed). In the midst of this stands a further antithesis (arm/leg) which we may find immediately familiar: *Aristoteles brachio exerto, Xenocrates crure collecta*, 'Aristotle with arm bared, Xenocrates with leg pulled back'. This is the same pairing as we see on the right-hand side of the mosaic, where Xenocrates' left leg is indeed pulled back, and Aristotle conspicuously has one arm bared.

Encouraged by this match with the mosaic, we can turn to Sidonius' very first pairing: *curva cervice Speusippus* [the accepted emendation for MSS *Zeuzippus* and *Zeuti(p)pus*], *Aratus panda*: 'Speusippus with neck *curva*, Aratus with it *panda*'. Both adjectives that I have left untranslated mean 'bent', but in the present context they must differ sufficiently to provide an appropriate contrast. The antithesis of *curvus* and *pandus* is one that Sidonius favours elsewhere in the *Letters*, with *curvus* sometimes indicating outward curvature or convexity, *pandus* inward curvature or concavity.[33] Dare we conjecture that, just as the arm/leg pairing referred to the two figures at the right-hand end of the mosaic, so the two differently bent necks are those of the two figures at the left-hand end? For there the standing figure is bending his neck down towards the seated Speusippus, which from the viewer's perspective is an inward curvature. And Speusippus for his part, listening to the standing figure, has his own neck erect but outwardly rotated.

A problem facing this suggestion is that the standing figure can hardly be Aratus,[34] a poet who was unconnected with the Academy, and who in any case lived two or more generations after the others depicted in the scene. Even worse, being known mainly for his wildly popular *Phainomena*, a versification of Eudoxus' account of constellations and weather signs, Aratus was sometimes classed as an astronomer and sometimes as a poet, but never as a philosopher. And this makes his very presence in Sidonius'

---

[33] At *Ep.* 4.8.5, with regard to a fluted silver cup, Sidonius wonders whether the verses he has been asked to compose are to be inscribed in the troughs (*ventribus pandis*) of the flutings, or, better, on their summits (*curvis ... capitibus*). At 1.6.3 someone bending to use a scythe is described as *panda curvus falce*, which seems to contrast the outer curvature of the back (*curvus*) with the inner curvature of the blade (*panda*).

[34] By pure coincidence, it seems, there has been a proposal, on grounds unrelated to the Sidonius text, to identify as Aratus the figure widely agreed to be Plato: see Wilson 2006: 310–16.

50                                    DAVID SEDLEY

otherwise entirely philosophical list anomalous.[35] We therefore have
grounds for suspecting a second MS corruption at this point, immediately
adjacent to the distorted spelling of 'Speusippus' (see above). One might
hypothesize a damaged line in the archetype, and a scribe who lacked the
philosophical knowledge to recognize either of these juxtaposed names. But
if not Aratus, then who? A strong candidate must be Archytas, given his
name's visual similarity to that of Aratus.

Back to the mosaic. The standing figure on the left with an exotic
headdress has long been suspected to be a Pythagorean, and Archytas was
undoubtedly both the leading Pythagorean of Plato's day and a close
associate (though not member) of the Academy.[36] Indeed, Rashed has
already argued, on independent grounds, that the figure depicted is
Archytas.[37] The figure's pose, in which he mimes the playing of an absent
cithara,[38] is likely to be another identifier of Archytas, known not as a
musical performer but as the greatest musical theorist of his day.[39]

In short I propose that Sidonius, in his selection of philosophers from various
famous paintings, is including four of the seven philosophers whom we see in
the mosaic, in a sentence whose relevant parts should be read as follows:

> curva cervice Speusippus, Archytas panda ... Aristoteles brachio exerto,
> Xenocrates crure collecto

> with neck bent round, Speusippus; with it bent in, Archytas. ... Aristotle
> with arm bare, Xenocrates with leg pulled back.[40]

---

[35] The Euclides in Sidonius' list (see n. 31) is likely to be Plato's so-named friend, the founder of the
Megaric school of philosophy, and not Euclid the geometer.

[36] See Schofield 2014: 71–8. Significantly, the presumed Archytas is standing just outside the
Academy boundary as marked by the gateway (I thank Philip Hardie for the point). If the
mosaic image is accepted as evidence that Archytas was still alive in 347, the conjectural date of
his death (see Huffman 2005: 5) needs to be brought down by a few years. But I would not press
the point: his depicted influence on Speusippus could well be represented as continuing after
his death.

[37] Rashed 2013a: 38–42, who builds largely on the fact that in the Sarsina mosaic the Archytas-figure
is holding a snake – an element that may well not have been in the archetype, given the many other
deviations in the Sarsina version. My main divergence from Rashed, however, as also from Gaiser,
regards their shared view that this figure is commanding the attention of the other figures. As I read
it, he is busy drawing Speusippus away from the Platonic circle.

[38] The observation that this figure is playing air-cithara I owe to Ilaria Romeo. It makes less likely the
conjecture that in the archetype he was shown holding a snake (see previous note), since he
apparently did not have a free hand to do so.

[39] For the testimonies, see Huffman 2005: 402–82.

[40] The very fact that these two pairs are less obviously antithetical than the other groups listed may be
thought to strengthen the conjecture that their linking was encouraged by their juxtaposition in
the painting.

## 2.6 Speusippus and Archytas

There is moreover a further, and stronger, confirmation that the figure on the far left is Archytas. As I have already stressed, almost every figure in the image is identified by a symbol vertically above his head. On the same horizontal plane as these icons, the epistyle of the Academy gateway is festooned with a row of four very curious objects. At first sight they are four of a kind, and in so far as they have attracted any comment at all they have been assumed all to be vessels of some sort, perhaps offerings to the Muses or to other local deities.

There are strong reasons for not being satisfied with this. For one thing, any such assumption risks breaching the otherwise exceptionless principle, as I have argued it to be, that everything in the upper stratum has an iconic value bearing on the identity of the figure below. Those who see vessels here have found no more precise explanation of their presence than that they somehow help convey the sanctity of the locale.[41] I do not suggest that this is *entirely* wrong, since no doubt the familiarity of such ritual practices explains why the apparent presence of a fairly uniform row of vessels above the Academy gateway would not have looked incongruous. But that cannot be all. So thin a decoding seems inadequate by itself to do justice to the picture's very sophisticated semiotics.

Secondly, when we apply the icon principle with sufficient discrimination, by following the pillars downwards as we have learnt to do, it becomes clear that two distinct identifications have been juxtaposed. As we saw in Section 2.3, on the gateway the right-hand object is connected, by the pillar above which it sits, to Speusippus. But the three objects to the left of it are linked, by the other pillar, to the Archytas figure. The initial impression of uniformity among the objects is undoubtedly intentional: they are just a row of pots. Nevertheless, as we deepen our acquaintance with the picture's symbolism and explore its numerous significant details, we are being invited to see beyond the uniformity.

Once we have noticed that Speusippus' icon is set apart from the other three, we should also see that it, and it alone, is symmetrical in shape. It seems to be a bronze cooking vessel, circular in the horizontal plane, with an ornate central lid and handle, and almost certainly also a pair of matching side-handles (presumably for carrying it while hot), although, apparently to increase the initial impression of overall uniformity among the row of objects, the artist has allowed its right handle to be hidden by

---

[41] E.g. Gaiser 1980: 11; Mattusch 2008.

the tree. What might have motivated this assimilation is a question that I must put on hold for now.

The remaining three objects to the vessel's left, despite their prima facie resemblance to it, are in fact all asymmetric in shape and turn out, I am convinced, to be a row of bird-shaped figures, facing to our left. The clue lies in their wings. The left wing of each is readily discerned because of its lighter colour. Their small heads are admittedly harder to make out, for a reason to which I shall return shortly. There is a virtually full side-on view of two bird figures, and to the far left we can glimpse a third,[42] which given the dimensions of the epistyle is probably the last in the row.

At this point it will be helpful to compare the Sarsina mosaic (Figure 2.3), which, although two or more centuries later in date, undoubtedly stems from the same archetype. Its depiction of the scene is very different in its overall style, and selective in its depiction of the individual figures and objects. Gone, for example, are the tree and the scrolls. But we do still have, however differently portrayed, most of the salient features seen in the Pompeian mosaic: seven figures occupying an exedra in a peaked formation, a (smaller) globe resting on a stand or small table (not a box), to which one of them, this time on the far right, is pointing with a stick; a sundial on top of a pillar; and some indeterminate stone structures top right. However, much the most detailed resemblance to the Pompeian mosaic is found on the far left.[43] It seems as if the Sarsina mosaicist is drawing on an incomplete recall of the classic painting, having memorized the contents of the left side more meticulously than the remainder.

There on the left we find once again a gateway consisting of an epistyle resting on two square pillars, topped by a row of three small-headed bird figures, facing left, and a vessel standing to their immediate right. The correspondences are so detailed as even to include the cutting-off of the final bird figure's head at the mosaic's left margin. Again, as in the Pompeian mosaic, the bird figures on the epistyle are linked, when the eye travels down the left-hand pillar of the gateway, to a standing philosopher on the far left, while the vessel sits over the right-hand pillar, which links it

---

[42] The gate's perspectival ambiguity can make it hard at first glance to be sure which of its two pillars is the closer to us. But it must in fact be the right-hand one, or the cornice of the epistyle would be wrongly positioned in relation to the left-hand pillar. Once assured of this perspective, we can easily spot the third bird figure, partly hidden by the second.

[43] The Sarsina mosaic has undergone a degree of restoration, resulting in some strangely beardless and (to all appearances) insecurely affixed male heads; but it seems from the information supplied by Gaiser 1980: 13–14 that there has been no restoration of the gateway or of the objects above it.

Figure 2.3 The Sarsina mosaic. Rome, Villa Albani Torlonia.
© Fondazione Torlonia. Reproduced with permission

instead to a second, seated philosopher. Finally, so far as correspondences are concerned, the bird figures and the vessel once more so strongly resemble each other that interpreters have regularly, as with the earlier mosaic, assumed that they are four matching vessels. Yet only the one on the right can be seen to have a lid, and thus be clearly recognized as a vessel.

The Sarsina bird figures do also differ from those in the Pompeian mosaic in at least one prominent regard: they are long-necked. The reason seems to be that the vessel's one visible side-handle, at any rate as we witness it in the earlier mosaic, looked sufficiently like an extended bird-neck to encourage the Sarsina artist to pick it out as a point of resemblance between vessel and birds. For both mosaic copies, each in its own style,

54                                    DAVID SEDLEY

place the same emphasis on uniformity among the four items, while also ensuring that the vessel is kept subtly distinct from the bird figures.

This parallel image provides quite strong confirmation that in the Pompeian mosaic too the identity icon unambiguously linked to the putative Archytas really is, as the clearly discernible wings already suggest, three bird figures of some sort. What, if so, are they?

An answer readily presents itself. Archytas, noted for his contributions to applied as well as to pure mathematics, was celebrated for his invention of a kind of mechanical wooden pigeon which, it was said, actually flew.[44] Once one has this story in mind, it becomes possible to recognize the winged and comically pigeon-chested figures as a trio of his wooden pigeons, perched on top of the gateway. Their exaggerated rotundity and small heads serve to strengthen their prima facie resemblance to the circular, lidded cooking pot. Even the two colours of the particular woods the bird figures are made of exactly match the two colours with which the mosaicist has captured the shiny surface of the bronze cooking vessel. This is incidentally yet another subtlety that is carefully replicated in the Sarsina version, albeit with one uniform bronze shade rather than two.

There has been much dispute about how Archytas' wooden pigeon could have been thought able to 'fly'.[45] If the evidence of the mosaic's

---

[44] Archytas 47A10a DK = Favorinus fr. 93 Barigazzi = Gellius 10.12.8–10, incorporating a verbatim testimony from Favorinus: *nam et plerique nobilium Graecorum et Favorinus philosophus, memoriarum antiquarum exsequentissimus, affirmatissime scripserunt simulacrum columbae e ligno ab Archyta ratione quadam disciplinaque mechanica factum volasse; ita erat scilicet libramentis suspensum et aura spiritus inclusa atque occulta concitum. libet hercle super re tam abhorrenti a fide ipsius Favorini verba ponere:* Ἀρχύτας Ταραντῖνος τὰ ἄλλα καὶ μηχανικὸς ὢν ἐποίησεν περιστερὰν ξυλίνην πετομένην. ὁπότε καθίσειεν οὐκέτι ἀνίστατο. μέχρι γὰρ τούτου. Favorinus' description here is: 'Archytas of Tarentum, being among other things an engineer, made a flying wooden pigeon. When it landed it did not take off again: for that's how far.' This, with its asyndeton and aposiopesis, is in the condensed note-form of a scholion, which I suggest Gellius read in the margin of a book belonging to his teacher Favorinus. Editors have been mistaken, if so, to restore it to regular grammar and to postulate (sometimes even fill) a textual lacuna at the end. For a comprehensive survey of the scholarship on Gellius' testimony see Huffman 2005: 570–9.

[45] The favoured view has been that Archytas' pigeon could 'fly' only as part of a mechanical structure that moved it, complete with hidden counterweights. But (a) that leaves unexplained its asymmetric capacity for landing but not for taking off (Favorinus, quoted in the previous note), and (b) the image in the mosaic, if at all accurate, suggests that each pigeon was freestanding. Gellius' far-fetched account of how the mechanism worked is introduced with *scilicet*, 'no doubt', and is therefore probably his own speculation, based on no more than general knowledge of other pneumatic automata in a tradition that is usually traced back to Ctesibius. His explanation has, if so, been taken too seriously in modern reconstructions. His only hard information about how the pigeon functioned seems to be what he extracts from the Favorinus passage itself. Cf. the well-founded scepticism of Berryman 2003: 350, 354–5; and Berryman 2009: 96. However, I am not sure of her reason for understanding περιστερά as merely Archytas' *name* for a device which could in reality have been a type of war engine. For Archytas' device in the context of other ancient mechanical wonders, see Mayor 2018: 190–2.

## An Iconography Of Xenocrates' Platonism

depiction is added to our exiguous other data, it becomes plausible that it descended under its own weight on a string, whose unwinding turned an internal mechanism designed to make the wings flap and the bird itself perhaps circle round, thus appearing to fly. In the Pompeian mosaic (as also, if distortedly, in its Sarsina counterpart) the strings in question can in fact be seen protruding from the tops of the pigeons' heads – heads whose strangely rectilinear features may in any case suggest that they have been manufactured to house a mechanism, below which the pigeons' wings would be pivoted. The artist has at any rate made quite sure that we will not mistake them for real living birds.

Given the reported fame of Archytas' invention, it is reasonable to assume that the picture's original viewers were expected to recognize the mechanical-bird icon and its allusion. By doing so they could appreciate just how belittling of both Archytas and Speusippus their icons really are. Archytas' corpulent pigeons, no doubt portrayed as if they were fattened up for the cooking pot,[46] and Speusippus' cooking pot itself have here been so closely assimilated to each other that we can scarcely tell them apart. The alliance of Speusippus and Archytas is mockingly reduced to a shared fondness for pigeon!

While Archytas' skills have been squandered on the (from a Platonic perspective) intellectually inferior discipline of applied mechanics,[47] and more specifically on the imitation of lowly if appetizing fowl, the Academy's intellectual resources have, on the contrary, been channelled into the complex mathematics of the supremely rational heaven itself. This is a contrast that the eye is able to register as it travels from the left to the centre of the image, where it will find the Academy's achievements celebrated with a celestial sphere and a sundial. It is to this segment of the picture that I now turn.

## 2.7  The Astronomical Heritage

At the centre of the scene, just as Plato and his true heir Xenocrates are mutually linked by their very similar appearance and posture,[48] so too we

---

[46] In Gellius' report it is usual to render Archytas' mechanical περιστερά as a 'dove', but when used specifically, and not as a genus name, the term designates the domestic pigeon (see Thompson 1895: 142), which would be kept primarily as a food source.

[47] This Platonist derision of Archytas is in keeping with the findings of Burnyeat 2005, and of Huffman 2005: esp. 83–9.

[48] Plato as well as Xenocrates is shown with one leg drawn back, his foot resting on the sitting surface of the exedra, whether because Xenocrates really did mimic the pose of his master (cf. Plut. *Adul.* 53C), or, more likely, because the artist wants to strengthen the special bond between them by making the pupil the master's mirror image.

see, rising above them, a second pair, linked not only by their mutually similar postures but also by a shared style of dress that sets them apart from all the others present. Of these two, as noted earlier, the one on our right has been correctly recognized as the astronomer Eudoxus, inventor of the *arachnē* sundial, which is presumed to be the one shown directly above him and firmly linked to him by a pillar. It seems likely, then, that the one on our left is an astronomer too. Their matching heavy attire, I conjecture, serves as a virtual uniform for a profession, which did after all require year-round outdoor work at night. We may compare a third-century AD Roman mosaic from Trier (Figure 2.4) in which Aratus, pictured in the company of the Muse of astronomy, and therefore represented as himself an astronomer, is enveloped in a similarly thick mantle, as in fact is the Muse herself![49]

Who, then, is the second astronomer in the Academy mosaic? I propose that he is Timaeus, the eponymous speaker in Plato's key doctrinal dialogue.[50] On what grounds?[51] First of all, he stands at the very apex of the entire philosophical group, a palpable allusion to the dialogue's description of Timaeus as 'having reached the summit (*akron*) of all philosophy' (*Ti.* 20a4–5). Second, Timaeus is also there called the 'most accomplished astronomer' (*astronomikōtatos, Ti.* 27a3–4) among those present in the dialogue, and this too, given the principle that greater elevation symbolizes closer kinship with the heaven (cf. *Ti.* 90a), is encoded in the picture when the artist places him higher even than the great Eudoxus.

Eudoxus was nevertheless the leading astronomical *theorist* of the day, and this is captured by his suitably reflective pose. He has pushed aside the star-watcher's night-time attire sufficiently to enable his chin to rest pensively on his right hand.[52] As a contemporary member or associate of Plato's circle, he is shown perched on the exedra with the rest of the Academic elite.

Timaeus, by contrast, is not actually on the exedra at all but behind it.[53] If, as seems likely, this marks his as a symbolic and not a literal presence,

---

[49] Fig. 3 = Richter 1965: vol. 2, fig. 1656; cf. her figs.1653, 1655, and description on pp. 239–41.

[50] An alternative astronomer one might consider instead of Timaeus is Philip of Opus, posthumous editor of Plato's *Laws* and presumed author of the *Epinomis*. Berti 2012: 33 does in fact propose to identify this figure as Philip, though without reference to astronomy. I cannot easily imagine Philip being ranked above the great Eudoxus, let alone above Plato himself.

[51] I especially thank Francesco Verde for helping me answer this question.

[52] For this and similar poses, see Zanker 1995: ch. III. Eudoxus himself appears to have been in a similarly pensive pose in the Budapest torso inscribed with his name, Richter 1965: vol. II, 244, fig. 1679.

[53] Cf. Gaiser 1980: 62, Rashed 2013a: 38.

Figure 2.4 *Aratus and Urania*, mosaic. Rheinisches Landesmuseum Trier.
Photo by Th. Zühmer. Reproduced courtesy of Die Generaldirektion Kulturelles Erbe Rheinland-Pfalz, Direktion Rheinisches Landesmuseum Trier

that could be in part because he belongs notionally to an earlier generation and is therefore present in spirit, not in the flesh. More importantly, however, it seems like an acknowledgement of Timaeus' being primarily Plato's literary alter ego rather than a distinct historical figure.[54] Whatever surprise the viewer may have initially felt at the artist's daring to place anyone other than the divine Plato at the philosophical summit, that reaction should dissolve once we realize that this venerated figure is not a competitor to Plato but speaks with Plato's own authoritative

---

[54] Cf. preceding chapter, p. 18.

## 58 DAVID SEDLEY

philosophical voice. It is probably no accident that the Timaeus figure even *looks* rather like Plato.[55]

The two astronomers are keeping watch over Plato's lesson to Xenocrates. Thanks to their presence, Xenocrates' understanding of the world's astronomical zone has the best possible pedigree. It enjoys not only Plato's blessing, but also that of Eudoxus, the leading astronomical theorist of the day. For details see Chapter 1, Sections 1.5 and 1.10, where among other things I argued that the eleven rings shown here on the celestial sphere represent Xenocrates' exegesis of the eleven divine self-movers portrayed in the *Phaedrus* myth. Thanks to the concord of Plato, Timaeus and Eudoxus in the scene now laid out before us, we are invited to work out that Plato himself regards the celestial mathematics of the *Phaedrus* not just as compatible with Timaeus' cosmography, but even as a welcome enrichment of it.

Let us now return to the plane tree. It is most closely tied to Plato, not only by its name *platanos*, as already mentioned, but also by the usual vertical link, the trunk attaching it to him as his identity symbol. Even so, it is not attached *exclusively* to Plato. In contrast to its withered branch stretching above the scorned Speusippus, on the other side beneath its lush greenery stands Timaeus. In the *Phaedrus* almost the entire conversation, the myth included, takes place under a tall plane tree (229a–230b). If on this ground we take the tall plane tree in the mosaic to allude not just to Plato, but also more specifically to the *Phaedrus*,[56] the presence of Timaeus beneath it can be recognized as symbolic of Xenocrates' Platonist canon. For, to repeat, Xenocrates' canon consisted in the content of the Timaean creation myth, not taken in isolation but interpreted and developed in the light of the *Phaedrus* myth. Placing the protagonist of the former dialogue beneath the tree that symbolizes the latter seems to be the artist's way of encapsulating that canon.[57]

---

[55] I thank Susanna McFadden for this observation.

[56] This draws on Rashed's inspired proposal. The long bare trunk and high foliage – the latter extending beyond the top margin of the picture – seem intended to capture the tallness of the particular plane tree described in the *Phaedrus*. For the potential tallness of plane trees, with reference to a contemporary though still young specimen in the Lyceum, cf. Theophrastus, *Hist. plant.* 1.7.1.8–14: ἐν τῷ Λυκείῳ ἡ πλάτανος ἡ κατὰ τὸν ὀχετὸν ἔτι νέα οὖσα ἐπὶ τρεῖς καὶ τριάκοντα πήχεις ἀφῆκεν ...

[57] The scene reassures us of Timaeus' status as the transmitter of Plato's own doctrines, as Xenocrates took him to be, rather than as an extraneous (perhaps Pythagorean) source of authority. Although Timaeus came to be regarded as a historical Pythagorean (e.g. Cic. *Rep.* 1.16, *Fin.* 5.87), and his eponymous dialogue consequently as a Pythagorean source text, there is no evidence of that tradition's going back to the fourth century BC, there being, for example, no sign of it in Aristotle's many references to the dialogue (see Bonitz 1870: *s.v.* Τίμαιος ὁ Λοκρός). For Timaeus

## 2.8 Xenocrates

Consider next the three-level stratification of the scene. (1) Spatially as well as axiologically, the central focus is a Platonic inner circle, consisting of Plato himself, Timaeus, Eudoxus and Xenocrates. The white hill behind them, by combining with them to complete a geometrical circle, serves to underline that point. (2) Placed in the foreground, Archytas and Speusippus are both in one way or another represented as outsiders to the circle, and Aristotle as in the very process of leaving it. (3) As already emphasized, there is a top stratum as well, in which the philosophers below are identified by symbols, placed in a horizontal sequence above them. From right to left, Aristotle's icon is the *peripatos* of his future school; Eudoxus is labelled by his sundial; Plato (and along with him his literary persona Timaeus) by the *platanos*; Speusippus both by the dead branch of Plato's tree (see Section 2.3) and, above that, on top of the gateway, by a bronze cooking vessel which I have suggested symbolizes his lack of self-control; and finally Archytas by his mechanized wooden pigeons. Anomalously, Xenocrates alone has no such identifying icon, despite being in a way the most important figure present.

Xenocrates, this seems to suggest, was at the time of the original painting too well-known and recognizable a public figure to need his own label. That familiarity no doubt originated from his constant visibility at Athens during the many years he taught in the public spaces of the Academy, and was reinforced by an iconographic tradition which showcased the famously severe countenance that had made him a byword for moral rectitude and dignity. The evidence for this pictorial celebrity includes Plutarch's story of a courtesan who so revered Xenocrates for his self-control that she refused to perform any unseemly act in front of his image, and Synesius' reference to 'the images of Xenocrates' as the very paradigm of a dignified gaze.[58] Even for those who enjoyed the advantage

---

himself as neither Pythagorean nor historical, see the brief but incisive remarks of Zhmud 2012: 415–16.

[58] Plut. fr. 85 Sandbach = test. 79 IP²; Synesius, *Epist.* 154 = test. 78 IP². For Xenocrates' severe facial expression see also DL 4.6 < test. 2 IP². Possible further evidence of his recognizability in paintings is a comic fragment of Alexis (fr. 99 = test. 46 IP²), dated to 307 BC by its praise for the decree of Sophocles of Sunium against philosophers which was in force just during that year, beginning 'This is the Academy, this Xenocrates' (τοῦτ᾽ ἐστιν Ἀκαδήμεια, τοῦτο Ξενοκράτης). Since at the dramatic date Xenocrates himself had been dead for eight years, it seems plausible that in the now lost context the speaker (direct or reported) was pointing to or recalling a painting of Xenocrates teaching in the Academy. (In his full discussion of the fragment Arnott 1996: 259–63 defends the – to my eye less attractive – traditional editorial expedient of punctuating the line as a rhetorical question which implicitly deplores the present state of *all* philosophy.)

60                                   DAVID SEDLEY

of direct visual familiarity with him, the existence of this iconographic
tradition helps explain why the much younger Xenocrates of 347 BC, as
shown in the mosaic, was expected to be instantly recognized too.

In short, Xenocrates was himself an iconic figure, the living embodiment of self-control, and did not need a further icon to identify him. The
artist could take viewers' recognition for granted, and concentrate instead
on depicting Xenocrates' philosophical pedigree. Alternatively the painting's title, if it had one, may have already identified its subject as
Xenocrates, leaving viewers to work out from the various icons who the
other six were.

The image preserved for us by the mosaic has turned out to be a tableau
designed to affirm the transmission of Plato's philosophical legacy via his
true successor, Xenocrates. At the same time it seeks to show how
Speusippus and Aristotle had, in effect, ruled themselves out of contention
for this particular role. Speusippus' formal succession is assured, no doubt,
but his moral failings and excessive leaning towards Pythagoreanism make
him unsuitable, and it is not he but Xenocrates who has been entrusted
with taking Plato's heritage forward.

In the preceding chapter I proposed that during Speusippus' headship
the young Xenocrates, in the interests of the school's presenting a united
Platonist front, worked towards a system that would minimize the differences between his own version of Platonism and Speusippus' significantly
different doctrines. The mosaic image's vilification of Speusippus suggests
that, after the latter's death and Xenocrates' accession, this narrative
receded and was replaced by one according to which Xenocrates was from
the start Plato's one true philosophical confidant and anointed successor.
We know that those who valued Speusippus' standing as a necessary link
in an unbroken Platonic succession continued to view him, however
implausibly, as a doctrinal follower of Plato.[59] But the pro-Xenocratean
lobby had considerable success in perpetuating its alternative narrative. To
the evidence of the mosaic itself we may add the words of the late
Neoplatonist commentator Hermias when commenting on the critique
of written discourse in Plato's *Phaedrus*:

> Starting here [*Phaedrus* 275d] he compares soulless and ensouled discourse.
> I call 'soulless' what he also calls 'illegitimate': discourse in writing. The one
> I call the legitimate and ensouled brother of internal discourse is the one

---

[59] E.g. DL 4.1, who reports that Speusippus, although inferior to Plato in moral character, did agree
with him doctrinally. Similarly Antiochus as represented at Cic. *Acad. post.* 34, and Numenius *ap.*
Euseb. *Praep. evang.* 14.5.1 (727b5–9) < fr. 24 des Places. Cf. preceding chapter p. 15–17.

inserted into the soul of the learner, when one can point to one's pupil, as Socrates could to Plato, Plato to Xenocrates, Xenocrates to Polemo, and so on according to the succession. (Hermias, in *Phdr.* 272.2–7 Lucarini & Moreschini; cf. 273.11–14)

Notice the absence of Speusippus from this succession. For one last time the *Phaedrus* (albeit no longer its myth) has come to Xenocrates' aid. The authentic transmission of philosophy, Hermias makes clear, is achieved not solely through written texts but by spoken discourse.[60] As the mosaic's message strongly implied, and as Hermias is found reaffirming many centuries later, Xenocrates' uniquely deep insight into Plato's thought came to him not just through the latter's writings, but also as a direct oral legacy, conferred by the master upon his true intellectual successor. It was therefore of the utmost importance to demonstrate, as the mosaic aspires to do, that Speusippus had been no more than the temporary, disinterested and indeed unworthy caretaker of the Academy, and that it was not to him but to Xenocrates that Plato had bequeathed the insights necessary for the system's completion.

Nor is it just a question of completion. Those who had studied under Plato might in principle be expected to bear authoritative witness, from the master's own lips, to the correct interpretation of his philosophy. Yet this expectation of an authorized Platonism had been disappointed: to take just the most famous example, Xenocrates and Aristotle, despite all the years they had spent with Plato, differed radically as to whether he had held the world to be sempiternal, or the product of a single past creative act. In such cases, the mosaic image implies, Xenocrates is the one to trust. For in it he alone is shown paying attention to Plato's teaching, and indeed specifically to his teaching regarding an astronomical doctrine of sempiternal self-movers as sketched in the *Phaedrus* myth. Aristotle meanwhile, having already left Plato's side in anticipation of his approaching apostasy, was entirely deaf to the lesson.

## 2.9 Date and Context

That the original from which the mosaic derives was a painting has long been assumed, and we have seen it corroborated by Sidonius (Section 2.5), along with the information that as late as the fifth-century AD copies of the painting remained on public view in Athens and perhaps other cities. There can be little doubt that it had the status of a classic artwork.

---

[60] Cf. n. 13.

62                                    DAVID SEDLEY

Can we date this archetype? Here four factors converge. First, on the basis of the image's depiction of the Lyceum we have seen reason (Section 2.5) to date it between 335, when Aristotle founded the Lyceum, and 174, when building of the Olympeion resumed. Second, the upper end of that date range has a significant overlap with the era that Quintilian identifies as the golden age of classical painting, roughly 360–280 BC.[61] Third, although such a painting could in principle have played a significant part in the Academy's internal debates about its true philosophical legacy at any time until the 260s, when under Arcesilaus' headship doctrinal Platonism ceased to be taught, nevertheless the rivalries encapsulated in the image must have become somewhat less important by the end of the fourth century, with Aristotle twenty years dead and Speusippus' interim headship a distant memory – especially as by then a growing challenge came instead from sceptical readings of Plato, a threat seemingly unrepresented in the painting.

The fourth and final consideration is also the most speculative. In Chapter 1, Section 1.10, I proposed that the celestial sphere to which Plato is shown pointing operates with a system of eleven prime movers jointly turning forty-one spheres, and that this is likely to have evolved in competition with Aristotle's count of movers as we meet it in *Metaphysics* $\Lambda$ 8. Aristotle initially names Eudoxus as his authority, and in striking parallel to this the mosaic image shows Plato teaching Xenocrates his own system of movers under the gaze of, and with the implicit approval of, that same Eudoxus. Evidently the counting competition, thanks to starting within the Academy, assumed the Eudoxan system as its common basis. However, while Xenocrates was fully committed to a calculation which, drawing on the *Phaedrus* myth, he attributed to Plato himself, Aristotle was able to refine his own calculation of the number of movers by explicitly adding the latest corrections to the Eudoxan system, established in the meantime by Callippus, a follower of Eudoxus (1073b32–8).[62]

It is hard to see how Xenocrates could have struck back. Had he followed suit and incorporated Callippus' corrections, he would almost inevitably have been abandoning his commitment to Plato's authority. And that he in fact did not continue the debate is to some extent confirmed by the fact that Hermias, in his commentary on the *Phaedrus*,

---

[61] Quintilian 12.10.

[62] According to Aristotle, Callippus' revision of the Eudoxan system adds seven spheres, to which Aristotle in turn expects to add further, counteracting spheres, reaching a grand total of fifty-five, although he sees some scope for bringing this number down (according to a controversial MS reading) to forty-seven (1073b32–1074a17).

shows no apparent familiarity with the Xenocratean interpretation of the eleven-gods motif. It may well be, then, that Xenocrates allowed this theory of movers, or at least its mathematical details, to lapse into obscurity. If so, the dating of the mosaic image, in which Xenocrates' theory of movers is still implicitly lauded as his own special legacy from the master, would have to predate Aristotle's composition of *Metaphysics* Λ 8, whose own *terminus ante quem* is 322, the year of Aristotle's death.

It thus seems entirely credible that the archetype was painted in Xenocrates' own lifetime, in or around the decade 335–325 BC. And if Xenocrates was indeed alive at the time, we might reasonably assume that he himself actively encouraged, or at least condoned, this pictorial affirmation of his own unique authority to voice Plato's philosophical creed.

Although we can hardly hope to identify the artist, we can at least ask ourselves whether he was a committed Platonist, or simply a technician hired to do a job under strict philosophical instruction. The former by now seems overwhelmingly the more credible option. The complex network of philosophically nuanced symbols and allusions is clearly the artist's own speciality. Moreover, it stems ultimately from the *Laws* 6 passage prescribing what an ageing legislator should do to secure his legacy. The significance of this is that Plato's speaker in that passage explains his point by an analogy with a supposedly more familiar case, that of a painter appointing a successor to maintain and perfect his paintings after his own death (769a4–c9). This is one of many painter analogies in the Platonic corpus, and by no means the most famous. Who is likelier to have remembered it, and to have remained alert to its potential for prefiguring Plato's philosophical legacy, than the painter himself?

To end, let me fast-forward four centuries. At the time of the great eruption of Vesuvius in AD 79, during the post-Hellenistic period that saw doctrinal Platonism's long-delayed return, someone in that largely Greek-speaking region of Italy owned a fine mosaic replica of a classic philosophical painting. As the owner was surely aware, the image it transmitted was a Platonist tableau, graphically depicting Xenocrates' credentials as the authorized voice of Plato's philosophical system. Such a tableau surely deserves to become a valued part of our evidence for the much-debated origins of Middle Platonism.

CHAPTER 3

# Arcesilaus' Appeal to Heraclitus as a Philosophical Authority for His Sceptical Stance

*Anna Maria Ioppolo*

In *Adversus Colotem* (1121F), Plutarch suggests that Colotes – in his polemical work against some of the eminent philosophers up to Epicurus – accused Arcesilaus of attributing his own sceptical views not only to Socrates and Plato but also to Parmenides and Heraclitus. Since Colotes' list dated back to Arcesilaus' time, it seems likely that Colotes derived the list from Arcesilaus himself. However, Heraclitus does not figure at all among Arcesilaus' illustrious predecessors in Cicero's *Academica*. This absence is puzzling not only because Heraclitus had a 'pervasive impact' upon Plato's philosophy, and because Arcesilaus strongly appealed to Plato, but also because Heraclitus was a key figure for the Stoics exactly at the time of Arcesilaus and Arcesilaus' quarrel with the Stoics over their philosophical predecessors. I will set out to detect if and to what extent Arcesilaus made use of Heraclitus in his own philosophy.

The plan of the paper is as follows. In Section 3.1, I will examine the testimony from the *Adversus Colotem* by comparing it to that provided by Cicero in the *Academici libri*, so as to establish possible points of contact or divergence. In Section 3.2, I will show how an important testimony from Cleanthes, who associates Zeno's doctrine with that of Heraclitus, is closely connected to a passage from Plutarch's *De communibus notitiis*, which offers an Academic criticism precisely of Cleanthes' position. A careful investigation of both testimonies suggests that the interpretation of Heraclitus' doctrine was an object of debate among Stoics and Academics from the very beginning. In Section 3.3, I will show that Zeno and Cleanthes appropriated some important arguments in Plato's *Theaetetus* by interpreting them in dogmatic terms, and that this dialogue became a bone of contention between the Stoics and Arcesilaus. In Section 3.4, I will show that Arcesilaus deployed some arguments from the *Theaetetus*, purely ad hominem, to oppose the interpretation of Heraclitus put forward by Cleanthes – namely the view of Heraclitus as

*Arcesilaus' Appeal to Heraclitus* 65

a theorist of universal flux – and hence that Arcesilaus may be identified as the author of the anti-Stoic argument that Plutarch reports. Finally, in Section 3.5, I will come back to Plutarch's testimony in the *Adversus Colotem* to conclude that Arcesilaus' appeal to Heraclitus is entirely justified.

### 3.1 Cicero and Plutarch's Account of Arcesilaus' Appeal to Presocratics

Plutarch's testimony is particularly important because it is based on a text by the Epicurean Colotes, a contemporary of Arcesilaus.[1] In this work, dating back to roughly 260 BC, when Arcesilaus' philosophical career was in full swing, Colotes attacked the doctrines of some earlier philosophers who, in his view, made life impossible. These included Parmenides, Empedocles, Melissus, Democritus, Socrates, Plato and Stilpo, as well as some philosophers of Colotes' day, the Cyrenaics and Arcesilaus, whose name he cautiously avoided mentioning.[2] Plutarch reports that Colotes, vexed by the fame that Arcesilaus had achieved as the most popular philosopher of his day,[3] had accused him of having 'nothing of his own to say' (μηθὲν γὰρ αὐτὸν ἴδιον λέγοντα). Plutarch takes Arcesilaus' side:

> Yet Arcesilaus was so far from loving any reputation for novelty or arrogating to himself anything belonging to the ancients, that the sophists of his time accused him of rubbing off his views on *epoché* and *akatalépsia* on Socrates, Plato, Parmenides and Heraclitus, who did not need them; whereas he attributed them, as it were, by way of confirmation, to famous men. On this behalf, then, we thank Colotes and everyone who asserts that the Academic discourse reached Arcesilaus from the past.[4] (*Adv. Col.* 1121F–1122A, trans. L&S 68H, slightly modified)

---

[1] I have defended the reliability of the *Adversus Colotem* in reconstructing Arcesilaus' philosophy in other studies, which I will refer to: Ioppolo 1986: 121–56; 2000: 333–60; 2004: 289–310. See too Hankinson 1995: 88. Other crucial arguments in support of this thesis may be found in Corti 2014: 115 ff.

[2] *Adv. Col.* 1120C (trans. L&S 68H): 'Having done with the ancients, Colotes turns to his contemporary philosophers, without naming any of them' (ὁ Κωλώτης ἀπὸ τῶν παλαιῶν τρέπεται πρὸς τοὺς καθ' ἑαυτὸν φιλοσόφους, οὐδενὸς τιθεὶς ὄνομα).

[3] Ibid. 1121E–F (trans. L&H 68H): 'who was more highly regarded at the time than any other philosopher' (ἐν τοῖς τότε χρόνοις μάλιστα τῶν φιλοσόφων ἀγαπηθέντος).

[4] ὁ δὲ Ἀρκεσίλαος τοσοῦτον ἀπέδει τοῦ καινοτομίας τινὰ δόξαν ἀγαπᾶν καὶ ὑποποιεῖσθαί τι τῶν παλαιῶν ὥστε ἐγκαλεῖν τοὺς τότε σοφιστὰς ὅτι προστρίβεται Σωκράτει καὶ Πλάτωνι καὶ Παρμενίδῃ καὶ Ἡρακλείτῳ τὰ περὶ τῆς ἐποχῆς δόγματα καὶ τῆς ἀκαταληψίας οὐδὲν δεομένοις, ἀλλὰ οἷον ἀναγωγὴν καὶ βεβαίωσιν αὐτῶν εἰς ἄνδρας ἐνδόξους ποιούμενος. ὑπὲρ μὲν οὖν τούτου Κωλώτῃ χάρις καὶ παντὶ τῷ τὸν Ἀκαδημαϊκὸν λόγον ἄνωθεν ἥκειν εἰς Ἀρκεσίλαον ἀποφαίνοντι. Brittain & Palmer 2001: 61 provide a different translation of the expression ἀναγωγὴν καὶ

# 66                    ANNA MARIA IOPPOLO

Instead of rejecting the charge levelled by those so-called sophists who accuse Arcesilaus of seeking to attribute his views on *epochē* and *akatalēpsia* to his predecessors, Plutarch accepts this criticism and thanks Colotes for stressing the continuity between Arcesilaus' philosophy and the Socratic-Platonic tradition. Plutarch's show of gratitude is ironic, as practically all interpreters have noted. This irony is disclosed by the scathing sentence Plutarch writes a little later, when he voices his suspicion that Arcesilaus' arguments on impulses and assent may have had the same effect on Colotes as lyre music on an ass.[5] Plutarch is stigmatising the philosophical obtuseness of Colotes, who has not realised that his accusation of Arcesilaus, far from slandering him, confirms his philosophical continuity with the previous tradition. Arcesilaus' strategy is a subtle and shrewd one: in wishing to establish a close connection with the whole tradition of his school – as suggested by the fact that, alongside Socrates and Plato, he mentions Parmenides and Heraclitus – he de facto sought to prevent anyone who did not adhere to the Academic doctrine from appealing to those philosophers. Note that Arcesilaus' claim is based on a philosophical analysis intended to ensure not historical accuracy but rather self-legitimation. This claim becomes clearer in the light of a very important fact, namely that the Stoics, too, laid claim to the same predecessors, although they painted a very different picture of these philosophers.

The ill feelings and disappointment shown by Zeno and the Stoics towards Arcesilaus' attempt to cast himself as the heir of the most distinguished philosophers of the past are pointed out by Cicero, a particularly authoritative source of information from within the sceptical Academy and one earlier than Plutarch.

In the *Academica*, Cicero confirms that the disagreement over how to interpret the preceding philosophical history lies at the origin of the

---

βεβαίωσιν αὐτῶν εἰς ἄνδρας ἐνδόξους ποιούμενος: 'but in fact he was, so to speak, making restitution and giving security for these views to men of good reputation'. They note that 'Plutarch's legal metaphor (the idiom βεβαίωσιν ποιεῖσθαι) seems to have escaped some of his English translators: Einarson-De Lacy, L&S'. In my view, one must bear in mind that Plutarch attributes the expression ἀλλὰ οἷον ἀναγωγὴν καὶ βεβαίωσιν to the sophists and not to Arcesilaus; and it is always the 'sophists' who refer to *epochē* and *akatalēpsia* as *dogmata*. The dogmatic language, therefore, belongs to the 'sophists', as Plutarch himself implicitly emphasises by referring to Arcesilaus' philosophy as τὸν Ἀκαδημαϊκὸν λόγον: see Corti 2014: 209. With regard to the meaning of the expression Ἀκαδημαϊκὸν λόγον, Donini 2002: 268 acutely observes: 'la cautela di Plutarco, che passa dall'attribuzione dell' ἐποχή e dell' ἀκαταληψία ad Arcesilao, alla formula τὸν Ἀκαδημαϊκὸν λόγον in riferimento agli antichi, comporta che egli non intendesse attribuire tali e quali quelle dottrine ai filosofi precedenti, ma che dagli antichi ad Arcesilao era giunto un generico suggerimento, un'indicazione di metodo, non quelle precise dottrine'. See too Babut 1994: 576.

[5] See *Adv. Col.* 1122B.

## Arcesilaus' Appeal to Heraclitus

epistemological controversy between Zeno and Arcesilaus. Significantly, in the *Lucullus*, too, Arcesilaus is accused of seeking to buttress his own doctrines by tracing them back to illustrious men. Lucullus compares the sceptical Academics to the *seditiosi cives* and Arcesilaus to Tiberius Gracchus. Just as the *seditiosi cives* attribute their populist ideas to illustrious men of the past 'in order to make themselves look like them',[6] the Academics invoke Empedocles, Anaxagoras, Democritus, Parmenides, Xenophanes and even Plato and Socrates in an attempt to subvert this well-established philosophy.[7] Just as Tiberius Gracchus threw the State into turmoil, concealing this upheaval behind the authority of illustrious men of the past, Arcesilaus overthrew the established philosophy.[8] Arcesilaus, therefore, is guilty of *calumnia* for the *way* in which he appeals to the *veteres physici*, attributing his own doctrines to them. In the *Varro*, however, Cicero explains and defends Arcesilaus' interpretation of the history of philosophy by contrasting it with the Antiochean version.

> It was with Zeno, so we have heard, that Arcesilaus began his entire struggle not out of obstinacy or desire for victory – in my opinion at least – but because of obscurity of the things which had brought Socrates to an admission of ignorance; and before him already, Democritus, Anaxagoras, Empedocles, and almost all the ancients (*omnes paene veteres*), who said that nothing could be grasped or cognized or known, saying that the senses are restricted, the mind weak, the course of life short and that (to quote Democritus) truth has been submerged in an abyss, with everything in the grip of the opinions and conventions, nothing left for truth and everything draped in darkness. (*Acad. post.* 44, trans. L&S 68A)[9]

The dispute between Zeno and Arcesilaus, owing to the desire of each to lay claim to the legacy of previous philosophers and to defend their own positions, revolves around the figure of Socrates, while also concerning the interpretation of Presocratic philosophy. Against the dogmatic Socrates of Cynical and Xenophontean origin described by Zeno, a figure possessing

---

[6] Cic. *Acad. pr.* 13: *cum ueteres physicos nominatis, facere idem, quod seditiosi ciues solent, cum aliquos ex antiquis claros uiros proferunt, quos dicant fuisse popularis, ut eorum ipsi similes esse uideantur.*

[7] Ibid. 14: *Similiter uos, cum perturbare, ut illi rem publicam, sic uos philosophiam bene iam constitutam uelitis, Empedoclen, Anaxagoran, Democritum, Parmeniden, Xenophanen, Platonem etiam et Socraten profertis.*

[8] Ibid. 15.

[9] *Tum ego 'Cum Zenone' inquam 'ut accepimus Arcesilas sibi omne certamen instituit, non pertinacia aut studio vincendi ut quidem mihi videtur, sed earum rerum obscuritate, quae ad confessionem ignorationis adduxerant Socratem et [vel ut] iam ante Socratem Democritum Anaxagoram Empedoclem omnes paene veteres, qui nihil cognosci nihil percipi nihil sciri posse dixerunt, angustos sensus imbecillos animos brevia curricula vitae et ut Democritus in profundo veritatem esse demersam, opinionibus et institutis omnia teneri nihil veritati relinqui, deinceps omnia tenebris circumfusa esse dixerunt.*

68                    ANNA MARIA IOPPOLO

knowledge and moral wisdom, Arcesilaus refers to Socrates' irony and
protestations of ignorance. Arcesilaus' Socrates is the aporetic Socrates of
Plato's dialogues, who disavows certain knowledge and is on a constant
quest for truth. It is rather surprising, therefore, that Heraclitus is not
listed among the Presocratic forerunners of Academic scepticism mentioned by Cicero,[10] considering not only his significant impact on
Plato's philosophy, but also the fact that the Stoics had claimed
Heraclitus for themselves, painting a dogmatic picture of the philosopher
to suit their point of view. Leaving aside the difficult issue of the extent to
which the Stoics were indebted to Heraclitus or, conversely, to what degree
they contributed to introducing new elements into Heraclitus' philosophy
because of the obscure way in which the latter's thought had been
transmitted,[11] there is no doubt that by Arcesilaus' day they had turned
Heraclitus into a key figure in their philosophical tradition. Cleanthes, in
particular, had devoted an in-depth study to Heraclitus, who had considerably influenced his philosophy and language. However, it may be argued
that Heraclitus' influence shaped the whole history of the Stoa from Zeno
to Marcus Aurelius, albeit it to different extents.[12] Zeno and Cleanthes
portray Heraclitus as a cosmologist, theorist of fire, and source of inspiration for Stoic physics, as well as – given the unity of the Stoic philosophical
system – for the doctrines of virtue and the soul as exhalation
(ἀναθυμίασις). Nevertheless, it is difficult to believe that Arcesilaus
refrained from countering this portrait of Heraclitus with that of the
philosopher as the theorist of flux, to whom Plato himself had assigned a
significant role in the *Theaetetus* when outlining his theory of perception as
knowledge. At this stage, it might be hypothesised that the discrepancy

---

[10] Except for a very fleeting mention of Heraclitus in *Acad. pr.* 118, as the philosopher who established
fire as the first principle, he is never mentioned in the *Academica*. Lévy 2014: 9 points out: 'On
notera que la présentation en première position de Parménide comme inventeur d'une doctrine
explicitée du feu principiel, aboutit à diminuer l'originalité d'Héraclite dont la *doxa* est exprimée
avec la plus extrême concision.' Brittain & Palmer 2001: 62 observe: 'That Heraclitus together with
Parmenides features more prominently in Plato's own dialogues than any of the other Presocratics
appealed to in the *Academica* might seem to make their relative absence from this work seem even
more strange.'

[11] On the problems of the transmission of Heraclitus' 'words', see Long 1996.

[12] See Long 1996: 35. While no other work by Zeno devoted to Heraclitus is attested, the ancient
sources report that Zeno regarded Heraclitus as an important philosophical authority: see
Numenius fr. 25 des Places (*apud* Euseb. *Praep. evang.* 14.5.12). Cleanthes' interest in Heraclitus
is confirmed, moreover, by the four-book work τῶν Ἡρακλείτου ἐξηγήσεις τέσσαρα (DL 7.174 =
*SVF* 1.481). In all likelihood, the heterodox Stoic Aristo, a contemporary of Arcesilaus and
Cleanthes, was also the author of a work Περὶ Ἡρακλείτου, mentioned by Diogenes Laertius
(DL 9.5, on which see Ioppolo 1980: 318 and Long 1996: 39 n. 15); a work Περὶ Ἡρακλείτου
in five books is also attributed to Sphaerus: see DL 7.177 (*SVF* I.620).

between the two Academic sources, Cicero and Plutarch, when it comes to the mention of Heraclitus among Arcesilaus' illustrious predecessors, depends on the fact that these two sources appeal to the philosophers of the past within two completely different contexts. The testimony provided by the *Adversus Colotem* is polemical, since it refers to the accusation levelled by his opponents and by the so-called sophists, who criticise Arcesilaus for his attempt to attribute his own 'doctrines' to his predecessors,[13] thereby also disputing his claim that his school was a continuation of the philosophical tradition whose name it bore.

It is noteworthy that the names of the precursors to which Arcesilaus appeals are listed in reverse chronological order, as this inversion would appear to stress the conceptual priority of the Socrates–Plato pair over the Parmenides–Heraclitus one.[14] The priority of the appeal to Socrates and Plato highlights Arcesilaus' belonging to his school, whereas the appeal to Parmenides and Heraclitus, which emphasises the significant role played by the two illustrious Presocratics with respect to Plato's philosophy, is designed to uphold Arcesilaus' interpretation of their philosophy. This hypothesis also finds confirmation in Socrates' portrayal in the *Adversus Colotem*, where he undoubtedly displays the distinguishing features of the Platonic-sceptical Socrates that may be traced back to Arcesilaus.[15] Therefore, it cannot be ruled out that Arcesilaus likewise described Heraclitus as a forerunner of scepticism.

In the *Academica*, Lucullus highlights the astute strategy adopted by Arcesilaus to explain the philosophical continuity between Academic scepticism and the conception of nature of the Presocratics, so as to reinforce and support his own position.[16] The one feature which, according to Arcesilaus, the most illustrious Presocratics shared was distrust of the ability of the human faculties to attain knowledge. This led Socrates to

---

[13] The same charge is levelled against Arcesilaus in Cic. *Acad. pr.* 15. With regard to the reliability of Plutarch's testimony, Donini 2003: 334 notes: 'Ci sono buone ragioni per pensare che questo fosse l'albero genealogico che Arcesilao presentava a difesa e a illustrazione della propria posizione filosofica e, a quanto a prima vista apparirebbe dalle pagine di *Adv. Col.*, Plutarco non ha nulla da obiettare alla ricostruzione dell'accademico', referring to *Adv. Col.* 1124D–E, in which all four philosophers are mentioned.

[14] See Burnyeat 1997: 296, and n. 54.

[15] In the *Adversus Colotem*, two contrasting pictures of Socrates emerge: the picture painted by Colotes, which may be traced back to Arcesilaus and which presents Socrates as a sceptical philosopher, and the one painted by Plutarch. I will briefly get back to this point later on. For a more detailed discussion of the issue, see Ioppolo 1995: 97; 2004 and, with different emphases, Opsomer 1998: 85–6 and 101–2; Warren 2002: 333–4; Donini 2003: 334 nn. 5 and 6, and Corti 2014: *passim*.

[16] See *Acad. pr.* 13: *ut eorum ipsi similes esse uideantur*.

# 70                    ANNA MARIA IOPPOLO

state that he *knew* that he knew nothing,[17] and Arcesilaus to disavow the one bit of knowledge Socrates had left himself. However, upon closer scrutiny, the *Academica* does not rule out the possibility that Heraclitus, too, may be included in Arcesilaus' list.[18]

Cicero suggests that the list is not limited to Democritus, Anaxagoras and Empedocles, but may be extended, as it includes *almost all the ancients* (*omnes paene veteres*).[19] Moreover, given that – as is widely known – the *Academica* has not survived in its entirety, we cannot exclude that Heraclitus was mentioned in the sections now lost. Besides, the history of earlier philosophy is presented in the surviving portion of the *Academica Posteriora* (44–5) as Arcesilaus' response to Zeno's Stoic version, although it is difficult to imagine how this narrative was developed.[20] The hypothesis that the absence of Heraclitus' name is due to the fact that 'the Academics as represented in the *Academica* are concerned with the actual Presocratics'[21] is not a crucial one, given that, if this explains the presence of Parmenides on the list, it should also account for the absence of Heraclitus.

We are thus dealing, on the one hand, with Cicero's regrettably incomplete testimony, which does not allow us to positively rule out that Arcesilaus also appealed to Heraclitus, and, on the other, with Plutarch's

---

[17] Cf. Pl. *Ap.* 21d3–6.

[18] Bonazzi 2018: 133 too mentions this possibility, but then explains Heraclitus' absence as a matter of fact, in the sense that 'Héraclite pouvait certes être mentionné par les Académiciens, mais pas pour autant en cela qu'il pouvait constituer un point de référence important.'

[19] See *Acad. post.* 44, quoted above. In *Acad. pr.* 72–4, Cicero responds to the accusation brought against the Academics in 13–15, but Heraclitus is not mentioned in the list of the Academics' predecessors. In §75, Cicero ends his response with a personal consideration: *Videorne tibi, non ut Saturninus, nominare modo illustris homines, sed imitari numquam nisi clarum, nisi nobilem? Atqui habebam* molestos uobis, *sed minutos, Stilponem Diodorum Alexinum, quorum sunt contorta et aculeata quaedam sofismata: sic enim appellantur fallaces conclusiunculae. Sed quid eos colligam, cum habeam Chrysippum, qui fulcire putatur porticum Stoicorum?* In this context, it is obvious that Stilpo, Diodorus and Alexinus are not part of the Academic 'genealogy' to which Arcesilaus appealed, less still Chrysippus. The appeal to this last group of philosophers comes from Cicero himself, who makes ironic use of it *contra Stoicos* – not to mention the fact that Arcesilaus could not have appealed to Chrysippus, for obvious chronological reasons. See Corti 2014: 222 and n. 84.

[20] Brittain & Palmer 2001: 46 note: 'For even if we come to accept that both editions offered more or less the same historical picture, it is still possible, if not likely, that it may have been deployed for somewhat different ends … The history in the extant portion of the *Academica Posteriora* is presented as a way of explaining Arcesilaus' motivation for his sceptical innovations … yet it is also a response to a critical question posed against the background of Varro's own Antiochean version of the history of philosophy.'

[21] Cf. Brittain & Palmer 2001: 62–3: 'Precisely because of their prominence in Plato, when Arcesilaus appealed to Parmenides and Heraclitus, he likely based his appeals on their representations in the dialogues … The Academics as represented in the *Academica*, by contrast, are obviously concerned with the actual Presocratics.'

## Arcesilaus' Appeal to Heraclitus

testimony in the *Adversus Colotem*, which is the only text we have that claims Heraclitus is an important antecedent for Arcesilaus' philosophy, and, as such, should not be sufficient for us to make this case.[22] Nor does the fact that Heraclitus was regarded as an authority by the Stoics seem a plausible reason to rule out that Arcesilaus appealed to him,[23] given that even Socrates was an authority for the Stoics,[24] and yet Arcesilaus claimed strongly to be his heir. So it is worth examining whether any surviving testimonies show that Arcesilaus drew upon Heraclitus' philosophy *in any way* for his dialectical arguments. And given that Arcesilaus' dialectical method was to allow his interlocutor to speak first, and only afterwards put forward the argument contrary to the one advanced by him,[25] it is worth setting out from the Stoic testimonies and then move on to examine Arcesilaus' counterarguments.

### 3.2 Cleanthes' Interpretation of Heraclitus' River Fragment (DK B12) Meets the Criticism of the Academics

Starting from a comparative analysis of a testimony from Cleanthes concerning Zeno's doctrine of the soul and a passage from Plutarch's *De communibus notitiis* which illustrates the Academic criticism of Cleanthes' position, I will endeavour to show that both the Stoics and the sceptical Academics made use of Heraclitus with the purpose of reinforcing their own philosophical position. In this respect, Cleanthes' testimony might represent a significant starting point in the epistemological dispute between Arcesilaus and the Stoics.

By examining Zeno's physics in the light of that of the most illustrious natural philosophers, Cleanthes expounded Zeno's theory of the soul, which he compared to Heraclitus':

> Concerning the soul, Cleanthes, setting out the doctrines of Zeno for comparison with the rest of the natural philosophers, states that Zeno says that the soul is a perceptive exhalation (αἰσθητικὴν ἀναθυμίασιν), just as

---

[22] For the view that Arcesilaus constitutes the ultimate source of Plutarch's list and that therefore the Academic genealogy presented in *Adv. Col.* is more reliable than Cicero's – which is based on a more generic Academic tradition – see Donini 2002, now in Donini 2011: 391 n. 70.

[23] Lévy 2001: 309 believes that Heraclitus is one of the few Presocratics to whom Arcesilaus did not appeal, because 'ce philosophe était une autorité de référence de l'adversaire stoïcien'.

[24] On Socrates' influence in shaping Zeno's philosophical outlook, see DL 7.2 (= *SVF* 1.1), 7.31 (= *SVF* 1.6); on the Stoic claim to be Socratics, see Philod. *De Stoicis* col. 13 (ed. Dorandi 1982, *PHerc.* 135 and 339: 107).

[25] See Cic. *Acad. post.* 45; *Fin.* 2.2; *De or.* 3.67; *ND* 1.11.

## 72 ANNA MARIA IOPPOLO

Heraclitus [*sc.* says]. For wishing to show that souls in being exhaled become always new (νεαραὶ ἀεὶ γίνονται),[26] likened them to rivers, speaking as follows: 'Upon those who step in the same rivers different and different waters flow', and 'souls are exhaled from moisture' (καὶ ψυχαὶ δὲ ἀπὸ τῶν ὑγρῶν ἀναθυμιῶνται).[27] Zeno, then, like Heraclitus, shows that the soul is an exhalation, and says that it is perceptive for the following reason: because its leading part is susceptible both of being modified by the external realities through the organs of sensation and of receiving the impressions. These in fact are properties peculiar to the soul. (Arius Did. fr. 39 *apud* Euseb. *Praep. evang.* 15.20.2–3 = fr. 39 Diels = *SVF* 1.141, 519)[28]

Cleanthes quotes Heraclitus' river fragment (B12 DK) in order to establish an analogy between the constant flow of the river's water, which he interprets as a metaphor for the continuous renewal of souls exhaled from moisture, and Zeno's doctrine of the soul, according to which the soul is an exhalation of breath capable of perceiving.[29] Here I do not wish to address the issue of whether the content of the fragment exemplifies Heraclitus' doctrine of conflict or rather his doctrine of the soul or of flux, or indeed whether – and to what extent – Cleanthes distorted Heraclitus'

---

[26] I accept the correction νεαραί proposed by Meerwaldt 1951: 53–4 in place of the νοεραί we find in the manuscripts.

[27] I agree with those scholars who believe that the phrase καὶ ψυχαὶ δὲ ἀπὸ τῶν ὑγρῶν ἀναθυμιῶνται is not part of the Heraclitus quote, because of the verb ἀναθυμιάομαι, whose use is not attested before Aristotle: see (among others) Kirk 1983: 367–9; Marcovich 2001: 206–14; Kahn 1979: 166–8; Fronterotta 2013: 84. Aristotle credits Heraclitus with the thesis of the origin of the soul by ἀναθυμίασις: see *De anima* 1.2.405a24. As Festa 1935: 120 notes: 'il ragionamento di Cleante è fatto per provare l'identità dell'intuizione zenonea con l'eraclitea, nonostante che i termini usati non siano perfettamente identici'.

[28] Περὶ δὲ ψυχῆς Κλεάνθης μὲν τὰ Ζήνωνος δόγματα παρατιθέμενος πρὸς σύγκρισιν τὴν πρὸς τοὺς ἄλλους φυσικούς φησιν ὅτι Ζήνων τὴν ψυχὴν λέγει αἰσθητικὴν ἀναθυμίασιν, καθάπερ Ἡράκλειτος. βουλόμενος γὰρ ἐμφανίσαι ὅτι αἱ ψυχαὶ ἀναθυμιώμεναι νεαραὶ ἀεὶ γίνονται, εἴκασεν αὐτὰς τοῖς ποταμοῖς λέγων οὕτως ποταμοῖσι τοῖσιν αὐτοῖσιν ἐμβαίνουσιν ἕτερα καὶ ἕτερα ὕδατα ἐπιρρεῖ· καὶ ψυχαὶ δὲ ἀπὸ τῶν ὑγρῶν ἀναθυμιῶνται. ἀναθυμίασιν μὲν οὖν ὁμοίως τῷ Ἡρακλείτῳ τὴν ψυχὴν ἀποφαίνει Ζήνων, αἰσθητικὴν δὲ αὐτὴν εἶναι διὰ τοῦτο λέγει, ὅτι τυποῦσθαί τε δύναται [τὸ μέγεθος] τὸ μέρος τὸ ἡγούμενον αὐτῆς ἀπὸ τῶν ὄντων καὶ ὑπαρχόντων διὰ τῶν αἰσθητηρίων καὶ παραδέχεσθαι τὰς τυπώσεις. ταῦτα γὰρ ἴδια ψυχῆς ἐστι. This testimony has a complex provenance, because the quote from Cleanthes, reporting Zeno's doctrine, has Arius Didymus as its source, who in turn is quoted by Eusebius in the *Praeparatio Evangelica*. On the reliability of Eusebius' testimony, which reports 'a securely attested fragment of Arius Didymus', see Algra 2018: 70. It is impossible to safely establish from which of Cleanthes' works the quote is drawn, whether it be from his four-book commentary on Heraclitus' philosophy (τῶν Ἡρακλείτου ἐξηγήσεις τέσσαρα), from his treatise *On the Physiology of Zeno* in two books (Περὶ τῆς Ζήνωνος φυσιολογίας δύο), or from his *Physical Notes* (Ὑπομνήματα φυσικά), mentioned by Plut. *Stoic. rep.* 1034D, on which see Festa 1935: 115 and 122–3. On the reliability of Cleanthes' testimony, which reports B12 DK in its original form – compared to Pl. *Cra.* 402a, which inserts a δίς – see Kahn 1979: 168; Kirk 1983: 374; Marcovich 2001: 206.

[29] See also DL 7.157 (*SVF* 1.135).

# Arcesilaus' Appeal to Heraclitus

73

thought.[30] What I wish to highlight is the prominent role which Cleanthes assigns to Heraclitus because of the support the latter provides to his Stoic doctrine.[31] The analogy which Cleanthes wishes to establish between Zeno's doctrine of the soul and Heraclitus' one is not confined to the fact that both philosophers envisage the soul as an exhalation; rather, it also extends to the soul's property of being *aisthētikē*, as *aisthētikē* is a constitutive part of the definition of the soul.[32] It is important to bear in mind that, before quoting the river fragment word by word, Cleanthes anticipates his interpretation of it by stating that Heraclitus likened the souls to rivers 'wishing to show that souls in being exhaled become *always new*'. Hence, the claim that 'souls become always new' stems from Cleanthes' exegesis of fragment B12.[33] Cleanthes' chief concern is to show that the analogy between Heraclitus' conception of the soul, according to which the soul is ἀναθυμίασις ἀπὸ τῶν ὑγρῶν, and Zeno's view that the soul is constantly nourished by blood via exhalation,[34] is centred on the idea of the constant renewal and replacement of the vaporous substance of the soul. The conclusion that the capacity to be modified by external objects and the capacity to receive impressions are properties (ἴδια) of the soul once more clearly reveals that Cleanthes is expounding the Stoic doctrine.[35] Besides, even admitting that the river fragment is a metaphor for

---

[30] Already Pearson 1891: 138 noted: 'It is doubtful whether the doctrine of nourishment of the soul by the blood was held by Heraclitus and from him derived by Zeno . . . It is best . . . to regard this as Stoic innovation.' See too Kahn 1979: 260: 'The only safe conclusion is that Cleanthes allows himself great freedom in reading Stoic doctrines into Heraclitean texts.' The use of allegory, applied to the reading of poets, constitutes another well-known example of the strategy of appropriation of other thinkers' doctrines adopted by Zeno and Cleanthes for their own purposes: see Ioppolo 1980, Algra 2001.

[31] See Hahm 1977: 151, 219–20.

[32] I do not share the thesis of Tarán 1999: 25, according to which 'Cleanthes first summarizes and limits the similarity between Heraclitus and Zeno to ἀναθυμίασις and immediately afterwards discusses the soul's perceptive powers according to Zeno's theory only.' *Contra*, in my view, Cleanthes affirms that a perfect analogy is to be found between Zeno's definition of the soul and Heraclitus' view of the soul as αἰσθητικὴ ἀναθυμίασις twice: before quoting fragment B12 DK (καθάπερ Ἡράκλειτος), and after quoting it (ὁμοίως τῷ Ἡρακλείτῳ). The fact that fragment B12 DK does not contain any reference to the perceptual power of the soul and that Cleanthes expounds the mechanism of perception in Stoic terms confirms that Cleanthes sought to draw upon Heraclitus in support of Stoic doctrine.

[33] Plut. *Comm. not.* 1085A reveals that this interpretation of Heraclitus' doctrine was formulated by Cleanthes, as we shall soon see.

[34] See Gal. *PHP* 2.8.166.12–14 (*SVF* 1.140; 521): τρέφεσθαι μὲν ἐξ αἵματος . . . τὴν ψυχήν, οὐσίαν δ' αὐτῆς ὑπάρχειν τὸ πνεῦμα. Long 1996: 55: 'Zeno probably held that the soul as *pneuma* is principally nurtured from the blood and his use of ἀναθυμίασις to describe the process of vaporisation may well owe more to Aristotle and medical theory than to Heraclitus.' See too Pradeau 2002: 249.

[35] DL 7.175 (*SVF* 1.481) transmits a work by Cleanthes entitled Περὶ ἰδίων, the content of which remains unknown.

74 ANNA MARIA IOPPOLO

the constant renewal of souls exhaled from moisture, it contains no reference to the *perceptual* capacity of souls.[36]

The hypothesis that Cleanthes' aim is to affirm the thesis that the substance of the soul – precisely insofar as it is a constantly renewed *pneuma* – is capable of perceiving things finds confirmation in a testimony from Plutarch.[37] This is a very important piece of evidence to reconstruct the polemic between the Stoics and the Academics before Chrysippus' time. Plutarch expounds and criticises the Stoic view of the soul, offering some important clues to identify both the promoter of the doctrine and the author of the criticism.

> Conception is a kind of presentation (φαντασία) and a presentation is an impression (τύπωσις) in the soul; but the nature of soul is exhalation (ἀναθυμίασις) on which it is difficult to make an impression on account of its fineness and for which to receive and retain an impression is impossible. For since its nourishment and its genesis is from liquids, it is in a continual process of accretion and consumption; and its mixture with the air of respiration is *always making the exhalation new* (καινὴν ἀεὶ ποιεῖ τὴν ἀναθυμίασιν)[38] as this is altered and transformed by the current which rushes in from without and withdraws again. For one can more easily suppose a stream of running water preserving shapes and imprints and forms than a breath being changed by vapours and moistures within and continually being blended with another, as it were, inert and alien breath. The Stoics, however, are so heedless of themselves as to define conceptions as a kind of stored notions and memories as abiding and stable impressions and to fix absolutely firm the form of knowledge as being unalterable and steadfast and then to posit a base and foundation for these things of a substance that slides and scatters and is always in motion and flux (οὐσίας

---

[36] This view is endorsed by Tarán 1999: 25, with whom I agree on this point: 'Yet even if it possible that Cleanthes found evidence of the "perceptive" powers of the soul in some fragments of Heraclitus, he *here* says nothing about it.'

[37] I disagree with Colvin 2005: 265, according to whom Cleanthes quotes the river fragment in order to describe 'the Stoic theory of the soul *production* by exhalation'; hence, in my view, it cannot be granted that 'what he has described with the word "vapour" is the transformation of πνεῦμα-as-φύσις into πνεῦμα-as-ψυχή'. Cleanthes is referring to the soul, to the soul as such and in its already constituted form, as is shown by the reference to the *hēgemonikon*, or reason, which has among its properties that of perceiving *because it is constantly exhaled*. One element in support of this interpretation is the fact that Cleanthes bases his analogy between Zeno's and Heraclitus' definitions of the soul on the soul's property of being *aisthētikē*, as a constitutive part of both definitions. With regard to the Stoic doctrine of the production of the soul, Long 1999: 564 writes: 'Breath, blood, heart – these make an essential contribution to metabolism and to "nourishment" of the *psuche*, but it is neither identical with them, nor supervenient on them. The psychic *pneuma* is an independent physical principle with causal powers intrinsic to itself.'

[38] As is evident from a comparison with the passage from Eusebius (*Praep. evang.* 15.20.2–3) just discussed, in which the same expression occurs, Plutarch is referring to Cleanthes' doctrine.

## Arcesilaus' Appeal to Heraclitus

ὀλισθηρᾶς καὶ σχεδαστῆς καὶ φερομένης ἀεὶ καὶ ῥεούσης). (*Comm. not.* 1084F–1085A = *SVF* 2.847)[39]

The doctrine which Plutarch criticises – by generically assigning it to the Stoics – concerns Cleanthes' interpretation of Zeno's doctrine of the soul, as is shown by a comparison with the testimony from Eusebius I have just discussed. Plutarch focuses his attack on the fact that the theory of the soul as a vaporous exhalation in constant flux is in conflict with the Stoic doctrine of conceptions. He sets out from Zeno's definition of representation as *typōsis*,[40] because conceptions find their origin in representations. Plutarch advances two objections: the soul, as an exhalation, could hardly receive external impressions given its tenuous nature; and even admitting that it did receive them, it would be incapable of preserving them. Plutarch explains the reasons for this. The corporeal soul is nourished by the exhalations from blood,[41] which entail a constant alternation of the increase and consumption of moisture.[42] By mixing with an external *argon kai allotrion pneuma*, the internal *pneuma* constantly *makes the exhalation new*.[43] The soul, therefore, owes its continuity and existence to the exhalation from blood and bodily humours, a flow of vaporising moisture.[44] What is noteworthy here is not just the fact that Plutarch presents the doctrine of the soul as *anathymiasis* by providing more details than Eusebius, but also – and especially – that he displays a very in-depth knowledge of technical Stoic terminology. This suggests that he was relying on a well-informed source, which he followed faithfully. The defining feature of Stoic doctrine that Plutarch criticises is the idea of a

---

[39] φαντασία γάρ τις ἡ ἔννοιά ἐστι, φαντασία δὲ τύπωσις ἐν ψυχῇ· ψυχῆς δὲ φύσις ἀναθυμίασις, ἣν τυπωθῆναι μὲν ἐργῶδες διὰ μανότητα, δεξαμένην δὲ τηρῆσαι τύπωσιν ἀδύνατον. ἥ τε γὰρ τροφὴ καὶ ἡ γένεσις αὐτῆς ἐξ ὑγρῶν οὖσα συνεχῆ τὴν ἐπιφορὰν ἔχει καὶ τὴν ἀνάλωσιν, ἥ τε πρὸς τὸν ἀέρα διὰ τῆς ἀναπνοῆς ἐπιμιξία καινὴν ἀεὶ ποιεῖ τὴν ἀναθυμίασιν, ἐξισταμένην καὶ τρεπομένην ὑπὸ τοῦ θύραθεν ἐμβάλλοντος ὀχετοῦ καὶ πάλιν ἐξιόντος. ῥεῦμα γὰρ ἄν τις ὕδατος φερομένου μᾶλλον διανοηθείη σχήματα καὶ τύπους καὶ εἴδη διαφυλάττον ἢ πνεῦμα φερόμενον ἐντὸς ἀτμοῖς καὶ ὑγρότησιν, ἑτέρῳ δ' ἔξωθεν ἐνδελεχῶς οἷον ἀργῷ καὶ ἀλλοτρίῳ πνεύματι κιρνάμενον. Ἀλλ' οὕτως παρακούουσι ἑαυτῶν ὥστε τὰς ἐννοίας ἐναποκειμένας τινὰς ὁριζόμενοι νοήσεις μνήμας δὲ μονίμους καὶ σχετικὰς τυπώσεις τὰς δ' ἐπιστήμας καὶ παντάπασι πηγνύντες ὡς τὸ ἀμετάπτωτον καὶ βέβαιον ἐχούσας εἶτα τούτοις ὑποτίθεσθαι βάσιν καὶ ἕδραν οὐσίας ὀλισθηρᾶς καὶ σχεδαστῆς καὶ φερομένης ἀεὶ καὶ ῥεούσης.

[40] See SE *M* 7.230, 236 (*SVF* 1.58).

[41] See the testimonies collected in *SVF* 1.518, which according to Cleanthes prove the corporeality of the soul. Zeno defined the soul as a warm or innate *pneuma* (see *SVF* 1.135–8) and Cleanthes retained Zeno's definition of the soul as *pneuma* (see *SVF* 1.521, 525).

[42] See again Gal. *PHP* 2.8.166.12–14 (*SVF* 1.140), quoted at n. 34, from which it may be inferred that the moist substance is blood.

[43] This observation by Plutarch would confirm the reading νεαραί proposed by Meerwaldt 1951: 53–4, instead of νοεραί in the Arius Didymus passage.

[44] See again Gal. *PHP* 2.8.166.12–14 (*SVF* 1.140), cit.

76 ANNA MARIA IOPPOLO

continuous flow and of the mobility of the soul, which always makes the exhalation new, as Cleanthes argues when comparing Zeno's doctrine of the soul with Heraclitus'.[45] Plutarch counters that if the soul were 'a substance that slides and scatters and is always in motion and flux', it would not be able to exercise its function of cognition, because it would be incapable of receiving and retaining any impressions. Plutarch, therefore, ironically concludes that flowing water can preserve figures, impressions and forms better than *pneuma*.

### 3.3 Plato's *Theaetetus* is a Bone of Contention between the Stoics and Arcesilaus

I will now show that Zeno and Cleanthes appropriated some significant outcomes of the *Theaetetus*, which they interpreted in dogmatic terms, and hence that the *Theaetetus* became a bone of contention between the Stoics and Arcesilaus.

In order to appreciate the importance which Cleanthes assigns to the soul as an exhalation,[46] it must be borne in mind that Cleanthes' primary concern is to explain the physical mechanism of cognition. Zeno had defined representation as an impression, which is to say as the imprint mechanically produced by the impression of an object upon the soul, compared to a wax tablet.[47] This conception of representation as an impression, however, runs up against a number of problems widely attested in the sources, as is shown by the fact that Zeno's immediate disciples held conflicting views as to how the notion of impression was to be understood.[48]

It is worth bearing in mind that the metaphor of representation as an impression had been employed effectively by Plato in the *Theaetetus*

---

[45] See Euseb. *Praep. evang.* 15.20.2–3 (*SVF* 1.141, 519), already quoted.

[46] The essence of the soul is its *pneuma*, whereas the exhalation from blood is its nourishment: see Galen in *SVF* 2.783.

[47] On the attribution of the analogy between the *hēgemonikon* and a wax tablet to Zeno, see Anon. *in Pl. Tht.* 11.27–31 (ed. Bastianini & Sedley, p. 290), with Ioppolo 1980: 120–3 and Bastianini & Sedley 1995: 498. Zeno also traced the origin of the definition of representation as *typōsis* back to the metaphor of the impression left by a signet ring on wax: see DL 7.45 (*SVF* 2.53): τοῦ ὀνόματος οἰκείως μετενηνεγμένου ἀπὸ τῶν τύπων τῶν ἐν τῷ κηρῷ ὑπὸ τοῦ δακτυλίου γινομένων ... Cf. SE *M* 7.373 (*SVF* 2.56): εἰ γὰρ κηροῦ τρόπον ἡ ψυχὴ φανταστικῶς πάσχουσα. This metaphor was far from new to Greek thought (cf. Democritus A135 DK) and was effectively used by Plato in the *Theaetetus* (191c ff.). On the influence of Plato's *Theaetetus* among the Stoics and the latter's use of it, as well as Arcesilaus' refutation of the dialogue, I will refer to Ioppolo 1990: 433–49.

[48] SE *M* 7.228: φαντασία οὖν ἐστι κατ᾽ αὐτοὺς τύπωσις ἐν ψυχῇ, περὶ ἧς εὐθὺς καὶ διέστησαν; 8.400 (*SVF* 1.484): παρ᾽ αὐτοῖς διαπεφωνῆσθαι τὸ τί ποτ᾽ ἐστιν ἡ φαντασία.

## Arcesilaus' Appeal to Heraclitus

(191c ff.), when discussing one of the definitions of opinion, envisaged as the encounter between an actual image and the impression of a past image upon the soul, compared to a wax tablet. This model of opinion is rejected in the *Theaetetus*, on the grounds that it cannot account for purely intellectual errors of judgement. However, if it refers to things that are perceived at the present moment, things that do not involve a memory process, it is adequate (192a–b). The main drawback, already highlighted by Plato, is that successive imprints end up cancelling the previous ones.[49] To avoid this objection, Cleanthes, on the one hand, emphasises the mechanical and physical aspect of representation, understanding impression in the literal sense 'as involving depression and elevation, just as does the impression made in wax by seal-rings';[50] on the other hand, he stresses the structure of the soul as an exhalation that constantly renews itself.

Perception faithfully reproduces all the features of an object by impressing them upon the *pneuma* of the soul via direct contact. What this means is that the soul does not have a limited capacity, like wax, particularly with respect to the number of impressions it can receive, because, being an exhalation in constant flux, its capacity to receive impressions is continually renewed. And because in order to ensure the reliability of perception it is necessary for the representation to faithfully reproduce the characteristics of the object by impressing them upon the soul *at the present moment*, the fact that the exhalation is in constant flux does not constitute a problem. According to Cleanthes, this explanation is enough to counter the objection that new impressions erase previous ones. In support of his thesis, Cleanthes invokes Heraclitus' doctrine and the parallel between the soul and the river, a particularly useful analogy to confirm his interpretation on account of the authority of the source.[51] The soul is like a river, which constantly changes through the inflow of new water, yet remains constant precisely in virtue of this incessant flowing of new currents. However, this explanation does not satisfy Cleanthes' opponents, who criticise the thesis

---

[49] See Chrysippus' criticism of Cleanthes' doctrine of representation in SE *M* 7.229, 372–5; cf. *PH* 2.70, where the same criticism is reported without mentioning its author.

[50] SE *M* 7.228: Κλεάνθης μὲν ἤκουσε τὴν τύπωσιν κατ᾽ εἰσοχήν τε καὶ ἐξοχήν, cf. 8.400, *PH* 2.70 (*SVF* 1.484). Note that, in describing representations as σχήματα καὶ τύπους καὶ εἴδη, Plutarch (*Comm. not.* 1085A) implicitly refers to Cleanthes' definition of representations as impressions.

[51] Long 1996: 56 stresses Cleanthes' eagerness to appeal to Heraclitus: 'Nor should we overlook the possibility that Cleanthes' interest in Heraclitus and other past writers was stimulated by the need to protect Stoicism against attack from the Academic sceptics. By associating Heraclitus with his own views he could present a more united front against scepticism.' See also Tarrant 1985: 81: 'It should be noted that it was in the time of Arcesilaus rather than that of Aenesidemus that Heraclitus was a key figure for the Stoics.'

of the soul as an exhalation by raising the objections featured in the passage from Plutarch just discussed. The constant flow of the soul's *pneuma* does not allow it to retain and preserve impressions, but prevents the accumulation of representations, which is the precondition for the establishment of memory, and hence for the formation of conceptions and any further cognitive process.

Plutarch's criticism is very acute, as it turns Cleanthes' conception of the soul as an exhalation in constant flux on its head by posing the following dilemma: either the soul is an exhalation in constant flux that, in becoming always new, cannot receive and preserve impressions, in which case it is not percipient; or it *is* percipient, in which case it cannot be an ever-new exhalation in constant flux. Consequently, as according to Cleanthes the soul is an exhalation in constant flux, it does not possess the property of being *aisthētikē*. Far from demonstrating that the leading part of the soul 'is susceptible to being impressed by the outside world through the sensory organs and receives the impressions', the thesis of the soul as an exhalation in constant flux engenders quite the opposite conclusion.

This objection, which proves very effective against Cleanthes' conception of representation, ignores Chrysippus' interpretation. According to Chrysippus, representation is a modification (*alloiōsis*) or alteration (*heteroiōsis*), meaning a qualitative change of the soul's *pneuma*, which in virtue of its inner tension admits of countless alterations:

> For it is no longer absurd that, when many presentations coexist in us at the same moment, the same body should admit of innumerable alterations. For just as the air, when many people are speaking simultaneously, receives in a single moment numberless and different impacts and at once undergoes many alterations also, so too when the *hēgemonikon* is the subject of a variety of impressions it will experience something analogous to this. (SE *M* 7.230–1 = *SVF* 2.56)[52]

Representations, therefore, are dynamic states of the soul's *pneuma* that can coexist at the same moment and endure. As Plutarch's critique is not effective against this definition of representation, it is evident that the source ignores Chrysippus' correction and his definition of representation as a stable and permanent alteration of the *pneuma*. Therefore, the target of this criticism cannot be Chrysippus' doctrine. Moreover, it is worth noting

---

[52] See Sambursky 1959: 25: 'We have thus to interpret Chrysippus' "modifications of the soul" as different dynamic states of the *pneuma*, existing by virtue of the latter's inherent tension and admitting of superposition which preserves each of them individually.'

## Arcesilaus' Appeal to Heraclitus

that Chrysippus presents his definition as the correct interpretation of Zeno's metaphor of representation as an impression, and above all as a correction of Cleanthes' erroneous interpretation.[53] Against the latter, he resorts to the same arguments as Plutarch:

> If the soul when affected by presentations is imprinted like wax, the last motion will always keep overshadowing the previous presentations, just as the impressions of the second seal is such as to obliterate that of the first. But if this is so, memory is abolished, it being 'a treasury of presentations', and every art is abolished ... but it is not possible for many and different presentations to subsist in the regent part, when its mental impressions vary from time to time. (SE *M* 7.373)[54]

Chrysippus, therefore, is familiar with and accepts the criticism formulated by the Stoics' opponents and reported by Plutarch, and seeks to neutralise its effectiveness. By applying the well-known dialectical strategy which distinguishes his philosophy, Chrysippus appropriates his opponents' objection,[55] passing this off merely as the internal correction, or interpretation, of a controversial Stoic doctrine.

### 3.4 Arcesilaus Counters Cleanthes' View of Heraclitus by Making ad Hominem Use of Some Arguments from the *Theaetetus*

I will now show that Arcesilaus countered the interpretation of Heraclitus put forward by Cleanthes, which is to say the view of Heraclitus as the theorist of universal flux, by making ad hominem use of some arguments from the *Theaetetus*. As is widely known, Arcesilaus engaged in a heated epistemological polemic with Zeno and his immediate disciples, which for obvious chronological reasons excludes Chrysippus.[56] At the beginning of the *De communibus notitiis* (1059B), Plutarch states that, according to the Stoics, Providence had sent them Chrysippus after Arcesilaus and before Carneades precisely because Chrysippus had been able to successfully respond to Arcesilaus' objections, adducing many arguments in support of perception and clearing the confusion between *prolēpseis* and *ennoiai*.

---

[53] SE *M* 7.229 (*SVF* 2.56): Χρύσιππος δὲ ἄτοπον ἡγεῖτο τὸ τοιοῦτο; cf. 7.373: εἰ μὲν κατ' ἐξοχὴν καὶ εἰσοχὴν ὑφίσταται, ταῦτα ἀκολουθήσει τὰ ἄτοπα.

[54] Chrysippus' doctrine of representation as ἑτεροίωσις was also criticised by later sceptics, who probably took their lead from Carneades: see SE *M* 7.377–80.

[55] On Chrysippus' dialectical strategy of incorporating Arcesilaus' criticism within his own doctrine, so that it might go unnoticed, see Ioppolo 1986: 11–12 and *passim*.

[56] See Ioppolo 1986, 1997 and Long 2006, who has particularly insisted on the prominent role played by Aristo of Chios in the dispute on knowledge with Arcesilaus.

# 80 ANNA MARIA IOPPOLO

Besides, precisely because the doctrine of common conceptions plays a fundamental role in the Stoic system – from epistemology to physics and ethics – it is most likely that it had already been developed by Zeno, and hence that it was the object of Arcesilaus' criticism, as is witnessed by the argument adumbrated by Plutarch.[57] In this regard, one must not overlook the fact that the author of the anti-Stoic argument (henceforth, A.) begins his attack by showing that the doctrine of the soul as a vaporous exhalation in constant flux – a thesis upheld by Cleanthes – conflicts with the Stoic doctrine of *ennoiai*.[58] Indeed, conceptions find their origin in representations. But a *pneuma* in constant flux cannot receive and preserve representations, which is the essential precondition for the formation of memory and hence of conceptions. It is evident that A. is familiar with Cleanthes' interpretation of Heraclitus' river fragment, because he offers a detailed and pertinent criticism of this interpretation.[59] However, it is equally evident that A. is delivering his criticism from a different perspective, namely one that takes Heraclitus as the theorist of universal flux, following Plato's account in the *Theaetetus*: 'According to Homer, Heraclitus, and all of their tribe, all things flow like streams.'[60] A. does

---

[57] Plutarch's testimony in the *De communibus notitiis* shows that the Stoic doctrine of common conceptions had already been developed by Zeno or at least Cleanthes, *pace* Brittain 2005: 167 n. 11. Besides, Plutarch testifies to the fact that Arcesilaus directed his harsh polemical attacks against certain Stoic doctrines that conflicted with the idea of common conceptions. In 1078B–C, Plutarch explicitly mentions Arcesilaus with regard to criticism of the Stoic doctrine of κρᾶσις δι' ὅλων, against which Arcesilaus is said to have made repeated use of a very ridiculous example, that of Antigonus' fleet 'sailing through the leg that has been severed putrefied thrown into the sea and dissolved'. A few chapters later (1083B–C), he mentions the well-known argument of growth (αὐξανόμενος λόγος), which is based on the doctrine of the radical instability of the sensible world associated with Heraclitus and Plato (cf. *Tht*. 152e), and which Arcesilaus reportedly made use of against the Stoic ἰδίως ποιόν. This argument, which may be traced back to Epicharmus, sets out from the Stoic premise that 'all individual substances are in flux and motion, releasing some things from themselves and receiving others which reach them from elsewhere'. As David Sedley has explained in his excellent 1982 article, 'The Stoic Criterion of Identity', to which I refer the reader, Arcesilaus was the first to formulate the argument against the Stoics and 'Chrysippus is the first Stoic reported to have tackled the question: he devoted a whole work to the Growing Argument' – as attested by Plutarch's discussion in *Comm. not*. 1083A–1084A. Cf. Anon. *in Pl. Tht*. col. 71.12–35.

[58] This shows that the first to attack the Stoic doctrine of common conceptions was not Carneades but, long before him, Arcesilaus.

[59] It is important to bear in mind that, in defining representation as an impression, Zeno appropriated one of the definitions of opinion formulated by Plato in the *Theaetetus* and altered its meaning by drawing upon Heraclitus. Long 2006: 224 agrees that the debate between Zeno and Arcesilaus emerged because 'Arcesilaus found Zeno recycling and meddling with material in Plato's *Theaetetus*, and interpreting the dialogue's findings positively rather than sceptically.'

[60] Pl. *Tht*. 160d7–8: οἷον ῥεύματα κινεῖσθαι τὰ πάντα. Cf. Arist. *Metaph*. A 6.987a29–b7, tracing Plato's philosophical education back to Cratylus and to the Heraclitean doctrines according to which ὡς ἁπάντων τῶν αἰσθητῶν ἀεὶ ῥεόντων καὶ ἐπιστήμης περὶ αὐτῶν οὐκ οὔσης.

## Arcesilaus' Appeal to Heraclitus

not dispute the assumption that the soul is an exhalation in constant flux, but rather that it is percipient, thereby leading the constant flow of the soul and its capacity to perceive into a contradiction. A. evidently wishes to put the Stoics in a tight spot, exactly as Plato does in the *Theaetetus* with the Heraclitean champions of the doctrine of universal flux, by forcing them to admit that knowledge does not coincide with perception. He thus opposes the interpretation put forward by Cleanthes, who attributes to Heraclitus the theory of the permanence and unity of the river despite the incessant flow of water that is always different and new, by invoking Heraclitus' statement that 'nothing ever is, yet always becomes'[61] – which is the image of the river in a perpetual flux of becoming and the endless changing of its waters. That Plato in the *Theaetetus* wishes to refer precisely to Heraclitus' doctrine is also suggested by the fact that immediately afterwards he explains that there is evidence for this doctrine in the fact that 'the hot or fire' generates and controls everything (153a7–10).

A. bases his criticism on the description of the Heracliteans' position in the *Theaetetus*. If everything changes through a constant flux, neither the subject nor the object have a permanent identity, and perception is the outcome of the intercourse between the two motions, 'the one having the *dynamis of* acting, the other having the *dynamis* of being acted upon'.[62] Things are mere aggregates of things that are constantly becoming. This means that neither the subject nor the object exists outside of their mutual interaction. Each thing becomes, and becomes in relation to something else. Nothing is ever still even for a moment; neither objects nor the subjects perceiving them have a continuing identity through time; and two given things never meet again in the same way. The properties 'hard', 'hot' etc. are nothing in themselves, and each perceptual change in the perceiving subject replaces the original subject with a new one (156e7–160a4).[63] To ensure the infallibility both of perceptions and of perceptual judgements, Heraclitean ontology requires that all things be in constant flux in every respect, undergoing both spatial movement and alteration. This also makes language impossible: given that there is nothing

---

[61] Cf. Ibid. 152e1: ἔστι μὲν γὰρ οὐδέποτε οὐδέν, ἀεὶ δὲ γίγνεται. While it is true that Plato attributes this doctrine not just to Heraclitus but to all wise men except Parmenides, as well as to the best comic and tragic poets, Epicharmus, and Homer, the content of the text recalls Heraclitus' river metaphor, B12 DK – which I have already repeatedly mentioned. See too Pl. *Cra.* 402a8–10 and the relevant observations made in Sedley 2003a: 104 n. 22.

[62] Ibid. 156a3–7: τὸ πᾶν κίνησις ἦν καὶ ἄλλο παρὰ τοῦτο οὐδέν, τῆς δὲ κινήσεως δύο εἴδη, πλήθει μὲν ἄπειρον ἑκάτερον, δύναμιν τὸ μὲν ποιεῖν ἔχον, τὸ δὲ πάσχειν.

[63] This lack of identity over time breaks the subject down into a temporal succession of distinct individuals, erasing his continuity and memory: see 159b–e.

stable that may be described as being in one way rather than another, there is nothing to which language can be anchored. Therefore, if the champions of the total flux theory wish to speak, seeing that they cannot make any assertions, or even say 'in this way' and 'not in that way' without making things motionless, even if only for that moment, they must adopt a different language enabling them not to assign properties to things, but rather to speak in an indefinite sense.[64]

While the image of Heraclitus that emerges from this description is a controversial one, since Plato himself contributed to shaping it for his own purposes,[65] what matters is that Arcesilaus draws upon this interpretation of Heraclitus,[66] and opposes it to the one put forward by Cleanthes.

### 3.5 Arcesilaus Is the Author of the Anti-Stoic Argument Reported by Plutarch

At this stage, I believe it is possible to identify Arcesilaus as the author of the anti-Stoic argument reported by Plutarch. Getting back to Plutarch's testimony, we have seen how the criticism which A. directs against the Stoic doctrine of the percipient soul – at any rate as this appears to emerge from the analysis conducted so far – seems very similar to the criticism that Plato directs against the thesis that 'everything is changing all the time' in the *Theaetetus*.[67] A. objects that if the soul is governed by two currents that constantly alter it – an internal current, the exhalation nourishing it, and an external one, the respiration that keeps it alive – it is a 'substance that slides and scatters and *is always in motion and flux*' and which therefore cannot perceive anything. Not only is this argument not redundant, but it fits as a missing piece within Arcesilaus' argumentative arsenal against Stoic epistemological theory.

As is well known, in his debate with Zeno on the existence of the Stoic criterion of truth, Arcesilaus makes dialectical use of Platonic arguments,

---

[64] See *Tht.* 183a9–b5 and Sedley 2002b: 98 n. 11.

[65] See, among others, McDowell 1973: 129–30.

[66] The picture of Heraclitus as the theorist of flux is transmitted not just by Plato, but also by Aristotle. We know that Arcesilaus frequented the Peripatos and was a pupil of Theophrastus before joining Crantor's Academy: see DL 4.29. According to Rapp 2017, Aristotle's dislike of Heraclitus is due to the fact that he was the originator of something like a flux theory, i.e. the claim that all things are in motion, and that the radicalising of the theory of the constant flux of the sensible world had given rise to the Heracliteans' extremist views: see Arist. *Metaph.* Γ5.1010a10–15.

[67] Indeed, already the anonymous commentator of the *Theaetetus* identifies the Stoics as the polemical target of *Tht.* 151–87: see Anon. *in Pl. Tht.* col. 3.7–12, p. 266 Bastianini & Sedley, with the *ad loc.* Commentary (p. 486).

some of which are drawn precisely from the *Theaetetus*. These arguments do not directly concern Heraclitus' philosophy, but apply to the consequences of Heracliteanism, as this is presented by Plato in the first part of the dialogue. In particular, Arcesilaus focuses his criticism on the Stoic definition of *katalēpsis* as assent to cataleptic representations.[68] Arcesilaus objects that if representation is understood in a physical sense as an impression upon the soul, assent as the judgement of reason cannot grant the truth of a *typōsis*, which is to say of a mere affection. Only a proposition can be recognised as true, and only to a proposition can the attributes of true and false belong.

Now, the argument used by A. shows the incompatibility between the physical-ontological structure of the soul as a perceptual exhalation and the nature of representation as an impression, and highlights the absurd consequences that arise for the Stoic epistemological doctrine from the ontology of flux. It constitutes an implicit premise that Arcesilaus takes as already given in his definitive refutation of the existence of the cataleptic representation, which ultimately establishes the irrationality of representation, which is incapable of conceptualising its object.[69] *Katalēpsis* does not exist not only because representation is incapable of expressing its content in a propositional and articulate form, but also because the very physical-ontological *conditions* for it to occur are lacking: if representation is an impression, it cannot be imprinted upon, and endure within, a transient substance such as the flow of vaporising moisture.

### 3.6 Arcesilaus' Appeal to Heraclitus Is Found in Heraclitus' Response to the Delphic Motto

At this stage, it is worth returning to the *Adversus Colotem* to examine whether Arcesilaus' appeal to Heraclitus finds any further confirmation within the Plutarchean testimony from which we began our enquiry. Heraclitus' name occurs in the section on Socrates, and Socrates is one of the predecessors to whom Arcesilaus is accused of attributing his own doctrine. An analysis of the testimony on Socrates reveals that Arcesilaus appealed to Heraclitus as a philosophical authority, and not just because of the role Plato had assigned to him in his dialogues. Significantly, the

---

[68] For a detailed analysis of Arcesilaus' arguments, partly drawn from Plato's *Theaetetus*, see Ioppolo 1990, 2009: 82–93, 2018: 36–50. e 2018,

[69] See SE *M* 7.151–4.

84 ANNA MARIA IOPPOLO

Socrates described by Colotes is not Plato's Socrates, or that of Socratic literature, but a figure displaying unambiguously sceptical traits, who rejects the evidence from perception and is therefore exposed to the charge of *apraxia*.[70] Later on, this accusation is brought against Arcesilaus himself (1122A–B), who is certainly the polemical target Colotes has in mind when attacking Socrates. Colotes' attack on Socrates revolves around three points – the oracle's response, the criticism of perceptions, and the investigation of man – which are designed to undermine the distinguishing features of the sceptic portrayal of Socrates provided by Arcesilaus' interpretation. Here I do not wish to delve into the details of Colotes' attack against Socrates, but only to focus on the significance of the Heraclitus quote within the context of this attack.

What is particularly noteworthy, in this respect, is the fact that Plutarch criticises the origin of Socrates' impulse to philosophise twice, by identifying it first with the response given by the oracle of Apollo and then with the Delphic inscription. The oracle had pronounced Socrates to be the wisest man (*sophōtatos*) because he was aware of knowing nothing, at any rate judging from the interpretation which Socrates himself provides in the *Apology*.[71] Socrates had thereby overturned the most common and widely accepted meaning of wisdom, turning it into a profession of ignorance. Colotes harshly criticises the episode of the oracle, which he regards as a crass and sophistic account lacking any credibility,[72] since a profession of ignorance cannot consistently be espoused without running up against considerable difficulties when it comes to its practical application. It is surprising, therefore, that at the end of his attack Colotes chooses to criticise Socrates' impulse to philosophise once more, this time by tracing it back to the Delphic inscription. He mocks Socrates, accusing him of speaking rashly because he seeks 'what man is' and 'professes with youthful self-assurance not to know even himself'.[73] Against the sarcasm of Colotes, who ridicules the Socratic profession of ignorance, Plutarch takes Socrates' side by quoting Heraclitus and recalling the famous saying 'I examined

---

[70] Significantly, Plutarch defends Socrates against the accusation of *apraxia* using the same arguments that Arcesilaus employs to defend himself (cf. 1122E–F). He objects that Socrates' behaviour is not due to a firm belief on his part that each thing is exactly as it appears to be, but rather that it 'is guided in every action by what appears (κατὰ τὸ φαινόμενον)' (1118A). More generally, it may be noted that the terminology and conceptual apparatus adopted in Colotes' section on Socrates are typical not of Socratic philosophy but rather of sceptical Academic thought.

[71] See Pl. *Ap.* 20e–23b.     [72] *Adv. Col.* 1116E–F.

[73] Ibid. 1118C: κομιδῇ διαγελᾷ καὶ φλαυρίζει τὸν Σωκράτην ζητοῦντα τί ἄνθρωπός ἐστι καὶ νεανιευόμενον, ὥς φησιν, ὅτι μηδὲ αὐτὸς αὑτὸν εἰδείη.

myself (ἐδιζησάμην ἐμεωυτόν),[74] which Heraclitus is said to have uttered in response to the Delphic instruction 'know thyself (γνῶθι σαυτόν). To lend authoritativeness to the claim that Socrates received the impulse to philosophise from the Delphic inscription, Plutarch quotes Aristotle's testimony *en tois Platōnikois*.[75] It is a matter – he explains – of answering the philosophical question par excellence, namely 'What is man?' The question 'what a human being is and what is proper for such a nature to do or bear different from any other' is established as the central subject of philosophical research in the so-called digression of the *Theaetetus*.[76] This section of the dialogue is not only presented as Plato's reflection on some distinctly Socratic themes but, insofar as it serves the immediate purpose of responding to Protagoras' thesis of man as the measure of all things, it also entails an enquiry into the human capacity to acquire knowledge.[77] The portrayal of Socrates as someone searching for 'what man is' points to the *Theaetetus* and suggests that Plutarch found the reference to Heraclitus in his sceptical source.[78] This hypothesis might further be confirmed by the fact that there is a difference between Arcesilaus' and Socrates' interpretations of the oracle's response proclaiming in the *Apology* that Socrates is the wisest man. Arcesilaus goes beyond Socrates' profession of ignorance, insofar as he does not even allow for himself what Socrates had,[79] namely the fact of knowing that he does not know. He, therefore, would appear to have justified his aporetic stance in terms of his obedience to the Delphic motto, which urges man to acknowledge his own limits and not overstep them. Indeed, the appeal to Heraclitus reveals an affinity with Socrates, as it is precisely the Delphic motto that marks the beginning of Socrates' aporia and philosophical research; yet, at the same time, it also points to one significant difference.[80] Whereas, in the *Apology*, the philosophical

---

[74] B101 DK. Marcovich 2001: 57 observes: 'Against the interpretation of the saying as an answer to the Delphic command "Know thyself" …, it can be said that neither δίζησθαι means the same as γιγνώσκειν, nor ἐμεωυτόν as ψυχή.'

[75] *Adv. Col.* 1118C: καὶ τῶν ἐν Δελφοῖς γραμμάτων θειότατον ἐδόκει γνῶθι σαυτόν, ὃ δὲ Σωκράτει τῆς ἀπορίας καὶ ζητήσεως ταύτης ἀρχὴν ἐνέδωκεν, ὡς Ἀριστοτέλης ἐν τοῖς Πλατωνικοῖς εἴρηκε. The reference here is to Περὶ φιλοσοφίας fr. 1 Rose = fr. 1 Ross.

[76] Pl. *Tht.* 174b1–6. Cf. *Phdr.* 229e–230a, which recalls the Delphic maxim 'know thyself', but says nothing about the Socratic question 'What is man?'

[77] See Polanski 1992: 139.

[78] See Long 2013: 222: 'Heraclitus was the true precursor of Plato's Socrates. Both thinkers require the persons they engage with to follow their respective logos wherever it leads. Again like Socrates, Heraclitus revels in paradoxes, meaning controversions of standard opinions.'

[79] See Cic. *Acad. post.* 45: *Itaque Arcesilas negabat esse quicquam quod sciri posset, ne illud quidem ipsum, quod Socrates sibi reliquisset.*

[80] B93 DK: 'The lord to whom the oracle at Delphi belongs neither tells nor conceals but gives a sign.' Cf. Pl. *Ap.* 21b3–4: Τί ποτε λέγει ὁ θεός, καὶ τί ποτε αἰνίττεται;

86         ANNA MARIA IOPPOLO

research which leads Socrates to an awareness of not knowing coincides with Socrates' reaction to the response from the oracle of Apollo, here the beginning of Socrates' philosophising is seen to lie in his obedience to the Delphic maxim that requires man not to overstep his limits. It is a matter not just of investigating oneself, but of extending this investigation to man as such and his cognitive capacities. Man possesses no wisdom at all, not even the kind of wisdom that Socrates refers to in the *Apology* as *anthrōpine sophia*.[81] This acknowledgement of the limits of human wisdom, for which the divine wisdom of the Socrates of the *Apology* constitutes a point of reference, finds correspondence in the digression of the *Theaetetus*, which refers to God as the measure of all things. The *Theaetetus* shows that ultimately the model of strong and infallible knowledge offered by science eludes human intellectual faculties. The gulf between the nature of man and that of God proves that truth belongs only to divine intellect.[82]

It may be objected that the quotation from Heraclitus might come from Plutarch himself, who – as is well known – was closely acquainted with Delphi and its religious traditions and rites, as is evidenced by his writings on Delphic issues and by the very fact that he served as a priest in the sanctuary of Apollo.[83] Nevertheless, some elements suggest that in this case the quotation comes from Plutarch's sceptical source. First of all, the context in which the γνῶθι σαυτόν motif is introduced and the quotation from Heraclitus is given is still part of the sceptical defence of Socrates. Plutarch himself marks the boundaries of the argument at the beginning, when he emphasises the obtuseness of Colotes, who has never considered the problem of the investigation of man,[84] and at the end, when he brings the argument to a close by noting, 'Colotes finds this ridiculous'.[85] This last observation clearly signals a transition to Plutarch's exposition of his own opinion, by which he seeks to connect the 'know thyself' motif to the religious one of the search for the soul. Secondly, the motif is perfectly functional to Arcesilaus' need to justify his aporetic stance and distinguish it from that of Socrates. Finally, the 'know thyself' motif is introduced in a way that sets it in continuity with the investigation into 'what man is'

---

[81] Pl. *Ap.* 23a.

[82] Epiphan. *Adv. haeres.* 3.29 (p. 592 Diels): 'Arcesilaus said that what is true is attainable only to the god, while this is not possible for human beings' (Ἀρκεσίλαος ἔφασκε τῷ θεῷ ἐφικτὸν εἶναι μόνῳ τὸ ἀληθές, ἀνθρώπου δὲ οὔ).

[83] See *Quaest. conv.* 7.2.2. Plutarch not only frequently referred to Delphic questions in his writing but also devoted several works to these issues, most notably *De E apud Delphos, De Pythiae oraculis* and *De defectu oraculorum.*

[84] *Adv. Col.* 1118C: δῆλός μέν ἐστιν αὐτὸς οὐδέποτε πρὸς τοῦτο γενόμενος.

[85] Ibid.: Κωλώτῃ δὲ γελοῖον δοκεῖ.

## Arcesilaus' Appeal to Heraclitus

thematised in the *Theaetetus*, Arcesilaus' favourite dialogue, as well as exhibiting his conception of Platonism.

If the analysis of the texts examined thus far is plausible, what it shows is that Heraclitus can rightfully be included in the list of those predecessors to whom Arcesilaus appealed. Arcesilaus' Socrates – as he emerges from Colotes' representation – does not coincide with the Platonic Socrates, even though he is inspired by the latter. Likewise, Heraclitus stands as a forerunner of Arcesilaus not merely on account of the philosophical position assigned to him by Plato, especially in the *Theaetetus*, but also because he was one of the Presocratics to have seriously doubted the human capacity to acquire knowledge.[86]

What remains to be explained is Heraclitus' absence from the list of predecessors to whom Arcesilaus appealed in Cicero's *Academica*.[87] Here I can only outline a few hypotheses on the basis of the conclusions reached by some scholars. Cicero's list of the forerunners of Academic scepticism is more extensive than Plutarch's and, even though it may be traced back to Arcesilaus,[88] it may have been influenced by later Academics, not least Cicero himself. However, it seems unlikely that the omission of an important forerunner such as Heraclitus would have gone unnoticed, or that it was due to negligence rather than to a conscious choice. In this case, the omission may be related to the fact that, in order to demolish Stoic epistemology, Arcesilaus made dialectical use of the distinctly Heraclitean argument according to which 'each thing constantly changes in all respects'.[89] This point of view entails unacceptable consequences on both

---

[86] See B123 DK: φύσις κρύπτεσθαι φιλεῖ. As Graham 2003: 178–9 explains, 'Heraclitus is saying that the nature of things is hidden from view, without necessarily making that nature an accomplice in its own concealment.' Arcesilaus attributes the thesis that the truth is hidden in the abyss to the Presocratics, and in particular to Democritus: see Cic. *Acad. post.* 44. Democritus is again mentioned in *Acad. pr.* 32 in relation to his claim that 'nature has concealed the truth in the abyss'. As noted by Brittain & Palmer 2001: 47, the various pronouncements about the unintelligibility of things in the *Academica* cannot be traced back to individual Presocratics, because 'we have here a set of claims intended to represent the kind of scepticism manifested among these Presocratics collectively'. However, the statement φύσις κρύπτεσθαι φιλεῖ would fully justify Heraclitus' inclusion in the list of Arcesilaus' predecessors. Cf. *Acad. post.* 44, *omnes paene veteres*.

[87] Already Reid 1885: 157, referring to Cic. *Acad. post.* 44, observed: 'Those of Heraclitus were considerable, but curiously enough are not mentioned definitely by Cicero, though from him probably came the sceptic vein in Plato, principally at least.' See also Lévy 2014: 10 n. 5: 'Il est remarquable qu'Héraclite, un philosophe si célèbre dans l'Antiquité et si important pour Platon, ne figure pas dans les doxographies néo-académiciennes proposées par Cicéron.'

[88] See Donini 2003: 336–7 with notes, and Brittain & Palmer 2001: 42 n. 7. One example of Cicero's interference is provided by *Acad. pr.* 75 (see n. 19). See also Spinelli 2010: 10–11.

[89] Let us bear in mind here that in Cic. *Acad. pr.* 16 Arcesilaus is accused of making what is most evident obscure (*conatus est clarissimis rebus tenebras obducere*), because he demolishes Zeno's

# 88 ANNA MARIA IOPPOLO

the level of action and that of language, and presents Arcesilaus as a radical sceptic.

Nevertheless, Heraclitus' absence from the list of predecessors to the Academics can quite reasonably be explained as a personal choice of Cicero's, who thought that Heraclitus was obscure for his own sake, and not because of the 'obscurity' of nature, as is confirmed by the quotations from Heraclitus in Cicero's works.[90] Cicero is assuming that Heraclitus expressed himself in an intentionally obscure way – a terrible reproach for a philosopher.[91] This approach, if Heraclitus were really guilty of it, would be almost the opposite of the well-known complaint that the truth and essence of things are deeply hidden, as in an abyss. Obviously, only this latter attitude can be regarded as a preliminary stage to scepticism. Intentionally unclear language has nothing to do with a sceptical attitude! So, if Cicero assumed that Heraclitus' 'darkness' was due to an intent (and not grounded in the darkness of the matter itself), then he had a very plausible reason not to consider him an authoritative precursor of Academic scepticism. However, this conclusion does not imply that Cicero's opinion of Heraclitus is the same as Arcesilaus', as I have tried to show in this paper. The question of Arcesilaus' place within the history of the Academy of Cicero's day is too large a topic for me to cover here, as it would require an in-depth study of the *Academica*.

---

definitions. On the hypothesis that Cicero regards Arcesilaus' ἐποχὴ περὶ πάντων as untenable, see Ioppolo 2008: 21–4 and 2009: 193–208. See too Görler 1997: 46 and 2004: 100 n. 31, with additional arguments.

[90] All Cicero's passages about Heraclitus have been collected by Lévy 2014: 6–24, which I refer the reader to.

[91] I am indebted to Woldemar Görler, who suggested this hypothesis to me and whom I warmly thank. See Cic. *Fin.* 2.15: *quod duobus modis sine reprehensione fit, si aut de industria facias, ut Heraclitus, 'cognomento qui* σκοτεινός *perhibetur, quia de natura nimis obscure memoravit', aut cum rerum obscuritas.* Cf. DL 9.6: 'He deposited it [*sc.* the book] in the temple of Artemis, as some say, having purposely written it in a rather obscure style so that only the competent might approach it, and lest a common style should make it easy to despise' (ἀνέθηκε δ' αὐτὸ εἰς τὸ τῆς Ἀρτέμιδος ἱερόν, ὡς μέν τινες, ἐπιτηδεύσας ἀσαφέστερον γράψαι, ὅπως οἱ δυνάμενοι <μόνοι> προσίοιεν αὐτῷ καὶ μὴ ἐκ τοῦ δημώδους εὐκαταφρόνητον ᾖ). Lévy 2014: 11 points out: 'Héraclite est pour Cicéron le représentant de l'obscurité intentionnelle: c'est l'auteur qui ne parle pas aussi proprement et aussi ouvertement qu'il en serait capable.'

CHAPTER 4

# Authority beyond Doctrines in the First Century BC[*]
## Antiochus' Model for Plato's Authority

### Federico M. Petrucci

After some decades of transition, in the first half of the first century BC, (almost) everything changed. This happened in the Stoa, where non-Athenian scholarchs felt the need for new perspectives, and for a clearer integration of Plato's doctrine.[1] This happened in the Garden, which found new life in Italy with Philodemus' 'adaptation'.[2] This happened in the Peripatos, where both the recovery of Aristotle's esoteric writings (in whatever form this may have occurred) and the introduction of a new approach to Aristotle's philosophy ushered in a new era.[3] More generally, the so-called decentralisation of philosophy strongly affected all schools, and determined the need for new ways of thinking and new approaches to authoritative texts.[4] Arguably, however, this traumatic passage had a particularly strong impact on those philosophers who claimed Plato's legacy for themselves: according to the standard view, the first century BC was the age of the revival of a dogmatic conception of Plato's philosophy, that is of the rejection of all Academic forms of scepticism (even the Philonian one).[5] Plato made a comeback with a set of doctrines

---

[*] I am grateful to Cambridge University Press's anonymous readers for their remarks, and to Lloyd Gerson and David Sedley for their insightful comments on my talk in Würzburg. I also owe a debt of gratitude to Mauro Bonazzi and George Boys-Stones, who read an earlier version of this paper and provided me with some very helpful suggestions.

[1] Panaet. T1, T120, T160–3 Alesse; Posid. 186–7; 190; 194–5; 197–214; 266 Edelstein & Kidd. See Reydams-Schils 1999: 85–115, and Sedley 2003b: 20–4. Although this aspect should not be pushed too far (see e.g. Tielemann 2007, on Panaetius), a particular interest in Plato and focused attempts to appropriate his thought are widely acknowledged and well testified to by available sources.

[2] See Erler 1992.

[3] For an overview of the much-debated puzzle of the alleged rediscovery of Aristotle's writings, see Hatzimichali 2013; on the importance of the first century BC in the history of the Peripatos, see Hahm 2007 (addressing the issue indirectly) and, above all, Falcon 2013.

[4] See Frede 1999 for an overview and esp. Sedley 2003c.

[5] One exception is the pioneering study by Tarrant 1985, who claimed a fundamental role in the rediscovery of Platonist dogmatism for Philo's Academy (but see now Brittain 2001); however, Tarrant himself now seems more inclined to identify Antiochus as the 'noble father' of the Platonist movement (Tarrant 2007). On Philo's role in my narrative see p. 93–4 and 105–6.

90 FEDERICO M. PETRUCCI

and claims, and from this moment until the end of Antiquity Platonism established itself as a dominant philosophical tradition.

This very general point granted, the impact of this shift in the Platonist tradition has been conceived in two ways. On the one hand, it has been argued that this new conception only really entered the Platonist tradition in the first century AD, especially with Plutarch, since Antiochus promulgated Stoic doctrines and *for this reason* was actually a Stoic, while Eudorus was a sort of Pythagorean maverick.[6] On the other hand, scholars have tried to trace the origins of Platonism – that is, Middle Platonism – back to either Antiochus or (more frequently) Eudorus,[7] by invoking the fact that these two philosophers proposed *Platonist doctrines* (albeit to different extents). Here our problem arises, however, for all these approaches are conditioned by a rather odd shortcoming. In general, it can be risky to define a philosopher's affiliation in the Imperial age by referring just to his doctrines: the appropriation of the claims made by other schools was a widespread practice, and only the overall economy of a philosopher's system, along with his self-perception, can really testify to his affiliation – the examples of Aspasius and of Apuleius' translation of the Peripatetic treatise *De mundo* are telling in this respect.[8] But in the first century BC the situation is even harder to read, for in the process of transition of philosophical schools towards a new identity we also witness the foundation almost *ex nihilo* of movements, such as Potamo's eclecticism, whose doctrines someone *could* trace back to Stoicism, by stretching them only a little.[9] Similarly, the Stoics tried to appropriate sempiternalism,[10] while with Philodemus it is possible to speak of Epicurean rhetoric and music. With the issue of Platonism itself there is even a further puzzle: at least

[6] This has been well argued by Boys-Stones 2001, but the idea that, properly speaking, Platonism only emerges in the first century AD is also put forward in Frede 1999: 776–8. In a recent paper (2016), however, George Boys-Stones has also argued that some kind of Platonist identity, above all with respect to the Peripatetic and the Stoic schools, is already present in Eudorus, although without falling into a traditional teleological representation of the history of philosophy.

[7] This is quite a widespread view. After Dillon 1977 and Donini 1982: 71–5 (on Antiochus) and 100–3 (on 'Alexandrian Platonism') – in whose view Platonism was born in Alexandria with Eudorus, although Antiochus rediscovered dogmatism – see Bonazzi 2005, 2012, 2013 (on Eudorus, who lies 'at the origins of Imperial Platonism'), 2015: 15–68.

[8] For the former, see esp. Donini 1974: 63–125 and Moraux 1984: 261–70. For the latter, see Petrucci 2018: 93–6. More generally, since the seminal study by George Boys-Stones (2001: esp. 97–151), a specific feature of Middle Platonist philosophy has emerged, that is, the appropriation of the tenets of rival schools: see Reydams-Schils & Ferrari 2014 for a brief but effective survey.

[9] This is especially the case with Potamo's epistemology and physics (DL 1.21) – for a valuable analysis of which see Hatzimichali 2011 (whose conclusions, however, have been criticised by Dorandi 2016).

[10] See Panaetius T130–4, T131 referring also to Boethus.

Authority beyond Doctrines in the First Century BC

before Middle Platonism, whenever it may have started, there was no Platonism at all in the sense of a shared set of doctrines which were recognised as Platonist.[11] Accordingly, the point is not only that in the first century BC philosophers were prepared to appropriate the doctrines of other schools in order to refashion their own models, or to create new ones, but also that traditional assessments of Platonist doctrines in the first century BC are circularly based on our appraisal of the Platonism of the next centuries, and it might well be possible that in this century no Platonism (in the sense of the adherence to a system of doctrines which we would regard as 'Platonist') existed at all. So, the fact that the doctrines of a first-century BC thinker coincide – or do not coincide – with those which we regard as Platonist according to later sources tells us almost nothing about his conscious commitment to a certain philosophical perspective, for nothing attests that in the first century BC these doctrines were regarded as Platonist. For all these reasons, a full understanding of what Platonism was in the first century BC can only be reached through a new approach, that is by leaving doctrines aside. In this paper I shall mainly focus on Antiochus, showing that he provided some crucial material for Platonism in the qualified sense that he coined a model of Plato's authority, in a dogmatic perspective, that preceded and had priority over the various doctrines which were to be embedded into it.[12] I will then briefly turn to Eudorus in order to confirm my point – extant sources, however, prevent me from producing anything more than this kind of treatment.

If my view is correct, it is bound to have significant consequences with respect to our conception of the history of Platonism. On the one hand, one should backdate the theoretical construction of a conception of Plato as a dogmatic authority after the sceptical period of the Academy to the first century BC (Xenocrates' Platonism, discussed by David Sedley in Chapter 1 of this volume, was in any case overturned by Arcesilaus, who – as shown by Anna Maria Ioppolo in Chapter 3 – rethought Plato's authority in terms which did not imply any construction of a

[11] To the best of my knowledge, the only consistent reference to this puzzle is to be found in Frede 1999: 776–8. I shall get back to this problem with respect to the Early Academy in due course.

[12] Tsouni 2018 provides a new account of Antiochus' notion of Plato's and Aristotle's authority. Although we agree on several points (e.g. on the importance of the idea of direct teaching within the Academy, but we also disagree on the authority which Antiochus really ascribed to Aristotle and Zeno), we provide quite different accounts and pursue different aims. So I would invite the reader to take that paper, too, into account for a different reading of the issue. Nonetheless, a shared conclusion of our papers is the fact that Platonist exegesis developed after Antiochus and within the framework of the conception of authority established by Antiochus.

# 92 FEDERICO M. PETRUCCI

positive system). On the other hand, however, we are in a better position to detect in what sense Middle Platonism arose only in the first century AD, namely in terms of the application of shared exegetical methods and a commitment to a set of crucial (yet *very* general) philosophical tenets.

## 4.1 Antiochus: A New Model for Plato's Authority

Until recently, the most authoritative position on Antiochus was that of Jonathan Barnes (1989), who, in his ground-breaking paper, regarded him as having introduced a poor form of syncretism.[13] After David Sedley's collective book (2012a), scholarship has undergone a huge number of developments, but the clearest of them is that it is hard to find more than two specialists who agree on the same interpretation not only of Antiochus' epistemological and cosmological doctrine, but also of his philosophical identity.[14] The point is that, in some sense, the two leading interpretations of Antiochus both have very good cases to make. After all, those who assign Antiochus a Platonist identity insist on the Platonist nature of some of his cosmological views (for instance, his commitment to some kind of theory of Forms in *Acad. post.* 33–5)[15] and downplay the *Lucullus*, or appeal to passages in Sextus, which however only some readers take to be ascribable to Antiochus.[16] On the other hand, the supporters of Antiochus' Stoic identity focus on his epistemology as presented in the *Lucullus* or offer refined – perhaps over-refined, though – interpretations of the reference to the Forms in the *Varro*, and substantially restrict the range of passages attesting Antiochus' doctrine.[17] At the same time, it must be emphasised that almost all scholars would accept the idea that Antiochus appropriated Peripatetic ethics, as Piso's speech in Book 5 of *De finibus* shows – but,

---

[13] A valuable and charitable reworking of this reading is proposed by Inwood 2012; I shall return to this point in due course (pp. 111–12).

[14] Needless to say, the aim of the book was not to propose a unifying view of Antiochus (Sedley 2012a: 1). However, a particularly unique (and thrilling) narrative may be gained by consecutively examining Sedley 2012b, Brittain 2012, Inwood 2012, Boys-Stones 2012, and Bonazzi 2012.

[15] See especially Bonazzi 2012 and 2015: 15–68.    [16] See e.g. Sedley 1981 and 2012b: 88–101.

[17] See especially Brittain 2012 (insisting on the *Lucullus*) and Boys-Stones 2012 (focussing, in quite an innovative way, on the *Varro*). Interestingly, also their reference to sources ascribing to Antiochus an affiliation to Stoicism is puzzling (see e.g. Brittain 2012: 104–13), for even in these cases (e.g. Plut. *Cic.* 4; Num. fr. 28 des Places; SE *PH* 1.235; Aug. *C. acad.* 3.41 and *De civ. D.* 19.3) the implication is that Antiochus' doctrines are Stoic. In this sense, these passages would end up confirming my view, for the polemic against Antiochus consists in the accusation that he introduced *Stoic doctrines* within the framework of the Academy – an accusation which probably relied on the fact (recently confirmed by the papyrological research in Fleischer 2015) that Antiochus attended Mnesarchus' lectures, but which does not imply that Antiochus regarded himself as a Stoic.

*Authority beyond Doctrines in the First Century* BC          93

curiously enough, no-one would conclude on this basis that Antiochus *was* a Peripatetic![18]

For certain, one of Antiochus' major concerns was to refute Academic scepticism and the Philonian idea that the whole Academy, since Plato's day, had been 'sceptical':[19] it is widely agreed that his agenda was oriented towards the general goal of outlining a unitary dogmatic tradition extending all the way back to Plato via the Early Academy, Aristotle and the Stoics, and excluding the Hellenistic Academy from Arcesilaus to Philo. In this sense, it is certain that a crucial aspect of Antiochus' strategy was to show that his opponents were sceptics and to counter their positions with a consistent set of doctrines which he upheld dogmatically – that is, positively and not provisionally – and which in his view coincided with the truth and deserved a strict commitment.[20] Indeed, in this attitude some scholars have detected Antiochus' main contribution to the formation of Platonism.[21] However, this representation risks being too broad and grasping only a part of Antiochus' strategy. As a matter of fact, just claiming that there is a truth that one can grasp in terms of a set of doctrines, and that one must commit oneself to these doctrines, says nothing about Antiochus' construction of a philosophical identity, one laying claim to the legacy of the Early Academy. In this case, his operation would be strategically and philosophically poor, for the mere assertion of the possibility of a positive philosophical system would represent an arbitrary reaction to the Academics, which they would be in a position to counter just as they used to counter the Stoics' positions, that is by resorting to the argument from disagreement. Rather, it seems to me that what Antiochus did was establish some specific requirements whose fulfilment would ensure a thinker's authority against all sceptic positions, and above all show that *only* Plato was in a position to meet these requirements.

Hence, let us begin our analysis from the generic and uncontroversial claim that Antiochus sought to outline a philosophical system which one

---

[18] See esp. Irwin 2012 and Schofield 2012. On Antiochus and Peripatetic ethics see now the excellent contribution by Tsouni 2019.

[19] Of course, in the sense of his peculiar version of Academic scepticism: see Brittain 2001: 169–254 on this. On Philo's theory of the unity of the Academy and the so-called *Sosus affaire* see also the traditional account of Glucker 1978: 13–97. In this paper, I shall use the label 'Early Academy' for the historical Early Academy, while I will use 'Old Academy' to refer to Antiochus' representation of the Early Academy.

[20] This represents a shift with respect to scepticism, even the Philonian one: although Academic sceptics claimed to be Plato's heirs with various arguments (see esp. Bonazzi 2003: 56–97), it may be argued that for them sound reasoning was the only authority (see esp. Brittain 2001: 73–128 and 220–54, on the Fourth Academy).

[21] See esp. Tarrant 2007.

94    FEDERICO M. PETRUCCI

could be in a position to be positively committed to. This idea was not new at all, for such a description of a philosophical system was already typical, for instance, of the Stoics. Significantly, in Cicero one can discover quite an explicit statement of what the commitment to a philosophical system entails, that is the strenuous defence of the set of doctrines established by a noble founder, a move key to the preservation of the whole system:

> In discussion it is not so much weight of authority as force of argument that should be demanded. Indeed, the authority of those to profess to teach is often a positive hindrance to those who desire to learn; they cease to employ their own judgement, and take what they perceive to be the verdict of their chosen master as settling the question. In fact I am not disposed to approve the practice traditionally ascribed to the Pythagoreans, who, when questioned as to the grounds of any assertion that they advanced in debate, are said to have been accustomed to reply: 'He himself said so', he himself being Pythagoras. So potent was an opinion already decided, making authority prevail unsupported by reason. (*ND* 1.10, trans. Rackham 1967)[22]

The fact that in this case Cicero is not referring to a philosophical system which he regards positively, but to the Pythagoreans, does not diminish the importance of the passage. Of course, the Pythagorean attitude is criticised for its blind adherence to authority, and in this sense the passage has a clear polemical flavour. This is the reason why Cicero must have referred to the Pythagoreans, who represent a sort of extreme application of the principle of authority, in order to undermine a *general* idea of the priority of authority over reasoning ('they cease to employ their own judgement, and take what they perceive to be the verdict of their chosen master as settling the question'). Accordingly, when the passage is deprived of his polemical nuances, one can draw from it the idea that, in Cicero's account, being committed to a thinker's authority means defending a set of views ascribable to him. It is not surprising that, while in the case of the Pythagoreans such representation cannot but remain quite vague, for a thinker of the end of the Hellenistic age such an account was easily

---

[22] *Non enim tam auctoritatis in disputando quam rationis momenta quaerenda sunt. Quin etiam obest plerumque iis qui discere volunt auctoritas eorum qui se docere profitentur; desinunt enim suum iudicium adhibere, id habent ratum quod ab eo quem probant iudicatum vident. Nec vero probare soleo id quod de Pythagoreis accepimus, quos ferunt, si quid adfirmarent in disputando, cum ex eis quaereretur quare ita esset, respondere solitos 'Ipse dixit'; 'ipse' autem erat Pythagoras: tantum opinio praeiudicata poterat, ut etiam sine ratione valeret auctoritas.* See also *Acad. pr.* 137, a polemical statement against the Antiochean attitude. These texts, however, encapsulate a sort of ideological pattern around which the notion of authority in antiquity (and especially in the Hellenistic Age) revolves: see Sedley 1989.

# Authority beyond Doctrines in the First Century BC

applicable to the philosophical school which most explicitly defined its own identity by appealing to the notion of system: this is a cornerstone of Stoic philosophy, which was established, even beyond the content of these doctrines, by referring to the fact that they are consistently and reciprocally articulated.[23]

Interestingly, this is exactly the background to Piso's account of Antiochus' ethics in *De finibus* 5.7 and 5.13–14.[24] First, Piso provides an overall picture of some major figures featuring in 'his' Old Academy:

> 'Perhaps' said Piso 'it will not be altogether easy, while our friend here' (meaning me) 'is by, still I will venture to urge you to leave the present New Academy for the Old, which includes, as you heard Antiochus declare, not only those who bear the name of Academics, Speusippus, Xenocrates, Polemo, Crantor and the rest, but also the early Peripatetics, headed by their chief, Aristotle, who, if Plato be excepted, I almost think deserves to be called the prince of philosophers. (*Fin.* 5.7, trans. Rackham 1931)[25]

Apparently, this is nothing more than a list. However, we can draw from it at least the following information. First, Antiochus did represent himself as being the member of and heir to a school having a well-defined identity. Second, this school had noble origins, coinciding with Aristotle, the early Peripatetics, and the Academics. Third – and most importantly – there is a figure who stands out in this school, that is Plato, the actual *princeps philosophorum*. From this, therefore, a sort of family portrait emerges, and we have a clear appraisal of the fact that Plato is the *pater familias*.

Then, Piso goes on:

> Let us limit ourselves to these authorities. Their successors are indeed in my opinion superior to the philosophers of any other school, but are so unworthy of their ancestry that one might imagine them to have been their own fathers. To begin with, Theophrastus' pupil Strato set up to be a natural philosopher; but great as he is in this department, he is nevertheless for the most part an innovator, and on ethics he has hardly anything. . . .

---

[23] While the Stoics did not agree on the number of parts of their system and their priority (see e.g. DL 7.39–41, Plut. *Stoic. rep.* 1035A = *SVF* 2.42), all of them would have agreed that Stoic philosophy is a consistent and comprehensive sum of doctrines, entailing a specific and – to put it with Posidonius – 'biological' interaction (SE *M* 7.19 = Posid. fr. 88).

[24] Scholars agree on the fact that Cicero makes Piso the spokesman of Antiochus' ethics in the *De finibus*, as explicitly stated in *Fin.* 5.1–3 and 7–8.

[25] *Tum Piso: 'Etsi hoc', inquit, 'fortasse non poterit sic abire cum hic adsit' (me autem dicebat), 'tamen audebo te ab hac Academia nova ad illam veterem vocare, in qua, ut dicere Antiochum audiebas, non ii soli numerantur qui Academici vocantur, Speusippus, Xenocrates, Polemo, Crantor ceterique, sed etiam Peripatetici veteres, quorum princeps Aristoteles, quem excepto Platone haud scio an recte dixerim principem philosophorum.*

> I pass over a number of writers, including the learned and entertaining Hieronymus. Indeed I know no reason for calling the latter a Peripatetic at all: for he defined the chief good as freedom from pain: and to hold a different view of the chief good is to hold a different system of philosophy altogether. ... Our master Antiochus seems to me to adhere most scrupulously to the doctrine of the ancients, which according to his teaching was common to Aristotle and to Polemo. (5.13–14, trans. Rackham 1931)[26]

Antiochus exploits the idea that Plato and his direct and distinguished students, including Aristotle, agreed on a consistent set of doctrines. In Antiochus' far from disinterested representation of the story, the decline of this unitary school began when innovation was introduced: even when innovation is due to a good thinker, it must be condemned if it *really* changes the system shaped by the master. Piso's way of putting the matter is not too sharp, and – as the cases of Theophrastus and Strato show – a certain degree of flexibility is admitted: if one still moves within certain philosophical boundaries, the system, albeit modified, is still preserved. There is, however, a cut-off point which cannot be transcended. More specifically, as the case of Hieronymus shows, the disagreement cannot reach the point of violating a core doctrine of the system (in this case, the doctrine of the *summum bonum*). Of course, the point is not that Hieronymus' innovation destroyed the system as such; rather, his modifications of the system he had inherited were radical enough as to transform it into something different, which could no longer be regarded as 'Peripatetic' (or Academic, in Antiochus' perspective). Indeed, in Piso's account the reason why Hieronymus cannot be called a Peripatetic is that he diverged from fundamental tenets of Peripatetic ethics. The consequence is that radically innovating a system implies demolishing it and substituting it with something different – and wrong, as the passage implies.

Independently from the specific case of Hieronymus, the argument can be generalised in the following terms: adhering to a school implies being committed to a set of key doctrines, which constitute the core of the system. So, the underlying general idea is arguably that, while some aspects

---

[26] *Simus igitur contenti his. Namque horum posteri meliores illi quidem, mea sententia, quam reliquarum philosophi disciplinarum, sed ita degenerant ut ipsi ex se nati esse videantur. Primum Theophrasti, Strato, physicum se voluit; in quo etsi est magnus, tamen nova pleraque et perpauca de moribus. ... Praetereo multos, in his doctum hominem et suavem, Hieronymum, quem iam cur Peripateticum appellam nescio; summum enim bonum exposuit vacuitatem doloris; qui autem de summo bono dissentit, de tota philosophiae ratione dissentit. ... Antiquorum autem sententiam Antiochus noster mihi videtur persequi diligentissime, quam eandem Aristoteli fuisse et Polemonis docet.*

*Authority beyond Doctrines in the First Century* BC                97

of a system can be readdressed and rethought within the school, radically modifying its cornerstones implies destroying the system itself. The reason for this is that a system has certain core doctrines, each of which is intrinsically related to all others, so that the destruction of any core doctrine would lead the whole system to collapse. Therefore, Piso is projecting onto the Academy the requirements which a standard model of authority implies: the whole Academic doctrine is perfect and consistent, and one must defend its core against radical modifications, for otherwise the system as a whole might perish. This has two implications. On the one hand, the person who radically modifies the system is in turn a bad follower of a philosophical tradition and of the master(s) who first developed it, since the commitment to certain doctrines implies an acknowledgement of the master's authority. On the other, what ensures the authority of the ancients (and, in turn, Antiochus' adherence to the tradition of the 'Old' Academy), is the fact of adhering 'most scrupulously to the doctrine of the ancients' (*antiquorum autem sententiam ... persequi diligentissime*).

Interestingly enough, this also explains why the Stoics, while endorsing the very same doctrines as the Academics and the Peripatetics (in Antiochus' view), are described in negative terms, as thieves who unlawfully appropriated the system (*Fin.* 5.74): they were right inasmuch as they did not radically modify the doctrines, but were wrong inasmuch as they tried to separate the recovery of the system from the acknowledgement of those thinker(s) who had first conceived it. But this also explains why priority is clearly granted to the Early Academy, Aristotle, and Theophrastus (again *Fin.* 5.7): Aristotle is the *princeps philosophorum* after Plato, and the others are outstanding thinkers, simply because they maintained a certain system and – in Antiochus' view – acknowledged its origins.

If this is the case, however, a starting point in the history of the 'preservation' of the system must be established. Of course, the Stoics cannot represent this starting point – in fact, they did not acknowledge their debt at all, though recovering the Academic system. Neither is there any reason to regard any of the Academics – from Speusippus to Crantor – as the founder of the system: in *De finibus* 5.7, as we have seen, none of them is granted any kind of priority and, interestingly enough, it is quite clear that Piso refers to them consistently with the succession of scholarchs (Crantor being somewhat 'added' to the series). In other words, if one of the Academics is to be regarded as the founder of the Academic system, only Speusippus would be a good candidate, but it is clear that Piso is not making this point. The last candidate, then, would be Aristotle, who is certainly highly rated by Piso (*Fin.* 5.14), and who also had a very faithful student, namely Theophrastus, who is praised for his adherence to his direct master's doctrines. If this were the case, however, Aristotle would be the *princeps philosophorum*, which is definitely not the case, for this honour, as we have seen, can only properly be granted to another thinker, namely Plato. And in this case it cannot be anyone but Plato who deserves the role of founder of the 'Academic' system. Indeed, this is the only option which makes good sense in the light both of the description of Aristotle's secondary role with respect to Plato, and of the unqualified mention of the Academics, who are essentially said to have preserved a system, even though none of them is regarded as its actual founder. All in all, then, it turns out that the Academic system was originally proposed by Plato and was preserved (in the flexible way I have indicated above) by Plato's heirs. Moreover, both the Academics and Aristotle must be credited not only with the preservation of the system, but also with a somewhat conscious acknowledgement of Plato's authoritative role as its founder, for they are not at all described as 'thieves'. Therefore, by invoking shared premises with regard to the notions of 'authority' and 'system', Antiochus can produce the following reasoning: if there is a school, or tradition, inspired by a master, there *must* also be a positive philosophical system; but Plato is recognised as the founder of a seminal school; therefore, he must also have established a positive philosophical system. Such a reasoning, moreover, is able to make good sense of Antiochus' references to different schools – the Early Academy, the Peripatos, and the Stoa – with the aim of unifying them: Antiochus is not just saying that there are several schools, but also that they are to be unified by assigning them a single authoritative origin. Indeed, in the light of my argument, one can ascribe to Antiochus the following views: (a) being part of a school implies being committed to certain key doctrines, which constitute the core of a system; (b) each system of doctrines stems from a founder who is regarded as an authority because of this. If one takes these points for granted, assuming that the Peripatetics and the Stoics operate within the 'Old' Academy amounts to saying: (a) that the Academics, the Peripatetics and the Stoics were all committed to certain key doctrines of a single system and (b) that Plato, being the *princeps philosophorum* who coined these views, is *the* fundamental philosophical authority for all these philosophers. Moreover, the argument not only has the effect of representing Plato as the founder of a dogmatic system, but also delivers a blow against the sceptical Academy and Philo, who (to different extents) stressed Plato's role as the ancestor of a sceptical current within the Academic tradition.

Still, one could argue that this representation is not able to establish that Plato has any *specific* priority over the other masters: after all, as we have seen, Antiochus apparently only projects onto Plato's system those requirements which Cicero too presents as being applicable to *all* dogmatic philosophies. By 'breaking' the continuity between Plato, Aristotle, and Zeno, one would simply be left with three competing dogmatisms. Antiochus' point, however, is more complex, and it is based on the establishment both of a link between Plato, the Early Academics, Aristotle, and Zeno, and of a sort of hierarchy between them. In this case, too, Antiochus resorts to a canonical representation of philosophical schools. On the one hand, it is widely known that only with Alexander and Plotinus did Aristotle emerge as a definitely more important figure than his first pupil, Theophrastus, who was perceived as a faithful student of Aristotle's and whose writings were widespread and regarded as a consistent development of Aristotle's thought. This view can easily be discovered also in Antiochean sources, which indicate a decline of the Peripatos from Strato onwards, while Theophrastus is depicted as endorsing Aristotle's philosophy (again *Fin.* 5.13–14, but also 4.3).[27] On the other hand, the standard representation of the *diadochē* of the first three heads of the Stoa entailed the idea of a consistent development of Zeno's philosophy on the part of Cleanthes and Chrysippus against some heterodox Stoics – especially Aristo and Herillus – who were blamed for their divergences from Zeno. The case of the Stoa is particularly relevant, for it shows that the founder is granted a special priority even though the excellence of other figures – especially Chrysippus – was already widely recognised by the ancients (and by Antiochus, of course, who usually only refers to Zeno when discussing the Stoics).[28] All in all, each school is such because the heirs of the master preserve his system, and they do so by having been instructed via direct teaching. Therefore, we obtain the following narrative: a dogmatic system entails a set of doctrines, which *the founder* coined in a proper way; such doctrines are transmitted to outstanding and faithful pupils via direct teaching; these pupils preserve the system, and in this way they also maintain its overall consistency and philosophical meaning; in some cases, the system suffers either internal attacks, which faithful students attempt to avert, or a decline due to bad

---

[27] This is true, after all, also when Theophrastus does something more than Aristotle: with regard to the Forms, for instance, he pushes Aristotle's changes further (*Acad. post.* 33: *vehementius etiam fregit*) – I shall get back to this point in due course.

[28] See Sedley 1989 and 2003b: 8–18.

100 FEDERICO M. PETRUCCI

pupils (i.e. pupils who do not correctly play the role which I have just outlined).[29]

Now, we have already seen that Plato is the best candidate for the role of founder of the Academic system, and for this reason Antiochus must have regarded him as *princeps philosophorum* (again Cic. *Fin.* 5.7). This crucial view is confirmed by other testimonies, which allow us to frame it within the wider argument for Plato's authority *over his heirs*. Indeed, when presenting the philosophy of the Old Academy, the Antiochean spokesman Varro explicitly ascribes its formulation *to Plato himself*,[30] and its recovery is ascribed to Plato's followers from Speusippus onwards:

> But originating with the authority of Plato, a thinker of manifold variety and fertility, there was established a philosophy that, though it had two appellations, was really a single and uniform system ... But both schools [the Peripatetics and the Academics] drew plentiful supplies from Plato's abundance, and both framed a definitely formulated system of doctrines ... (Cic. *Acad. post.* 17; trans. Rackham 1967, modified)[31]

Although Antiochus acknowledges that some elements of the doctrine were already available to Plato (I shall get back to this point in due course), he stresses the fact that the responsibility of fashioning a consistent system out of these elements is entirely Plato's (*Fin.* 5.87–8).[32] Consistently with this, Varro emphasises that the very foundation of the Academic system, namely its tripartite structure, derives directly from Plato himself (*Acad. post.* 19: *fuit ergo iam accepta a Platone philosophandi ratio triplex*): it is first of all *in this very sense* that Plato left the Academy a *perfectissima disciplina* (*Acad. pr.* 15).[33] Moreover, the very place in which the philosophy of the Old Academy was founded, that is the Academy, recalls *first* Plato, and

---

[29] In historical terms, such a perspective is also typical of the Garden, where it probably reflects Epicurus' programmatic commitment to the education of the 'friends': the defence of orthodoxy on the part of the *kathēgemones* and their students reproduces the pattern emerging from the other traditions. Even in this case, moreover, such a regular pattern of transmission of the system is broken – in the representation given by the ancients – by some internal dissident Epicureans, who put the tradition at risk, thereby proving bad Epicureans.

[30] As in Piso's case, scholars acknowledge that Varro is, in Cicero's intention, an Antiochean spokesman; moreover, this is explicitly indicated by Cicero in his *Letters*: see Griffin 1997. On the historical relationship between Varro and Antiochus see Blank 2012.

[31] *Platonis autem auctoritate, qui varius et multiplex et copiosus fuit, una et consentiens duobus vocabulis philosophiae forma instituta est ... Sed utrique* [the Peripatetics and the Academics] *Platonis ubertate completi certam quandam disciplinae formulam composuerunt ...*

[32] Interestingly, the claim that Plato produced a substantial shift with respect to his predecessors is clearly meant to be a criticism of Philo's – and other sceptics' – idea, that Socrates *and* Plato stand together at the origin of the unitary tradition of the sceptical Academy (see again Brittain 2001: 169–219, for the various 'sceptical' narratives about the origins of Academic scepticism).

[33] See p. 94–5 for the importance of this aspect for the formation of a philosophical system.

only secondly the recovery of his teachings by his first pupils (*Fin.* 5.2).[34] Therefore, the first argument of Antiochus' claim for Plato's authority consists in establishing that the *Old Academy* has an authoritative founder, with whom everything started.[35]

This allows Antiochus to go one step further by introducing the idea that Plato's first pupils, namely Speusippus, Xenocrates, and Polemo, recovered Plato's system *without changing it in any way*.[36] This is true not only as a general statement, but also in relation to all the specific fields which are taken into account in the *Academica* and *De finibus*. This crucial point clearly emerges both in the *Varro* (*Acad. post.* 17, containing a mention of Speusippus and Xenocrates), and in the *De finibus* (5.7, where *Speusippus, Xenocrates, Polemo, Crantor ceterique* are mentioned). This emerges clearly through a comparison with Aristotle's attitude. Indeed, while in these passages Aristotle too is mentioned as a direct heir to Plato, we know that Antiochus regarded him and Theophrastus as having modified Plato's system to some extent, namely as concerns the theory of Forms (*Acad. post.* 33). On the contrary, the Academics' recovery of Plato's doctrine is characterised by a complete adherence to Plato's teachings, and their attitude is singled out precisely for this reason, distinguishing them from other outstanding figures within the tradition:

> On the other hand Speusippus and Xenocrates, the first inheritors of the system and authority of Plato, and after them Polemo and Crates, and also Crantor, gathered in the one fold of the Academy, were assiduous defenders

---

[34] *Venit enim mihi Platonis in mentem, quem accepimus primum hic disputare solitum; cuius etiam illi propinqui hortuli non memoriam solum mihi afferunt sed ipsum videntur in conspectu meo ponere. Hic Speusippus, hic Xenocrates, hic eius auditor Polemo, cuius illa ipsa sessio fuit quam videmus.* As confirmation of the application of a standard model to the special case of Plato's Academy on the part of Antiochus, one might further note that also Pomponius recovers Piso's 'perception' of the Academy by applying it to the Garden as the place where Epicurus himself used to teach (ibid. 5.3).

[35] Interestingly enough, in Plutarch's representation (*Brut.* 2.2–3 = Antioch. T8 Sedley) Brutus is depicted as a follower of Antiochus, which implies that to be a follower of the philosopher is to be a follower of those who come ἀπὸ Πλάτωνος. It has been argued (Sedley 2002a) that Antiochus' system, especially with respect to his physics, strongly draws on Polemo. This view is controversial (see e.g. Inwood 2012; Sedley has strengthened his case in Sedley 2012a and 2012b). Even if it were correct (as I am partly inclined to believe), my view would not be negatively affected precisely because Antiochus would have ascribed this content to Plato himself: the point is not who the most influential Academic was for Antiochus, but who Antiochus wanted to be the authority according to his narrative and argumentative strategy.

[36] Antiochus can make this move since, as we have seen on p. 95–7, he allows a certain degree of flexibility in the recovery of a system, ranging from a perfectly faithful recovery to the introduction of certain – non-destructive – modifications. To express it through the image introduced in *Fin.* 5.12–14, it is one thing to slightly modify Aristotle's philosophy, as Theophrastus and Strato did, but quite another to make it collapse, as Hieronymus did.

of the doctrines that they had received from their predecessors. (*Acad. post.* 34; trans. Rackham 1967)[37]

*This* is the reason why the Academy recalls the founding of the system by Plato, and *then also* recalls its recovery by Speusippus, Xenocrates, and Polemo (again *Fin.* 5.2). What distinguishes Plato's direct students in the Academy, then, is the fact that they just kept Plato's system as it was *in all its aspects.* So, there is indeed a true founder of the Old Academy, that is Plato, and one can identify some outstanding pupils of his, who recovered his system without altering it in any respect, as well as other pupils, such as Aristotle, Theophrastus, and Zeno, who slightly modified it in certain ways, yet without putting the whole system at risk.[38]

Interestingly enough, if *this is the difference* that makes the case of the Early Academy so special, we have also discovered the reason why Antiochus frequently invoked its representatives while granting Plato special priority, and why he insisted on the Early Academy as a whole – not only Speusippus and Xenocrates, but also Crantor and Polemo – as opposed to Plato alone. Indeed, such a description leads Antiochus to make two fundamental cases both against a sceptically oriented narrative of the Academy and in favour of the priority of Plato above all other successive thinkers. First, the image of Plato as a teacher, and of his students as faithful custodians of the system transmitted, implies that Plato committed himself to teaching some specific – that is, positive – doctrines: the Early Academy is the living picture of Plato's dogmatism and positive philosophising. Second, the complete agreement characterising the Early Academy de facto ensures the possibility of avoiding the risk of divergence and distortion: in Antiochus' representation, Plato's good students were in a position to completely agree on all Platonic doctrines, without producing any misunderstandings or quarrels. What Antiochus shows, therefore, is that the transmission of Plato's system in the Early Academy (in modern terms, Speusippus, Xenocrates, Polemo, etc.) did not encounter any kind of *diaphōnia*, and this allows him to make a fundamental case against both a sceptic interpretation of Plato's philosophy and the alleged self-inconsistency of dogmatism due to *diaphōnia*. Indeed, if all the direct and most faithful students of Plato's agreed on a single doctrine,

---

[37] *Speusippus autem et Xenocrates, qui primi Platonis rationem auctoritatemque susceperant, et post eos Polemo et Crates unaque Crantor in Academia congregati, diligenter ea quae a superioribus acceperant tuebantur.*
[38] On the specific case of Aristotle's, Theophrastus', and Zeno's treatment of the issue of Forms, see p. 103–4 just below.

then those who produced a shift and some disagreement were precisely Arcesilaus and his followers: Plato's scepticism never existed, and the Academic scepticism was the cause of the disagreement within the Academy and with respect to Plato.

But there is also more to it, for here Antiochus' representation of the Academy and the distinction between the Early Academy and the other followers of Plato (namely, Aristotle, Theophrastus, and Zeno) have the strongest impact, insofar as they disprove the sceptical counterargument based on *diaphōnia* (see e.g. *Acad. pr.* 115). As we have seen, Antiochus' account of Plato's authority leads him to conclude that the Academics, the Peripatetics, and the Stoics all belong to the same school, in the sense that they are committed to the key doctrines of a single system and hence have Plato as their authoritative founder. In this framework, Antiochus could have argued something more than simply that Plato's Academy has a blatant chronological priority over the Peripatetics and the Stoics, implying that Plato precedes all other school founders and, hence, all *diaphōniai*.[39] Indeed, in Antiochus' representation the relationship between Plato and the other schools entails specific teaching links, implying the direct transmission and reception of doctrines, and revolving around the Early Academy.

A first case can be made with respect to Aristotle. He is among Plato's students, and plays a privileged role in the history of the tradition, since he preserved Plato's doctrine, as in the case of ethics. One could argue that in some fields he might also have disagreed with Plato and the Academics, as in the case of the theory of Forms (*Acad. post.* 33: *Aristoteles primus species quas paulo ante dixi labefactavit, quas mirifice Plato erat amplexatus, ut in iis quiddam divinum esse diceret*). But here Antiochus' narrative of the history of Plato's school proves effective, for he was in a position to set this (partial) modification in contrast to the strict respect which Speusippus and Xenocrates showed for this doctrine (*Acad. post.* 34, quoted above). On the one hand, we must assume that, *if* – as is widely acknowledged – Antiochus' idea was that a single system was shared by all dogmatics, then Aristotle's, Theophrastus', and Zeno's treatment of the Forms, puzzling though it may have been, did not really modify the core of Plato's system. On the other hand, this does mean – as I have shown – that complete adherence was not regarded as a more suitable philosophical attitude.

---

[39] According to Boys-Stones 2001 this is, after all, the way in which Middle Platonists from Plutarch onwards granted priority to Plato, whom they believed to have recovered a body of ancient lore by establishing a perfect system, demolished by subsequent philosophers.

Now, whatever the doctrines presented in this controversial passage may amount to,[40] while Aristotle changed Plato's doctrine *to some extent* – and Theophrastus, following him, pushed this change even further, albeit without revolutionising it – the fact that Plato's closest and most faithful students recovered it without any modification attests the fact that possible changes were not due to a lack of clarity or to any intrinsic deficiency of Plato's system. Accordingly, in some fields Aristotle, as a good pupil, recovered certain doctrines from Plato, while in other fields he diverged from Plato just by changing some aspects of his system: Aristotle's doctrines are either the same as Plato's, or modifications thereof, and this is ensured by the fact that Aristotle was a student of Plato's. Moreover, Antiochus' narrative explains Aristotle's modifications without leaving room for the idea that Plato's doctrines were unclear or self-contradictory, for they were maintained by a number of distinguished direct students of his.

A similar pattern can be applied to the Stoics' reception of Plato's thought. Antiochus emphasised that Zeno was not simply the founder of the Stoa, but also a student of Polemo's, who in turn was among the most faithful students of Plato (*Acad. post.* 35).[41] Now, Stoic ethics are regarded as essentially coinciding with those of Plato, the Academy and the Peripatos: the fact that the Stoics changed only the terms in which these doctrines were expressed (*Fin.* 5.74; see also *Acad. pr.* 15: the Stoics diverged *verbis magis quam sententiis*) does not disprove this point, but rather confirms it. This could even be the case with cosmology, ontology, and epistemology: if those who regard Antiochus' doctrines in these fields as being fairly Stoic are right, Antiochus' way of conceiving their pedigree must have entailed that Zeno only recovered them thanks to his Academic education. If, on the contrary, Antiochus regarded Stoic doctrines as entailing a real change, he in any case had an alternative explanation at hand, which was similar to that applied to Aristotle's modifications of the theory of Forms: Zeno's doctrines in any case stem from Academic ones, so that Zeno's modifications cannot amount to the production of a different system and do not introduce any *actual* disagreement.[42] Finally, as said above, both in Aristotle's case and in that of Zeno, the

---

[40] The import of this passage is one of the *vexatae quaestiones* in the interpretation of Antiochus' affiliation. For a Platonising reading see Bonazzi 2015: 15–68; for a Stoicising one Boys-Stones 2012.

[41] On Polemo's potential role in this story see n. 35.

[42] This interpretation is also consistent with the exegetical crux represented by *Acad. post.* 35, where it is said that Zeno *corrigere conatus est disciplinam*, namely Plato's theory of Forms. Boys-Stones 2012:

# Authority beyond Doctrines in the First Century BC          105

modifications introduced were not strong enough to really alter the system, for otherwise the general idea of a unitary tradition of Academic philosophy (as expressed e.g. in *Fin.* 5.13–14 or *Acad. pr.* 15) would be utterly meaningless.

If my reading is correct, Antiochus' historiographical model of Plato's authority is effective against two views, which were key to the self-representations respectively of the sceptical Academy and of Philo. First, it is able to undermine Philo's theory of the unity of the Academy under the sign of (his peculiar version of) scepticism.[43] Indeed, such a view is impossible to uphold if one states that the unity of the tradition is based on the transmission of the teaching of a positive system of doctrines, leaving no room for any kind of scepticism. In other words, if one wishes to affirm the unity of the Academy, the only way to do so is to adhere to Antiochus' representation. Second, and more generally, Antiochus' representation is not only able to leave aside the argument from disagreement by identifying Plato as the *origin* of the clear and consistent system which the first Academics recovered without any modification, but can also show that the only actual disagreement is the one introduced by scepticism *against Plato*. This demolishes the possibility of any kind of link between Plato and Arcesilaus:[44] of course, Arcesilaus himself was an indirect student of Plato's (via Polemo, and with Zeno: *Acad. post.* 35), but in Antiochus' account he becomes the *only* student of Plato's who really disagreed with

---

232 n. 42 insists on the fact that *corrigere* necessarily implies a positive evaluation of the changes made to the corrected object, whereas Bonazzi 2012: 313–14 denies that this is the case. As a matter of fact, although in principle Bonazzi could be right (*never say never!*), it is true that *corrigere* generally entails an idea of improvement. There are, however, a general and a more specific point. In general, as emphasised by Donini 2012: 155–6, it is true that Zeno's *correctio* is introduced with a *sed*, indicating a certain diffidence on Varro's part, and above all by suggesting that Zeno's *correctio* is related to his relationship with Arcesilaus at Polemo's school and testifies to Zeno's excellence as a dialectician. In other words, it does not seem as though Varro regards Zeno's *correctio* as positive in absolute terms. But the specific point is even more important, for Varro emphasises that Zeno wanted (*conatus est*) to correct the doctrine. Given that *conatus est* is used by Varro in order to introduce some subjective exigence, and given that Zeno *did* modify the doctrine to some extent, the only 'subjective' aspect entailed by the expression concerns the positive import of his modification: in Varro's narrative, as far as the issue of forms is concerned, Zeno did modify Plato's doctrine, and *believed* that this modification would ameliorate it. All in all, even if *corrigere* and *correctio* have a positive nuance, they describe how Zeno regarded his own move, and not what Antiochus thought of it. Such an explanation, moreover, has the huge advantage of reconciling the possible positive meaning of *correctio* and *corrigere* with the overall tone of the passage.

43 See p. 100 n. 32.

44 This is quite an effective point, for from Arcesilaus onwards the Academic sceptics attempted to portray themselves as the direct heirs of Plato, who in turn was depicted as a sceptic: see e.g. Cic. *Acad. pr.* 15 and 46, and *De or.* 3.67; DL 4.22 and 32; Phld. *Ind. Ac.* 15.9, with Bonazzi 2003: 97–138.

106                     FEDERICO M. PETRUCCI

him to the point of abolishing his system. Arcesilaus plays the role
Hieronymus plays in the Peripatos (*Fin.* 5.13–14, quoted at p. 95–6) –
and this does not sound like a flattering comparison. Nonetheless,
Antiochus' model is not just a polemic tool deployed against the sceptical
Academy and Philo, for it positively produces a new model of Plato's
authority. Plato's system was consistent and perfect in its original formulation and reception, and has only undergone a few modifications, which
however amount to changes made to a single set of core doctrines and
according to a single theoretical trajectory. In this representation, the Early
Academy plays a fundamental role: the reception of Plato's doctrine by
Speusippus, Xenocrates, and Polemo attests that Plato formulated a positive system, that this system was primarily received without modifications,
and that any modifications were just natural occurrences of a single
tradition, flowing through the branches of the Peripatos and the Stoa via
the teaching of Plato himself or his pupils. And this, in turn, ensures that
Plato's system can be assigned all the features of a good philosophical
system: it was consistent, entailed a set of doctrines and philosophical
milestones, was open to teaching and transmission, and was endorsed by
some good students, who preserved it. And this whole narrative, as we have
seen, paints a dynamic picture not only of Plato's authority, but of the
possibility for Plato to be the only philosophical authority.[45] Only the
sceptics introduced an actual shift against Plato: *they* essentially betrayed
Plato's system, deviated from the chain of direct teaching, and for this

---

[45] A possible counterargument could be drawn from the existence of one dogmatic philosophy which
in any case remains outside the Academy, that is the Epicurean tradition. Concerning Antiochus'
evaluation of Epicureanism we only have a couple of scattered pieces of evidence. For sure, he did
not regard this school with favour, as is clearly shown by *Acad. post.* 5–8, where Epicurean
philosophy is taken as a negative term of comparison. This rejection probably lies at the basis of
Cicero's criticism of the reliability of the senses, as proposed at *Acad. pr.* 79 ff., where he ironically
suggests that the Antiochean has only one strong authority for the reliability of the senses, that is
Epicurus. Of course Antiochus would not have agreed on such a point, for the Epicurean doctrine
of perception is implicitly ridiculed in *Acad. pr.* 19–20. A possible and quite general explanation
might be to ascribe to Antiochus the idea that Epicureanism is not a real competitor for the 'Old
Academy': its system and philosophical instruments are, as stated in *Acad. post.* 5–8, too simplistic
to be seriously taken into account. *Acad. pr.* 19–20, however, might suggest a solution to the puzzle:
Lucullus argues against the sceptics that sense perception is absolutely reliable if the senses are fit,
and for this reason he does not deal with the typical arguments of the bent oar or the pigeon's neck,
which he would rather leave to the Epicureans, who take all sense-perceptions to be true. This
amounts to saying that the Epicureans are compelled to take such arguments seriously, as the
sceptics did: while the Academics were consciously sceptic, the Epicureans ended up being sceptics
too, albeit unwittingly. If this explanation were correct, here we would have an antecedent for
Plutarch's associating of Epicureans and Pyrrhonists (see esp. *Quaest. conv.* 3.5 and *Adv. Col.*
1108D–F, with Bonazzi 2015: 73–88: of course, Plutarch adapted the argument to his goal, namely
to distinguish the Academics from the Pyrrhonists).

## Authority beyond Doctrines in the First Century BC — 107

reason are fully responsible for the introduction of *diaphōnia* and for putting the unity of the Academy at risk.

## 4.2 Echoes from Alexandria

Although extant witnesses of Antiochus are quite puzzling, the fact that one of the most renowned claims of his concerned the new representation of the history of Plato's Early Academy provides enough evidence for us to discuss his position on the issue. The same cannot be said of another obscure figure within the Platonist revival of the first century BC, that is Eudorus of Alexandria, whose view on this issue is much less well represented in extant sources. Nonetheless, in this paragraph I will suggest that Eudorus probably applied a strategy similar to Antiochus' in his own attempt to establish Plato's authority. On the one hand, this will leave room for us to regard the model of authority I am outlining as a somewhat shared strategy, making new sense of the idea of a Platonist revival.[46] On the other, detecting a shared (though possibly polygenetic) strategy will be particularly important, for Antiochus' philosophy and Eudorus' are, famously, almost the opposites of each other in terms of content. In this sense, it will be clear that the model of authority I am detecting is prior to, and not dependent on, the doctrinal contents it frames.

When dealing with Eudorus' views of Plato's authority, it would be tempting to bring into play the well-known claim that Plato was *polyphōnos* but not *polydoxos* – a claim reported by Stobaeus (2.7.3f and 4a) and often ascribed to Eudorus – or the historiographical view that Plato was the one who best formulated a dualist cosmology compared both to his predecessors and to Aristotle, a notion which occurs twice in Plutarch (*De Is. et Os.* 369A–370C and *De procr. an.* 1026B–D) and has been traced back to Eudorus.[47] Unfortunately, however, these would be unstable and somewhat circular foundations for my case, and I prefer to leave them aside. What we *do* know for sure is that Eudorus regarded himself as an Academic (T1), but also that this did not imply any endorsement of

---

[46] By establishing this parallel I do not wish to revert to the idea that Antiochus taught at Alexandria, which Glucker 1978: 90–7, demonstrated to be unwarranted (although new readings of *PHerc* 1021 of Philodemus' *Historia Academicorum* apparently suggest that Antiochus did produce some kind of 'Academic' legacy in Alexandria: see Fleischer 2016). My point is that Antiochus' and Eudorus' strategies for dismissing scepticism share a common core, namely the construction of Plato's authority through the reference to a chain of teachers and a shared legacy.

[47] See Mansfeld 1992: 282–6, and above all Donini 1992: 84–90.

scepticism.[48] I would suggest that Eudorus was more interested in the role of the Early Academy than is usually believed, and that this interest played a strong argumentative role in his attempt to establish Plato's authority.

Now, it is widely known that Eudorus was a major source for Plutarch's *De procreatione animae in Timaeo*. When presenting the semipiternalistic perspective, however, Plutarch expands on Xenocrates' and Crantor's interpretations, and then adds that Eudorus found *neither* of them to be unlikely (1012D–F). Even admitting that Plutarch had access to these views independently of Eudorus, the passage attests that Eudorus himself invoked the Early Academy as an authority for his semipiternalistic reading of Plato. Such a move, moreover, had a huge argumentative potential for him given that, as a well-known passage of the *De natura deorum* (1.19–24) shows, the temporal reading became standard in the Hellenistic Age.[49] In this sense, Eudorus must have regarded the Early Academy's semipiternalistic position as an argument from the authority of the first students of Plato, who agreed on it, despite minor divergences: although many people take Plato to have upheld a temporal perspective, the agreement of his direct students testifies that he rather endorsed a semipiternalistic doctrine. Significantly, Plutarch has no counterargument from authority to oppose to Eudorus' point, and the only course of action open to him is to completely change the game and (speciously) claim that he is proposing a *new* – and correct – interpretation of Plato's cosmogony (*De procr. an.* 1013B). A confirmation of this reading comes from Philo of Alexandria's polemic against the semipiternalist interpretation presented in the *De aeternitate mundi* (14–17).[50] Indeed, Philo supports his argument not only by invoking Plato's text (*Ti.* 41b), but also by emphasising that *a most distinguished student of Plato*, that is Aristotle, took Plato's cosmogony to be temporal. This very remark allows Philo to accuse the supporters of the semipiternalistic interpretation of twisting Plato's words (σοφιζόμενοι), that is of depriving them of any external authority. Now, given the Alexandrian context in which both Eudorus and Philo were operating, and given the spread of the temporal interpretation in the Hellenistic Age, Philo's target could hardly be anyone else but Eudorus. But if this is the case, Philo's point confirms that Eudorus' invocation of the Academy counted as an argument from the authority of Plato's students: Eudorus'

---

[48] On the broad category of 'Academic' and its later replacement with that of 'Platonist', see Bonazzi 2003. Eudorus' texts are quoted according to Mazzarelli's collection.

[49] See Petrucci 2018: ch. 1.

[50] On Philo's exegesis of Plato's cosmogony and psychogony, see Runia 1986: 91–176 and 2001: 1–43.

*Authority beyond Doctrines in the First Century* BC    109

appeal to the Early Academy, that is to Plato's pupils, was not effective as an argument from authority because the case of Aristotle – *a student of Plato* – contradicted it. Similarly, it can hardly be by chance that in Eudorus' reading of the *Categories*, and especially in his appropriation of Aristotle's categories from a Platonist perspective, Eudorus takes the Academic opposition between καθ' αὐτό and πρός τι as his starting point.[51] The point is not whether, and to what extent, Eudorus was committed to this classification more than to Aristotle's one; the point, rather, is that, apart from Plato's hint in the *Sophist* (255c–d), this doctrine of categories was formalised only in the Academy, and to regard it as fairly Platonic is to assume that the Early Academy authoritatively attests Plato's authentic thought. Thus, we are back to the situation emerging from Eudorus' psychogony: Plato's thought is best expressed by its Academic interpretation, and this implies that Plato's thought was positive, consistently structured, understandable, and recoverable by his direct students. In Eudorus' view, therefore, the Early Academy recovers the consistent legacy of Plato via direct teaching, and through this direct transmission the positive and uncontroversial nature of Plato's thought is ensured.

If this is correct, we can also better explain another typical operation of Eudorus, namely the appropriation of Aristotle and, partly, of the Stoics.[52] As a matter of fact, if the reception of Plato's system is based on the progressive recovery of his doctrines through intermediate teaching, one can regard both Aristotle and the Stoics as links in this chain, which is to say as philosophers who either recovered and further developed aspects already implicit in Plato's system, or else distorted them. Such a representation allowed Eudorus not only to consistently appropriate certain Aristotelian and Stoic doctrines, but also to reject other ones, for in the process of transmission some alteration of the original core was quite acceptable. And this, in turn, ensured a very safe way out of the argument from disagreement and quite a strong attack against all sceptical narratives of the continuity of the Academy.

Therefore, Eudorus seems to stress aspects which already Antiochus regarded as key means to re-establish Plato's authority and avoid the risks of the argument from disagreement. But it is likely that he pushed the point even further. Antiochus already regarded Plato as having recovered – yet also supplemented and construed into a system – ideas of previous

---

[51] See esp. Chiaradonna 2009 on this aspect of Eudorus' philosophy.

[52] On his appropriation of Aristotle, see again Chiaradonna 2009 and Bonazzi 2005; on his appropriation of Stoic ethics, see Bonazzi 2007.

thinkers, namely Pythagoras and Socrates (Cic. *Fin.* 5.87–8). With Eudorus we observe a much greater insistence on this point, for – as is as widely known – Plato becomes an heir to the Pythagoreans (T3–5).[53] This attempt to 'Pythagoreanise' Plato is perfectly consistent with the production of a set of Pythagorean *pseudepigrapha* in Eudorus' circle.[54] It is first worth noting that this does not imply that in Eudorus' view Plato was less of an authority than the Pythagoreans; rather, Plato is taken to have recovered from them a core of ancient lore, but the production of a set of Pythagorean texts encompassing Platonic doctrines (i.e. the doctrines Eudorus ascribed to Plato) was a way to ensure a Pythagorean pedigree for him. It was Plato's authority, therefore, which was ultimately emphasised.[55] Now, if we insert this aspect into the narrative I have been outlining, Eudorus' operation becomes much clearer. Plato's system is proven to be positive and consistent not only because the Early Academy faithfully recovered it, but also because it stands in continuity with ancient Pythagorean lore, encompassing the core of Plato's doctrine. This continuity, extending from the Pythagoreans to the Academy via Plato's key role as a systematiser, ensures that his system is consistent, just as Cicero required; that it entails a set of doctrines and specific theoretical milestones; and that, as such, it may be recovered and understood in a nonequivocal way. It is in this very sense that Eudorus could dismiss all a priori sceptical arguments,[56] while at the same time attempting to integrate aspects of subsequent philosophies into his representation of Plato.

### 4.3   Back to the Doctrines

At this point, however, we are also in a position to reassess the role of doctrines in Antiochus' and Eudorus' philosophy. Indeed, if each of them was committed to affirming this historiographical narrative, which was crucial to establishing and ensuring Plato's authority, they must also have sought to build a system complying with this framework. Two centuries of scepticism had almost destroyed the idea that Plato's authority entailed a positive system of doctrines, and even in the Early Academy no shared Platonist philosophy really emerged: while in some fields (e.g. the sempiternalistic interpretation of Plato's psychogony and cosmogony) a

---

[53] See Bonazzi 2005 and 2013.     [54] See Bonazzi 2013, Ulacco 2017: 10–16, Centrone 2014.

[55] See also Centrone 2000a, more generally, on the need to avoid the category of 'Neo-Pythagoreanism'.

[56] The role of Eudorus' interest in Pythagoreanism as a weapon against scepticism has been emphasised by Bonazzi 2013, albeit on other bases.

# Authority beyond Doctrines in the First Century BC

mainstream Early Academic doctrine was probably available,[57] in most cases this was not the case at all (as regards the theory of Forms, for instance: as shown by David Sedley in Chapter 1 of this volume, Xenocrates' Platonism diverged from, and looked critically at, Speusippus'). Accordingly, before building up the doctrinal content of a Platonist system, one had to construct a Platonist identity, that is Plato's authority: and Antiochus and Eudorus did so in the way I have described. At this stage, however, the doctrines not only had to meet specific requirements – that is, comply with the specific philosophical views held by Antiochus and Eudorus – but also, and most crucially, they had to fit the new model of Plato's authority. It is hardly a coincidence that Eudorus' psychogony and his doctrine of categories fit very well with the role of both the Academy and Aristotle I have outlined.

Similarly, the reading I am proposing allows us to grasp why Antiochus opted for a Stoic, or Stoicising, epistemology:[58] he must have regarded such a theory as being more easily projectable back onto Plato, while a different form of epistemology, namely one renouncing all empiricism, would have been impossible to project onto the Stoics, and this would have broken the chain of the Academic tradition. A similar point must also come into play in Antiochus' interest in the Forms. As is widely known, just after Plato the theory of Forms became quite a controversial issue, and it would be difficult to take it as representing a shared Academic commitment. The reason why we expect it to feature in a Platonist revival – and to do so in a form which is comparable with that attested in later Platonism – is simply that it became very important in Middle Platonism, but this says nothing about the reason why Antiochus took it to be – to some extent, and in some form – part of Plato's system (*Acad. post.* 33–5). I would submit that Antiochus introduced it (in whatever form he may have done so) because this put him in a position to suggest some kind of continuity – albeit with substantial fluctuations – from Plato to the Stoics: whether Antiochus was committed to a Stoic ontology or to some sort of Platonist cosmology, he must have regarded interest in universals as a constant feature of 'Academic' philosophy (i.e. of philosophy from Plato to the Stoics),[59] and the modifications affecting it can well be read according to

---

[57] At least to some extent, for it is likely that some kind of temporal stance had been proposed already in the Early Academy: see Sedley 2002b and Petrucci 2018: 27–32.

[58] In this sense, at least in the case of Antiochus, the idea of a 'fair' syncretism (as proposed e.g. by Inwood 2012) is probably correct, provided that we regard this syncretism as a way to fill the ideological framework of Plato's authority with suitable doctrines.

[59] Of course, this does not imply that the authentic Stoic view of universals (on which a huge debate has been developing: see e.g. Sedley 1985 and Caston 1999) stood in any way in continuity with

the historiographical model he outlined. The same analysis could be extended, for instance, to Antiochus' ethics, but my point should already be clear. When there is no specific doctrine that is firmly ascribable to Plato – indeed, when it is not even a widespread view that any doctrine at all may be ascribed to Plato – the first move for any self-styled heir of Plato is to build up Plato's very authority as the master and founder of a system, for otherwise no doctrine at all could be ascribed to him. Only *then* will the philosopher in question be in a position to build up a suitable set of doctrines, and these doctrines must first satisfy a single requirement, that of consistently fitting with the model of authority which has been established. At the same time, what one can deduce from the analysis I have been developing is that Antiochus regarded himself as a Platonist and his doctrines as Platonist in nature.

## 4.4 Authority, Exegesis, and Argument: The First Century BC and Middle Platonism

From the point of view of doctrines, the distance between Antiochus and Eudorus is huge: not least because of this divergence, dating the origin of Platonism to the first century BC would be risky and, ultimately, arbitrary. Moreover, it is clear that both philosophers had some main polemical targets to challenge: although, as I have shown, both Antiochus' and Eudorus' models were able (or, at least, designed) to challenge Academic scepticism, in the case of Antiochus the issue of disproving Philo's narrative of the unity of the Academy must have been even more pressing. Granted all this, the positive aspects which have been emerging as crucial in both representations of Plato allow us to detect aspects of the conception of authority that bind together Antiochus' and Eudorus' approaches to Plato, while respecting the specificities of their philosophies. Indeed, both representations of Plato's authority and the history of the Academy share certain remarkable aspects. Both understood that the only way to effectively present Plato as a dogmatic philosopher proposing a positive system of doctrines was to dismiss the argument from disagreement by ascribing a key role in the narrative to the Early Academy. Furthermore, they addressed this issue by reconstructing a chain of teaching and faithful

---

Plato's theory of Forms. What is important here is that the view according to which Stoic concepts were regarded as a replacement for Plato's Forms is attested in antiquity (without assuming that Antiochus upheld a doctrine of Forms such as that of Plato or the Middle Platonists), and that this view may have been at the basis of Antiochus' reasoning, whether he regarded the entities in question as 'Platonist Forms' or rather as concepts (or as something in between the two).

reception that found its authoritative apex in Plato. They interpreted the alternative views which had emerged after Plato as being either plain recoveries of core ideas already to be found in Plato's writings or slight and consistent developments *of them*. Within this theoretical framework, moreover, we can make much better use of the notion of 'appropriation', which has been introduced over the last few years as a key for understanding both Antiochus' and Eudorus' approaches to Hellenistic philosophies.[60]

But what, then, is the role of Antiochus (and Eudorus)'s conception in the Platonist revival? It would be hard to regard them as the founders of a set of doctrines characterising Middle Platonism as a consistent movement: although some valuable attempts have been made in this sense, it is very hard even to identify a common core of doctrines shared by almost all Middle Platonists.[61] So, any attempt to establish a starting point for Middle Platonism from the point of view of doctrines would be a desperate and self-contradictory endeavour. If, however, we focus on the conception of authority, we find that the model I have outlined for Antiochus and Eudorus did endure in Middle Platonism, and that to some extent it stood at the basis of the movement. A similar conception of post-Platonic history as a response to the argument from disagreement has indeed been detected from Plutarch onwards,[62] and the idea that Plato has said everything necessary in the best possible way is a fundamental tenet from Plutarch (e.g. *De Is. et Os.* 370E–F) and Taurus (T14.7 and T24.1 Petrucci) to Atticus (e.g. fr. 1 des Places). Therefore, Antiochus and Eudorus designed a suitable framework for a new Platonist identity, a framework which is deeply rooted in the polemical engagement with other philosophies and scepticism, just like Middle Platonism.

As far as I can see, however, this is not enough to take Antiochus and Eudorus as Middle Platonists even from a formal point of view, for there is an element which is lacking in Antiochus and is only very partially exploited by Eudorus: textual exegesis. This is a point which one cannot leave aside, for such an approach represents the path followed by all

---

[60] See p. 90.

[61] For instance, the pursuit of transcendence is too generic a concept, while a commitment to the idea of divine craftsmanship (on which scholars have recently insisted: see e.g. Opsomer 2005a, Michalewski 2014, O'Brien 2015) in my view only applies to some Platonists, such as Plutarch, Numenius, and Atticus, and in any case obscures the complexity of the Middle Platonist debate on cosmology: see Petrucci 2018: ch. 3.

[62] See the fundamental study by Boys-Stones 2001, who however uses this principle in order to establish a late starting point for the movement: see also p. 90.

Middle Platonist philosophers. The Middle Platonists of the first century AD could rely on the conception of Plato's authority which Antiochus and Eudorus had shaped; now they had to discover new methods to look into Plato's writings in order to develop a new Platonist doctrinal system. In this sense, the detachment from the Hellenistic background and the discovery of new forms of philosophy reveal themselves as a progressive and to some extent contradictory process. Antiochus' effort to build up Plato's authority, which lies at the basis of his system, is in any case grounded in dialectical arguments.[63] With Eudorus we witness an attempt to support the dialectical argument for Plato's authority with some kind of exegesis, and certainly with the direct use of texts. However, as far as we know, the fundamental features of Middle Platonist exegesis are still lacking: this is not a matter of philosophical style, but of the way in which these philosophers perceived their own role within the Platonist narrative once Plato's authority and the rejection of scepticism had been granted *as an extra-exegetical framework*. This does *not* mean that Antiochus and Eudorus represent a provisional and imperfect stage of Middle Platonism, which would imply a teleological and somewhat *naïve* representation. Rather, the point is that Antiochus and Eudorus had a specific exigency, namely to create a dogmatic Plato *from scratch*, and to do so against sceptical stances and/or rival dogmatic schools: before producing any exegesis, and before arguing in favour of a certain way of understanding Plato's text, it was fundamental for them to enable Plato to be regarded as a credible authority; and this could only be achieved by introducing a dialectical representation of Plato's role. So while a philosophical model of Plato's authority was already available in the first century BC, Middle Platonist exegesis emerged not as a way to appropriate a Platonist identity, but as a way to imbue this identity with suitable arguments and doctrines. But this is the beginning of another story.

---

[63] Sedley 2012b: 89–101 suggests that Antiochus did, at least to some extent, invoke some Platonic passages in order to build up his doctrine. One of the reasons why I am not addressing this point is that David Sedley mainly refers to a passage, namely SE *M* 7.141–260, which not all scholars accept as Antiochean (but he also refers to *Acad. post.* 30–2 as being inspired by *Timaeus* 27d–28a). My point would be, however, that the (very likely) fact that Antiochus was acquainted with Plato's dialogues, and that he was inspired by them, does not imply that he built up his system by means of direct philosophical exegesis rather than in a dialectical way. It seems to me, after all, that the conclusions of Chiaradonna 2013 on the dialectical nature of Antiochus' reference to Aristotle may well be extended to his overall approach to philosophical debate.

CHAPTER 5

# Authority and Doctrine in the Pseudo-Pythagorean Writings[*]

### Bruno Centrone

Within the Pythagorean tradition the supreme source of authority is, needless to say, Pythagoras himself. The Pythagoreans are the only Presocratics named after the founder of their brotherhood. However, if one takes into account the amount of extant Pythagorean literature, which is for the most part apocryphal – as is well known, the amount of apocryphal Pythagorean literature by far exceeds the few fragments which can be considered authentic and safely attributed to ancient Pythagoreans – the predominant name is that of Archytas, who was undoubtedly a prominent figure, although not one as authoritative as Pythagoras. Moreover, a great number of pseudo-Pythagorean writings go under the name of largely unimportant, or otherwise unknown, authors. Nonetheless, this apocryphal literature considerably contributed to lending the necessary authority to a very influential tradition that extended over the centuries. In this contribution I will endeavour, among other things, to explain (a) how Archytas came to be regarded as a major source of authority; (b) why the authors of Pythagorean forgeries made recourse to names which apparently were anything but authoritative; (c) more broadly, what kind of criteria may have guided the authors in building the pseudo-Pythagorean corpus; (d) what relationship exists between these writings and the Platonist tradition.

## 5.1 The Authoritativeness of Pythagoras and of the Writings Attributed to Him

The creation of authority usually requires some written reference texts, but it is certain that no authentic writings by Pythagoras have been handed down to posterity. Yet the question of whether Pythagoras had left any

---

[*] I am grateful to Carl Huffman and Federico Petrucci for their previous reading of this contribution and their helpful comments.

# 116 BRUNO CENTRONE

writings behind was much debated in Antiquity (and still is nowadays). Another question is whether the ancient authors critical of Pythagoras' alleged writings believed that (1) Pythagoras had written nothing (or at most a few letters), or at any rate shared the opinion that (2) all of the works circulating under his name were apocryphal. The latter belief could imply that there once existed some writings by Pythagoras, but that these were not divulged by him or were lost for contingent reasons. It is not clear to what period we can trace back the idea that Pythagoras intentionally left no writings; according to Christoph Riedweg,[1] this belief only surfaced for the first time in the first century BC, with the revival of Pythagoreanism. Indeed, the very production of apocryphal writings presupposes that their addressees did not rule out Pythagoras' activity as a writer. But an inclination to favour thesis (1) could easily originate from thesis (2) with a minimal shift, and the two theses are not always easily distinguishable (as is clear, for instance, from Porphyry's *Life of Pythagoras* 57): a statement such as 'there was no writing of Pythagoras himself' (οὔτε γὰρ αὐτοῦ Πυθαγόρου σύγγραμμα ἦν) is ambiguous in itself and could imply either belief.[2]

Contrary to Riedweg's contention, I believe that a thesis which is very close to the first (even though it assigns a few letters to Pythagoras) can safely be attributed to Sosicrates, as is suggested by a comparison between two passages from Diogenes Laertius' *Lives*. In 1.16, tackling the topic of philosophers who wrote nothing, Diogenes claims that according to some authors Pythagoras and Aristo of Chios did not leave any writings behind, except a few letters;[3] in 7.163 the champions of this thesis are identified as Panaetius and Sosicrates as far as Aristo is concerned,[4] and this would take us to roughly the second half of the second century BC – or, at any rate, to a period before the Pythagorean revival. But in all likelihood this tradition goes back to an even earlier period.[5]

---

[1] See Riedweg 1997.

[2] More unambiguous are the *anonymi* in DL 8.6 (see n. 8) and in particular Plutarch, *Num.* 22.3 (φασὶ μηδὲ τοὺς Πυθαγορικοὺς εἰς γραφὴν κατατίθεσθαι τὰ συντάγματα). Posidonius' statement in Galen, *PHP* 5.6.43.1–4, according to which 'no writing of Pythagoras has been safely transmitted to us' (αὐτοῦ μὲν τοῦ Πυθαγόρου συγγράμματος οὐδενὸς εἰς ἡμᾶς διασωζομένου) instead seems to endorse the opposite view, that originally there existed some writings by Pythagoras.

[3] 'While others wrote nothing at all . . . some add Pythagoras and Aristo of Chios, except that they wrote a few letters' (οἱ δ' ὅλως οὐ συνέγραψαν, ὥσπερ . . . κατά τινας Πυθαγόρας, Ἀρίστων ὁ Χῖος, πλὴν ἐπιστολῶν ὀλίγων).

[4] 'Panaetius and Sosicrates consider his [*sc.* Aristo's] letters to be alone genuine; all the other works named they attribute to Aristo the Peripatetic' (Παναίτιος δὲ καὶ Σωσικράτης μόνας αὐτοῦ τὰς ἐπιστολάς φασι, τὰ δ' ἄλλα τοῦ περιπατητικοῦ Ἀρίστωνος).

[5] One must concede that it is not perfectly clear whether Sosicrates thought that Pythagoras *intentionally* left no writings. Riedweg's contention is that the attribution to Pythagoras of a principled position against writing appeared only later. But ὅλως οὐ συνέγραψαν rather suggests

## *Authority and Doctrine in the* Pseudopythagorica 117

Be that as it may, until the third century BC no alleged writings by Pythagoras were available to ancient authors – regardless of whether they believed that Pythagoras had written anything. A testimony in Porphyry (*VPyth.* 19), which probably goes back to Dicaearchus,[6] shows that the latter could not rely on authoritative written sources: what Pythagoras told his audiences cannot be determined with certainty, for he enjoined silence upon his hearers. In fact, the firm belief that Pythagoras left no writings, or that alleged writings of his were not divulged, could easily be derived from the tradition of the Pythagorean practice of secrecy, which was surely more ancient.[7] For those who maintained that Pythagoras had left some writings, historical facts such as anti-Pythagorean attacks and the burning down of Pythagorean houses could also buttress the belief that some written material had been destroyed and lost. At the same time, the very idea of Pythagorean secrecy later made the work of forgers easier, as it was used to explain why allegedly authentic material had suddenly cropped up again after centuries.

The production of Pythagorean forgeries begins in the Hellenistic age; only from the third century BC onwards is the circulation of writings bearing the name of Pythagoras well attested. The remnants of these forgeries are too scanty to allow us in all cases to clearly decipher the aims and purposes of their authors; it is certain, however, that they endeavoured to fill an embarrassing gap, given the unquestionable prestige enjoyed at that time by the figure of Pythagoras. The work of the forgers was, at least in some cases, successful. In his life of Pythagoras, Diogenes Laertius (or his source, which in this case is probably Neanthes of Cyzicus) claims that some people absurdly insisted that Pythagoras had left no writings.[8] Diogenes then lists three books by Pythagoras, which he considers genuine, and mentions the more generous position of Sotion-Heraclides Lembus, who held other works, too, to be authentic.

Be that as it may, none of the alleged writings of Pythagoras could easily withstand athetesis. Criticism of allegedly genuine Pythagorean material is

---

    an intentional avoidance of the practice. The fact that Sosicrates attributes some letters to Pythagoras is compatible with the view that Pythagoras left no writings. Evidently, what is meant here is treatises or poems, for otherwise the ἔνιοι would be contradicting themselves.

[6]  See Burkert 1972: 122 and n. 7. The attribution of section 19 to Dicaearchus has been rejected by Rathmann and Wehrli.

[7]  See for instance Aristotle fr. 192 = Iambl. *VP* 31; Aristox. fr. 43 Wehrli = DL 8.15.

[8]  DL 8.6: 'Some people absurdly claim that Pythagoras left no writing at all' (Ἔνιοι μὲν οὖν Πυθαγόραν μηδὲ ἓν καταλιπεῖν σύγγραμμά φασιν παίζοντες); but διαπεσόντες is another possible reading. For a more detailed analysis of this passage, see Centrone 1992, 4188–90.

118 BRUNO CENTRONE

attested before the first century BC,[9] and, as we have just seen in relation to Diogenes Laertius, it did not always rely on the conviction that Pythagoras had left no writings at all.

So there were different attitudes towards the alleged writings of Pythagoras. Some authors firmly maintained that he had not written anything at all, or that none of his works had survived, while others accepted only a few writings as genuine; but less critical and more generous positions are attested as well. The former belief, along with a widespread scepticism towards the alleged writings of Pythagoras, which fuelled a more generally critical attitude towards the authenticity of Pythagorean material, probably discouraged the production of apocryphal texts in Pythagoras' name and favoured the composition of writings bearing the names of other Pythagoreans. But this is only part of the story.

## 5.2 The Pseudo-Pythagorean Corpus and the Creation of Authority

If we now take the whole pseudo-Pythagorean corpus into account, what we find is some very heterogeneous material, which is hard to trace back to a common origin and date.[10] A basic distinction within this corpus can be drawn between writings attributed to Pythagoras himself or members of his family, and writings that bear the names of other, more or less renowned, Pythagoreans (this was the criterion used by H. Thesleff for his edition of the pseudo-Pythagorean texts). The latter group is made up of philosophical treatises in the Doric dialect that form a rather homogeneous corpus within the apocrypha. Some of them are preserved in their entirety, while others are only fragmentary – though in some cases the fragments are rather extensive. Concerning their doctrinal content, it

---

[9] Neanthes, for instance, questioned the authenticity of Telauges' letter (DL 8.55 = Neanthes, *FGrHist* 84 F 26: 'But which of the Pythagoreans it was who had Empedocles as a pupil he did not say. For the letter commonly attributed to Telauges and the statement that Empedocles was pupil of both Hippasus and Brontinus he held to be unworthy of credence'; τίνος μέντοι γ᾽ αὐτῶν ἤκουσεν ὁ Ἐμπεδοκλῆς οὐκ εἶπε· τὴν γὰρ περιφερομένην πρὸς Τηλαυγοῦς ἐπιστολήν, ὅτι μετέσχεν Ἱππάσου καὶ Βροντίνου, μὴ εἶναι ἀξιόπιστον.)

[10] On pseudo-Pythagorean literature in general see Thesleff 1961 and 1965; Burkert 1961 and 1971; Moraux 1984; Centrone 2000b and 2014; Zhmud 2019. The proposed chronologies fluctuate wildly between the fourth century BC and the second century AD, but the time limits for the composition of the Doric treatises considered here have mostly been narrowed down to between the first century BC and the first century AD: see Baltes 1972 on Ps.-Timaeus; Szlezàk 1972 on Ps.-Archytas' *Categories*; Moraux 1984: 606–7; Centrone 1990 on the ethical treatises; Ulacco 2017. As for the geographical provenance of the writings, the best candidates are Rome, southern Italy and Alexandria.

*Authority and Doctrine in the* Pseudopythagorica 119

mainly consists in a combination of Platonic and Aristotelian doctrines, and the interaction between these two components is difficult to explain.

For specific reasons, I will focus only on these writings: the material is much richer, and allows for more detailed conclusions. But, above all, the Doric treatises are decidedly philosophical in content, and this offers an appropriate context within which it is possible to deal with the question of philosophical authority. The two types of writings mentioned above, which reflect different perspectives and ways of recreating authority, are to be traced back to different branches of the tradition. One branch of the apocryphal tradition attempted to fill the gap by producing forgeries bearing the name of Pythagoras himself. As is shown by the aforementioned passage from Diogenes Laertius, other authors instead shared the belief that Pythagoras had left no writings at all or, at any rate, acknowledged the difficulty of producing reliable forgeries in his name. It became necessary, therefore, to build authority in a different way. And it is here that the name of Archytas comes to the fore. None of the Doric treatises bears Pythagoras' name; some of them are attributed to insignificant or otherwise unknown authors,[11] but Archytas' name is largely predominant, so much so that H. Thesleff even spoke of a *corpus archyteum*.[12] Surely some of these writings have been lost, and the extant ones are for the most part fragmentary, but neither the absence of Pythagoras' name, nor Archytas' predominance can be fortuitous.

In such a scenario some major questions arise: (1) Why is Pythagoras' name systematically avoided? (2) How is Archytas' predominance to be explained? (3) Given that names such as Philolaus or Archytas were rather influential on their own, what kind of authority could have been exercised by such minor or sometimes possibly unknown figures, such as Theages or Callicratidas? How authoritative could a text circulating under the name of one Cleinias or Metopus be? Why did someone choose to attribute these works to such obscure figures? And why did the forgers employ a range of

---

[11] A particular case is represented by Ps.-Timaeus Locrus' *De natura mundi et animae*, whose authoritativeness was of course guaranteed by its alleged author being the main character of Plato's dialogue and hence the original source of the *Timaeus*. The composition of this forgery fitted very well with the report according to which Plato paid a lot of money for a little Pythagorean book, on the basis of which he composed the *Timaeus* (Timon, fr. 54 = Philolaus A8 DK): see Baltes 1972: 3. Later authors such as Proclus came to consider the Timaeus Locrus authentic, regarding it as the model followed by Plato: see the relevant testimonies in Marg 1972. On the Timaeus Locrus see further Ulacco & Opsomer 2014.

[12] One particular case is represented by Philolaus. As is widely known, many of the fragments attributed to him are spurious, and therefore various apocrypha must have been circulating under his name. In the current corpus of Doric *Pseudopythagorica*, however, the material bearing his name is scant compared to that attributed to Archytas.

different names? (4) Why is a system combining Platonic and Aristotelian doctrines attributed to ancient Pythagoreans?

Concerning question (3), Thesleff put forward the hypothesis that we are faced here with dissenting voices critical of theses maintained in other writings by the alleged 'Archytas'. According to him, these dissenting voices 'seem to have behaved very modestly in choosing names which nobody would find more authoritative than that of Archytas'.[13] However, Thesleff's observation actually reveals the implausibility of his thesis: otherwise unknown names may suggest authenticity, but hardly lend authoritativeness. Moreover, some writings bearing the name of Archytas apparently hold views that are at variance with other treatises by 'Archytas'; in addition, for the most part treatises bearing the names of the unknown authors, instead of conflicting with doctrines of 'Archytas', by and large agree with them. The hypothesis, then, of dissenters using alternative names does not hold. I believe, instead, that some definite convictions guided the authors' choice, and this explains the absence of Pythagoras' name as well.

Regarding question (1) (Why is Pythagoras' name systematically avoided?), it is probable that the authors shared the view that Pythagoras had left no writings, or at least were sceptical about the possibility that the alleged writings of Pythagoras could easily be accepted as authentic. The legend of Pythagorean secrecy was widespread, along with the conviction that at least in the first stage of the history of this school (until Philolaus) the Pythagoreans had not divulged its doctrines;[14] for this reason alone, writings bearing the name of Pythagoras were automatically open to the suspicion of being spurious. However, the conscious avoidance of Pythagoras' name could reveal different attitudes, implying either that (a) the doctrines in question were in fact to be traced back to Pythagoras himself, who nonetheless had avoided writing them down, or that (b) the doctrines professed by the historical Pythagoras were to be identified with those belonging to the acousmatic tradition – a tradition of which, as a matter of fact, there is no trace in the Doric *Pseudopythagorica*. It is difficult to reach any certainty on this point, but I am inclined to favour the second option, for reasons I will soon explain.

With reference to question (3), the use of different names possibly serves the purpose of fostering in the readers the belief that there existed a single Pythagorean philosophy, with slight variations, that was shared by all the members of the school. I have argued elsewhere that, despite some

[13] Thesleff 1961: 76.     [14] See p. 116 n. 3.

# Authority and Doctrine in the Pseudopythagorica

apparent inconsistencies between some of the treatises, a single coherent philosophical system is at work in the Doric *Pseudopythagorica*, even in the political writings, where discrepancies seem more evident (I will soon get back to this point).[15] This is confirmed by the very centrality of the notion of *systēma* in the treatises (the only possible parallel for this, to my knowledge, is what survives of Chrysippus' philosophy). By comparing different *Pseudopythagorica*, it is possible to reconstruct the general notion of *systēma*. A *systēma* is a complex structure made up of many different parts brought together under a common golden rule. So it is defined by Callicratidas:

> a system is composed by opposites and dissimilar elements, is ordered towards something that is one and the best thing, and is oriented to the common advantage.[16]

The definition particularly stresses the fact that in a *systēma* the better ought to direct and the worse ought to be governed and obey, while intermediate entities must both govern and be governed.[17] The authors seek to discover this same structure at work in all realities across the universe, applying this schema to the political community and the family, as well as to individual life. To sum up, the use of many different voices repeating the same basic doctrine in slightly different forms serves the purpose of proving the inner consistency and unity of the school – an ideal well attested for Pythagoreanism.

As for the political writings, I have argued elsewhere that the kingship treatises, in which monarchy is extolled, are not inconsistent, upon closer scrutiny, with the ideal of a mixed constitution championed by Ps.-Archytas in *On Law*, but only mirror different perspectives within the same single fundamental orientation.[18] Such a tension is already present in Plato (see *Plt.* 301a–e and 302e; *Leg.* 875c–d): kingship is the best form of government if, by divine decree, the state is ruled by a wise king who is the living embodiment of the law; but given the difficulty of finding such a king, it is preferable for the laws to have full authority; hence the predilection for a mixed form of government, combining monarchy and democracy, which still represents only a second-best. Here I only wish to

---

[15] Centrone 2000b and 2014.

[16] Cf. Callicratidas, *De dom. felic.* 103.20–3: (σύσταμα δὲ πᾶν ἔκ τινων ἐναντίων καὶ ἀνομοίων σύγκειται, καὶ ποτὶ ἕν τι τὸ ἄριστον συντέτακται, καὶ ἐπὶ τὸ κοινὸν συμφέρον ἐπαμφέρεται).

[17] This is, to my knowledge, the only attempt ever made in antiquity to *define* the very notion of *systēma*.

[18] See Centrone 2000c: 573–5 and 2014: 335–6.

underline that perhaps it is no chance that a treatise propounding a mixed constitution goes under the name of Archytas, who was the representative of a democratically oriented version of political Pythagoreanism in Tarentum. If we turn to consider the attribution of the treatises on kingship, it is rather remarkable that the names of Diotogenes and Sthenidas are not otherwise attested (one Sthenonidas of Locri is listed in Iamblichus' catalogue, *VP* 267). One Ecphantus of Croton appears in Iamblichus' catalogue, but is otherwise unknown (Ecphantus of Syracuse in Diels-Kranz, the upholder of a geocentric theory, was perhaps only a character in a dialogue by Heraclides Ponticus).[19] The monarchical ideal could hardly have been ascribed to Archytas. Thus, selecting names that pose no problems in this respect, while projecting the reader into an indefinite past, was probably an intentional strategy.

It should be remarked that our authors did not limit themselves to attaching Pythagorean names to their forgeries, but intentionally gave these writings a Pythagorean veneer in order to convey an impression of authenticity, most notably by using an (artificial) Doric dialect. Some minor strategies should also be mentioned, such as the use of examples with suitably Pythagorean contexts (e.g. 'in Tarentum' as an example of the 'where' category, in Ps.-Archytas' treatise *On the Whole System* 22.29 Thesleff). It is striking, then, that many of the names employed, such as Aristombrotos, Diotogenes, or those of alleged Pythagorean women, such as Phyntis and Pempelus, are not otherwise attested, or appear only later, possibly thanks to these very writings (as in the case of Myia in Lucian).[20] As has been pointed out,[21] in the apocryphal literature the very rarity of a name sometimes suggests authenticity.

### 5.3 Archytas' Authoritativeness and Iamblichus' Account (*VP* 250–67)

Turning to question (2) (How is Archytas' predominance to be explained?), it must be recalled that the first centuries BC and AD were the period of Archytas' greatest fame in antiquity, and he soon became an unquestioned authority.[22] In some sporadic cases this might also be a *consequence* of the vast number of writings circulating under his name, but it is far more likely that treatises came to be forged in Archytas' name owing to his fame, which was based on the tradition of his connection to

[19] Burkert 1972: 341 n. 17.    [20] See Centrone 2005: 573–4.    [21] Syme 1972.
[22] See Huffman 2005: 21–5 and 324–31.

## Authority and Doctrine in the Pseudopythagorica 123

Plato. As a matter of fact, the references to Archytas in texts from the first centuries BC and AD (Cicero above all) do not reflect doctrines found in the pseudo-epigraphical treatises. Therefore, the main reason for Archytas' prominence was Plato's traditional proximity to him, which hardly needs to be further investigated here – a few hints will suffice. According to a well-known tradition, during his journey to Sicily Plato became acquainted with Archytas, who was his main source of Pythagorean doctrines.[23] Diogenes Laertius presents the correspondence between Plato and Archytas in his *Life of Archytas* (DL 8.79–80). In the first of these letters the Pythagorean claims:

> We attended to the matter of the memoirs and went up to Lucania where we found the true progeny of Ocellus. We did get the works *On Law*, *On Kingship*, *Of Piety*, and *On the Origin of the Universe*, all of which we have sent on to you. (DL 8.80, trans. Hicks 1925)

All of the works mentioned here can safely be identified with the Pythagorean *Pseudepigrapha* of our corpus. The letter was thus forged with the main aim of guaranteeing the authenticity of these writings and explaining their transmission, while also providing a Pythagorean pedigree for Plato.[24] Thus, in the anonymous biography from Photius' library (249.438b16–19) Plato is presented as a disciple of Archytas (the elder!) and as the ninth scholarch, followed by Aristotle, in a Pythagorean line of succession that starts with Pythagoras. Archytas became the most direct link between Pythagoreanism and Plato: under his name writings were composed that presented those Platonic doctrines which Plato could not have derived from Socrates' teachings.[25]

In the process of selecting (or making up) the names of the authors of apocrypha, an important role must have been played by the tradition stretching back to Aristoxenus, whose interest in the figure of Archytas is well known.[26] It is to be remarked that most of the names occur in Iamblichus' catalogue of Pythagoreans, whose source the vast majority of scholars have identified as Aristoxenus.[27] But we can go one step further,

---

[23] See for instance Cic. *Rep.* 1.16; *Fin.* 5.87; Apul. *De dog. Plat.* 1.3; Photius 249.438b.

[24] A different explanation is proposed by Thesleff 1962: according to Thesleff the aim of the letter is to extol, in opposition to the Romans' supremacy, the origins of the Lucanians, by making Plato himself dependent on the Lucanian Ocellus.

[25] Zhmud 2019.

[26] Aristoxenus wrote a *Life of Archytas* (fr. 47–50 Wehrli) which had a considerable influence on the later tradition; see Huffman 2005: 4–5.

[27] Iambl. *VP* 267: Archytas, Brontinus, Bryson, Butherus, Charondas, Cleinias, Eccelus, Ecphantus, Euryphamus, Eurytus, Criton, Metopus, Ocellus, Onatas, Philolaus, Zaleucus, Dios (cf. Endios and Odios), Sthenidas (cf. Sthenonidas), Theages. Cf. *VP* 257 and 261.

## 124  BRUNO CENTRONE

by taking into account the report of the end of the Pythagorean school found in Iamblichus (*VP* 250–1), which goes back to Aristoxenus: after the burning down of Milon's house, the Pythagoreans departed from Italy, except for Archytas.[28] The most celebrated of them were Phanto, Echecrates, Polymnastus, Diocles, and Xenophilus. At first they dwelt together in Rhegium and 'preserved the Pythagorean *mathēmata*' (ἐφύλαξαν ... τὰ μαθήματα), but then the sect completely disintegrated. Here I only wish to remark that perhaps it is not by chance that none of these ancient Pythagoreans appear among the authors of *Pseudopythagorica*; if one is to trust reports of this kind, Archytas remained the only intermediary for the transmission of Pythagorean doctrines.

But another section of Iamblichus' work is perhaps even more worthy of consideration. Chapters 265–6 of *The Pythagorean Life* come after a section (254–64) based on Apollonius, whose work Iamblichus draws upon in order to provide an alternative version of the anti-Pythagorean attacks. At 267 Iamblichus provides his renowned list of Pythagoreans, whose source has long been recognized to be Aristoxenus. The source of chapters 265–6, instead, is difficult to ascertain. In this section a brief survey is given of the history of the school, focusing on the succession of Pythagorean scholarchs/*diadochoi*. According to Iamblichus' report, everyone unanimously acknowledged that Pythagoras' successor was Aristaeus, son of Damophon, who had married Theano. The next scholarchs were Mnemarchus, Boulagoras, and Gartydas. After some time the direction of the school was taken up by Aresas Lucanus. To him came Diodorus of Aspendus, who was accepted into the school because of its small number of affiliates. On his return to Greece, Diodorus divulged the Pythagorean sayings. Distinguished members of the school included Cleinias and Philolaus at Heraclea, Thearides and Eurytus at Metapontum, and Archytas in Tarentum.

---

[28] 'Except Archytas of Tarentum, the rest of the Pythagoreans departed from Italy, and dwelt together in Rhegium. But in course of time, as the administration of public affairs went from bad to worse? *** the most celebrated were Phanto, Echecrates, Polymnastus, and Diocles, who were Phliasians, and Xenophilus Chalcidensis of Thrace. These Pythagoreans nevertheless preserved their pristine manners and disciplines; yet soon the sect began to fail, till they nobly perished,' trans. Guthrie (οἱ δὲ λοιποὶ τῶν Πυθαγορείων ἀπέστησαν τῆς Ἰταλίας πλὴν Ἀρχύτου τοῦ Ταραντίνου· ἀθροισθέντες δὲ εἰς τὸ Ῥήγιον ἐκεῖ διέτριβον μετ' ἀλλήλων. προϊόντος δὲ τοῦ χρόνου καὶ τῶν πολιτευμάτων ἐπὶ τὸ χεῖρον προβαινόντων *** ἦσαν δὲ οἱ σπουδαιότατοι Φάντων τε καὶ Ἐχεκράτης καὶ Πολύμναστος καὶ Διοκλῆς Φλιάσιοι, Ξενόφιλος δὲ Χαλκιδεὺς τῶν ἀπὸ Θράκης Χαλκιδέων. ἐφύλαξαν μὲν οὖν τὰ ἐξ ἀρχῆς ἤθη καὶ τὰ μαθήματα, καίτοι ἐκλειπούσης τῆς αἱρέσεως, ἕως εὐγενῶς ἠφανίσθησαν.)

Authority and Doctrine in the Pseudopythagorica 125

According to Rohde,[29] this section too went back to Apollonius, who had invented the whole account. This view has recently been taken up by some scholars,[30] whereas others have linked this section with Timaeus, who in his *Histories* (566F16 = T9) had dealt with the figure of Diodorus. In this respect, it should be noted, first of all, that the end of the section going back to Apollonius (and hence, perhaps, to a different source) is clearly marked in Iamblichus' text (264.16–18): '*and thus much* concerning the attack which was made on the Pythagoreans' (περὶ μὲν οὖν τῆς κατὰ τῶν Πυθαγορείων γενομένης ἐπιθέσεως τοσαῦτα εἰρήσθω). The list of Pythagorean scholarchs, then, must derive from a doxography concerned with the genre of successions (*Diadochai*) – which does not seem to have been one of Apollonius' main interests. Sosicrates, for instance, in the third book of his *Succession of Philosophers*, had dealt with Diodorus as the champion of an innovative way of life, differing from that of earlier Pythagoreans.[31] It seems improbable, then, that the list goes back to Apollonius. However, whether this list of Pythagorean scholarchs – none of whom is mentioned in Aristoxenus' catalogue – is wholly fanciful and a late (Hellenistic) invention, as was maintained e.g. by Corssen,[32] is a question that is best left open. Regardless of whether the whole report is historically reliable, I would suggest that it is precisely a tradition of this sort that might have underpinned the building of the apocryphal corpus and guided authors in their choice of Pythagorean pseudonyms.

It is remarkable, in this respect, that almost all the names of the Pythagoreans mentioned in Iamblichus' passage (Aristaeus, Aresas – these two are not mentioned in other ancient sources – Cleinias, Philolaus, Eurytus and obviously Archytas) appear as authors of apocrypha. The only exception, represented by Diodorus, is easily explained: Diodorus, who was accepted in the school *faute des mieux*, is seen as the popularizer of the Pythagorean *phōnai*, which were oral precepts and instructions belonging to the genre of *akousmata*. According to a standard view, this tradition was rejected by Aristoxenus, or (as recently argued by Carl Huffman)[33] not

---

[29] Rohde 1872: 58–9.    [30] Zhmud 2012: 132 n. 26.

[31] Sosicrates, fr. 20 (= Athenaeus 163F–164A): 'And Sosicrates, in the third book of the *Succession of Philosophers*, relates that Diodorus used to wear a long beard, and a worn-out cloak, and to keep his hair long, indulging in these fashions out of a vain ostentation. For the Pythagoreans before him wore very handsome clothes, and used baths, and perfumes, and hair of the ordinary length' (Σωσικράτης δ' ἐν τρίτῳ Φιλοσόφων διαδοχῆς βαθεῖ πώγωνι χρήσασθαι τὸν Διόδωρον ἱστορεῖ, καὶ τρίβωνα ἀναλαβεῖν, κόμην τε φορῆσαι, κατά τινα τῦφον τὴν ἐπιτήδευσιν ταύτην προσαγαγόντα, τῶν πρὸ αὐτοῦ Πυθαγορικῶν λαμπρᾷ τε ἐσθῆτι ἀμφιεννυμένων, καὶ λουτροῖς καὶ ἀλείμμασι, κουρᾷ τε τῇ συνήθει χρωμένων).

[32] Corssen 1912: 348–9.    [33] Huffman 2014a: 285–95.

rejected at all by him, but traced back to Pythagoras himself, while at the same time being distinguished from the mathematical strain of Pythagoreanism. It is certain, in any case, that Aristoxenus rejected radical ascetics such as Diodorus. It is hardly fortuitous, then, that a name such as Diodorus' is absent from the pseudo-Pythagorean corpus: Diodorus, the representative of a non-scientific branch of Pythagoreanism, could not be credited with writings which aspired to philosophical validity. The same applies to the subsequent information concerning Epicharmus, who is said to have been not a fully-fledged member of the association, but only a foreign listener. Because of Hiero's tyranny, he refrained from philosophizing in public, but he wrote down the Pythagorean doctrines in metre and disclosed Pythagoras' occult dogmas in his comedies.[34] Accordingly, none of the Doric *Pseudopythagorica* considered here bear the name of Epicharmus. Iamblichus' report on the succession of Pythagorean scholarchs fits very well with the two main strands of the Pythagorean tradition: philosophical Pythagoreanism extends until Archytas, while Diodorus is the divulger of the *akousmata*. Accordingly, philosophical treatises were composed by forgers using the names of the main exponents of the first current, while the champions of the acousmatic tradition (or 'degenerate' Pythagoreans such as Diodorus) do not find any place in the circle of philosophical writers.

We may state, then, that the authors of the apocrypha, when endeavouring to lend authority to their writings, rely on a tradition stretching back to authors like Aristoxenus, or to other Hellenistic writers of *diadochai*, whose reflections are confusedly mirrored in Iamblichus. The prominent role of Archytas and the proliferation of pseudo-Pythagorean names have their roots here. For many concurring reasons Pythagoras' name was unsuitable for lending authority to strictly philosophical doctrines: the image of him as a wonder man or miracle-worker was well established, and his name was associated with the *akousmata*, which were perceived by many as a foreign body and a stumbling block, a superstition incompatible with philosophical doctrines. The belief that he had left no

---

[34] Iambl. *VP* 266.11–16: 'Epicharmus was also said to have been one of the foreign hearers, but he was not one of the school. However, having arrived at Syracuse, he refrained from public philosophizing in consideration of the tyranny of Hiero. But he wrote the Pythagorean views in metre, and published the occult Pythagorean dogmas in comedies' (τῶν δ' ἔξωθεν ἀκροατῶν γενέσθαι καὶ Ἐπίχαρμον, ἀλλ' οὐκ ἐκ τοῦ συστήματος τῶν ἀνδρῶν· ἀφικόμενον δὲ εἰς Συρακούσας διὰ τὴν Ἱέρωνος τυραννίδα τοῦ μὲν φανερῶς φιλοσοφεῖν ἀποσχέσθαι, εἰς μέτρον δ' ἐντεῖναι τὰς διανοίας τῶν ἀνδρῶν, μετὰ παιδιᾶς κρύφα ἐκφέροντα τὰ Πυθαγόρου δόγματα).

*Authority and Doctrine in the* Pseudopythagorica     127

writings was probably already widespread in the Hellenistic age, and the tenet of Pythagorean secrecy also contributed towards this outcome.

Nonetheless, other authors firmly believed that the fundamental doctrines of philosophical Pythagoreanism could be traced back to Pythagoras himself, and this is an ancient tradition too, which endured for a long period of time. For a number of reasons, Numenius, for instance, regarded Pythagoras as the primary source of philosophical wisdom.[35] Significantly, those scholars who have more recently chosen to present Pythagoras as a philosopher have credited him with a doctrine whose outline is bound to remain very vague – a philosophy quite different from the dominant picture of Pythagorean philosophy in antiquity.[36]

## 5.4   The *Pseudopythagorica* in the Platonist Tradition

We now come to our last question, (4): why is a system combining Platonic and Aristotelian doctrines attributed to ancient Pythagoreans? What purpose does the attribution of this system to ancient Pythagoreans serve? How is the aforementioned blending of Platonic and Aristotelian doctrines to be explained? First, it is difficult to ascertain whether our authors were relying on first-hand knowledge of Plato's and Aristotle's writings; Platonic doctrines in the *Pseudopythagorica* are mostly mediated by the Academic tradition, which profoundly shapes the basic orientation of the treatises towards systematization and classification. The theory of principles plays a fundamental role in all spheres of knowledge, but its very formulation contains innovative elements which make the pseudo-Pythagorean system more than simply a repetition of early Academic doctrines.

The presence of Aristotelian doctrines, particularly in logic and ethics, is substantial in the treatises. Nonetheless, as I have argued elsewhere, a constant effort is made to integrate them within a Platonizing system. Here I can only recall the most basic features of this system.[37] A theory of two principles of Academic derivation – one ordering and determining things, the other being the principle of disorder and indetermination – provides the background for all the treatises, finding application in every domain: in cosmology, ethics, and politics (Arch. *De princ.* 19.5–20.17). The Aristotelian doctrine of categories is integrated into a Platonic-

[35] Numenius, fr. 24 des Places; see also Alexandra Michalewski, Chapter 6 in this volume.
[36] See for instance Kahn 2001: 11–38.
[37] For a more in-depth investigation, I will once again refer to Centrone 2014.

oriented system. Aristotle's hylomorphism is interpreted in the light of the doctrine of Ideas – identified with the Aristotelian Forms – and traced back to these two fundamental principles. In theology, although God is described in terms that fit the conception of the first mover moving the sphere of the fixed stars (Onat. *De deo* 139.11–140.5), he is conceived in Platonic fashion as a demiurge who impresses form upon matter. Also distinctly Platonic is the notion of God's direct action upon the world and of his providential care of man. The Aristotelian idea of a division of the cosmos into two regions is adapted to the two-principle scheme: the ever-moving part, the superlunary region, belongs to the limiting nature, the ever-passive one, which is always subject to corruption, to the undetermined (Damipp. *De prud.* 68.21–25). In ethics, the Platonic precept of assimilation to God (*homoiōsis theōi*) as the goal of human life, while not found in the *Pseudopythagorica* quite in these terms, is dealt with and endorsed in the treatises on kingship. Fundamental notions such as the right mean, and its opposite, whose species are excess and deficiency, are brought back to the original pair of principles. The political treatises too, while reflecting a variety of influences, are essentially of Platonic inspiration.

Since the Aristotelian doctrines are constantly integrated within a Platonizing system, it is tempting to frame these writings within the Platonic tradition. This combining of Platonic and Aristotelian doctrines is typical of so-called Middle Platonism – as is well known, a problematic historiographical category – from the first century BC onward. Indeed, recent scholarship is inclined to view these writings within the framework of Middle Platonism. More precisely, the hypothesis of their attribution to Eudorus' circle is now widely accepted.[38]

The attribution of Platonic and Aristotelian doctrines to ancient Pythagoreans was intended to secure an *imprimatur* of authority, thereby enforcing the idea of the continuity between Pythagoreanism and Platonism. By being traced back to illustrious figures from this philosophical tradition, Platonic doctrines were given an aura of authoritativeness, in accordance with a tendency already established within the Early Academy by Plato's successors. If the hypothesis that has been put forward here with regard to the construction of the Pythagorean *diadochē* is correct, then the overall purpose of the operation was to establish an unbroken continuity

---

[38] That they may have originated in Eudorus' circle, whose main aim was to reconcile Platonism and Aristotelism by tracing them back to Pythagoreanism, is a concrete possibility: see recently Bonazzi 2005: 152–60 and 2013, and Centrone 2014: 338 with further references.

between the ancient Pythagorean doctrine and the Platonist tradition through the essential mediation of Archytas. At the same time, the aim was also to highlight, on the one hand, the harmony between Plato and Aristotle and, on the other, the idea of the internal unity of the Platonist-Pythagorean tradition, notwithstanding the presence of different voices that disagreed on certain details yet shared the same, ultimately unitary doctrine.

CHAPTER 6

# Constructing Authority[*]
## A Re-examination of Some Controversial Issues in the Theology of Numenius

*Alexandra Michalewski*

In a recent article, George Boys-Stones (2018b) offered an interesting definition of the Imperial Platonist conception of authority. According to him, contrary to the members of the other Hellenistic schools, the Middle Platonists do not aim to acquire a sum of propositional knowledge to be preserved within the school. Plato's authority was for them not that of a founder of a school, but that of a man who had seen the intelligible Forms and discovered a truth to which all subsequent Platonists aspired. According to Boys-Stones, this conception of authority goes hand in hand with a certain epistemological perspective, the traces of which we can find in the fragments of Numenius, most notably in how he thinks of the relation between the second and the third God (fr. 11 des Places). The perspective of this paper is slightly different. We will first recall the way in which Numenius retrospectively constructs a lineage of authority in order to support his triadic theology. We will then examine how this architecture is later critiqued by Proclus, who places Numenius in a lineage of exegetes who betrayed the spirit of Plato's thought and, in doing so, provides a new lineage of epistemic authority.

The history of the transmission of Platonic doctrines is, according to Numenius, a story of betrayal which, having begun in the ancient Academy, never stopped spreading. This interpretation is known thanks to Eusebius of Caesarea,[1] who in Numenius finds confirmation of many of his own convictions: paganism is marked by dissent, and the best things in Hellenism themselves derive from previous sources, the Greeks having simply looted a more ancient religious heritage. Eusebius readily attributes

---

[*] I would like to thank the editors of this volume, as well as G. Karamanolis for his accurate remarks during a previous presentation of this paper in Vienna, and G. Reydams-Schils, F. Jourdan, J. Opsomer and M.-A. Gavray for their reading of the first draft of this paper. The English translation has greatly benefitted from the help of S. Fortier.

[1] On the sources available at the Caesarea library and Eusebian citation standards, I refer, for a *status quaestionis*, to Morlet 2015.

to Numenius a formula which later came to be associated with him, stemming from the question 'For what is Plato but Moses speaking Attic Greek?'[2] Eusebius' excerpts quoted in the *Praeparatio evangelica* were carefully chosen by Eusebius to buttress his apologetic project:[3] on the one hand, they aim to show that the truth of Platonism – which, for him, is the pagan doctrine which best agrees with Christianity – has its roots in previous revelations (transmitted by sages such as Moses and Pythagoras) and, on the other hand, they aim to track milestones in the history of the reception of those revelations. Eusebius also finds support for his general argument in Numenius' pamphlet *On the Dissension between the Academics and Plato*.[4] According to Numenius, one of the worst changes which Platonic doctrine has undergone is that which the scepticism of the New Academy has inflicted upon it. In *Praep. evang.* 14.4, Eusebius reveals how Numenius worked so as to distance Plato as well as his teacher, Socrates, from the interpretations given by the Academics, creating the image of Socrates the theologian, a disciple of the religious teachings of Pythagoras. While what is at stake, for Numenius, is to show the fundamental error of the neo-Academic dissidents, for Eusebius it is a matter of highlighting how much Plato and Socrates had distanced themselves from traditional religion – and hence, indirectly, how Plato had struck a secret agreement with Mosaic Revelation. The excerpts chosen by Eusebius bring to light Numenius the theologian, who sees in Plato a source of authority which in turn derives from previous and more legitimate sources which, from where he stood, were perfectly reconcilable with Christian dogma.

This paper, which is composed of two parts, will be organised as follows. After having explained the background against which Numenius' position arises, we will then examine how the theology he fashioned was later received. First of all, with the aid of some Eusebian excerpts, we will examine the issue of the construction of Socrates' theological authority by Numenius. We will show how Numenius, in order to justify his own triadic theological architecture, establishes a history of Platonism which rests on a genealogy of successive figures of authority: Pythagoras, Plato, and Socrates, of whom Numenius presents himself as the legitimate heir.

---

[2] Num. fr. 8.13. All fragments are cited following des Places 1973. Unless otherwise noted, I am following the translations proposed in BS. This definition of Plato as Moses speaking Attic Greek will become popular during the Renaissance, only to later be made the object of severe criticism by J. Brucker. On this history, see Laks 2010. I refer also to Whittaker 1984: VII 200–1, who indicates that 'one cannot exclude the possibility that Numenius was also using the Septuagint designation to indicate the namelessness and incomprehensibility of God'.

[3] On Eusebius as excerptor, see Jourdan 2015.     [4] On this point, see Karamanolis 2014: 179–80.

This triadic theology, as we shall see in the second part of this article, was later strongly criticised by Proclus when presenting his own interpretation of the figure of the demiurge. In this regard, we should make the following distinction: in the Neoplatonic commentaries, one must distinguish between sources that have *revealed* the truth – such as Plato, but also the Orphic tradition or the Chaldean Oracles – and the figures of exegetical authority, that is, authors who have more or less *approached and understood* these revealed truths. Thus, concerning the interpretation of the demiurge of the *Timaeus*, Proclus acknowledges two figures of exegetical authority, who are not at the same level: Syrianus, Proclus' master and the highest exegetical authority, and then Plotinus, the first to propose a philosophical interpretation of the demiurge. Indeed, Proclus both simplifies the elements of Numenian theology and makes them fit into a history of the interpretations of the nature of the demiurge which culminates with his teacher, Syrianus, who follows a path paved by Plotinus. If, according to Proclus, it is Plotinus who really marks the beginning of the history of the philosophical interpretation of the demiurge of the *Timaeus*, it is because he views this figure within the context of a metaphysical architecture based on a theological reading of the second part of the *Parmenides*. For Proclus this dialogue is the key to all Platonic theology: the One is not only the first principle, devoid of any multiplicity, but it is above all a principle beyond all analogy, which is not coordinate with what derives from it. Thus, in *in Ti.* 1.303.27–306.15, Proclus offers a privileged example of the construction of Platonic authority: using as his reference the theology inspired by the *Parmenides*, he manages to make Numenius an author who, far from having inspired Plotinus (as some of his contemporaries maintained),[5] is actually an exegete to be grouped with Atticus, who establishes no difference between the demiurge and the Good.

### 6.1   Socrates the Theologian

In his treatise *On the Dissention between the Academics and Plato*, Numenius establishes a line of transmission of authority which runs from Pythagoras to Plato via Socrates. This exegetical move testifies to a prodigious intellectual effort. Indeed, in a certain sense, Plato's dependence on Pythagoras is not a completely unusual thing in genealogies of Platonism in the Imperial age;[6] however, the presence among these genealogies of Socrates – a key figure for the Academic conception of *epochē* – is rather

---

[5] Porphyry, *VP* 17.1–3.    [6] See Dillon 1996: 367.

## Constructing Authority in the Theology of Numenius    133

surprising. A symbol of the one who *tends towards* wisdom – reminding us that wisdom about divine realities is the object of a quest which is ever-renewed, rather than an assured possession – Socrates urges us to protect ourselves against all epistemological dogmatism. Besides, the association between Socrates and Pythagoras brings specific issues into play. As P. Donini has shown,[7] the definition of Socrates as a theologian is the result of a long process of reappropriation of the image of Socrates within a Pythagorising Platonism. Thus, we see it at work e.g. in Apuleius, who finds confirmation of the truth of Socrates' experience in the doctrines of the Pythagoreans, according to which it is possible to 'see a demon'.[8] In the following excerpt reported by Eusebius, Numenius goes even further, providing a portrait of Socrates as a theologian who professed the existence of three Gods, and made speeches suited to the nature of each one.

> Socrates posited three Gods, and discussed them in a style appropriate to each. Those who heard him did not understand, and thought that he was saying it all without order, directed by the winds of chance as they blew here and there at random. (Num. fr. 24.52–6 = 1F BS)

Socrates' disciples did not understand the principle according to which to each divine level there corresponds a specific type of discourse. Also, they fragmented his theology, incapable as they were of seeing the big picture, i.e. of ascending to the unity of its true sources. Of all of his students, only Plato was able to do so, because he knew the Pythagorean origin of the Socratic discourse.

> But Plato followed Pythagoras ('Ο δὲ Πλάτων πυθαγορίσας) and knew that that was precisely where Socrates got it all from, and that he knew what he was saying. (Num. fr. 24.57–9 = 1F BS)

But whereas Pythagoras' direct disciples remained faithful to their master's teachings, Plato's disciples (like Socrates')[9] only managed to stray from them, partly because of their incomprehension, and partly because they were driven by a spirit of rivalry and contention (interestingly, this passage has been chosen by Eusebius to highlight, beyond the case of Plato's heritage, a typical example of dissent among the *diadochoi* of pagan

---

[7] On this history, from the Socrates we find in Plutarch's *Adversus Colotem* – which revives the association between Socrates and the *epochē* established by Arcesilaus – to his progressive adaptation to the context of Pythagorising Platonism, see Donini 2003 and Bonazzi 2006: 241–4.

[8] Apuleius, *De deo Soc.* 20.

[9] Mansfeld 1992: 298 sees in these lines confirmation of the fact that, for Numenius, Pythagoras remains the primary authority, even above Plato: 'Plato and Pythagoras are almost put on a par but Pythagoras still comes out the more important person.'

schools). By reducing the multifaceted aspects of the Platonic heritage in the Academy to a series of disputes caused by the lack of knowledge of Plato's true core doctrines, Numenius builds the image of an exclusively Pythagorean Plato. Reading Plato while seeing him as a repository of Pythagoras' teachings – as Numenius himself does, thus justifying his approach – is the only correct method:[10] this method is the very same one which Plato employed to grasp the unity and coherence of Socrates' words, which Socrates' other disciples failed to grasp. Also, Numenius' project consists in separating (*chōrizein*) Plato from his successors, and taking him as he is, i.e. in light of his Pythagorean source:

> We should apply our thought elsewhere and, as we set out to distinguish him [Plato] from Aristotle and Zeno, so now, with the help of god, we shall distinguish him from the Academy, and let him be in his own terms, a Pythagorean. As things stand, he has been torn apart in a frenzy more crazed than any Pentheus deserved, and suffers if considered as a collection of limbs – although, taken as a whole, he never changes back and forth with respect to himself considered as a whole. (Num. fr. 24.67–73 = 1F BS)

Compared to his heirs, who seek to 'tear him apart', Plato remains as impassible and unchangeable as the intelligible itself with respect to the material world. To grasp the intelligible in its truth, one must separate it from what has been added to it and from what prevents us from understanding it in its purity.[11] This operation of separation is an indispensable step to achieving what Numenius considers to be authentic Pythagoreanism: thus, for example, concerning the theory of cosmological principles and the question of the relation between the Dyad (matter) and the One, Numenius stands in stark opposition to the exegetes who misunderstood the Pythagorean doctrine, conceiving a relationship of derivation between the two.[12] To these champions of derivation he opposes a dualism of principles, which he detects in book 10 of the *Laws*, where Plato, according to him, theorised the existence of two 'world souls', one beneficent and one maleficent.[13]

---

[10] Frede 1987: 1044–5.

[11] O'Meara 1989: 12: 'This assimilation suggests that the changeability and disputatious behaviour of Plato's followers is testimony to their error, and that the unchanging integrity of Plato's doctrine is a sign of its truth, a truth which, despite the distortions inflicted on it in the history of the Academy, remains intact and unaffected, just as the Platonic Forms transcend and are independent of the fragmentary images of them reflected in matter.'

[12] Calc. *in Ti.* 295–7 (= Num. fr. 52). On other aspects of Numenius' project aiming to restore Plato's interpretation, which he thought matched his true Pythagoreanism, differing from that of the Academics and that of certain Pythagoreans or neo-Pythagoreans, see Jourdan 2017–2018.

[13] Pl. *Leg.* 10.897a–c. Plato's text does not talk about 'two world souls'; on this issue, I refer to Brisson 1974: 299–300, and to Zambon 2002: 205–7.

Building a genealogy which makes Socrates and Plato two heirs of Pythagoras also allows Numenius to postulate a certain definition of Platonic identity: leaving aside the novelties and exegetical blemishes inflicted upon Plato by the Academics, to be Platonic is to ascend to the primary source of Plato's doctrines, which Numenius seeks to restore in all its purity. As we have seen, the exegetical decision to consider the core of Socratism to reside in theology serves a polemical goal, namely to challenge the image of Socrates painted by the neo-Academics. In the polemical perspective which Numenius adopts in his treatise against the Academics, this decision aims at nothing less than purely and simply excluding the Hellenistic Academy from the Platonic tradition.[14] Fragment 23 offers additional clarifications on Socrates' theology and its presentation by Plato. This text is the sole excerpt from the lost treatise *The Secrets in Plato*, where Numenius – for the first time in Antiquity – detects a Platonic criticism of traditional religions in the *Euthyphro*:[15] a criticism which Plato disguises by attributing the prevailing conceptions about the Gods to Euthyphro, a mediocre character. This strategy, consisting in opposing the beliefs of the city without showing any direct disagreement, is – according to Numenius – typical of Plato, who was caught between his desire not to renounce the truth and his desire not to meet the same fate as his teacher, Socrates. He thus hid his writings behind a veil of obscurity.[16] Nevertheless, this voluntary obscurity had severe consequences, in part causing the *diastasis* which spread among all his heirs. Indeed, in the *Euthyphro*, while feigning respect for Athenian religious traditions, Plato actually criticises them systematically, indirectly placing them in opposition to his true interpretation of the nature of the Gods. That is where he brings Socrates into play as his spokesperson: Plato's master has no trouble dealing with the arguments proposed by Euthyphro, who is a hopeless theologian.[17]

By evoking a Pythagorising theology by Socrates, founded upon the existence of three Gods, Numenius justifies a posteriori his own theology, for which he finds confirmation in Plato's texts – as well as in texts attributed to Plato, such as the *Second Letter*.[18] Indeed, according to Numenius, Plato was the only one to truly understand Socrates' tripartite

---

[14] Bonazzi 2006: 241. This exegetical strategy, which consists in separating Plato from Aristotle and the Academics, is directed not only towards the Academics but also towards the conciliating project of someone such as Antiochus, as G. Reydams-Schils has pointed out to me.
[15] Van Nuffelen 2011: 74–5.    [16] Num. fr. 23.12–14.    [17] Num. fr. 23.15.
[18] As Jourdan 2017–2018 points out. It should be noted that this pseudo-epigraph text was considered an authentic Platonic work by Numenius, as well as by the Neoplatonic tradition.

theology and to transcribe it allusively in the *Euthyphro*. Now, to interpret Platonic writings in such a manner, Numenius must partly reinvent, as it were, the oral teachings of Plato and, through them, those of his teacher, Socrates. Indeed, as F. Jourdan has shown, Numenius' strategy consists not merely in relying on the oral tradition, but in turning this tradition into a kind of 'pretext to justify Plato's Pythagoreanism'. In other words, in order to establish the truth of his own theological triad, Numenius develops a version of what might have been the content of the unwritten tradition based on its primary authoritative source, the original word of Pythagoras.[19] Through an impeccable rhetorical construction, Numenius draws a sort of portrait of the extremes with respect to which Plato appears to constitute a stylistic middle ground, born out of the mix between Socrates and Pythagoras: between Pythagoras' hieratic dignity (which is *semnos*) and Socrates' demotic cheerfulness. This image of Plato as the mean between two opposites also manifests itself in his art of 'chiaroscuro', insofar as Plato deliberately fosters a relative obscurity.[20]

> As a man who struck a mean between Pythagoras and Socrates, he reduced the solemnity (τὸ σεμνόν) of the one to make it humane, and elevated the wit and playfulness of the other from the level of irony to dignity and weight. He made this mixture of Pythagoras with Socrates, and proved himself more accessible than the one and more dignified than the other. (τοῦ μὲν δημοτικώτερος, τοῦ δὲ σεμνότερος ὤφθη) (Num. fr. 24.73–9 = 1F BS)

Thus, the authority attributed to Socrates by Numenius derives from a careful construction aiming to establish the former within a line of doctrinal and theological transmission which goes from Pythagoras to Plato: Plato is not the first source of authority, but rather derives his authority from that of Pythagoras.[21] These instances themselves are taken as reference points by Numenius to confirm his own analyses. Before concluding this section dedicated to Numenius' construction of authority, I would like to address a further point regarding the organisation of his triadic theology.

---

[19] Jourdan 2017–2018: 164.
[20] On the subject of Platonic obscurity in Numenius, see Mansfeld 1992: 205. Petrucci 2018: 57–9, presents a comparative analysis of how Plutarch, Numenius and Taurus, respectively, dealt with Plato's obscurity, in relation to the issue of the generation of the world in the *Timaeus*. According to him, Atticus' plea in favour of Plato's clarity is a consciously polemical and falsely naive reaction to the interpretative subtleties developed by Taurus on the question of the different meanings of the term *genēton*.
[21] Moreover, as Karamanolis 2014: 179 has noticed, 'in some respect Eusebius is similar to Numenius, in that the latter ascribes more value to Pythagoras than to Plato, as Eusebius does to the Scriptures'.

# Constructing Authority in the Theology of Numenius 137

In a passage from the treatise *On the Good*, preserved by Eusebius, Numenius defines the three Gods in this way:

> The first God, being in himself, is simple (ἁπλοῦς), and being together with himself throughout can never be divided. The God who is the second and third, however, is one (εἷς). (Num. fr. 11.11–14 = 6V BS)

This passage has occasioned numerous discussions in the secondary literature.[22] While I shall not dwell on it, since it does not directly concern the topic at hand, I would mention that Numenius, in this passage, establishes a distinction between the first God in his absolute simplicity, and the other, the second God, who doubles himself. The evocation of this hierarchy of three distinct Gods presented by Numenius, as the legacy of authoritative sources, could serve Eusebius' purpose: to find traces in some pagan exegetes of a dim prefiguration of the trinitarian doctrine.[23]

What I would like to do now is to show how Numenian theology – at least as far as it is possible to reconstruct it – is in turn presented by Proclus in the *Commentary on the Timaeus*. We are indeed confronted with the following paradox: on the one hand Proclus, apart from a few quotations in Eusebius, is an essential source of our knowledge of the theology of Numenius, while, on the other hand Proclus is at the origin of the *damnatio memoriae* – because of his radical dualism in ethics and cosmology and of his rejection of Aristotelian doctrines – to which Numenius was condemned in later Neoplatonism, and from which he would not soon recover.[24] Unlike Eusebius, Proclus does not subordinate Plato's authority to that of someone else. Proclus, interestingly enough, does not present exactly the same triadic organisation of Numenian theology: he does not take into account the unity of the second and third Gods and instead stresses what he sees as Numenius' conflation of the first God and the demiurge. Proclus interprets divine hierarchies through the lens of Plotinian theology. In the framework of a philosophical history of interpretations of the demiurge, Proclus offers a quick presentation of Numenian theology which he fiercely criticises in order to better highlight, by contrast, the authoritative figure from which a rigorous history of interpretations of the demiurge can truly begin, namely Plotinus.

---

[22] I would refer the reader to the fundamental study of Frede 1987. For a discussion of the problems posed by this fragment, see Michalewski 2014: 93–6.

[23] Karamanolis 2013.

[24] For a discussion of the reception of Numenian theology and Proclus' work seeking to undermine what Boys-Stones has called a certain 'pan-Numenianism' running from Amelius to Iamblichus, see Athanassiadi 2018: 203–5.

## 6.2 The Demiurge in Numenian Theology

A reconstruction of Numenius' theological doctrine is hard to achieve, given the fragmentary and partially indirect state in which his doctrine has reached us. Going into the details of this reconstruction would lead me far beyond the scope of this contribution:[25] rather, I would like simply to recall certain elements textually reported by Eusebius before examining the choices made by Proclus in Numenius' doctrines.

There is a first God, exempt from all productive activity (ἀργός),[26] and even from all intellective duality.[27] In the Numenian excerpts selected by Eusebius, we found evidence of a distinction between the first God and the demiurge linked to the production of the world: a distinction which Eusebius himself uses in a Christian context, when he distinguishes the figure of God the Father from that of God the creator.[28] The second God is himself divided into two different figures: one only exercising intellectual functions, the other being the demiurge of the sensible realm, who has the task of subjecting matter to the intelligible order.[29] This hierarchical distinction allows Numenius to spare the first intellect the burden of acting like an artisan with respect to the matter of the world, the supreme God not being apt to create in the manner of a mere craftsman.[30] Proclus, while acknowledging that Numenius establishes this distinction between the first and the second God, highlights that this distinction is *in fine* ineffective, because he does not take into account that the first principle must be located beyond being and intellect. In *in Ti.* 1.303.27–306.15, Proclus refers to a selection of Middle Platonic testimonies extolling, by

---

[25] On this difficult point I refer to Opsomer 2006a.

[26] Num. fr. 12.13. On the use of the adjective *argos* in this fragment, see Flamand 1992: 158 and Staab 2009: 76–81, who carefully investigates the Pythagorean nature of this distinction between the first God, who is *argos*, and the second, who is involved in the production of the world.

[27] Num. fr. 22. On this question and the meaning of *proschrēsis*, see Frede 1987: 1062 and Michalewski 2012: 36–7. More recently, Calabi 2017 has studied the Numenian distinction between the first and the second God through the prism of the image of the planter and the sower in fr. 13. For a detailed study of the textual problems posed by this fragment, see Whittaker 1984: VIII.

[28] For a more detailed analysis of this point, and of the reception of Numenian theology in the Patristic tradition, I refer to Mathieu 2007: 259–61. As Whittaker 1984: VIII 153 points out, in the context of the late second century, 'this Platonic debate on the acceptability of the notion of divine paternity is an essential presupposition of the Arian controversy. It was precisely the view of Arius that only metaphorically can God be described as Father.'

[29] Num. fr. 12.2–4. Beyond the question of divine levels and of the Numenian hierarchy, Petrucci 2018: 114–15 examines the question of Plutarch's demiurgy (as God's ordering of irrational matter) and, from a broader perspective, the Epicurean criticism of the origin of the order of the world.

[30] On this question, I refer to Opsomer 2005a. See also Zambon 2002: 221–2; Dillon 1996: 366–72; Boys-Stones 2018a: chap. VI.3.4.

# Constructing Authority in the Theology of Numenius 139

contrast, the excellence of Plotinus,[31] whom he turns into the first link of the truly philosophical history of the interpretation of the figure of the demiurge.[32] Reading Plato according to an interpretative perspective proposed by his authoritative teacher Syrianus, Proclus presents a summary of Numenius' theses in *in Ti.* 1.303.27–304.22, which, taken in the general doxographic presentation of *in Ti.* 1.303.27–305.16, ends up achieving a paradoxical reversal: even though Numenius conceives of the first principle as being unified and isolated from the sensible world, as an author he should be grouped not so much with Plotinus as with Atticus, who brings together the demiurge and the Good into a single entity. What justifies such proximity is the fact that all Middle Platonic theologies share the same fundamental mistake: a misunderstanding of the nature of the first principle, which is always thought of as an entity 'in relation to' something, i.e. an entity which we can coordinate in a series.[33]

This passage is found within the framework of the commentary on *Timaeus* 28c3–5. Before dealing with the *lexis*, i.e. the examination of the meaning of the terms employed by Plato in this section of the text, Proclus sets out by reminding us of the numerous difficulties posed by the identification of the figure of the demiurge and the articulation of the terms 'Father' and 'Maker' which, according to his reading, do not refer to two distinct entities, but to two ways of exercising causality.[34] The passage which we are tackling here is found immediately after the *lexis* and opens the very long section on *theōria*, which itself rests on the architecture of a whole structured on multiple levels: a kind of 'prehistory' of the interpretations of the demiurge, corresponding to the Middle Platonic readings, the philosophical history of which begins with Plotinus and follows a non-linear development. The true interpretation of the nature of the demiurge manifests itself in stages and finds its culmination in Syrianus' presentation. Within this history, Platonic thinkers before Plotinus serve as supporting actors, so to speak. Proclus chooses three of them: Numenius, Harpocration, and Atticus. These authors are not discussed in chronological order, but rather in a progression which illustrates in detail the

---

[31] The Proclean selection and the interpretation of Numenius provided by the Neoplatonic commentator is studied by Tarrant 2004: 184–5, in a different perspective from the one proposed here. Tarrant highlights Proclus' biases in order to show that he undoubtedly had no first-hand access to Numenius' texts, but was probably using Porphyry's testimony as his starting point.

[32] Procl. *in Ti.* 1.305.16–17.    [33] Procl. *in Ti.* 1.304.6–7.

[34] Procl. *in Ti.* 1.300.8–13. On the inversion of the Platonic formula of *Ti.* 28c3 (ποιητὴν καὶ πατέρα, 'Maker and Father') by Numenius, see Ferrari 2014.

140 ALEXANDRA MICHALEWSKI

consequences of the conceptions which make the first principle an intellect or an intelligible reality. Atticus is presented as the one who commits the quintessential Middle Platonic mistake of confusing the demiurge with the Good. In this three-stage progression, starting from Numenius and ending with Atticus, Harpocration is seen to be familiar with – and to return to – the theses of these two great exegetes, combining their different aspects. It thus seems as though, for Proclus, only one intermediate author, Harpocration, is enough to make Numenius and Atticus' proximity understood. In a nutshell, Proclus returns to that which, in Numenius, can corroborate a doxographical presentation of the nature of the demiurge within the context of the commentary on *Timaeus* 28c3–5 – even if it is not certain that Numenius had properly commented on this passage of the *Timaeus*.[35] He briefly indicates that Numenius distinguishes between three Gods: the first called *patēr*, the second *poiētēs*, and the third *poiēma*.[36]

> Numenius celebrates three Gods. The first he calls 'Father', the second he calls 'Maker', the third he calls 'Product', for in his view the cosmos is the third God. As a result, according to him the Demiurge is double, the first God and the second, while what is produced by him is the third God. (Procl. *in Ti.* 1.303.27–304.3, trans. Share in Runia & Share 2008)[37]

The identification of a third God with the world is an aspect which is not of significant interest to Proclus: instead, it is mostly his interpretation of the double epithet of *Ti.* 28c3–5 which is subject to criticism. The reasoning is very terse, as is shown by the almost immediate use of the conjunction 'as a result' (*hōste*): Proclus does not bother to justify his logical reasoning or to clarify certain details. Here is his argument: 'Father' and 'Maker' are two epithets which both apply to the demiurge of the *Timaeus*. Numenius interpreted this doubling of the terms as referring to

---

[35] Cf. Dillon 1991: 144. Tarrant 2000: 85 suggests that it is likely that Numenius had not presented his exegesis in actual commentaries, which would explain the fact that the later commentators only sparsely mention it. According to Tarrant, Proclus essentially presents the Numenian theses through the lens of what Porphyry had grasped – that is, in his interpretation of the prologue of the *Timaeus* and the Atlantis story.

[36] For a discussion of the identification of the world with the third God, which is perhaps related to the fact that Plato, in the *Timaeus* (92c7), calls the world a *theos aisthētos*, I refer to the analyses by Opsomer 2006a: 270. This scholar points out that, in all likelihood, the world is not called a God in reference to its material dimension, but rather with respect to its order (an order which may be identified with the soul of the world). In particular, he discusses Festugière's (1954: 124) interpretation, according to which it is the world as it exists in the demiurge's mind which is a God.

[37] Νουμήνιος μὲν γὰρ τρεῖς ἀνυμνήσας θεοὺς πατέρα μὲν καλεῖ τὸν πρῶτον, ποιητὴν δὲ τὸν δεύτερον, ποίημα δὲ τὸν τρίτον· ὁ γὰρ κόσμος κατ᾽ αὐτὸν ὁ τρίτος ἐστὶ θεός· ὥστε ὁ κατ᾽ αὐτὸν δημιουργὸς διττός, ὅ τε πρῶτος θεὸς καὶ ὁ δεύτερος, τὸ δὲ δημιουργούμενον ὁ τρίτος.

## Constructing Authority in the Theology of Numenius 141

two distinct entities, the 'Father' and the 'Maker'.[38] While Numenius is not wrong in distinguishing different divine levels, he carries out this task incorrectly. In distinguishing the 'Maker' from the 'Father', he needlessly doubles the figure of the demiurge and completely misses the real nature of the first principle, the One, which is itself the origin of the fatherly function of derived principles. With this erroneous distinction that separates the Father from the Maker, Numenius considers each of these entities as being one demiurge. This is where his main mistake lies: in attributing a common characteristic to the first God and to the maker of the sensible world. Furthermore, there is evidence of this procedure in the excerpts reported by Eusebius.[39] In *Praep. evang.* 11.22, Eusebius shows how Numenius, starting from an analysis of book 6 of the *Republic*, conceives divine hierarchies in an analogous way: just as there is a demiurge responsible for becoming, there is a 'demiurge of being'.

> And if the demiurge of *becoming* is good, well of course the demiurge of being will be the good-itself, an innate feature of being. (Num. fr. 16.8–10, my translation)[40]

Proclus develops a whole different reading of the *Republic* in connection to the second part of the *Parmenides*, according to which the Good is beyond any and all relation and any and all analogy. What he highlights is the fact that, by calling the first God 'Father', Numenius bestows upon him a trait which belongs to the demiurge. In doing so, he engenders confusion between the first God and the demiurge and relegates the first principle to an inferior level, making the Good a cause, so to speak, comparable to another demiurgical cause, which considerably weakens its transcendence.[41] Thus, it is not right to call the first principle 'Father' for two reasons: (1) the fatherly principle is posterior to the One and (2) 'Father and Maker' are not two distinct realities, but two names for the same demiurge.[42] Numenius is wrong to confuse the two levels, dissociating the Father from the producer. However, as Proclus remarks, he is not so much

---

[38] This doubling does not agree with previous interpretations, e.g. Plutarch's (*Quaest. Plat.* 2.1001A4–B6), for whom these two terms refer to two distinct aspects of divine demiurgy. For him, the production of the world, which is a living thing, is irreducible to a simple artisanal fabrication: this is the reason why God is simultaneously the producer and the father of the world.

[39] On this point, see Bonazzi 2004 and Opsomer 2005a.

[40] Εἴπερ δὲ ὁ δημιουργὸς ὁ τῆς γενέσεώς ἐστιν ἀγαθός, ἦ που ἔσται καὶ ὁ τῆς οὐσίας δημιουργὸς αὐτοάγαθον, σύμφυτον τῇ οὐσίᾳ. On this point, see Reydams-Schils 2007: 253–5, who examines the parallels between the Numenian hierarchies and Calcidian theology.

[41] Opsomer 2006a: 269–70.   [42] Procl. *in Ti.* 1.304.13–22.

## 142 ALEXANDRA MICHALEWSKI

to blame when he uses this vocabulary in relation to the demiurge as when he presents the divine hierarchies with the aid of unsuitable terminology:

> ... for it is better to speak in this way rather than to say in his theatrical manner: grandfather, child (ἔγγονος), grandchild. (Procl. *in Ti.* 1.304.3–5, trans. Share in Runia & Share 2008)[43]

M. Bonazzi has advanced the hypothesis that the term ἔγγονος could mean that, in explaining the divine hierarchies, Numenius had not only the *Timaeus* in mind, but also the *Republic* (506d7–507a5), where Socrates defines the sun as the ἔγγονος of the Good.[44] To this hypothesis another one can be added without contradiction. According to A. Longo, the use of divine names could be the trace of an allegorical reading of the Hesiodic myth of Ouranos – which would come from Numenius' Pythagorean affiliations – in which Ouranos is the grandfather, Kronos his son, and Zeus the grandson.[45] Numenius would have given these God-principles the same family ties as those established in the Hesiodic myth.

Numenius' criticism allows Proclus to introduce the interpretations of Harpocration – a Platonic author about whom we are ill-informed.[46] Proclus attributes to Harpocration a view very similar to Numenius', in whose footsteps he follows: he also accepts three Gods, he duplicates the demiurge (1.304.25–6), and he develops an allegorical exegesis of Hesiodic theogony.[47] His way of duplicating is, however, slightly different because he duplicates each one of the Gods, giving each a double name: he calls the first God 'Ouranos and Kronos', the second 'Zeus and Zen', the third 'Heaven (οὐρανός) and Cosmos'. Later, says Proclus (1.304.28), Harpocration changed his mind (μεταβαλών) in his interpretation. The

---

[43] ἄμεινον γὰρ οὕτω λέγειν, ἢ ὡς ἐκεῖνος λέγει προστραγῳδῶν, πάππον, ἔγγονον, ἀπόγονον.

[44] Bonazzi 2017–2018: 132–3; Tarrant 2004: 184–5.

[45] Longo 2017: 171–6. Hadot 1981: 124 rightly remarks that Numenius is following the advice given about this Hesiodic myth by Plato in the *Republic*: either to keep silent about it, or to reserve its interpretation to a few initiates. Only an allegorical reading of this myth reveals the theological meaning of divine filiations, obscured by the crudeness of the Hesiodic narrative. For a detailed explanation of the Plotinian interpretation of this myth, according to which Ouranos, Kronos, and Zeus are related to the three hypostases, see Hadot 1981 and Pépin 1995.

[46] In addition to his *Lexicon*, Harpocration had written a commentary on Plato's works in twenty-four volumes. For more details, see Whittaker 1984: XXIV and 2000; Dillon 1991: XIV; Gioè 2002; Petrucci 2014: 334; Lakman 2017: 122–7; and recently Ferrari 2018. Following Whittaker 1984, who brought attention to the opening lines of a summary of Psellus that mention Harpocration, Rashed 2016: IV 1 has recently edited and translated the text in its entirety, which he suggests is a scholium on Proclus' lost commentary on the *Phaedrus*. In this text, we find an indication that Harpocration was a source to which the geometer Serenus referred in order to understand Platonic thought, and more specifically, that Harpocration held that human souls change into animal souls as a punishment for their misdeeds, a hypothesis which Proclus rejected.

[47] On this point, see Gioè 2002: 483–4 and Longo 2017: 174–6.

verb *metaballō* (μεταβάλλω, here as the aorist participle μεταβαλών) is typical of Proclus' vocabulary, where it is used to highlight a contradiction found in an exegete. We find it, for example, a few pages later, in *in Ti.* 1.393.1, with regard to Atticus: after having initially stated that it is in the very nature of the divine principle to be productive (1.392.28–30), Atticus then changes his view, declaring that God can exist without producing anything. Harpocration too changed his mind, for after having called the first God 'Ouranos and Kronos', he called him 'Zeus and King of the intelligible realm'. The first God would therefore be named 'Ouranos and Kronos' as well as 'Zeus', whereas before 'Zeus' was only one of the names of the second God. Harpocration thus establishes, from Proclus' point of view, a dangerous confusion between the first and the second God by using the name 'Zeus' indifferently for both. Now, this confusion adds to a first confusion linked to the name *ouranos* itself, which serves both as a proper noun, as in the case of the first God, and as a common noun (the heaven, the world), in the case of the third God. Thus, Proclus can argue that Harpocration indifferently names the first God with names which also suit the second and third Gods, and he ironically asks himself whether Harpocration himself would had been satisfied with this disastrous classification. Actually, it is very unlikely that Harpocration contradicted himself in the same exegetical passage. On the other hand, it is more likely that Proclus, relying on Porphyry, proceeded to provide a reconstruction by summarising Harpocration's views – and especially by assembling different exegeses developed by this author in different contexts in order to immediately point to a contradiction.[48] Indeed, if we read the Proclean presentation, we find that from Numenius to Harpocration things worsen, so to speak: Numenius thinks of the first principle as a demiurge, which means that he uses an inferior category to think of a superior principle, and thus mingles distinct registers. Harpocration makes an even more serious mistake, for he no longer respects even Numenius' hierarchies and confuses all three levels of divinity.

This passage has sparked numerous discussions in the secondary literature. Two main options have been proposed. According to J. Dillon, Harpocration is highly reliant on Numenius with regard to the interpretation of divine hierarchies, where he opposes Atticus – whom he follows, however, on the question of the real genesis of the universe.[49] More recently, G. Boys-Stones has adopted the converse perspective, proposing that Harpocration's theses gain meaning if we consider the general

---

[48] Dillon 1991: 144.    [49] Dillon 1991: 143.

144 ALEXANDRA MICHALEWSKI

structure of the metaphysics of Atticus, his teacher, who gives a renewed interpretation of the divine hierarchies of *Cratylus* 395e–396c.[50] My own interpretation does not conflict with these two, but rather suggests that we shift our perspective, as it were. Instead of trying to bring Harpocration closer to either Numenius or Atticus, I would like to focus on Proclus' choice to assign him a middle ground between those two masters. Indeed, it seems to me that in presenting the three exegetes in a progression which is not chronological, Proclus gives Harpocration a particular role: to mark a transition between Numenius and Atticus. From Proclus' point of view, insofar as the demiurge is concerned, the Middle Platonists all belong to a period which precedes truly philosophical interpretation. This granted, Numenius and Atticus both developed one of the two sides of the same fundamental mistake. The former distinguishes the first God from the demiurge but brings the two together by assigning them demiurgic functions. The latter reunites them into one single entity but is later forced to establish complicated and aporetical distinctions between the two different levels.[51]

Atticus is mentioned last, despite his being Harpocration's teacher.[52] That is probably because Atticus represents, from Proclus' point of view, a kind of radicalisation of Numenius' and Harpocration's theses.[53] Contrary to the other two philosophers, he only admits one single demiurgic figure but, just like them, he strips the first principle of its transcendence, in a way, for he identifies the demiurge with the first principle. By pushing these theses to their extreme, Atticus serves as a foil to Plotinus who, for the first time, distinguishes very neatly the first principle from all other derivative realities: the One, the first principle, is beyond being, beyond intellect, and is completely different from all that derives from it. Atticus makes a fundamental mistake: the demiurge is surely called 'good' by Plato but being good (*agathos*) is not equivalent to being *the* Good (*to agathon*)[54] – that simply means that it participates of the Good. What all these mistaken interpretations have in common is the fact that they make the first God a reality which stands in relation to something other than itself. That ends up causing confusion between the first principle and the

---

[50] Boys-Stones 2011.   [51] Procl. *in Ti.* 1.305.11–16.

[52] As noted by Dörrie & Baltes 1993: 180–1, Harpocration was an erudite and prolific author, one who was attached to the *lexis* of the text, just like his master Atticus. His exegeses took the form of *aporiai kai lyseis*. According to a scholium on Procl. *In R.* 2.10.6 ff., Harpocration and Atticus interpreted the word γενητόν in *Ti.* 28b7 as indicating the generation of the world κατὰ χρόνον.

[53] Lernould 2001: 256.

[54] This distinction is presented by Numenius in fr. 20.4–7 (= Euseb. *Praep. evang.* 11.22).

## Constructing Authority in the Theology of Numenius 145

demiurgic level. According to Proclus, the demiurge corresponds to the activity of the intellective intellect, which itself derives from an infinitely superior power.[55] Proclus' chief achievement in this doxographic passage is that he manages to reconstruct an exegetical framework which allows him to associate Numenius' and Atticus' theories by postulating only a single intermediary between them, namely Harpocration.

Plotinus, who is mentioned immediately after, is presented as a figure who marks a break and contrast: Proclus only highlights the points of disagreement between the philosopher and his predecessors.[56] Now, according to Proclus, the break introduced by Plotinus is at the same time the beginning of a properly philosophical history of the exegesis of the Platonic demiurge, culminating with Syrianus. By establishing the foundations of a metaphysical structure inspired by a theological reading of the second part of the *Parmenides*, Plotinus inaugurates a philosophical tradition to which Proclus himself belongs. It is from this viewpoint that a more detailed exegesis of specific points in the Platonic text is later provided. Insofar as he has clearly dissociated the demiurge from the One, which lies radically beyond being and intellect, Plotinus represents the first figure to have authoritatively analysed *Timaeus* 28c. At this point in the commentary, Proclus does not mention the difference between his own conception of the demiurge (who corresponds to the lowest component of the first Intellective triad) and that of Plotinus, who does not establish such sophisticated hierarchies in the intelligible world. For Proclus, the important thing is that Plotinus places the demiurge in the intelligible realm, with no possible confusion with the One. Here, certain nuances are to be ignored, for it is a matter of underlining the difference between two moments in the history of the interpretation of the Platonic demiurge. According to Proclus, Plotinus – just like Numenius before him – theorises the existence of a 'double demiurge'.[57] But, unlike the Middle Platonic exegete, he proposes a correct interpretation of this: one demiurge remains in the intelligible, while the other governs the universe. Proclus' version is rather surprising. First of all, in his treatises, Plotinus never talks about a 'double demiurge'. We only find – in *Enn.* 4.4(28).10.1 – mention of a 'double ordering principle' (τὸ κοσμοῦν διττόν): the intellect and the world soul. While Plotinus, so to speak, empties the demiurge of all artisanal functions, he keeps the reference to the term 'demiurge' all the

---

[55] Trouillard 1958.
[56] Proclus ignores the fact that Plotinus also calls the One a 'father' – for instance in *Enn.* 5.1(10).8.4.
[57] Procl. *in Ti.* 1.305.17: ὁ φιλόσοφος διττὸν μὲν ὑποτίθεται τὸν δημιουργόν.

same – out of loyalty to Plato's text – which he identifies as the unmoved divine intellect that produces an image of itself all while remaining in itself.[58] Reserving the substantive *dēmiourgos* for the intellect, he nevertheless attributes to the soul (and to nature) the exercise of a *dēmiourgia* which consists in applying the forms to the sensibles. Proclus thus condenses and modifies Plotinus' views by attributing the theory of a *dēmiourgos dittos* to him.[59] The doubling of the demiurge is something that is achieved rather by Numenius, who talks about the internal division of the second God.[60] Yet, this theory is not preserved by Proclus, who attributes to Numenius another form of doubling, which he criticises: he blames him not for having split the second God, but for having unduly transferred certain features of the demiurge to the first principle. To a certain extent, this fundamental error, according to Proclus, is a typical Middle Platonic mistake. In his view, Plotinus was the first to interpret Platonic philosophy as a whole, and its hierarchies of principles, in the light of the second part of the *Parmenides*; as such, he marks the beginning of the true philosophical interpretation, which culminates with Syrianus. Indeed, Plotinus was the first to clearly distinguish the intellective level – that of the demiurge – from the One which, being absolutely first, is beyond all levels which derive from it. It is by leaning on these sources of authority that Proclus can, in retrospect, compose this Middle Platonic triptych, bringing together Numenius, Harpocration, and Atticus.

### 6.3   Conclusion

Numenius is an author whose work only survives in a few fragments, which have reached us through a complex process of indirect transmission: Eusebius, through the excerpts he selects, provides a particular perspective on Numenius' words, which are framed within the general context of the apologetic arguments of the *Praeparatio evangelica*. In these excerpts, Numenius is pictured as an author who established a relationship between

[58] For more in-depth developments on this question, linked to the abandoning of the artificialist model in cosmology and to the new interpretation, offered by Plotinus, of the causality of the intellect and of the Forms, I shall refer to Michalewski 2014: 185–97.

[59] For more details on the Proclean reading of Plotinus' supposed 'double demiurge', see Opsomer 2005b: 79–89 and 2006a: 271–3. He draws our attention to the fact that here, for contextual argumentative reasons, Proclus does not mention the difference between his own conception of the demiurge (which corresponds to the third of the three intellective Gods) and that of Plotinus, which does not establish a hierarchy in the intelligible, the important thing for Proclus being here that Plotinus places the demiurge in the intelligible, with no possible confusion with the One.

[60] See Dillon 1996: 367–72.

# Constructing Authority in the Theology of Numenius    147

different sources of authority, with the aim of updating the definition of Platonic identity as resting on a system of fidelity to a certain teaching supposedly derived from Pythagoras – and quite distinct from the successive changes introduced by the Academic *diadochoi*. What is striking in the passages of Numenius preserved by Eusebius is that Numenius posits three figures of authority: Pythagoras, Socrates, and Plato, which are perfectly compatible, since they each express in their own way one and the same truth. Presenting Socrates as a Pythagorean theologian, Numenius sets himself in relation to that authority in order to support his own theological triad, which in turn serves Eusebius' apologetical purpose. According to Proclus, this triadic theology leads to an erroneous interpretation of both the first principle and the demiurge. Instead of this wrong reading, Proclus presents his own interpretation of the demiurge, based on the exegetical authority of Plotinus and Syrianus. To be sure, Numenius and Proclus conceive the authority of Plato in quite different ways. However, both introduce, alongside a primary and fundamental source of authority, lineages of loyal exegetes on one hand and of unfaithful heirs on the other.

Bestowing authority on a source means establishing a selection and system aimed at bringing one's arguments in line with the source that is being invoked. While Numenius uses the authority of Socrates and Pythagoras to present himself as a real and legitimate heir to Plato, Proclus, for his part, uses the exegetical authority of Plotinus and Syrianus to extend to Numenius a criticism directed at other Middle Platonists. This procedure is evident in the doxographical presentation of *in Ti.* 1.303.27–305.16. If we compare the passage of Numenius' treatise *On the Good* (fr. 11) and this testimony of Proclus, it is clear that the divine triplicity is not presented in the same manner. In fragment 11, we get a close connection between the second and the third God, whereas Proclus emphasises the close connection between the first and the second God,[61] which better serves his specific polemical aim in this context. Proclus – who in all likelihood did not have first-hand access to Numenius' writing, but worked on Porphyrian material – reformulates elements of Numenius' allegorical theology in order to develop a criticism intended to show the weakness of the Middle Platonic interpretations of the demiurge. From Proclus' point of view, all Middle Platonists misinterpreted the nature of

---

[61] I would like to thank Gretchen Reydams-Schils for her suggestions on this point. The interpretation of Proclus, which is obviously controversial, finds, however, some confirmation in Numenius' texts, such as fr. 16, which establishes an analogy between the demiurge of being and the demiurge of becoming.

the demiurge and its true ontological status, even if this common error was formulated in different ways. By contrast, this criticism brings out the value of the interpretation proposed by Plotinus, who, by using the hypotheses from the second part of the *Parmenides* to think about divine hierarchies, marks the beginning of the properly philosophical history of the exegeses of the Platonic demiurge and retrospectively appears to be an authoritative source on this question.

CHAPTER 7

# *Plutarch's* E at Delphi
## *The Hypothesis of Platonic Authority*

### George Boys-Stones

## 7.1 Introduction

In his seminal article on philosophical authority published in 1997, David Sedley showed that, in antiquity, the founder of a philosophical school was taken as figure of 'authority' by subsequent members of the school, who would carefully avoid expressing disagreement with him. What is more, the reason for their deference was not purely formal, or political: the authority with which school-members invested the founder of their school was epistemic as well, in the sense that it involved some level of concern to know and be guided by their founder's views. But this is far from the end of the story. As Jan Opsomer and Angela Ulacco have been careful to describe subsequently, 'epistemic authority' ranges widely in sense and strength: from uncritical assent to the truth of whatever can be gleaned from the authority-figure within a given domain, to the belief that their views might help to point one in the right direction.[1] Where one stands on this question might make all the difference to the character of one's philosophical project.

On the face of it, Platonists seem to lie on the 'fundamentalist' end of the spectrum: it seems that they take Plato's views to be sufficient justification for the beliefs that they adopt. It seems this way, because Platonists appear more interested in the views of their founder than members of almost any other school, and less ready – in fact, altogether unprepared – to countenance disagreement with him. (There has been some debate in the literature over the extent to which this represents a point of divergence with other schools; but what is in question in this debate is more the flexibility of the other schools on the question than the rigidity of Platonists.) But in this paper I want to make the case that 'fundamentalism' is exactly the wrong conclusion to draw from the evidence. If it were

---

[1] Opsomer & Ulacco 2016: esp. 28.

149

the right conclusion, and Platonists took Plato's deliverances to be sufficient justification for their own beliefs, then there would be something 'fideistic' about Platonism.[2] But we know that Platonists were in fact appalled by the idea that one might allow oneself to be guided by blind faith: at least, that is the clear impression one gets from Celsus' reaction to the epistemic behaviour of Christians.[3] Instead, then, I want to make the case for a very different explanation for their behaviour towards Plato. Surprising at it may sound, the epistemic authority with which Platonists invested Plato actually lay on the 'weaker' end of the Opsomer–Ulacco scale. Platonists are philosophers who, for one reason or another, merely come to think or hope that Plato was right, or that he could point one in the right direction.[4] The reason that they seem more fundamentalist has to do with methodology. Having come to the view that Plato might be right, or stands a greater chance of being right than anyone else whose views are available to them, Platonists see that the natural thing for them to do is to *assume* Plato's being right, that is, as a kind of 'working hypothesis'. (One might think of this, in fact, as an adaptation of the very 'method of hypothesis' recommended by Plato in the Line image of the *Republic*, to which I shall return below.) The assumption of Plato's infallibility, in other words, is precisely that – an assumption; and, indeed, from time to time our texts make it very clear that Platonic exegesis is distinct from the search for epistemic justification – and in principle at least the day might come when the hypothesis is falsified.[5]

Another way of saying this is that Plato's epistemic authority for a Platonist is more like that of a teacher than that of a prophet: a pupil makes progress by relying on (assuming the truth of) what the teacher teaches her. But here is the real irony as far as the question of 'authority' is concerned: the pupil only knows that she did well to trust the teacher at the point where she grasps the truth for herself; or, to put this another way, the pupil can only be sure of the teacher's epistemic authority when she no longer needs it – that is, because she can see the truth for herself. And so it is for Platonists and Plato: Platonists submit to be guided by Plato, but aim

---

[2] This is the case even allowing that they might have explanations to give for how Plato acquired his knowledge, for example along the lines I suggested in Boys-Stones 2001: ch. 6.

[3] Origen, *Contra Celsum* 1.9; cf. 3.14, 18, 38.

[4] For example, they might come to the view that Plato deserves exploration as the only, or the most promising alternative to scepticism: see Boys-Stones 2001: ch. 7; 2018a: ch. 1.

[5] See esp. Plutarch, *De procr. an.* 1014A and Numenius fr. 1a des Places (= 2J and 2K BS respectively). The general position, that Platonist 'faith' in Plato is conditional not absolute is one that I first ventured in Boys-Stones 2001: ch. 7.

## The Hypothesis of Platonic Authority

to understand for themselves – and *can* only know that Plato was a reliable guide when they do.

This position on Platonic authority is, I believe, dramatically exemplified in Plutarch's *De E apud Delphos*. It has been remarked that this work has a special place in our understanding of Plutarch's philosophy – not least because the final speech, by the character Ammonius, gives us one of the clearest statements of what we have to assume is Plutarch's own metaphysical outlook.[6] But the stages leading up to the speech of Ammonius are important as well, because, as I hope to show, they map out the long intellectual ascent that leads to the position occupied by Ammonius – and in doing so, invite us to think about the role played by the teacher (which is the same in kind as the role played by Plato) in helping the student to get there.

### 7.2 Plato's Line and the *De E*

The programmatic status of the *De E* is clear from its very beginning. The work has a frame in which it is presented as the first of a series of discussions (the so-called Πυθικοὶ λόγοι) intended to form part of an exchange with Plutarch's friends in Athens:

> I am sending you – and by way of you to your friends there – some 'Pythian discussions' as first-fruits, so to speak; and I look forward to others from you – more and better, since you have the resources of a large city, more leisure among plentiful books, and the opportunity of all sorts of conversations. (*De E* 384E)[7]

The *De E* is in this way framed both to exemplify and also to create the conditions for philosophical discussion: it is the representation of a discussion (real or fictional, it hardly matters); and it is also the first move in a dialogue between Chaeronea and Athens – or, specifically, between Plutarch and his circle on the one hand and that of his addressee, Sarapion, on the other.

The *Pythikoi logoi* are sometimes referred to in English as the 'Pythian dialogues'; but the *De E* is not a 'dialogue' in the Platonic or Academic mould. It does not set up theories to put them to the test (as normally in

---

[6] Ferrari 1995: 39 calls the work a 'manifesto' for Plutarch's Platonism; cf. 2010: 71.
[7] ἐγὼ γοῦν πρὸς σὲ καὶ διὰ σοῦ τοῖς αὐτόθι φίλοις τῶν Πυθικῶν λόγων ἐνίους ὥσπερ ἀπαρχὰς ἀποστέλλων ὁμολογῶ προσδοκᾶν ἑτέρους καὶ πλείονας καὶ βελτίονας παρ' ὑμῶν, ἅτε δὴ καὶ πόλει χρωμένων μεγάλῃ καὶ σχολῆς μᾶλλον ἐν βιβλίοις πολλοῖς καὶ παντοδαπαῖς διατριβαῖς εὐπορούντων.

152 GEORGE BOYS-STONES

Plato); nor does it bring rival theories into debate with each other (as, for example, in Cicero). Instead, the discussion is structured as a more or less discrete series of attempts to explain its focal question: why models of the letter E had been dedicated to Apollo in his temple at Delphi.[8] But if they are discrete, in the sense that none directly addresses or corrects the philosophical content of any other, that is not to say that they are uncoordinated. In fact, it is very clear that they are arranged so that the explanations offered for the Delphic E increase in sophistication as the dialogue progresses, beginning as they do from a more or less frivolous suggestion by Plutarch's brother Lamprias and ending with the sublime essay on the nature of being put in the mouth of Plutarch's teacher, Ammonius.[9] It has also been noted that the explanations do not simply increase in their sophistication, but more specifically appeal to ever higher intellectual faculties as they do so, and that they map out stages on an ideal educational 'curriculum', leading us from the merely empirical, through the scientific, and finally to the metaphysical.[10]

It has usually been supposed that the structural inspiration for this curriculum is the 'ladder' which, in Plato's *Symposium*, takes us in stages from the empirical to the metaphysical (cf. esp. 211c).[11] But I want to make the case that Plutarch has another Platonic proof-text in mind, one less oriented towards the ontological status of the objects of study, and more towards the cognitive state of the student: the Line image in *Republic* 6.509d–513e.[12] If the Line has been overlooked by previous commentators, this is perhaps because, at first glance, the 'fit' with the speeches of the *De E* is not obvious. The Line has just *four* segments, corresponding to the cognitive faculties of *eikasia*, *pistis*, *dianoia* and *noēsis*. But there are, depending on how you count them, at least five and perhaps as many as seven contributions to the attempt to explain the Delphic E.[13] The voices,

---

[8] For historical discussion of the E, see Berman & Losada 1975.

[9] On Ammonius, who plays a vital role in the argument I shall be unfolding, see Opsomer 2009a.

[10] E.g. Bonazzi 2008: esp. 206 ('un vero e proprio *cursus studiorum*'); Simonetti 2017: 119, 123. Although my claim is that this pattern becomes in some sense the real theme of the *De E* itself (considered, that is, as a programmatic work), it is no coincidence that the very same pattern structures first-order discussions of philosophical 'problems' elsewhere in Plutarch: see e.g. Opsomer 2010.

[11] E.g. Moreschini 1997: 46; Simonetti 2017: 119.

[12] The suggestion that Plutarch has the Line in view is in no way exclusive with the suggestion that he is thinking about the *Symposium* too: in fact Plutarch elsewhere argues that the 'ascent' passage of the *Symposium* should be read against the Line (*Quaest. Plat.* 3.1002E; and cf. Alcinous, *Didaskalikos* 10).

[13] Commentators who count seven relevant positions include Babbitt 1936: 194–5. Lernould 2006 and Simonetti 2017: 119 count six (taking Eustrophus and Younger Plutarch together); I shall count five (eliding the Chaldean with Lamprias as well), as does e.g. Moreschini 1997: 46–7.

# The Hypothesis of Platonic Authority   153

certainly, are seven. These include: (1) Lamprias (who thinks that the E counts off five of the seven sages); (2) an unnamed Chaldean (who had apparently noted that E is the *second* of the vowels, and as such alludes to the *second* of the celestial bodies above the earth, namely the sun); (3) Nicander (who sees the word εἰ, 'if', in the E, and takes it to refer to questions addressed to the oracle about what will or ought to happen); (4) Theon (who agrees that the E means 'if', but construes it as a cardinal term in logical consequence ['if . . . then . . .'], and connects this with thinking both about geometry and fate, i.e. consequence in the realm of physical causality); (5) Eustrophus (returning to the idea that E is the numeral, 5, and connecting this to the study of arithmetic); (6) Younger Plutarch (as I shall refer to the speaker within the work, to distinguish him from Plutarch's authorial voice) (he develops Eustrophus' theme through a discussion of the mathematical sciences, and finally the Greater Kinds of the *Sophist*); and (7) Ammonius (for whom E = εἶ, 'you are', taken as an invitation to think about what it is *to be*, and especially for god to 'be').

If there are seven voices, however, it is not so clear that there are seven relevantly distinct positions. There is a strong case to be made that the number of relevant positions here is, in fact, just the number represented by E as a numeral: five. It is regularly and rightly observed that the two *characters* Eustrophus and Younger Plutarch count together as one *position*. As we shall see, the position is a slightly complex one, but the text is quite clear about their continuity. The authorial voice of Plutarch intervenes to comment that Eustrophus' position was framed to appeal to the position represented by this younger version of himself (387F); and Younger Plutarch takes over by affirming the solution offered by Eustrophus in the strongest possible terms: 'Eustrophus used number to give the best solution to the puzzle' (κάλλιστα τὸν Εὔστροφον τῷ ἀριθμῷ λύειν τὴν ἀπορίαν, 387F).

That brings the number of relevant positions down to six; but it seems to me that the text asks us to discount the 'Chaldean' as well. Modern readers have argued that the Chaldean brings astronomy to the table, and in this sense pushes us in a more scientific direction. One can dispute that in its own terms: there is nothing scientific about simply counting the sun as the second body from the centre of the universe (rather than, say,

---

Interestingly enough, Ammonius raises it as a question whether seven or five is really the most appropriate number for Apollo (391F), and the possibility of dividing out the positions to different effects (maximally seven, minimally five) might be related to this.

offering a proof that it is, or an explanation for why it is);[14] but more to the point, the characters within the *De E* quite clearly and explicitly assimilate the Chaldean theory with that of Lamprias, at least in terms of its intellectual level.[15] In fact it is mentioned, not as a contribution with its own right to be heard, so to speak, but only to say (a) that it is nonsense (ἐφλυάρει, 386A) and (b) that this is how we should think of Lamprias' theory which is the *same sort of thing* (ὅμοια ταῦτ' ἐστίν, 386A).

If all this is right, then the *De E* shows us *five* relevant positions – that is to say, five positions relevant to mapping an intellectual ascent. And whether or not the *Symposium* is also somewhere behind them, it is the cognitive taxonomy of the Line that gives us the vocabulary to describe them.

(1) Lamprias' explanation, to start with, is all 'report and hearsay' (ἱστορίαν καὶ ἀκοήν, 386A): in other words, it belongs in the arena of (bare) perception – but, more than this, of perception at second-hand. Lamprias has no experience of his own to draw on, and no evidence either. Ammonius suspects that it is a 'personal opinion' (ἰδίᾳ τὸν Λαμπρίαν δόξῃ κεχρῆσθαι, 386A: note that the lower portion of Plato's Line is 'the opinable', τὸ δοξαστόν, 510a): the point may be that it is a belief which is not shared just because there is no accounting for it. *Eikasia*, the lowest section of the Line, might be a fair description of the cognitive faculty behind it.

(2) Nicander's account (which is still *doxa*, but in this case an opinion which is shared: τὴν δὲ κοινὴν καὶ περιηγητικὴν δόξαν, 386B) differs from Lamprias' in kind, as being based in particular realities which are or can be experienced first-hand by petitioners to the oracle: what Nicander calls *pragmata* (386C), questions about what will happen, questions about what they ought to do, and expressions of what they wish would come about. It is just this level of thinking that Plato characterises as *pistis* (cf. τά τε περὶ ἡμᾶς, *Republic* 510a).

(3) Nicander contrasts his 'realities' with what he sees as the 'unreal' hypothetical concerns of the logician (386C) – and it is to defend the logician that Theon initially speaks up. But note that Theon does not only, or even principally, discuss logic.[16] He also brings in discussion of

---

[14] Having said this, it is worth noting that Plutarch himself probably agrees that the sun is the second of the stars (and cf. Plato, *Timaeus* 38c–d).

[15] One might make the case that the Chaldean view fails to find any real place in the dialogue at all: it is an anonymous position, remembered from *before* the dialogue started by someone unidentified within the *De E*.

[16] Baldassari 1993 not only exaggerates when he calls Theon's speech a small treatise in logic (esp. 41), but risks missing its real contribution to the economy of the work.

## The Hypothesis of Platonic Authority 155

geometry and fate – and in doing so he very clearly joins the company of those who work in the third portion of Plato's Line, 'people who busy themselves with geometry, reasoning (λογισμούς), and that sort of thing' (510c). This portion of the Line, *dianoia*, marks the transition from what is seen to what is thought (509e), and Theon makes just this point, that he is interested now not in what you can merely perceive, but what you can think (386E–387F).

This is a significant moment in the conversation; but it is important to recognise that, while Theon's contribution takes the discussion into properly philosophical territory for the first time, it goes no further than thought that is (a) discursive and (b) concerned with the empirical world. First, Theon's interest in logic here is confined to inference; but a Platonist will be keenly aware that it is a feature of inference that it can never take you in its conclusions to a higher ontological level than that on which the premises operate. Through inference you may be able to learn more things, but not as it were 'better' things. (Platonists by contrast recognised other procedures that fell under the rubric of 'logic' whose purpose was to bootstrap the mind from lower to higher cognitive states: especially, from experience of the world to contemplation of the forms.)[17] Secondly, Theon makes it clear that the level at which he is operating – and so, in which his logic is confined – is precisely that of the empirical world. He distinguishes perception (of which animals, too, are capable) from thought; but this thought is thought about the very same objects that animals perceive ('That it is day and light wolves and dogs and birds can perceive; that, if it is day, it is light only a human can understand,' 386F–387A). Similarly, when Theon talks about geometry, he has in mind geometry not as an abstract study, but as it might be applied to an empirical problem – in this case the doubling of a particular cuboid altar (namely, the altar at Delos: 386E).[18] Again, he can talk about fate in this context, because he thinks of logical inference as something that can track the sequence of empirical cause and effect which structures the unfolding of temporal events (387B).[19]

---

[17] See for example the procedures of 'induction' and 'analysis' in Alcinous, *Didaskalikos* 6 (= 14A [5.4–7] BS; cf. Boys-Stones 2018a: 406–8). Both procedures obviously have the roots in Aristotle, and although they are retooled in significant ways towards the Platonist ends for which Alcinous uses them, this might be one reason why Plutarch would want to characterise Theon's logic as Stoic (see n. 19: i.e. there is no danger that we might be tempted to think that he has relevant forms of induction and analysis up his sleeve as well).

[18] Contrast Eustrophus, who will phrase his own interest in numbers as an interest in the principle of things divine as well as human: 387E.

[19] In this context it is worth observing that Theon seems to be characterised quite specifically as a Stoic. For example, he uses the 'Stoic' term συνημμένον ἀξίωμα ('linked axiom') for a conditional proposition, rather than the Peripatetic πρότασις ὑποθετική ('hypothetical premise'). (It is a

(4) So far, the alignment between explanations for the E and sections on the Line has been straightforward enough. With Eustrophus and Plutarch, however, things are slightly different: for the complex of views they present does not correspond to a single, discrete section of the Line, but suggests studies which straddle the third and fourth divisions – in effect marking out our transition from 'dianoetic' thinking about the world to the divine realm, the realm of dialectic, just as Plato expresses it in the Line image itself (511a). We start in the realm of the mathematic sciences to which Theon has already introduced us: Eustrophus begins with arithmetic (387E). Younger Plutarch takes us in turn through topics which seem intended to track the curriculum of mathematical sciences described later in the *Republic* (book 7) as the training for dianoetic thought: music, geometry and stereometry.[20] Indeed, Plutarch's authorial voice underscores this association: twice it intrudes to emphasise that Younger Plutarch is concerned, not just with arithmetic, but with the *mathematical sciences* (387E–F, 391E). But this time, the study is not merely applied to events or objects in the empirical world, as was the case with Theon; this time we are put in mind of the mathematical sciences precisely as the means by which we can hope to approach the realm of the forms and the *noetic* thinking associated with dialectic (cf. *Republic* 510d). Younger Plutarch in fact finishes with a sustained account of the 'Greater Kinds' – the five architectonic forms.[21]

---

consciously syncretistic move on Galen's part to claim that the former is just a newer term for the latter: *Inst. log.* 3.4.) It is also to be noted that Theon's definition of εἰ (as a συναπτικὸς σύνδεσμος which allows the formation of a συνημμένον ἀξίωμα, and of which an example is εἰ ἡμέρα ἐστί, φῶς ἐστι), seems to be taken straight out of Chrysippus (DL 7.71). In case we have not got the point, Theon's appeal to Heracles (387D; Eustrophus at 387E suggests that he 'all but dressed in lionskin' – i.e. like Heracles – himself) is presumably meant to put us in mind of the totemic hero of the Stoics. But why does it matter? Plutarch's general point might equally have been made with terms that encompassed Aristotelian syllogistic as well: but to appeal to the Stoics in particular rules out any question that non-empirical entities (even Aristotelian 'forms') might be in question. (See also n. 17.)

[20] This is not quite the order from the *Republic* (geometry, stereometry, music), which authorial Plutarch certainly knows (*Platonic Questions* 3.1001E–F), but it has a parallel in Theon of Smyrna, who also introduces a branch of musical study which precedes geometry (*Mathematics* 16.24–18.2). In general, the speech of the Younger Plutarch does not display anything like the precision or technical sophistication in the mathematical sciences of which (authorial) Plutarch is capable: indeed, one might say that it does more to put us in mind of them than it does to show in any detail how they can elevate the level of one's thinking. But that is all it needs to do, at least for my purposes; and the intellectual deficit helps to emphasise the character of the Younger Plutarch as a student.

[21] See Schoppe 1994: ch. 4 for Plutarch's interest in the Greater Kinds both here and elsewhere in his work. It may be subtly hinted in the exchange at 391B that this is the point at which Plutarch pulls ahead of Eustrophus.

# The Hypothesis of Platonic Authority 157

(5) This, finally, paves the way for Ammonius to speak from a position squarely within the noetic section of the Line. But more than this: if the 'transitional' movement in stage (4) reflects the way Plato himself expounds the relationship between the two 'intelligible' portions of the Line, Ammonius traces a further and final transition that Plato traces within the top, dialectical portion:

> Then also understand that, by the other subsection of the intelligible, I mean that which reason itself grasps by the power of dialectic. It does not consider these hypotheses as first principles but truly as hypotheses – but as stepping stones to take off from, enabling it to reach the unhypothetical first principle of everything. (*Rep.* 511b)

Ammonius' discussion of god or the good as the very principle of being does not merely sit within the dianoetic realm, but clearly takes us to the *unhypothetical first principle* which is the limit of cognitive achievement – and, although he does not spell this out, what we will recognise to be the grounding condition for all other knowledge (cf. *Republic* 511b–c).

## 7.3   Ammonius' Authority

From Lamprias to Ammonius, then, we have made progress, not only in going from less to more sophisticated explanations for the E but also, as the presence of the Line makes clear, in tracing an ascent from 'eikastic' to 'noetic' thinking – and, just as importantly, from work based on hypotheses to the *self-validating* vision of the unhypothetical first principle (a principle which can be used to convert the hypothetical, or provisional, beliefs gained on the way up the Line into demonstrative certainties on the way down).[22]

For the purposes of this paper, no more needs to be said about the content of Ammonius' speech. What matters is only this: that he not only gives us the 'best' explanation of the E, but more importantly gives an explanation that makes him the paradigm of direct personal acquaintance with the first principle of the Line image. This is important because what it means is that Ammonius (at least, the idealised character Ammonius who occupies this totemic position within the *De E*) has a uniquely

---

[22] It is worth noting in this context that no speaker articulates a philosophical position whose content is challenged by any other, or need be challenged (in its own terms) by a Platonist. Opsomer 2006b argues that Stoic determinism is rejected in the course of the discussion, but in fact the operation of fate, at least in the sublunary realm, is something that Platonists recognise too: see Boys-Stones 2018a: ch. 12.

'authoritative' grasp of the philosophical content in the theory he expounds. Even where other people in the dialogue might be right in their convictions (for example, about logic or fate or the Greater Kinds), Ammonius is the only person in the dialogue in a position to speak with justified certitude – whether about his subject (being) or about those matters which happen to have been correctly addressed by the speakers who preceded him.

It is also an important part of the economy of the dialogue that Ammonius is a teacher. By this I mean to say that it is more than an incidental part of his characterisation, or the pretext for his use as a character at all. His status as a teacher is foregrounded by the way in which Younger Plutarch is a character in the work explicitly distinct from Plutarch's own authorial voice and, if my observations about the Line are right, clearly located at a lower level of epistemic attainment. (Even if my observations about the Line are not right, the authorial voice of Plutarch intervenes to tell us that Younger Plutarch was in need of Ammonius' help: 387E.) And we are in a position to see, now, what makes Ammonius ideally qualified as a teacher: he has seen, with his own intellectual eyes, so to speak, the truth towards which Younger Plutarch is striving. Yet this, of course, does not mean that Younger Plutarch only has to parrot what Ammonius says in order to find what he is looking for. Ammonius must surely be an 'epistemic authority' for him, in the sense that he follows his direction. But Younger Plutarch's faith in Ammonius is equally 'hypothetical' with his grasp of mathematical science and dialectic. And it will remain hypothetical until he finds the unhypothetical first principle for himself.

But what happens when Plutarch does finally encounter the unhypothetical first principle for himself? One thing is that Plutarch can finally be sure that Ammonius was right. But at the same time, if his understanding becomes transparently self-validating at this point, the whole question of (external) epistemic authority evaporates. Plutarch may still love and admire Ammonius, for example; but Ammonius will no longer be any sort of epistemic authority for him: Plutarch now has superior, in fact absolute, justification for his beliefs in his own immediate experience. There is a certain irony in this, but no paradox: it is only to say that Plutarch will no longer require a teacher. And this is, in effect, dramatised within the *De E* as well. For the authorial Plutarch, of whose existence we are kept in mind as he intervenes to comment, not least on the situation of Younger Plutarch, is as such the author of Ammonius' speech as well. Not to put too fine a point on it, Ammonius is here a mouthpiece for Plutarch

## The Hypothesis of Platonic Authority 159

every bit as much as Plutarch's own authorial voice. Younger Plutarch defers to Ammonius; authorial Plutarch speaks as his equal: literally speaks, in fact, *as* him.

### 7.4 Plato's Authority

It may by now be clear where all this is leading. As with Ammonius, so with Plato. Plato has epistemic authority for everyone who chooses to use him as a guide, and for just so long as they need guidance. But for anyone who has achieved their own vision of the unhypothetical first principle, for anyone (here is the irony) who is thereby in a position to know for sure that Plato is right, Plato, even if he remains a figurehead and object of reverence in other respects, has *no epistemic authority at all*.

Within the economy of the *De E*, what this ought to mean is that Plato functions as an authority for Younger Plutarch in much the same that Ammonius does, but not for Ammonius himself (that is to say, Ammonius in the enlightened state in which we find him in the *De E*). And this is not only consistent with the characterisation of the two figures, Younger Plutarch and Ammonius, but explains a curious difference in the speeches they give.

Younger Plutarch is the first person in the *De E* who bases his account of the E on the exegesis of Platonic texts. In fact, there is only one mention of Plato before Younger Plutarch speaks, when Theon invokes him as the source of the story that the oracle had told the Delians to double the size of their altar (386E) – a story from the anecdotal tradition, because it is not to be found in the dialogues. Younger Plutarch names Plato three times (389F, 391A, 391C); but more importantly he makes explicit reference to four of his texts: the *Timaeus*, *Cratylus*, *Sophist* and *Philebus* (all named).[23] And more still: Younger Plutarch does not just refer to these dialogues, he expounds them. He sets out the theory of the Greater Kinds in the *Sophist* (391B); and, having done that, just like a good commentator, he goes on to show how exactly the same theory can be found in the *Philebus* as well (391B–C). That is a striking move to make: it is not easy, partly because the language does not match, and partly because, as Plutarch acknowledges, Plato only explicitly refers to four 'kinds' in the *Philebus* passage anyway, leaving the possibility of a fifth unresolved.[24] But

---

[23] *Timaeus* is named at 389F (with a reference to 31a); *Cratylus* at 391A (with a reference to 409a); *Sophist* at 391B (for the Greater kinds: 254bff.); the *Philebus* (23c-e) at 391B–C.

[24] Obsieger 2013: 284–6 calls it 'abenteuerliche Exegese'.

160 GEORGE BOYS-STONES

nor is it necessary to Plutarch's argument, namely that there are *five* ('E') Greater Kinds: this can be read off the surface of the *Sophist* without any need of corroboration. Younger Plutarch, in fact, is mounting something like a *performance* of Platonism, a demonstration of how a Platonist proceeds, testing his reading of one Platonic dialogue by seeing how well it works to make sense of others as well. You would think from this that Younger Plutarch represents something like the ideal Platonist.

But we know that he does not: authorial Plutarch, no less, informs us of the fact. If anyone in *De E* is the ideal Platonist, it ought to be Ammonius. But Ammonius for his part – and here is the striking difference with Younger Plutarch – *does not mention Plato at all.* There is not a single use of his name, or reference to any dialogue; no Platonic quotation is alleged to support his theory.[25] That is not because Ammonius is in generally averse to making reference to the views of others, or even just of other philosophers: he quotes by name Heraclitus (392A), Homer (393C), Pindar, Euripides, Stesichorus and Sophocles (in quick succession at 394A–B). He even quotes a god – Apollo himself: for it is Apollo, Ammonius tells us, who says 'know yourself' (392A).

Now, as it happens, the claim that Apollo says 'Know yourself' and, more specifically, that this is his way of issuing a greeting to those who enter his temple, does have a precedent in Plato. Readers of the *De E* might recognise it from a very similar claim in Plato's *Charmides* (164c–165a), namely that 'Know Yourself' is Apollo's greeting. However, even as we entertain this parallel, it becomes evident that it does nothing to illuminate or explain what Ammonius is thinking. The speaker at this point of the *Charmides* is (not Socrates but) Critias, and it would be surprising to find that Ammonius took Critias as a mouthpiece for Plato, or (to put in more directly relevant terms) as a source for authoritative Platonic thought. That aside, Critias' gloss on 'Know yourself' and his reason for mentioning it stand in no useful relationship with what Ammonius has to say. Critias uses the injunction to make an ethical point: he wants to connect temperance and self-knowledge (so that 'Know yourself!' means 'Be temperate!'). Ammonius, by contrast, sees a metaphysical message within it: what

---

[25] This is not to say that Plutarch's own reading of Plato does not in fact inform the speech of Ammonius, and attempts have been made for example to relate it to exegesis of the *Timaeus* (Whittaker 1969; Ferrari 2010: 82–5). Nor is it to say that Plutarch wishes us to think that Ammonius has not himself read the *Timaeus*: on the contrary. My point is simply that Plutarch seems to be making a studious attempt not to make Ammonius *read* like exegesis of Plato, to emphasise that, by now, Ammonius no longer relies on Plato – in the way for example that Young Plutarch still does.

## The Hypothesis of Platonic Authority

we are to 'know' is the ontological inferiority of our own nature when compared with god – whose being is expressed in the real object of his interest, the E (394C). If the authorial Plutarch intended us to see a reference to the *Charmides* here at all, it is not because he thinks that his character, Ammonius, has any stake in it (because, for example, it provides authoritative backing for his own view). It can only be because the authorial Plutarch himself has a point to make: and his point is that just the opposite is the case. He wants us to see that Ammonius is precisely *not* expounding or relying on Plato, even at the one place in his speech where we are most likely to be put in mind of a particular Platonic text. Ammonius must know Plato; his knowledge of Plato might naturally inform his own way of speaking. But Ammonius speaks on his own authority.[26]

All of this is consistent with, and in fact explained by, my suggestion that Plato is no longer an epistemic authority for Ammonius. Having seen the unhypothetical first principle, Ammonius knows what he knows on his *own* authority. Plato was no doubt an epistemic authority for him in earlier life. No doubt too, Ammonius could be a very good expounder of Plato, and would use exposition of Plato with his own students. But the character of Ammonius in the *De E* represents someone who has, in philosophical terms at least, become Plato's epistemic equal – just as Younger Plutarch was to grow into the author who is the philosophical equal of Ammonius.

### 7.5  Envoi

David Sedley quoted Simplicius to support his argument that 'authority' was invested in Plato as scholarch: 'One should not seek to prove Aristotle totally and utterly infallible, as if one had enrolled in his school' (*in Cat.* 7.27–9; Sedley 1997: 107). What I hope to have shown is that we need to add to this, on pain of making Platonists as irrational as Celsus' Christians, that (a) the decision to enrol in Plato's school is, ideally at least, a deliberate decision to adopt a certain philosophical methodology, and not an act of as it were 'conversion' to a belief in Plato's infallibility; and (b) this methodology involves a theoretically falsifiable hypothesis that Plato is infallible –

---

[26] It is relevant to note in this context that Ammonius gives an etymology of 'Apollo' which is perfectly consistent with what Plato has to say about the god, yet at the same time not among any of the etymologies which Plato himself considers. Ammonius derives the name from *ἀ-πολλά, 'not-many' (393C: οἷον ἀρνούμενος τὰ πολλά); in *Cratylus* 405b–e Plato offers us ἀπολούων ('washing off'), ἀπολύων ('releasing'), ἁπλοῦν ('simple', which at least converges in sense with Ammonius), and ἁ (in the sense of ὁμοῦ) + πόλησις ('moving together').

which explains why Platonists typically seem to be committed to the position that he actually is infallible. To this, we can add that (c) adopting this hypothesis counts as investing Plato with epistemic authority, but it is epistemic authority in qualified sense; and in fact (d) the moment the hypothesis is no longer required – that is, when you can see the truth for yourself – Plato ceases to be for you an epistemic authority of any kind at all. For the successful Platonist, Plato becomes an epistemic peer.

Simplicius supplies a later proof-text for this point as well. At *in Cael.* 377.29–34, he says that, if you read Alexander's work superficially (*epipolaioteron*), you risk finding yourself in conflict with Plato's views, 'which is', he says, 'the same as to say [being in conflict] with Aristotle's doctrines and with the divine truth' (διαβεβλημένως ἴσχειν πρὸς τὰ τοῦ Πλάτωνος δόγματα, ταὐτὸν δὲ εἰπεῖν καὶ πρὸς τὰ τοῦ Ἀριστοτέλους καὶ πρὸς τὴν θείαν ἀλήθειαν). My attention was brought to this passage by Pantelis Golitsis, who explains it as follows (2015: 59):

> In Simplicius' view, Platonic truth, Aristotelian truth, and divine truth (say, the truth contained in the Chaldean Oracles) are interchangeable; and they are interchangeable because, in spite of being formulated differently, they are identical.

My argument has been that this applies to the earlier period too: in Plutarch's view, one might say, Platonic truth, Ammonius' truth, and divine truth (say, the truth contained in the deliverances of Apollo) are interchangeable; and they are interchangeable because, in spite of being formulated differently, they are identical. Plato is no more or less an epistemic authority than Apollo, Ammonius – or the author of the *De E* himself.[27]

---

[27] In Boys-Stones 2018b, of which this paper is in some sense a companion-piece, I argue that it is not only theoretically possible that Platonists might recognise epistemic authorities equal in status to Plato, but a demonstrable fact of Platonist practice (something which, of course, could not be the case if epistemic authority were inseparably bound up with Plato's status as 'founder' of the school).

CHAPTER 8

# *Aristotle's* Physics *as an Authoritative Work in Early Neoplatonism*
## Plotinus and Porphyry

### Riccardo Chiaradonna

## 8.1 The Middle Platonist Background

The distinction between Middle Platonism and Neoplatonism is controversial, but it remains helpful in that it makes it clear that there are important differences in the philosophical background of Platonist philosophers before and after Plotinus.[1] One of these differences resides in their knowledge of Aristotle's treatises. It can plausibly be argued that Platonist philosophers, from at least Eudorus of Alexandria onward (first century BC), regarded Aristotle as an authority, though not unqualifiedly so, and though his status was clearly inferior to that of Plato.[2] Eudorus of Alexandria was certainly involved in the early debates on Aristotle's *Categories*, and we know from Alexander of Aphrodisias (*in Metaph.* 58.25–59.8) that Eudorus proposed an emendation to Aristotle's report on Plato's theory of principles at *Metaph.* A6.988a10–11.[3] Further hypotheses are possible. So M. Bonazzi has argued that Eudorus' theory of principles, as reported by Simp. *in Phys.* 181.7–30 (= 3O BS), may be based on *Metaphysics* Λ, even though Aristotle is not explicitly referred to in the text.[4] In addition to this, M. Rashed and Th. Auffret have interestingly suggested that Eudorus of Alexandria prepared an edition of *Metaphysics* A which supplemented Aristotle's text with what Rashed and Auffret call 'un certain nombre d'ajouts à la tonalité pythagoricienne'.[5] As a matter of fact, Aristotle's theories were an important resource for the polemic against materialist philosophies, and Aristotle's writings were a crucial source of information on Plato, the Pythagoreans and the

---

[1] For criticism of these historical categories see, for example, Frede 1987 and Catana 2013. A persuasive defence of them can be found in Donini 1990 and Remes & Slaveva-Griffin 2014a. Further discussion in Boys-Stones 2018a: 2–6.
[2] See on this Karamanolis 2006.
[3] On Eudorus' work on Aristotle, see now Griffin 2015a: 78–97.   [4] See Bonazzi 2013.
[5] Rashed & Auffret 2014: 82.

163

philosophers of the Academy, i.e. on those whom Platonist philosophers regarded as their principal authorities. Aristotle's theories and vocabulary play an important role in some pseudo-Pythagorean treatises whose genesis has persuasively been traced back to Eudorus' teaching and can easily been interpreted as part of a general movement of return to the ancients which characterised philosophical debates around the first century BC.[6] Aristotle was one of the ancients whose authority was set in contrast with that of Hellenistic philosophers. Therefore, it is not surprising that Plutarch, possibly relying on Eudorus, regards Aristotle as a member of the Platonic-Pythagorean philosophical lineage in his *De Iside et Osiride* (see in particular *De Iside et Osiride* 382D = 13Q BS): this Pythagorising reading of Aristotle can further be confirmed by Plutarch's reference to Aristotle's *Metaphysics* in his *Life of Alexander* (7.9.668C).[7]

Before reaching any hasty conclusion about the integration of Aristotle in pre-Plotinian Platonism, however, some additional remarks are needed. We don't know of any Platonist commentary or proper exegetical work on Aristotle before Porphyry. There is no reason to suppose that Eudorus wrote a commentary on the *Metaphysics*. Eudorus' amendment of Aristotle's text must rather be connected with his Platonic-Pythagorean philosophical project. As said above, Aristotle's reports on Plato and the Academy were a source for any account of the Early Academic theory of principles, and Eudorus was predictably engaged in a close reading of these texts. In addition to that, the extant evidence suggests that, before Plotinus, Platonist philosophers only had limited direct knowledge of Aristotle's treatises. This of course does not mean that Platonist philosophers before Plotinus had no access to Aristotle's treatises. Independently of this fact, they were apparently not interested in reading them through and, with some important exceptions such as the *Categories* and the *De caelo*, their acquaintance with Aristotle's acroamatic writings was somewhat superficial (if indeed they were acquainted with them at all).[8] Here I will focus on a case study, that is, the reception of Aristotle's *Physics*.

Before Plotinus, Aristotle's *Physics* shines, so to speak, for its absence in Platonist debates. This remark does not refer to theories or tenets that can be traced back to Aristotle's natural philosophy. As a matter of fact, some examples show that Platonist or Platonising authors were happy to integrate Aristotle's hylomorphism into their accounts of the physical world.

---

[6] For details, see Szlezàk 1972 and Ulacco 2017.
[7] See Donini 1999 and, on Plutarch's passage on the *Metaphysics*, Chiaradonna 2017.
[8] For further details, see Chiaradonna 2011.

Aristotle's Physics *in early Neoplatonism* 165

A. Ulacco and J. Opsomer have focused on Ps.-Timaeus of Locri, whose paraphrase of Plato's elemental theory in the *Timaeus* makes distinctive use of the notions of matter, form and composite (see Ps.-Timaeus 206.5–7 Thesleff).[9] Certainly, reading Plato's elemental account against the background of Aristotle's hylomorphism is no neutral choice, but it is far from certain that the author of this treatise was aware of all the philosophical aspects and consequences of his move. He might only be adopting some school notions which, at first glance, make very good sense in order to explain Plato's views. This is not an isolated situation. The doxographical tradition was aware of Aristotle's four causes, famously designated by prepositional formulas (see Stob. *Anth.* 1.13.1b = Aët. 1.11.4 p. 310 Diels):[10] but, again, passages like these can hardly be seen as interpretations of Aristotle's *Physics*. In one passage from *Letter* 65, possibly deriving from some Platonist source, Seneca reports Aristotle's distinction of causes and notes that Plato had added a fifth cause to Aristotle's list, i.e. the paradigm:

> Aristotle thinks that cause is said in three ways. The first cause, he says, is the material itself, without which nothing can be produced. The second is the workman. The third is the form, which is imposed on each work as it is on a statue. For Aristotle calls this the form. 'A fourth cause,' he says 'accompanies these: the purpose of the entire product.' ... To these causes Plato adds a fifth, the model, which he himself calls an 'idea'. For this is what the artisan looked to in making what he planned to make ... (Sen. *Ep.* 65.4–7 in 5C BS, trans. Inwood 2007)

Seneca's account of causes reflects an influential tradition that lies behind Porphyry's later integration of Aristotle's *Physics* (*apud* Simp. *in Phys.* 10.25–11.3 = Porph. 120F Smith).[11] Unlike Seneca (or his source), however, Porphyry wrote an extensive commentary on Aristotle's *Physics* (more precisely, on the first four books of the work) and, as we shall see later, his integration of Aristotle's *Physics* into Platonism relies on a number of supplementary assumptions connected to the scientific status of physics and to the previous Peripatetic debates on hylomorphism. Terms and notions from Aristotle's physics are ubiquitous in Porphyry's extant writings and fragments. Nothing of this sort apparently happens before Plotinus' engagement with Aristotle's *Physics*. This emerges in a passage

---

[9] For a similar approach, see also Atticus fr. 5.39–41 des Places; Alcin. *Did.* 13.169.4–5.
[10] Mansfeld 2010: 401–2 argues that this lemma is to be attributed to Arius Didymus.
[11] See Dörrie & Baltes 1996: 142–6 (= *Bst.* 117); Mansfeld 2010: 402. See p. 171–2.

from Atticus, where he contrasts Aristotle's account of nature with Plato's world soul:

> He [*sc.* Aristotle] denies that nature is soul and says that, while things on earth are organised by nature, they are not organised by soul. For he claims that there are different causes for each thing: in the case of heavenly bodies, which always remain the same thing in the same way, he posits fate as cause; for sublunary things he posits nature; for human affairs, he posits intelligence and foresight and soul. ... Aristotle, then, said that there was something like this, which pervades everything as a principle of motion; but he would not allow that it is soul ... (Euseb. *Praep. Evang.* 15.12.2–4 = Atticus, fr. 8 des Places = 11B BS, trans. BS)[12]

Details are not relevant to the present discussion:[13] suffice it to remark that Aristotle's distinctive terminology is completely absent (this is no exception in Atticus' extant fragments), and Atticus' report is misleading to say the least (see e.g. his remark that Aristotle posits fate as the cause for heavenly bodies). Atticus' polemics against Aristotle's God actually seem to be addressed to later Peripatetic views such as that of the author of the *De mundo*, whereas Aristotle's distinctive theories and vocabulary do not emerge in this passage.[14]

Before Plotinus we find only one remarkable exception to this situation, i.e. Alcinous' *Didaskalikos*: Alcinous, whoever he may have been, was certainly very familiar with a number of texts from Aristotle's corpus. For example, his allusions to *Metaphysics* Λ are very clear, and his use of Aristotelian terminology is extensive.[15] However, there are simply no grounds to suppose that Alcinous' doctrines represent some kind of standard Platonist teaching before Plotinus (let alone some standard Platonist teaching in the second century AD: the chronology of this work is completely uncertain). Alcinous' familiarity with Aristotle's treatises represents an exception and not the norm.[16] That said, Aristotle's *Physics* was apparently not at the forefront of Alcinous' agenda. His section on matter is certainly inspired by Aristotelian notions and vocabulary. This emerges especially with the reference to potentiality at the end of the passage:

---

[12] For the Greek text, see des Places 1977: 66–7.

[13] See Michalewski 2017: 132–3; Boys-Stones 2018a: 323–6.

[14] Moraux 1984: 577–9 sees Atticus as depending on a doxographic tradition; Karamanolis 2006: 166 holds that 'Atticus' argumentation contains ... hints to widespread views at his time that he probably meant to target' (e.g. theological views such as those of the treatise *De mundo*). Taurus of Beirut provides a further interesting example of Aristotle's reception in Middle Platonism. On this, see now the judicious remarks in Petrucci 2018: 5, which are consistent with the present account.

[15] See Alcin. *Did.* 10.164.18–27 = 6A BS.     [16] Further discussion in Chiaradonna 2017.

And being such, it will be neither body nor incorporeal, but potentially body, just as we understand the bronze to be potentially a statue, because once it has received the form it will be a statue. (Alcin. *Did.* 8.163.8-10 = 4E BS, trans. Dillon 1993)

After all, the very identification between Plato's receptacle and Aristotle's matter comes from the *Physics* (4.2.209b11–12). Yet it is difficult to go beyond these minimal conclusions. For example, Alcinous makes no reference to the notion of privation (στέρησις), and Whittaker's *Index locorum* only provides a couple of references to Aristotle's *Physics*.[17]

## 8.2 Plotinus

Let us now move on to Plotinus. A quick comparison between *Indices* is instructive. Henry and Schwyzer's *Index locorum* has three columns of references to the *Physics*, and the list is probably partial.[18] This, however, is not the crucial fact. What really matters is that Plotinus is deeply aware of Aristotle's account of the physical world and shows a thorough familiarity with Aristotle's *Physics*. In addition to that, Plotinus is aware that Aristotle's views raise a number of challenges for a follower of Plato and Plotinus' critical dialogue with Aristotle's *Physics* is of crucial importance for his philosophy.

Plotinus actually engages with Aristotle's *Physics* in order to show that the corporeal world depends on extra-physical essential and productive principles, i.e. on precisely the kind of principles that Aristotle is not willing to accept in his account of nature. Furthermore, according to Plotinus such principles are necessary and sufficient conditions that ground the structure and the very existence of bodies. Therefore, there are no physical principles in addition to the extra-physical ones: there is no horizontal causation in addition to top-down vertical causation from intelligibles. As such, all principles are extra-physical.[19] This, however, is only half of the story, for Plotinus is at the same time heavily dependent on Aristotle's views, and his own account is mostly developed through a modified or qualified use of Aristotelian concepts, which Plotinus transposes into a different philosophical framework.[20] Here I will only focus on a limited number of texts that illustrate Plotinus' exegetical and critical approach to Aristotle's *Physics*.

---

[17] See Whittaker 1990: 170.    [18] See Henry & Schwyzer 1983: 336–7.
[19] For further details, see Linguiti 2014.    [20] See Chiaradonna 2014a.

168                    RICCARDO CHIARADONNA

The first text comes from the first part of Plotinus' tripartite treatise *On the Genera of Being* (6.1(42)). There Plotinus argues that the Peripatetic account of physical substance includes a list of merely factual features (see below) which actually do not make clear what the concept and the nature of substance really are

> But one might say that these are peculiar properties of substances as compared with other things, and for this reason one might collect them into one and call them substances, but one would not be speaking of one genus, nor would one yet be making clear the concept and nature of substance (τὴν ἔννοιαν τῆς οὐσίας καὶ τὴν φύσιν). (6.1(42).3.19–22, trans. Armstrong 1988)

In fact, according to Plotinus, the only satisfying way to make sense of the priority of substance is the Platonic one, which makes *ousia* metaphysically separate from the whole structure of sensible beings. Therefore, as fully emerges in 6.3(44), the *ousia* of *x* must not be something primary and essential in sensible particulars (i.e. something in sensible particulars which makes them what they are), but must rather be an extra-physical and self-subsisting principle (the *logos*) which acts as an essential and productive cause for that of which it is the *ousia* (the enmattered, qualitative and perceptible form) (see 6.3(44).15.24–38).[21]

At the very beginning of his discussion, Plotinus makes a cursory and indeed very cryptic allusion to Aristotle's characterisation of time as 'something belonging to motion' and to Aristotle's view that motion goes with the moved object:

> But what is this very 'something' and 'this here', and the 'substrate' and the not resting upon or being in something else as in a substrate, nor being what it is as belonging to another, as white is a quality of body and quantity belongs to substance, and time is something belonging to motion, and motion belongs to the moved (καὶ χρόνος κινήσεώς τι καὶ κίνησις τοῦ κινουμένου)? (6.1(42).3.13–16, trans. Armstrong 1988)

Plotinus' cursory list includes all features which, on his view, characterise Aristotle's substance without explaining the genuine nature of *ousia* (i.e. as an extra-physical incorporeal principle). The reference to Aristotle's *Physics* 4.11 seems unmistakable.[22] Yet, Plotinus' allusion to time and motion is

---

[21] More details can be found in Chiaradonna 2014b.

[22] 'Hence time is either movement or something that belongs to movement. Since then it is not movement, it must be the other. But what is moved is moved from something to something, and all magnitude is continuous. Therefore the movement goes with the magnitude. Because the magnitude is continuous, the movement too is continuous, and if the movement, then the time;

obscure, to say the least. The situation becomes clearer if we take this passage as having some kind of proleptic function: the very beginning of Plotinus' discussion points to what he will be arguing extensively in the following sections. The passage is exceedingly succinct and cryptic, but Plotinus' point is apparently that Aristotle's account of time is, so to speak, telescoped into motion and that motion is telescoped into the moving continuous magnitude. Both time and motion are continuous because the magnitude is continuous. Therefore, as Plotinus says, time is something belonging to motion and motion is something belonging to the moved object, i.e. to the sensible particular. So motion, according to this view, is ultimately nothing but the moving object in its successive states. In his discussion Plotinus aims precisely to dismantle this nexus which makes all fundamental aspects of the physical world ultimately dependent on the bodily and particular extended substance which is placed, so to speak, at the bottom of them. Here Porphyry's arrangement of Plotinus' treatises can be misleading, since Plotinus' critical discussion of Aristotle's physical views on substance, motion and time covers both the tripartite treatise 42–44 *On the Genera of Being* (6.1–3), where Plotinus focuses on substance and motion, and treatise 45 *On Eternity and Time* (3.7). These treatises are contiguous according to the chronological order, and develop, among other things, an extensive critical dialogue with Aristotle's *Physics*. To cut a rather long story short, Plotinus' main point is that the only adequate way to make sense of these notions is to separate them from their, so to speak, physical and extended instantiations and to refer them instead to extra-physical and incorporeal principles. So Plotinus takes issue with Aristotle's definition of motion as 'incomplete activity' (*Physics* 3.2.201b31–3) and argues that motion is a complete activity that should be distinguished from the change accomplished by the moving object, which is incomplete until it reaches its end (6.1(42).16.4–8).[23] As emerges in 6.3 (44), this complete activity is grounded, in turn, in an 'active moving power' (6.3(44).23.21: δύναμις τοῦ κινεῖν) which can be connected to the causative power of incorporeal principles. We find a closely parallel situation in the discussion about time. Again, Plotinus argues that Aristotle's account of time as the 'measure of motion' (see *Ph.* 4.12.220b32–221a1) misleadingly telescopes the nature of time into the movement accomplished by bodies.

---

for the time that has passed is always thought to be as great as the movement' (Arist. *Ph.* 4.11.219a8–14, trans. Hardie & Gaye in Barnes 1984).

[23] As Noble 2016: 259 remarks: 'when I go for a walk, there are two distinct motions in play, the energeia of walking, which is complete at all times, and the extended change of walking a stade, which remains incomplete until the whole distance has been traversed'.

# 170                          RICCARDO CHIARADONNA

It is worth noting that in this Plotinus raises an objection that is identical to
that raised against Aristotle's substance:

> Now, if it is a measure of this kind, then it has been said what time is a
> measure of, that it is a measure of movement, but we have not yet been told
> what it in itself (αὐτὸς δ' ὅ ἐστιν οὔπω εἴρηται). (3.7(45).9.10–12, trans.
> Armstrong 1980)

So the account of time as the 'measure of motion' does not make clear
what time is. Aristotle merely says what time is the measure of, i.e. of
movements, but he does not explain what time really is. Plotinus actually
holds that time, properly speaking, is the distinctive mode of being of the
world soul, which entails a succession of states, while this succession in
itself is not connected with the extended processes that occur in bodies (see
3.7(45).11).

This is but a sketchy account of Plotinus' tour de force in treatises
42–45. It should be reasonably clear that this situation is completely
different from what we find in authors like Atticus. Plotinus is unmistakably familiar with Aristotle's *Physics* and, even more interestingly, he makes
systematic use of Aristotle's *Physics* in his account of the natural world.
Until now we have seen how, according to Plotinus, intelligible causes
provide an adequate foundation for those concepts which Aristotle mistakenly telescopes into sensible particulars. There are two ways of interpreting this approach. (a) Plotinus could be arguing that we can well
preserve Aristotle's theories provided that we *supplement* them with genuine extra-physical causes. (b) Plotinus could be arguing that a genuine
account of extra-physical causes ultimately *supplants* Aristotle's theories
with a different account. I suggest that (b) actually reflects Plotinus'
approach and this for a reason that points, once again, to his engagement
with Aristotle's *Physics*. For in order to preserve Aristotle's account Plotinus
should at least admit that matter can be a suitable subject for the hylomorphic form and that sensible particulars are proper and continuous
subjects of change. This view, however, is precisely what Plotinus rejects
in his early treatise 2.4(12). D. O'Brien has shown that Plotinus offers a
subtle interpretation of *Physics* 1.9 which modifies Aristotle's account in a
crucial detail, since Plotinus (just like Aristotle's Platonist opponents)
identifies matter and privation (2.4(12).16.3–16) and regards matter as
changeless and incapable of receiving form.[24] In so doing, Plotinus suggests that no continuous subject of change can ultimately be found at the

---

[24] See O'Brien 1996: 178–81.

Aristotle's Physics *in early Neoplatonism*                                    171

level of bodies. In two recent valuable articles C. Arruzza and Ch. Noble have drawn attention to a passage from Simplicius' commentary on the *Physics* where Alexander of Aphrodisias' account of matter is contrasted with that of some anonymous Platonists (Simp. *in Phys.* 320.20–32). While Alexander argues that matter receives form 'according to an alteration' (κατὰ ἀλλοίωσιν) (in such a way that matter becomes the subject of formal properties), the anonymous Platonists deny precisely this fact.[25] Therefore their matter is not only without qualities in itself, but in addition it is unaffectable, so that it cannot in any way receive qualities from form: 'the Platonists, who speak of qualityless first matter, do not on any account grant that it is altered. For that which has been acted upon when it casts off one quality and takes on another is altered, but how could what is qualityless be altered?' (Simp. *in Phys.* 320.27–30, trans. Noble 2013: 239). Both Arruzza and Noble argue convincingly that those Platonists actually reflect Plotinus' account of matter as unaffectable, 'entirely separated and incapable of transforming itself' (2.5(25).5.10–13 trans. Arruzza 2015: 59). Should we infer that Plotinus' account of matter was developed as a reaction to Alexander's exegesis of Aristotle's *Physics*? Unfortunately, Alexander's commentary is lost,[26] but this is a reasonable hypothesis, which could indeed add a further piece to our jigsaw, i.e. that it was Alexander's exegetical work that laid the ground for Plotinus' engagement with Aristotle's *Physics*. To sum up, Plotinus develops a sort of pseudo-hylomorphism largely based on theories drawn from Aristotle's physics, while at the same time critically adapting these theories to a Platonist philosophical framework which is definitely anti-hylomorphic: for, according to Plotinus, the hylomorphic form is no substance; matter is no substrate; motion does not belong to any continuous magnitude; and time is no measure of motion.

### 8.3 Porphyry

This background helps us understand Porphyry's integration of Aristotle's *Physics* into Platonism. J. Mansfeld has persuasively suggested that Porphyry depends on the same tradition reflected in Arius Didymus and in Seneca's *Letter* 65.[27] As a matter of fact, Porphyry gives a list of

---

[25] See Arruzza 2011: 33; and Noble 2013: 238–40.     [26] See Rashed 2011.

[27] See Mansfeld 2010: 402. Note that, unlike Seneca, Porphyry speaks of principles and not of causes. The difference, however, should not be overestimated, since according to Porphyry 'principle' and 'cause' are spoken of in an equal number of senses; see Porph. *apud* Simp. *in Phys.* 11.4–5: ὁσαχῶς

Aristotle's principles and describes them through prepositional formulas (Simp. *in Phys.* 10.25–11.3 = Porph. 120F Smith). Like Seneca, Porphyry argues that Plato had added further principles to Aristotle's list: these are the paradigmatic principle, which also occurs in Seneca's list, and the instrumental one, which is only found in Porphyry's list. The parallel is unmistakable, but some further remarks are necessary. The first one is obvious, but it is nonetheless worth expressing it in full clarity. Porphyry's list of causes occurs in a commentary on Aristotle's *Physics* (as we shall see in more detail later on, Porphyry probably wrote a commentary on the first four books of the *Physics*) – it does not occur in some discussion about different accounts of causes.[28] It is a well-known fact that Porphyry is often dependent on the Platonist tradition before Plotinus, but this should not lead us to simply equate his approach with that of his predecessors.[29] Porphyry's exegetical project on Aristotle is something new in the Platonist tradition, and it is only from Porphyry onward that Platonists regard Aristotle's treatises as authoritative writings that deserve to be commented upon: it is Porphyry, and not Arius Didymus, who paves the ground for the Neoplatonist commentary work on Aristotle.[30] Whatever the reasons for this fact, its importance should in no way be underestimated. The second remark is connected to Porphyry's approach. Seneca (or rather his source) simply claims that Aristotle talks about four causes and Plato adds a further cause to the list: Aristotle's list and Plato's exemplary cause are, so to speak, merely juxtaposed. Porphyry apparently developed this issue and tried to answer the question of how Aristotle's account precisely relates to another superior account of principles. This is suggested by a short but extremely interesting passage in which Porphyry presents physics as a subordinate science that does not investigate the existence of its principles but accepts them as a given, whereas another superior science (that of the 'metaphysician' *tou anabebēkotos*) accomplishes the superior task that physics cannot perform, i.e. the investigation of the existence of physical principles which physics takes for granted:

---

δὲ ἡ ἀρχὴ λέγεται, τοσαυταχῶς καὶ τὸ αἴτιον (cf. Arist. *Metaph.* Δ1.1013a16–17). On this passage see also Karamanolis 2006: 272–7.

[28] Porphyry's commentary is lost (see Porph. 118–62T Smith): fragments of it are known through Simplicius' *in Phys.* and through evidence from Arabic sources: see Romano 1985; Moraux 1985; Karamanolis 2004: 111–14; Adamson 2007; Smith 2012.

[29] See on this Zambon 2002.

[30] For a general account of Porphyry's approach to Aristotle, see Chiaradonna 2016 and Karamanolis 2006: 243–330.

## Aristotle's Physics *in early Neoplatonism*

> Porphyry says that investigating if principles of the natural things exist is not proper to the natural scientist, but to someone who has ascended: for the natural scientist makes use of them as given. (Simp. *in Phys.* 9.11–12 = Porph. 119F Smith)[31]

This important passage raises some problems. (a) It would be interesting to know more about precisely what kind of relation subsists between physics and this mysterious superior science. And, of course, (b) it would be interesting to know just what this superior science is. I will postpone the answer to question (b) and start by addressing the first question. S. Menn has interestingly suggested that Aristotle's account of subordinate sciences lies behind this passage, so that the relation between physics and metaphysics would be the same as that which subsists between optics and geometry.[32] Physics posits things that are proved in metaphysics. This is a very plausible suggestion, which could receive further support by the hypothesis, recently raised by M. Chase, that Porphyry wrote a commentary on Aristotle's *Posterior Analytics*.[33] If this is the case, however, further problems emerge. In his classification of sciences in *Metaphysics* E1 Aristotle distinguishes physics from first philosophy, whose object is superior. Aristotle never suggests, however, that physics has the status of a subordinate science which takes its principles for granted, whereas another superior science investigates their existence. This is Porphyry's ingenious move, whose relation with Aristotle's original view about the status of physics is controversial, to say the least.

Before coming to the identity of the superior science, let us consider some supplementary remarks that can shed light on the relation between Porphyry and Plotinus. Porphyry's list of physical principles includes matter (see Simp. *in Phys.* 10.30–1). As said earlier, one of the main features of Plotinus' interpretation of Aristotle's physics resides in the account of matter, whose status Plotinus equates with that of privation. Plotinus possibly develops this view as a reaction to Alexander's account and the doctrine of matter as privation is crucial for Plotinus' criticism of Aristotle's hylomorphism, since it affects both the account of the form–matter relation (forms are not inherent in matter for the very simple reason that matter is no subject of inherence) and that of change (there is no continuous substrate for physical change). Plotinus never regards matter as a principle, except when he argues that matter is a principle of evil (see 1.8

---

[31] ὁ δὲ Πορφύριος οὐδὲ φυσικοῦ φησιν εἶναι τὸ ζητεῖν, εἰ εἰσὶν ἀρχαὶ τῶν φυσικῶν, ἀλλὰ τοῦ ἀναβεβηκότος· ὁ γὰρ φυσικὸς ὡς δεδομέναις χρῆται.
[32] See Menn 2013: 147 n. 10.   [33] See Chase 2012: 1355.

174      RICCARDO CHIARADONNA

(51)). To the best of my knowledge, in his extant works Porphyry never refers to Plotinus' distinctive account of matter as privation, not even in the *Sententiae*. And, in his commentary on the *Physics*, he follows Aristotle's view that privation is not identical to matter, but to a status of matter (the shapeless status of the bronze: see Simp. *in Phys.* 406.31–2 = 152F Smith). In addition to this, Porphyry accepts the Peripatetic account of the hylomorphic and essential form. So Porphyry says that the hylomorphic form is 'nature' in the most proper sense and argues that the composite itself can be designated as *physis* rather than matter since it has form in itself (Simp. *in Phys.* 277.24–7 = Porph. 148aF Smith). This passage is interestingly similar to a fragment from Porphyry's lost commentary on the *Categories*, where he criticises the early Peripatetic commentator Boethus of Sidon, who had equated Aristotle's form with some kind of non-essential property inherent in matter:

> Porphyry says that Boethus is mistaken in saying this, because <Boethus> claims that the form which is contradistinguished from matter and is called substance from Aristotle, is quality or one of the other accidents. For that which qualifies substance is substance-like and therefore substance (τὸ γὰρ ποιωτικὸν οὐσίας οὐσιῶδες καὶ διὰ τοῦτο οὐσία). For indeed the composite is substance most of all in virtue of the form. (Simp. *in Cat.* 78.20–4 = Porph. 58F Smith, trans. de Haas 2001)

Porphyry claims that the qualification of substance (τὸ ... ποιωτικὸν οὐσίας) is *ousia* and the composite is most properly *ousia* insofar as it has form in itself.[34] In all of these texts Porphyry never denies that matter is substance, that it is a subject and that it has the status of a principle in nature. At the same time, Porphyry argues that the hylomorphic form is 'substance' and 'nature' in the most proper sense. He criticises Boethus' earlier account of hylomorphic form as being outside substance, and in doing this Porphyry is probably indebted to Alexander of Aphrodisias.[35] In short: while Plotinus engages in a critical discussion of Aristotle's physics which ultimately aims to dismantle the key aspects of Aristotle's theory, we find nothing of the sort in Porphyry. His reading of Aristotle entails a careful exegesis of the text, and Porphyry never questions Aristotle's key ideas about principles in nature, although Porphyry clearly says that this is not the whole story, for Plato has further principles in addition to those in

---

[34] The expression τὸ ... ποιωτικὸν οὐσίας is closely parallel to Porphyry's characterisation of the specific differentia as 'essential quality' (ποιότης οὐσιώδης: Porph. *in Cat.* 95.17–20): see on this Luna 2001: 235; 240–1. On the text of Simplicius' passage, however, see now Chiaradonna & Rashed 2020: 37 and 162n.2 (= Boethus, fr. 18).

[35] On Boethus' ontology and Alexander's reaction against it, see Rashed 2013b.

Aristotle and, furthermore, physics merely accepts its principles as a given, whereas a superior science investigates their very existence.

We now come to the last question, i.e. what this superior science properly is. A possible candidate would be Aristotle's metaphysics or first philosophy. This hypothesis might find support in a famous passage where Aristotle says that 'The accurate determination of the first principle in respect of form, whether it is one or many and what it is or what they are, is the province of first philosophy' (*Ph.* 1.9.192a35–6, trans. Hardie & Gaye in Barnes 1984; cf. 2.2.194b9–15; 2.7.198a22–31). We don't know much about Porphyry's reading of Aristotle's *Metaphysics*, however: he certainly commented on *Metaphysics* Λ, but his interpretation is virtually unknown to us.[36] And, in addition to that, it is unclear how Aristotle's first philosophy, while being first and universal, can also be taken to investigate the existence of physical principles: certainly, the passage from *Ph.* 1.9 does not say this (rather, Aristotle's point implies that first philosophy focuses on what the formal principle properly is). If Porphyry was simply alluding to Aristotle's first philosophy, one might wonder why he didn't mention first philosophy and instead used the obscure expression *tou anabebēkotos*.

I would suggest, then, another solution which does not rule out the reference to Aristotle's first philosophy, but considers a further possible connotation for the expression *tou anabebēkotos*. It is in fact very interesting to compare Porphyry's references to form and matter in the fragments of his commentary on *Physics* with what we find in the fragments of his lost commentary on the *Timaeus*:

> Well then, the philosopher Porphyry, who took a contrary position <to these people> on these issues, says that in the course of procession the Forms are always being borne down into multiplicity and division and <eventually> acquire extension and undergo fragmentation of every kind. For this reason, when the intelligible essence proceeds into the cosmos, it ends in divided, coarse and enmattered plurality, even though above it is unified, without parts and monadic. Now, in the case of the Intelligible as a whole, nothing else was providing it with matter. It produced it itself, <and> therefore produced just as much as it could occupy. But in the case of Human-being-itself, it was this universe that was providing it with matter, <and> for this reason there was more matter than <was necessary> for one <human> ...
> (Procl. *in Ti.* 1.439.29–440.7, trans. Runia & Share 2008)

Whatever of the details of this exceedingly difficult passage, the difference is striking: for while in the commentary on *Physics* Porphyry takes matter

---

[36] Fragments in Smith 1992: 160–1 (= Porph. 163–4F Smith).

and form as given and shows how their mutual relation works, in the commentary on the *Timaeus* he illustrates their genesis from superior metaphysical principles.[37] So it is in Porphyry's commentary on the *Timaeus* that the cursory reference to the superior exemplary and instrumental principles mentioned in the exegesis of the *Physics* is fully explored, so that physical principles are now regarded as deriving from intelligible and metaphysical causes. If this is correct, then Porphyry would be suggesting that Aristotle's physics focuses on sensible beings and takes its principles as given, whereas Plato's account in the *Timaeus* shows that these principles exist insofar as they come from superior and intelligible causes. In doing so, Porphyry makes an interesting use of Aristotle's account of the subordination of sciences in order to illustrate the relation between Plato's *Timaeus* and Aristotle's *Physics*. From this perspective, it is also worth recalling that Porphyry's famous metaphysical excursus about Moderatus' account of principles did not come from his commentary on the *Physics*, but from a different work *On Matter* (see Simp. *in Phys.* 230.34–231.24 = Porph. 236F Smith = 4B BS).

This position could lie behind Porphyry's idea that Aristotle's *Physics* is divided into two parts: books 1–4 focus on principles, whereas books 5–8 focus on movement (see Simp. *in Phys.* 802.7–13 = Porph. 159F Smith). Apparently, Porphyry only commented on books 1–4, while he wrote a summary (σύνοψις) of the rest of the work.[38] On his view, perhaps, the first four books of the work, and hence the discussion that spans from the account of physical principles to that of time, represented a physical treatment of the topics which are metaphysically explored in Plato's *Timaeus*. Instead, the abstract account of motion and the demonstration of the prime mover in *Physics* 5–8 fall outside this scope. This is just an hypothesis: in any case, Porphyry's preliminary remarks in his lost commentary on the *Physics* probably hinted at the integration of Aristotle's *Physics* and Plato's *Timaeus*. Porphyry's move actually paves the ground for the later exegetical work on Aristotle's *Physics*. Aristotle's work is regarded as an authoritative text which deserves careful reading in itself and must be supplemented by a Platonist account of principles. With different emphases, later Neoplatonist interpreters also shared this view. Porphyry's project is remarkably different from the early Middle Platonist reaction to Aristotle's natural philosophy. As said earlier, it is Porphyry, and not

---

[37] For details, see Smith 2012.
[38] See Moraux 1985; Chase 2012: according to Romano 1985: 56, Porphyry's σύνοψις only included *Ph.* 5.

Arius Didymus, who sets the foundation for the Neoplatonic commentary work on Aristotle.

If what we have attempted to show in this contribution is correct, from Plotinus onwards Aristotle's *Physics* emerges as a reference work for Platonist philosophers, and this marks a genuine turning point in the reception of the text; from this point of view, Plotinus' engagement with Aristotle is a necessary condition for the subsequent Neoplatonist commentary tradition. Plotinus, however, makes free and ultimately very critical use of Aristotle. His account of the physical world is largely indebted to Aristotelian texts and theories, which are nonetheless critically discussed and even dismantled. The situation is different with Porphyry, who clearly regards Aristotle's works as authoritative texts (though not unqualifiedly so) which deserve to be covered by detailed commentaries. Porphyry probably aims to integrate Aristotle's physics within a larger framework in which Plato's account in the *Timaeus* has the position of a superior science. Whereas Plotinus develops a sophisticated internal criticism of Aristotle's hylomorphism, Porphyry integrates Aristotle's theories into his Platonist philosophy with a subordinate position: this project is based on Porphyry's commentary work on Aristotle, which paves the way for the later Neoplatonist commentary tradition.

CHAPTER 9

# Conflicting Authorities? Hermias and Simplicius on the Self-Moving Soul[*]

Saskia Aerts

Aristotle plays a highly authoritative role in Neoplatonic philosophy, second only to the almost undisputed authority of Plato. However, as any reader of Plato's and Aristotle's works knows, the views of the two philosophers often diverge and generate conflicts. These conflicts provide the Neoplatonic commentators with a serious interpretative challenge: although, as Platonists, their main goal is to defend Plato and the Platonist position, they are also hesitant to openly criticise Aristotle, who is regarded as a true adherent of Plato's philosophy. The commentators most prominently face such a challenge in the case of the self-moving soul, a core Platonic doctrine severely criticised by Aristotle, implicitly in *Physics* 8.5 and explicitly in *De anima* 1.3.

The key for dealing with these conflicting authorities lies in the exegetical act of explicating the 'harmony' that exists between the views of both philosophers. This approach relies on the idea that the philosophies of Plato and Aristotle are fundamentally in agreement, which comes to the surface when their texts are interpreted in the right way. 'Harmony' translates the Greek *symphōnia*, a term most notably used in this technical meaning by Simplicius.[1] However, the term 'harmony' is problematic, because it does not identify any absolute concept – instead, it can refer to any kind of agreement, ranging from mere compatibility to theoretical identity. What is more, the operative concept of harmony employed by modern scholars often bears the same ambiguity as its ancient

---

[*] This paper is part of a larger project on epistemic authority in the Neoplatonic commentary tradition, conducted by a research group of the KU Leuven, consisting of Jan Opsomer, Pieter d'Hoine, Irini Fotini Viltanioti, and myself. In order to get a better grasp on the phenomenon of epistemic authority, we have developed a theoretical model meant for the analysis of epistemic authority in textual traditions, as discussed in Opsomer & Ulacco 2016, Aerts & Opsomer 2017, and Aerts 2019.

[1] For instance, in his introduction to his commentary on Aristotle's *Categories* (2.15–25), Simplicius records that Iamblichus demonstrated the harmony (συμφωνία) between the doctrines of the Pythagorean Archytas and Aristotle's *Categories*.

counterpart.[2] Most studies do not reflect on the polysemy of the term, and the notion of harmony used is not always well defined, which may lead to pointless debates on terminological matters.[3] Moreover, the danger of overemphasising the unity of this 'harmonising tendency', as I. Hadot calls it, lies in failing to take proper account of the diversity of the commentators' approaches.[4]

In this paper, I will present two parallel Neoplatonic discussions of the apparent disagreement between Plato and Aristotle about the self-moving soul, namely those of Hermias of Alexandria in his commentary on Plato's *Phaedrus*, and Simplicius of Cilicia in his commentary on Aristotle's *Physics*.[5] Since both philosophers ultimately argue that there is agreement between Aristotle and Plato, I will elucidate (i) what specific kind of 'harmony' each of the commentators assumes, (ii) what reasons each provides for supposing such a harmony, and (iii) which exegetical methods they use to explicate this harmony.

The harmonising interpretations of Hermias and Simplicius on this issue have been discussed previously by S. Gertz, who claims that both commentators similarly argue that the disagreement between Plato and Aristotle is 'merely verbal, motivated by respect for the common usage of

[2] In her latest work on Neoplatonic harmonisation, Hadot 2015 states that 'in order to avoid misunderstandings, it is worthwhile insisting beforehand on the definition of the term "harmonization", for there is no unanimity on the subject' (p. 41). However, despite the fact that Hadot strongly argues against understanding 'harmonisation' as 'identification' (pp. 41–2), she does not provide any positive definition herself, as far as I can see. Gerson 2005 claims that the concept of harmony is 'necessarily somewhat vague' (p. 4), and in order to make the idea more precise he introduces three different senses of harmony (p. 5).

[3] An example might be Hadot's 2015 criticism of Helmig 2009, whom she accuses of understanding the term 'harmonisation' in the sense of 'identification' (p. 42). Although the sentence quoted of Helmig's article is indeed ambiguous when taken out of its context, Helmig carefully explains what he has in mind (p. 371) and actually emphasises the importance of qualifying the notion of harmony in order for it to be meaningful (p. 349).

[4] Hadot 2015: ix defines the aim of her work as follows: 'For my part, I would like to show that this harmonizing tendency, born in Middle Platonism . . ., prevailed in Neoplatonism from Porphyry and Iamblichus, and that it persisted in this philosophy until its end *without any known exception, but with some nuances*, which are due both to the proper personality of each of the Neoplatonists and to the stage of development of their doctrines' (my emphasis). Regarding this aspect, I share the concern of Helmig 2009: 349, who remarks that 'it is probably more promising to investigate "single" Neoplatonists and their particular features before speaking of general characteristics of the whole school'.

[5] To the possible objection that it may not be appropriate to compare remarks from commentaries on Plato to those from commentaries on Aristotle because of the difference in context, I would reply that this only poses interpretative problems insofar as the context radically changes the views of the commentators. Although I acknowledge that there might be differences of emphasis because of the different source texts, these are all differences within a unitary doctrine that each Neoplatonist traces back, confronts, and assesses in relation to the authoritative sources of Aristotle and Plato.

names'.[6] Although I agree that this is the kind of harmony that Simplicius assumes, my interpretation of Hermias' discussion differs from the one proposed by Gertz. Despite some evident similarities in their approaches, I will suggest that Hermias defends a much less radical form of harmony than Simplicius: whereas Simplicius claims that the views of Plato and Aristotle are verbally different but philosophically identical, Hermias only intends to show that Aristotle would have to approve of the self-moving soul to remain faithful to and consistent with his own doctrines. In addition to showing the individuality of these commentators' approaches in dealing with conflicting authorities, my analysis also aims at elucidating *why* it is so important for the commentators to defend the self-motion of the soul. As will become clear, the concept of self-motion is not only crucial in Neoplatonic psychology, but also indispensable in their explanation of physical motion.

## 9.1 Plato and Aristotle on Self-Motion

The most important source for Plato's concept of the self-moving soul is *Phaedrus* 245c5–d7, in which soul's self-motion is essential to prove its immortality. Contrary to other possible arguments for the immortality of the soul (such as those delivered in the *Phaedo*), this proof heavily relies on the connection between motion and life: what ceases to move, ceases to live. Only what is always moving has unending life and may be thereby called immortal. According to Plato, it is only possible for something never to cease moving if the cause of its motion is not external but in *itself*. Thus, only something that moves itself can continue moving, because it has the source of its motion in itself: since it cannot depart from itself, it will always move. For this reason, Plato concludes that the 'self-moving' must also be the principle of motion (ἀρχὴ κινήσεως) for other things that are in motion: not only is soul the first mover because it has no cause of motion prior to itself, but its everlasting self-motion also guarantees, by imparting it, the continuous motion of other things.

In book 10 of the *Laws* (894b–896c), the first mover is identified as a soul that moves both itself and other things. In order to show the priority of self-motion over all other types of motion, Plato first argues that there must be a first cause of motion that cannot be moved externally, because this would imply an infinite regress in the series of movers. Since the first cause cannot be something that is moved by another, it must be moved by

---

[6] Gertz 2010: 79–84 (cit. 84). I was not able to benefit from the recent contribution of Longo 2020 on this topic, which became available at a late stage of the editing process and could thus not be taken into consideration.

itself (894e4–895a3).[7] Second, let us imagine that everything suddenly became motionless: what type of motion would be the first to start again? If everything is motionless, it cannot be motion caused by an external agent. The first mover must then be the self-mover, as it is the only kind of mobile entity that can initiate its own motion (895a5–b7). By connecting the capacity for self-motion with life, Plato concludes that the self-mover, which is 'the cause of all change and motion in all things',[8] must be soul.[9]

Aristotle critically analyses the self-mover as the first cause of motion in *Physics* 8. In this book, Aristotle sets out to prove that everlasting natural motion is guaranteed by a first cause of motion, which is responsible for all motion in the universe. In a Platonic spirit, Aristotle notes that *if* this first mover is moved, it must be moved by itself.[10] This hypothesis triggers a critical investigation into the nature of self-motion in *Physics* 8.5, which leads Aristotle to conclude that primary self-motion is impossible. Primary self-motion entails being capable of *causing motion*, both in itself and others, while simultaneously *being in motion*. According to Aristotle, however, a whole cannot possibly move itself as a whole, since the self-mover would be causing and undergoing the same change.[11] This implies the absurdity that the same thing is both actual and potential in the very same respect at the same time. Instead, it is the case that what causes motion must already have in actuality what it imparts to others, while the moveable is moved in virtue of potentiality, not actuality.[12] Therefore, the mover and moved cannot be the same. To assert that the mover and moved are the same would come down to saying, to adopt Aristotle's own example, that the teacher learns what he is teaching. However, this implies that the teacher at the same time *has* and *does not have* knowledge of the same thing, which is impossible according to the law of non-contradiction.[13]

---

[7] Plato thus frames the question of the nature of the first mover in disjunctive form: it is *either* externally moved *or* moved by itself. Since the first option is impossible, he concludes that it must be moved by itself; Aristotle's proposal of an unmoved mover is not even considered. As Menn 2012: 57 comments: 'Plato either has never considered the possibility that something that is itself unmoved could set something else in motion, or else he regards it as not needing refutation'.

[8] Plato, *Leg.* 10.896b1: μεταβολῆς τε καὶ κινήσεως ἁπάσης αἰτία ἅπασιν. In the next sentence, Plato calls the self-moving soul again the 'principle of motion' (896b3: ἀρχὴ κινήσεως).

[9] Ibid. 895c1–13. The argument is that since living is *both* possessing the capacity of self-motion *and* possessing – or being – a soul, soul must be self-moving. See Mayhew 2008: 124.

[10] Aristotle, *Ph.* 8.5.256a19–21: 'If, then, everything moved is moved by something, and the first mover is moved, but not by another, it must be moved by itself' (εἰ οὖν ἅπαν μὲν τὸ κινούμενον ὑπό τινος κινεῖται, τὸ δὲ πρῶτον κινοῦν κινεῖται μέν, οὐχ ὑπ' ἄλλου δέ, ἀνάγκη αὐτὸ ὑφ' αὑτοῦ κινεῖσθαι – ed. Ross).

[11] Aristotle, *Ph.* 8.5.257b2–6.  [12] Ibid. 257b6–12.  [13] Ibid. 257a12–14.

182 SASKIA AERTS

The discussion leads Aristotle to affirm that self-motion is only possible in the sense that one part of the whole self-moving entity acts as an unmoved mover and the other part as the moved, as is the case for the living being.[14] The living being is indeed a self-mover in a *derivative* sense: the soul, as unmoved mover, imparts motion on its moved body. Overall, Aristotle's discussion of self-motion in *Physics* 8.5 is very abstract and does not seem to specifically target a concrete self-mover such as Plato's self-moving soul. The only concrete self-mover mentioned in *Physics* 8 is the living being, that is, the derivative self-mover defined by Aristotle's own criteria.[15] However, even though neither Plato nor his notion of the self-moving soul are explicitly mentioned, Aristotle's criticism is so general that it may easily apply to Plato's idea of self-motion. Indeed, late Platonists, such as Simplicius, are well aware of the difficulties that Aristotle's arguments pose for Plato's notion of the self-moving soul.[16]

It is in *De anima* 1.3 that Aristotle explicitly rejects the possibility of a self-moving soul. In this chapter, Aristotle argues that soul is the cause of motion for the body and is even capable of being in motion itself, but not in the way his predecessors, Plato included, think. First, soul can only be in motion *accidentally* (κατὰ συμβεβηκός), that is, by being carried around in a moving body, so not in its own right (καθ' αὑτήν). Only a magnitude (μέγεθος) can move in its own right, but soul is not a magnitude. Second, Aristotle agrees with Plato that soul is the principle of motion for bodies, but not because it is itself in motion. Instead, soul operates through activity (ἐνέργεια) rather than motion (κίνησις). In order to prove it impossible for physical motion to belong to the soul, Aristotle develops a series of arguments against the view that soul is in motion and in place in its own right.[17] I cannot go into the details of all the arguments here, but

[14] Ibid. 257b12–13; 258a1–8.

[15] The self-moving animal is already introduced in *Physics* 8 in ch. 2 (252b21–3), and enters back into the discussion in ch. 6 (259b1–19). Aristotle is specifically concerned with the question of how animals *initiate* their motion: the fact that animal movements seem to arise spontaneously without existing previously provides an *aporia* to Aristotle's view of the continuation of motion (ch. 2). He tries to solve this problem by arguing that, although these self-movers have their principle of motion and rest in themselves, this principle cannot trigger the motion but needs a stimulus from the environment (ch. 6). See Gill 1994.

[16] As Opsomer 2012 shows, Iamblichus already attempts to counter Aristotle's criticism of self-motion. For the reception of Aristotle's *Physics* in Plotinus and Porphyry, see Riccardo Chiaradonna, Chapter 8 in the present volume.

[17] Aristotle, *DA* 1.3.406a10 ff. Again, soul can only be in motion and in place accidentally, as present in a *body* that is in motion and in place. Aristotle's interpretation of Plato is right insofar as one might be justified in assuming that the motion that Plato ascribes to the soul is no different from the motion it imparts, i.e. physical motion that belongs to spatially extended objects. A Platonist like

## Hermias and Simplicius on the Self-Moving Soul

183

I would like to draw attention to one objection that provides a serious challenge to the Platonic view. The concept of motion, Aristotle argues, always implies a displacement (ἔκστασις) of the moving entity in the respect in which it is moved. If soul is both mover and moved in its own right, its motion can cause soul to move away from its own essence (οὐσία).[18] The essence of the soul can hardly remain unchanged if the soul would be continuously in motion.

This criticism is clearly aimed at Plato's inference in the *Phaedrus*, according to which only what moves itself, *since it does not depart from itself,* never stops moving, and can thus provide continuous motion to other things.[19] By connecting self-motion to the essence of the soul, Plato believes he has guaranteed the everlastingness of this motion. In this way, soul has the source of its motion safely stored in itself. By contrast, Aristotle replies that if soul could move itself, it would actually depart from itself, and thus from its essential nature as principle of motion. The motion that such an entity would impart would not be continuous at all, but rather interrupted and variable.[20] In order for soul to remain essentially the same, soul must therefore be unmoved. Nevertheless, even if one grants that soul is unmoved, Aristotle would still deny the Platonic thesis that soul is the first mover of all things: even a soul that is unmoved *per se* is still moved accidentally with the body, and thereby suffers too much change to cause continuous motion.[21] For this reason, Aristotle postulates a prime unmoved mover, indivisible, without parts and magnitude, which is unaffected by any change whatsoever. This first mover holds the same relationship to the moved continuously, causing everlasting, constant motion.[22]

### 9.2 Hermias

In his commentary on the *Phaedrus*, Hermias provides a detailed explanation of Plato's proof of the immortality of the soul (*Phdr.* 245c5–d7) by distinguishing two syllogisms.[23] According to Hermias, both syllogisms

---

Plutarch thus interpreted soul's self-motion as spatially extended circular motion: see Opsomer 2012: 263–4.

[18] Ibid. 406b11–15.

[19] Plato, *Phdr.* 245c7–9: μόνον δὴ τὸ αὑτὸ κινοῦν, <u>ἅτε οὐκ ἀπολεῖπον ἑαυτό,</u> οὔποτε λήγει κινούμενον, ἀλλὰ καὶ τοῖς ἄλλοις ὅσα κινεῖται τοῦτο πηγὴ καὶ ἀρχὴ κινήσεως.

[20] See Menn 2002: 97–8.   [21] Aristotle, *Ph.* 8.6.259b20–8.   [22] Aristotle, *Ph.* 8.10.267b2–6.

[23] According to Hermias, Plato's statement that 'all/every soul is immortal' (ψυχὴ πᾶσα ἀθάνατος: *Phdr.* 245c5) only pertains to the rational soul. In contrast to many modern interpreters, the question whether πᾶσα should be construed distributively ('every soul') or collectively ('all soul'), is not Hermias' main concern. Rather, he tries to define the kind of soul Plato has in mind. Hermias

# 184 SASKIA AERTS

show the indestructibility, and consequently the immortality, of the soul: the first demonstrates that soul cannot destroy itself, the second that it cannot be destroyed from outside either.[24] That soul cannot destroy itself, in the sense that it cannot suffer natural destruction, is deduced from soul's self-moving nature, which implies that soul is always moving and thus immortal.[25] That soul cannot be destroyed by something else follows from the fact that soul's self-moving nature makes it the principle of motion for other things, and a principle (ἀρχή) is by necessity ungenerated and thereby indestructible.[26] Both syllogisms are thus based on the premise that soul is essentially self-moving, which leads the commentator to the discussion of the controversial issue of soul's self-motion:

> Now, let us discuss separately on its own the first premise, common to both syllogisms, that says 'the soul is self-moving', which Plato will set forth as the last of the whole argument, and examine regarding the self-moving how it is the first of the things moved, since it was no random person who has raised doubts about the existence of the self-moved in general (ἐπειδὴ καὶ περὶ τοῦ εἶναι ὅλως αὐτὸ οὐχ ὁ τυχὼν ἀνὴρ ἠμφισβήτησεν). And perhaps a point will be found on which the philosophers do not disagree. For Aristotle too does away with all bodily motions of the soul, which we also consider to be very true, and Plato clearly declares that the motions of the soul are other than all bodily ones. For he says in the tenth book of the *Laws*: 'The soul drives all things in heaven and earth and sea by its own motions, of which the names are willing, investigating, caring, deliberating, opining correctly or falsely, being joyful or grieving, bold or fearful, hating or loving.' (Hermias, *in Phdr.* 109.30–110.9 Lucarini & Moreschini)[27]

explicitly rejects the views that Plato's ψυχὴ πᾶσα refers to every soul without qualification or only to the World Soul; instead, he argues that the argument is 'about all/every rational soul' (περὶ πάσης λογικῆς ψυχῆς: *in Phdr.* 108.13–14). Like Plato, Hermias does not make an explicit distinction between the distributive and collective senses, probably because any proof of the immortality of 'all rational soul' would for him equally apply to individual souls, which are clearly the focus of the rest of the palinode. Cf. Menn 2012: 55–7.

[24] Hermias, *in Phdr.* 108.21–109.29 (eds. Lucarini & Moreschini 2012). Hermias emphasises that each of the two arguments is complete in itself to prove soul's immortality, while also entailing the other, in the sense that what cannot destroy itself cannot be destroyed by another either, and vice versa.

[25] The first syllogism (*in Phdr.* 109.22–4) goes as follows: (1) Soul is self-moving; (2) What is self-moving is always moving; (3) What is always moving is immortal. → Therefore soul is immortal. Shortly afterwards, Hermias explicates what is already implicitly present in Plato's argument, namely that soul's self-motion is everlasting because the moved is always united with the cause of its motion (*in Phdr.* 114.13–17).

[26] The second syllogism (*in Phdr.* 109.25–8) reads: (1) Soul is self-moving; (2) What is self-moving is a principle of motion; (3) A principle of motion is ungenerated; (4) What is ungenerated is indestructible; (5) What is indestructible is immortal. → Therefore soul is immortal.

[27] All translations of Hermias' text are my own (the recently published English translation by Baltzly & Share 2018 was unfortunately not yet available to me at the time of writing).

## Hermias and Simplicius on the Self-Moving Soul 185

This passage introduces Hermias' discussion of soul as self-mover: an examination shaped by the initial question of how soul is the first of the things moved (πρῶτον ... τῶν κινουμένων). A sufficient and convincing answer to this question is necessitated by the fact that, as Hermias points out, a distinguished thinker, namely Aristotle, has raised doubts about soul's nature as self-mover. Notably, this passage shows that Hermias is perfectly aware of the disagreement (διαφωνία) that exists between Plato and Aristotle on the motion of the soul – in fact, acknowledging the tension, he expresses his hopes of finding some points on which the philosophers *do not* disagree (οὐδὲ διαφωνοῦσιν οἱ φιλόσοφοι). Then he immediately recognises a point of harmony that needs to be explained to the reader: both Plato and Aristotle believe that bodily motion could not in any way be ascribed to the soul. Hermias thus interprets Aristotle's criticisms in *De anima* 1.3 as directed against those who think that corporeal motions could be ascribed to the incorporeal soul, *not* against Plato's self-moving soul. Rather, those criticisms support Plato's claim in *Laws* 10 that soul has its own typical motions, such as willing or investigating, which are radically different from those found in bodies.[28]

Precisely because motion, qua physical motion, cannot apply to something incorporeal like soul, Aristotle argues that soul must be unmoved per se, and that soul imparts motion rather through its own distinctive activity than through any kind of motion. However, Hermias is not arguing for anything even remotely similar to Aristotle's conclusion. Instead of affirming that motion as such cannot apply to soul in any way, Hermias emphasises that motion *does* pertain to souls – just as Plato says – but that this psychic motion is of a completely different kind than physical motion. So, even when this point of agreement is granted, there still exists a crucial difference between the views of Plato and Aristotle. Whereas Plato regards the soul as the first of the things *moved*, that is, as suffering the motion – albeit in a psychic way – of which it is itself the cause, Aristotle grants that soul can cause motion but must be unmoved per se.

Before settling the issue whether the soul as principle of motion is self-moved or unmoved, Hermias provides arguments for the necessity of a principle of motion.[29] First, he shows that it is impossible to claim that all

---

[28] It is indeed the case that Aristotle criticises the Platonic concept of the soul only explicitly in the second part of *De anima* 1.3, so not in the first part which raises objections against the view that soul is moved in terms of one of the four types of physical motion. The second part (406b26 ff.) argues explicitly against Plato's *Timaeus*, and argues that soul cannot be described as magnitude (μέγεθος) since reasoning would be impossible for such an entity.

[29] Hermias, *in Phdr.* 110.10–21.

## 186                    SASKIA AERTS

things that move are moved externally, since this would lead to an untenable infinite regress.[30] Also circularity of causation – which, in its simplest form, comes down to A causing motion in B and B causing motion in A – can be excluded. Such circularity would indeed neglect the hierarchy of beings and put the effect on the same level as its cause.[31] Since both of these options have been shown to be impossible, Hermias concludes that there must necessarily be a principle of motion.[32] However, the arguments that Hermias puts forward to argue for a principle of motion only show the necessity of a first mover that is not *externally* moved, whether this would be an unmoved mover or a self-mover.[33] Since Plato and Aristotle agree that this principle of motion is soul, the real question is whether soul is self-moved (Plato) or unmoved (Aristotle):

> This principle of motion, which according to both philosophers is the soul, is called by Plato self-moved, by Aristotle unmoved. That the principle of motion needs to be put forth as the self-moved, even according to Aristotle's own doctrines, one could learn from the following argument. In all beings, nature does not advance immediately from contrary to contrary, like from winter to summer, but in every case a middle term must precede, now the spring, then the autumn. And it is similar for all corporeals and incorporeals. So, also here, where there is the externally moved and the unmoved, there must be a middle term too, which is the self-moved, that is one and the same in number and substratum. For, what Aristotle calls self-moved, namely the living being, is not what we are looking for right now. Since, insofar as according to him the living being is composed of the unmoved and the externally moved, he calls the whole self-moved. So that, if there is something that is in every way unmoved, i.e. the principle of all, and something that is externally moved, i.e. bodies,

[30] This argument for a first mover is used by both Plato (*Leg.* 10.894e4–895a3) and Aristotle (*Ph.* 8.5.256a13–21). Next to the fact that an infinite regress is simply begging the question, its rejection in antiquity has been dominated by Aristotle's view that the actual infinite is impossible. Thus Hermias: 'For, neither does infinity exist in being nor is there any knowledge of it' (*in Phdr.* 110.17–18).

[31] For the Neoplatonic position that every efficient cause should be superior to its effect, see Proclus, *ET* 7. In a similar though different way, Aristotle discusses the option of circular causation in the self-mover and concludes that this is impossible for several reasons. One of these reasons, similar to the one offered by Hermias, is that there would be no priority in movers when each entity would cause the motion of another, whereas it is clear that a prior mover is more of a cause of motion than what comes next in the series (*Ph.* 8.5.257b13–26).

[32] Proclus uses exactly the same arguments in *ET* 14 (lines 15–19) to argue for the existence of a first unmoved mover. For an enlightening discussion of *ET* 14–24 and its relation to Aristotle, see Opsomer 2009b: 203–9.

[33] Proclus, by contrast, leaps to the conclusion in *ET* 14 that these arguments show the necessity of a first mover that is itself *unmoved*. See Opsomer 2009b: 204–5.

## Hermias and Simplicius on the Self-Moving Soul     187

there shall be a middle, that is the self-moved, which shall be nothing other than soul. (Hermias, *in Phdr.* 110.21–111.3 Lucarini & Moreschini)

In this passage, Hermias makes an interesting interpretative move in order to argue for a specific kind of harmony between the conflicting views of Plato and Aristotle. After having testified to the philosophers' different ideas regarding the motion of the soul, Hermias defends Plato's view that the soul is self-moved. In doing so, Hermias also emphasises that the same conclusion, although in clear opposition to Aristotle's last predicament, should follow from Aristotle's own doctrines (δόγματα). Even without Aristotle drawing such a conclusion himself – Hermias seems to suggest – some Aristotelian principles admit, and can eventually lead us to understand, the soul as self-moving without any contradiction.

In order to get a clear grasp on the argumentative steps that Hermias takes, we should first recognise the crucial distinction between, on the one hand, the conclusions that Aristotle explicitly draws in his texts with regard to a specific issue, and on the other hand, the doctrines that he endorses throughout his texts that can be abstracted from their specific context and applied to other cases. The doctrine that Hermias uses to show that soul is indeed self-moved is the idea that changes in nature do not happen as a leap from contrary to contrary. Thus, winter cannot suddenly change into summer. This change rather occurs through an intermediate state, such as spring or autumn, that helps the transition to take place gradually. In the *Physics,* Aristotle indeed endorses the view that natural changes between contraries always happen continuously (συνεχῶς): after having departed from the initial state, the changing object must first arrive at the 'in between' (τὸ μεταξύ) before it can reach the end of the change.[34]

As an ingenious step in his exegetical strategy, Hermias applies this doctrine to the causal chain of motion, thereby making Aristotle an adherent of the Neoplatonic law of mean terms:[35] every cause produces things that are like, rather than unlike, itself; consequently, two contrary terms cannot be continuous, but need to be linked by an intermediate term that shares a characteristic with both.[36] In the case of motion, this means that, between the unmoved cause of motion and that which is only moved externally, there must be a middle term that connects the two extremes by being both mover and moved at the same time. Hermias

---

[34] Aristotle, *Ph.* 5.3.227a7–226b32 (as transposed by Ross).
[35] Designated as such by Dodds 1963: xxii.
[36] The relation between cause and effect is laid down by Proclus in *ET* 28. I follow and endorse the untraditional reading of this proposition as proposed by Opsomer 2015.

188                                   SASKIA AERTS

stresses that this self-moving entity must unite the capacities of causing and undergoing motion as *one single whole*, so not in the way that Aristotle conceives of the self-mover, which consists of an unmoved part that causes motion and a moved part that undergoes it. By contrast, the self-mover that Hermias has in mind has its own existence between the unmoved mover, Intellect, and the externally moved bodies.[37] Hermias then concludes on the basis of metaphysical and exegetic reasons that this middle place should be assigned to soul, which provides the link between the material and the immaterial realm.[38]

In the paragraph following the one cited above, Hermias provides additional support for his thesis that the existence of the self-moved can legitimately follow from Aristotle's own doctrines. Hermias shows that Aristotle himself allows certain beings to be the cause of an effect that is both affecting others and themselves.[39] A clarifying example from physical nature is the sun. The sun is indeed the cause of light for others, but also for itself; it does not receive its light from a prior cause.[40] Hermias explains that for Aristotle there are being, life, and intellect, just as there are for the Platonists. In all of these aspects, there are things that receive their life, being, or intellect from something else, like a human being whose life is given by another human being.[41] However, there are also things that do not have external causes of their life, being, or intellect, but grant these things to *themselves*. According to Hermias, it is evident that Aristotle accepts this thesis, since he insists that, for instance, the heavens are not generated by another cause, but are an ungenerated cause of their own being.[42] The same holds for intellect: whereas the potential intellect can

---

[37] Hermias describes this being that is 'in every way unmoved' (ὄντος τοῦ πάντῃ ἀκινήτου) as 'the principle of all' (τῆς πάντων ἀρχῆς; *in Phdr.* 111.1–2). Although the designation ἀρχὴ πάντων is usually reserved for the One, it would be odd if Hermias would characterise the One as unmoved, since the One stands beyond these categories altogether. Rather, he must have Intellect in mind, to which he will refer some pages later as the unmoved cause of soul's motion (115.31–3). Therefore, I do not think that πάντων in ἀρχὴ πάντων should be understood as *all things* without further qualification, but rather as all things *that move*, considering that the scope of the discussion is clearly limited to motion.

[38] Also Proclus in *ET* 14 (lines 23–6) appeals to the law of mean terms in order to argue for the necessity of a self-mover. Moreover, just like Hermias, he makes a threefold classification of movers in unmoved movers, self-movers, and things moved externally, which in prop. 20 he equates to the different levels in the metaphysical hierarchy, namely to Intellect, soul, and bodies, respectively.

[39] Hermias, *in Phdr.* 111.6–29.       [40] Ibid. 121.22–3.

[41] Hermias quotes Aristotle's favorite example that 'it takes a human being to generate a human being': e.g. *Ph.* 2.2.194b13; *Met.* Z 7.1032a25; Z 8.1033b32; Θ.8.1049b25–6; Λ 3.1070a8; N 5.1092a16.

[42] In *De caelo* 1.10–12, Aristotle argues that the heavens must be both ungenerated and indestructible.

only actualise its thinking with the aid of the active intellect (and thus receives its thinking externally), active intellect causes its own intellection and is even capable of intelligising *itself*.[43] So, just as there are entities that can cause their own being, life, and intellect, there must an entity that can cause its own motion: soul.

In short, Hermias argues for harmony between the doctrines of Plato and Aristotle in two argumentative steps. First, he emphasises that Plato and Aristotle agree that bodily motion cannot belong to the incorporeal soul. However, this assumption brings Aristotle to conclude that the soul is *unmoved*. Plato, by contrast, argues that motion *does* pertain to the soul in the form of a completely different kind of motion, psychic motion. As the name suggests, this type of motion originates in the soul itself, thus providing it with its *self-moving* nature. This point of disagreement requires a second step in order to explicate the assumed harmony: despite the fact that Aristotle claims the opposite, Hermias argues that it follows from Aristotle's own doctrines that the self-moved must exist as intermediate between the unmoved mover and the externally moved. The doctrines that Hermias has in mind are (1) the principle that two contrary terms are always connected by a mean term, which demands that the self-moved mediates between the unmoved and the externally moved; and (2) the assumption that certain entities cause their own being, life, and intellect, from which it follows by analogy that there is an entity that causes its own motion. Hermias' strategy in arguing for harmony between Plato and Aristotle thus consists in demonstrating that Aristotle, while not explicitly drawing this conclusion himself, shares all the philosophical assumptions that lead to the doctrine of the self-moving soul. Now, let us turn to Simplicius for a different approach in reconciling the conflicting authorities.

## 9.3 Simplicius

In *Physics* 8.5, Aristotle offers a critical discussion of self-motion, which leads him to the conclusion that primary self-motion is impossible. Simplicius, who writes a detailed commentary on the *Physics*, closely follows Aristotle's text. Only in the last pages dedicated to chapter 8.5 does Simplicius mention the apparent disagreement (διαφορά) between Aristotle's and Plato's views.[44] Before moving on to the analysis of this

---

[43] Possible references are: Aristotle, *DA* 3.4–5; *Metaph.* Λ 9.
[44] Simplicius, *in Phys.* 1247.27–1250.31.

disagreement, Simplicius enumerates the points on which the philosophers agree. First, he argues, Aristotle and Plato both insist that the self-moved is the principle of motion, as testified by passages from the *Physics*, and the *Phaedrus* and *Laws*.[45] Moreover, Plato and Aristotle also agree that the living being is self-moved, although they have radically different views regarding the cause of this self-motion. Aristotle, on the one hand, believes that what is 'primarily and properly' (πρώτως καὶ κυρίως) self-moved is the living being as combination of a moved body and an unmoved soul. Plato, on the other hand, holds that what is primarily and properly self-moved is the soul. For Plato, the living being's self-motion is nothing but an imprint (ἴχνος) and a mere appearance of the actual self-motion that belongs to the soul.[46]

In this respect, the views of the two philosophers seem to be in conflict and even irreconcilable. However, according to Simplicius, there is actually a compelling reason for Plato to assert that the soul is self-moved and for Aristotle that it is unmoved:

> The difference came about insofar as Plato grants that all change (μεταβολήν), both active and passive, is motion (κίνησιν). ... Aristotle, by contrast, who considers only physical changes (φυσικὰς μεταβολάς) worthy to be called motions, holds that the soul is active but is not moved (τὴν ψυχὴν ἐνεργεῖν, ἀλλ' οὐχὶ κινεῖσθαι). He clearly denies physical motions of the soul in Book I of *De anima* ... Yet Plato also denies them of the soul, enumerating them among the nine motions before those of the soul in the tenth book of the *Laws*, having transmitted the previously mentioned motions as those of the soul. And it is clear that Aristotle attributes these to the soul, and knows that they take place from it and toward it, but he calls them not motions (κινήσεις) but activities and affects (ἐνεργείας καὶ πάθη). (Simp. *in Phys.* 1248.21–1249.6, trans. Bodnár, Chase & Share 2012, slightly modified)

According to Simplicius, the reason why Plato calls the soul self-moved while Aristotle calls it unmoved is that each of them employs a very different concept when they speak of 'motion' (κίνησις).[47] Whereas Plato

---

[45] Ibid. 1247.29–1248.3. Simplicius quotes *Ph.* 8.5.257a28–30: 'If one had to examine whether the self-mover or the thing moved externally were the cause and principle of motion, everyone would suppose the former.' Of Plato, he quotes *Phdr.* 245c9, 'source and principle of motion', and *Laws* 10.895b3–6.

[46] Ibid. 1248.3–21. Cf. Proclus, *in Alc.* 225.12–15.

[47] The Greek term *kinēsis* can, dependent on the context, be translated as 'motion' or 'change'. The most significant difference with *metabolē* is that *metabolē*, 'change' or 'alteration', is mostly used as a more general term. Although Aristotle uses the two terms sometimes interchangeably, *metabolē* is strictly speaking an umbrella term for both *kinēsis* (motion or change with respect to quantity, quality, or place), and coming-to-be (*genesis*) and ceasing-to-be (*phthora*): see *Ph.* 5.1.

## Hermias and Simplicius on the Self-Moving Soul 191

ascribes the term 'motion' to every kind of change (μεταβολή), including psychic changes such as loving and willing, Aristotle reserves the term specifically for *physical* changes. For this reason, Plato calls the psychic changes discussed in *Laws* 10 motions, whereas Aristotle accepts these changes in the soul but rather calls them 'activities' (ἐνέργειαι) or 'affects' (πάθη). When insisting that soul is unmoved, Aristotle does not claim that soul remains completely unaffected by any change whatsoever, but rather that soul cannot change in a physical way. Like Hermias, Simplicius emphasises the harmony between *De anima* 1.3 and *Laws* 10, since he reads in both texts a rejection of the idea that bodily motion belongs to the soul. The difference in view regarding the motion of the soul comes about insofar as Plato's concept of motion allows him to ascribe a *different kind* of motion to soul, namely psychic motion, whereas Aristotle's narrower concept of motion prevents him from reaching the same conclusion. For Aristotle, if physical motion cannot be attributed to soul, and motion *is* physical motion, then soul must necessarily be unmoved. Thus 'motion' has a much broader meaning for Plato than for Aristotle.

Simplicius emphasises that Aristotle, 'who has philosophised so much about the soul', certainly knows about the changes that take place in the soul, such as knowing and bringing itself to perfection – however, unlike Plato, Aristotle does not want to call these changes 'motions'.[48] Aristotle's concept of motion is based on bodies, and the application of this concept to something incorporeal like the soul would lead to absurdities. For instance, with regard to bodies, Aristotle recognises that motion always implies a departure from a current state to a new one (τὸ ἐκστατικὸν τῆς κινήσεως).[49] It would be absurd to ascribe such a departure from its essence to the soul, and therefore Aristotle was completely right in criticising those who think of soul's motion as physical (*De anima* 1.3). In Simplicius' view, Plato would agree with Aristotle that soul is not in motion in the sense just described. Accordingly, Aristotle's criticism does not actually apply to the psychic motion of Plato's soul. As a result, the commentator concludes that the difference in views between the philosophers is in this case – like in most of the cases – not over a reality (πρᾶγμα), that is, the nature of the soul, but rather over a name (ὄνομα), that is, motion.[50]

The reason for this difference in name lies not so much in a difference of *understanding*, but rather in one of *method*. According to Simplicius, Aristotle starts his arguments from what is evident to the senses, and for

---

[48] Simplicius, *in Phys.* 1249.6–8.    [49] Ibid. 1249.8–12.    [50] Ibid. 1249.12–13.

this reason he maintains the ordinary use of words. Aristotle's inquiry into motion starts with physical nature; the concept that he develops is based on bodies, and therefore can only be appropriately applied to bodies. The ordinary use of the term 'motion' also designates changes of place, quality, or quantity that are observable in bodies, and Aristotle simply operates within this semantic context when he says that the soul cannot suffer this motion per se. By contrast, Plato often scorns what is evident to the senses, and rather resorts to intellectual theories (τὰς νοητὰς θεωρίας).[51] For Plato, 'motion' is an expression that, though it may be derived from physical nature, can also be applied just as easily to non-physical higher realities. Our lack of an adequate vocabulary to speak about these realities appropriately renders the analogical use of the word 'motion' in this context legitimate.

However, one should not immediately regard this remark of Simplicius as an implicit criticism of Aristotle, as if Aristotle would be accused of being a more 'low-minded' and 'this-worldly' thinker than the 'high-minded' or 'other-worldly' Plato. Rather, it is helpful to read this isolated comment in light of Simplicius' other discussions regarding the differences in terminology between Plato and Aristotle. Simplicius' comments at the end of his commentary on the *Physics*, regarding the different uses of the term 'generation', are especially enlightening.[52] The case is rather similar to the one discussed above: although both philosophers agree that the cosmos is eternal but changing, each of them uses a completely different terminology to describe it. Plato gives an account of the 'generation' of the cosmos in the *Timaeus*, which might give the wrong impression that he believes that the cosmos has a temporal origin. The reason for this is that Plato does not adhere to the ordinary use of the term 'generation'. Rather, he contrasts things that are generated to things that 'are', i.e. what is changing to what is always in the same state and condition. By contrast, Aristotle realises that qualifying eternal things as generated might give the wrong impression that they have a temporal origin. As a result, Aristotle refuses to use the term 'generation' with reference to the cosmos;[53] instead,

---

[51] Ibid. 1249.13–17. The reference to Plato's νοηταὶ θεωρίαι might be seen as an echo of Iamblichus' interpretative strategy called νοερὰ θεωρία ('intellective contemplation') but then on a higher level of the divine.

[52] Ibid. 1359.30–1360.23.

[53] Ibid. 1359.38–40: 'But this wonderful man seems to me clearly to refuse to apply the term "generation" to eternal things, because the imagination easily suggests a temporal origin for things that are said to be generated.'

he contrasts the unmoved with the moved, which is the same distinction as made by Plato but without implying any temporal origin.[54]

In Simplicius' view, Plato should be praised for having divine insight into the higher realities and for revealing this insight to others by means of familiar, ordinary expressions in order to facilitate its comprehension.[55] Nevertheless, he finds Aristotle's refusal to employ terms for the higher realm that cannot be properly attributed to realities belonging to this sphere equally commendable. Such broad use of language would not only be intrinsically inappropriate, but also misleading, since some people might mistakenly take these words literally. Although this would require further consideration, Simplicius might think that Aristotle's criticism of self-motion does not affect Plato's actual position, but only Plato's *apparent* position. This apparent position is a mistaken reconstruction of Plato's actual position and is the outcome of an overly literal and philosophical unrefined interpretation of ambiguous elements in Plato's texts. In this way, Simplicius could use Aristotle's remarks to clarify his own interpretation of Plato: to free the latter from potential criticisms and thereby firmly establishing the authority of Plato's position.[56]

## 9.4 Self-Motion Transformed

Thus far, I have focused on the two commentators' different approaches to explicating the harmony between Plato and Aristotle's views on the self-motion of the soul. However, some crucial questions regarding the Neoplatonic concept of self-motion are left unanswered. For instance, the commentators' solution to Aristotle's objection that motion cannot

---

[54] The interpretation of Plato's claim in the *Timaeus* that the world 'has been generated' (γέγονεν: 28b67) has been a matter of debate in the Platonic tradition, particularly in relation to the question of the eternity of the world. In his recent book on the Middle Platonist Taurus of Beirut, Petrucci 2018: 36–42 convincingly argues that Taurus, by providing a list of different meanings of γενητόν that do *not* imply temporal origin, demonstrates that the right, but still literalist, reading of the *Timaeus* passage shows that Plato believes in the eternity of the world. In Neoplatonist times, Porphyry quotes Taurus' meanings and adds some of his own, shifting the argument to fit his own metaphorical reading of the passage (Philoponus, *De aet. mund.* 148.7–149.16). It became Neoplatonic practice to list the meanings of γενητόν in order to show that the term is not exclusively used to refer to a temporal beginning, as done by Proclus (*in Ti.* 1.279.30–280.8) and Simplicius (*in Cael.* 92.33–97.17). For a discussion of this issue in Taurus and other Middle Platonists, and its echoes in Neoplatonism, see Petrucci 2018: 26–75.

[55] This is how the 'wise men' engage in cosmogony: Simplicius, *in Phys.* 1359.40–1360.6.

[56] To use the Arabic terminology introduced by Menn 2012, Simplicius uses Aristotle's criticism of Plato's apparent position in order to establish an interpretation of Plato that will be free of *tashbih*, i.e. the improper assimilation of divine things to lower things by attributing to them predicates which are appropriate only for lower things.

194 SASKIA AERTS

belong per se to the incorporeal soul is that the psychic motion meant by Plato is essentially different from the physical motion that Aristotle has in mind. But if this is the case, as both Hermias and Simplicius assert, what does this psychic self-motion actually amount to? Moreover, do any of Aristotle's objections against self-motion still apply to the reinterpreted self-motion of the soul, and if so, what would the commentators reply to them be?

In the following passage, Hermias gives some clues about the nature of soul's self-motion, both negatively (what this self-motion is *not*) and affirmatively. In the passage preceding this one, Hermias explained that whereas things naturally perish because they lose connection with their cause, soul can never suffer this kind of loss. The reason for this is that soul as self-mover unites the cause and effect of its motion in itself, which explains this motion's, and thus soul's, everlastingness.

> From this syllogism, it is shown that soul does not perish because of itself. This is not strange in the case of soul, since it is not the case that one part of it only moves, while another is only moved, but *every part of it, whichever one takes, both moves and is moved in the same respect.* But one may desire to learn more clearly what the motion in the soul actually is. That it is none of the bodily motions, not even the ninth, is clear, for these are not self-moved. But neither all the motions proper to the soul indicate the motion under discussion, such as volitions, opinions, spirited desires, or appetites: for it is not *always* moved regarding these, whereas we are looking for the motion that always belongs to it. . . . One might most of all grasp the soul's self-motion from its bringing itself to perfection and separate the rational soul in this respect from the irrational soul and from nature. For it belongs to the rational soul to *bring itself to perfection* and to *awaken itself* and to *revert upon itself* (τὸ ἑαυτὴν τελειοῦν καὶ ἀνεγείρειν καὶ ἐπιστρέφειν εἰς ἑαυτήν), which does not belong to any of the others. And with this interpretation it fits that he says 'about soul both divine and human', that is, about every rational soul and not about the irrational one or about nature. (Hermias, *in Phdr.* 119.16–34 Lucarini & Moreschini – my emphasis)

In this passage, Hermias points out that if we distinguished within this self-mover a part that moves and a part that is moved, as Aristotle does, the cause and the effect of the motion would become separated, and there is no guarantee that the link between the two, and the motion that it causes, would last forever. Therefore, Hermias insists that we should rather conceive of soul as a self-mover that moves itself as a whole in such a way that even when divided, each of its parts would be a self-mover *in exactly the same way* as the whole. In his view, soul is thus a primary self-

## Hermias and Simplicius on the Self-Moving Soul

mover that is potentially divisible in parts that are themselves primary self-movers.[57] Although this kind of self-motion is not directly discussed by Aristotle, he would most probably reply that the objection made against the self-mover moving itself as a whole would also apply to this self-mover: no matter if it concerns wholes or parts, it is impossible for the same thing to be actual and potential in the same respect. Hermias does not reply to this objection but, as will become clear shortly, Simplicius does.

Nevertheless, Hermias does provide some insight into what soul's self-motion exactly *is*. It has already become sufficiently clear that it is none of the eight bodily motions enumerated in *Laws* 10, nor can it be the ninth motion which is described by Plato as the motion that is 'capable of moving other things but *not itself*'.[58] In fact, not even the typical psychic motions such willing or opining are the true self-motion of the soul, since they are interrupted and thus do not always belong to it, whereas we are looking for an unceasing motion. Rather, the unceasing self-motion becomes manifest from soul's capacity of bringing itself to perfection (ἑαυτὴν τελειοῦν), which it accomplishes by means of *reverting upon itself* (ἐπιστρέφειν εἰς ἑαυτήν). This reversion upon itself, which amounts to its self-thinking, is the only true and proper motion of the soul. What is more, the fact that soul is capable of perfecting itself indicates that it can cause its own well-being (τὸ εὖ εἶναι), so it necessarily follows that soul is also the cause of its own being (τὸ εἶναι), that is, its life and, accordingly, its motion.[59] Soul thus constitutes its own motion by means of reflecting upon itself as cause of its being.[60]

Soul's self-causation is actually of crucial importance in understanding how soul functions as principle of motion when imparting motion to other things. As we have seen above, Hermias' harmonising strategy consists in showing that the self-moved as intermediate between the unmoved mover and the externally moved follows from Aristotle's own doctrines. Nevertheless, Aristotle did not draw this conclusion: in his view, the self-

---

[57] These parts only have a potential existence since soul as self-moving and thus self-constituting entity (see below) is an essential unity.

[58] Plato, *Laws* 10.894b8–9 (my emphasis). Hermias interprets the ninth as the motion of incorporeals in the realm of bodies (for instance, in processes of heating, cooling, and ensouling). This motion corresponds to the psychic motion of imparting life to bodies (in *Phdr.* 113.5–8), which belongs to the *irrational* soul, not to the self-moving rational soul (118.31–119.4).

[59] Hermias, in *Phdr.* 115.2–8. The assumption behind this reasoning is that what can grant itself the better (i.e. being good) can also grant itself the less (i.e. being).

[60] That soul is, to use Proclus' terminology, self-constituted (αὐθυπόστατος) does of course not mean that it is completely independent from superior causes such as the unmoved cause of all motion, Intellect.

moved is not only an impossible but also superfluous entity, for the unmoved mover can immediately impart continuous motion to the externally moved universe. Hermias, by contrast, considers it impossible for there to be continuous motion without the medium of the self-moving soul. Motion, he argues, originates from the contact that exists between the mover and the moved.[61] The most intuitive way for this contact to occur is when the mover 'approaches' (προσελθεῖν) the moved, like my foot can approach and move the stone. This type of contact can, however, not exist between the unmoved and the externally moved: the activity of the unmoved mover Intellect is always directed at itself, and it would go against the hierarchy of beings if the superior would turn to the inferior instead of the other way around. On the other hand, the externally moved cannot approach the unmoved source of motion either, simply because it does not possess the capacity of approaching anything when not yet in motion.[62]

Therefore, a middle term is needed, a first *moved* mover, whose motion serves as cause for the motion of the externally moved. That this middle term must be self-moved, follows from the assertion that in the case of a hypothetical standstill the self-moved soul is the only one capable of initiating motion: whereas neither the unmoved mover nor the externally moved can be the first thing *moved*, soul is united with the cause of its motion, and is thus the first moved mover.[63] In this sense, the self-moved is the first entity capable of actually *undergoing* motion, and exactly because it possesses this capacity, the self-moved is the efficient cause of all motion in the universe.[64] There would be no motion whatsoever without the self-moved as origin of passive motion.[65] However, this does not mean that soul's own motion is identical to the motion that it imparts to others. Rather, the motions of the soul serve as *paradigms* for the bodily motions identified by Plato in *Laws* 10.[66] Psychic motion thus has a crucial relation to corporeal motion as exemplar to image. So, without explicitly

---

[61] Note the Aristotelian framework and terminology used in this argument.

[62] Hermias, *in Phdr.* 115.28–116.12.

[63] Ibid. 112.7–14: δῆλον ὡς αὐτὸ πρῶτον κινηθὲν τἆλλα κινήσει. The unmoved mover cannot be the first moved simply because it is in any way unmoved, nor can the externally moved be the first moved since it does not have the capacity of approaching the source of motion.

[64] According to Hermias, soul is the cause of motion in all the different senses of cause, that is, efficient, paradigmatic, and final cause (*in Phdr.* 112.1–7). The text discussing self-motion as final cause is missing.

[65] Cf. Aristotle, *Ph.* 8.4.255b30–1. The idea of the self-moved as origin of passive motion is elaborated by Proclus in *PT* 1.14; cf. *ET* 14.23–4. See Opsomer 2009b: 213.

[66] The eight bodily motions and their psychic counterparts are: (1) generation – soul's ascent away from the realities down here; (2) destruction – soul's fall from the intelligible; (3) growth – the

*Hermias and Simplicius on the Self-Moving Soul* 197

naming Aristotle, Hermias raises objections against the Aristotelian hypothesis that the unmoved can impart continuous motion to the externally moved without the mediation of the self-moved. Interestingly, he takes up Aristotle's own distinction between active and passive potency to do so. In this way, the commentator makes use of Aristotle's philosophy in a strategic way: he employs, as it were, Aristotle's own philosophical notions against him in an implicit criticism of the idea that motion would be possible without the self-moving soul, thus re-establishing the correctness of the Platonic position.

Simplicius, on the other hand, attempts to disarm Aristotle's strong objection that primary self-motion is impossible because the same thing cannot be actual and potential in the same respect. However, he does not intend to overthrow Aristotle's critical point altogether – in fact, he agrees that in general it is impossible for a unitary and simple thing to be self-moved. Rather, his strategy consists in showing that this objection, which is in general legitimate, does not apply to the case of the soul, and that Aristotle himself actually agrees with this. According to Simplicius, it is possible for the soul to move itself as a whole, exactly *because* it is actual and potential at the same time. Namely, despite being an essential unity, soul contains a multiplicity of reason-principles (λόγοι), of which some are active and others at rest:

> After all, the soul, which possesses all the reason-principles (λόγους), has some of them close at hand and active, and others at rest and still in potency within it, and it moves the ones that are still in potency by those that are in act, but the latter are moved, so that the entire [soul] is said to be self-moved. Aristotle also concurs with these concepts, which are Platonic: for Aristotle as well, of the soul, one [part] is the intellect in potency, and another [the intellect] in act, and the one that is in potency comes to be in act by the one that is in act, with the soul teaching itself and learning from itself, and seeking and finding. For all discursive learning, as he himself teaches, that is, both seeking and finding, takes place from the pre-existent knowledge that is in accordance with the intellect that is then active. (Simp. *in Phys.* 1249.32–1250.4, trans. Bodnár, Chase & Share 2012, slightly modified)

Simplicius too portrays the true self-motion of the soul as soul's reversion upon itself, its self-thinking, which practically consists in the actualisation

---

multiplication of intellections by means of turning to higher things; (4) decay – the decay of these intellections by means of turning away from the higher things; (5) combination – simultaneous contemplation of the Forms; (6) separation – the grasp of one particular form; (7) (rectilinear) motion – rectilinear motion into the realm of becoming; (8) circular motion – the going around and unfolding of the Forms, and the re-establishment to the same position (*in Phdr.* 112.22–113.8).

of the pre-existent reason-principles that the soul possesses in potency. The already actualised reason-principles have, as it were, the capacity of 'moving', that is, actualising, the reason-principles that are there potentially; it is this change from potentiality to actuality that the soul suffers as a whole that we might call its self-motion. Simplicius argues that Aristotle agrees with these Platonic concepts, as his distinction between the intellect in potency and the intellect in act shows. It is exactly this twofold structure of intellect which makes it possible for soul to both teach itself and learn from itself by means of actualising pre-existent knowledge. In fact, according to Simplicius, when Aristotle argues against primary self-motion in a unitary and simple thing, he intentionally uses as his example the impossibility that such an entity could teach and learn at the same time, in order to show that soul cannot know itself qua one and simple, but only insofar as it is made up of potency and act.[67] So, soul has the capacity of knowing itself, and thus of moving itself, insofar as it combines potency and act, a twofold dynamic structure that allows for psychic change, but that does not refer to different *parts*.[68]

Yet, Simplicius asks, if Aristotle accepts that the soul progresses from potency to act in its self-thinking, why does he not accept that soul is in motion, considering that he himself defines motion as the 'actuality of what is potential qua potential' (ἐντελέχεια τοῦ δυνατοῦ ἦ δυνατόν)?[69] Indeed, the definition of motion that Simplicius paraphrases, provided by Aristotle in *Physics* 3.2, is much broader than the later definition that we find in *Physics* 8.5, which states that motion is the imperfect actuality of the moveable.[70] According to Simplicius, Aristotle rejects motion in the soul only insofar as he adheres to the more limited definition of motion of *Physics* 8.5, which Simplicius paraphrases as the 'actuality of the moveable qua moveable' (ἐντελέχεια τοῦ κινητοῦ ἦ κινητόν).[71] This definition, which Simplicius describes as the definition of motion qua motion, can only be applied to the specific case of physical motion, whereas the

---

[67] Ibid. 1250.5–16.

[68] It would go beyond the scope of this paper to address the question if Simplicius has a point here regarding the 'motion' that supposedly takes place in Aristotle's intellect when it 'moves' from potentiality to actuality, but it might be worth noting that in Aristotelian scholarship there is indeed mention of 'noetic motion' or even 'mind's self-motion', as the papers on this subject in Gill & Lennox 1994: 81–133 show.

[69] Simplicius, *in Phys.* 1250.19–22.

[70] Aristotle defines motion in *Ph.* 3.2.201a10–11 as the 'actuality of what is potentially, as such' (ἡ τοῦ δυνάμει ὄντος ἐντελέχεια, ἦ τοιοῦτον) and in *Ph.* 8.5.257b8–9 as the 'imperfect actuality of the moveable' (ἡ κίνησις ἐντελέχεια κινητοῦ ἀτελής).

[71] Simplicius, *in Phys.* 1250.22–31.

definition of *Physics* 3.2 can cover *all changes*, whether physical or psychic. So, the difference between Plato and Aristotle comes about insofar as Aristotle rejects that motion qua motion can belong to the soul, whereas he would accept that the soul is in motion in the broader sense of actualising what it possesses potentially. In the end, the views of Plato and Aristotle are thus in perfect harmony.

## 9.5  Conclusion

In this paper, I have presented two related cases of Neoplatonic commentators dealing in their own way with the conflicting authorities of Plato and Aristotle in the case of the self-moving soul. We have seen that both Hermias and Simplicius recognise harmony between the views of Aristotle and Plato as presented in *De anima* 1.3 and *Laws* 10, namely that bodily motions cannot belong to the incorporeal soul. In this way, the commentators can ingeniously explain Aristotle's criticism away as not applicable to the Platonic concept of the self-moving soul, but rather as aimed at other philosophers who believe that soul moves in a physical way or at those who misinterpret Plato's concept of the self-moving soul as such.

Nevertheless, on the assumption that physical motion cannot belong to the soul, Aristotle concludes that soul must be unmoved, whereas Plato insists that soul is self-moved, although its motion is of a different kind than the motion of bodies. On this point, the views of the philosophers still diverge, and the commentators need to provide a reply to this apparent doctrinal conflict between their authorities. Simplicius argues that there is no doctrinal conflict at all, but only a verbal difference because of the different concepts of 'motion' that the philosophers employ. Since Aristotle's terminology is actually more appropriate than Plato's, the commentator uses what we would consider Aristotle's criticism for his own purposes, in order to get both a better grasp on Plato's concept of self-motion and to free it from those elements that might provoke objections.

Whereas Simplicius argues for harmony in the sense of theoretical identity, the harmony that Hermias is arguing for is of a different kind. According to Hermias, Plato rightly asserts that the soul as principle of motion is self-moved, and the harmony between the two authorities consists in the fact that although this conclusion is not explicitly drawn by Aristotle, it *does* follow from his own doctrines. In other words, Aristotle shares the assumptions which lead Plato and the Platonists to assert that the soul is self-moved, so there is no conflict between this assertion and Aristotle's doctrines. Both commentators thus clearly accept the authority of Aristotle even when it comes to the core Platonic doctrine of the self-moving soul. However, while for Simplicius Aristotle's texts share the same truth as Plato's but in different terminology, Hermias' commitment to Aristotle's authority is of a more complex kind.

One might of course object that Hermias' interpretation of Aristotle is not really convincing since Aristotle explicitly draws a different conclusion. Unfortunately, Hermias does not give us any further clue on how to understand his provocative thesis with regard to Aristotle's own intentions. Should we understand it to mean that, according to Hermias, Aristotle actually believes that the soul is self-moved, despite the fact that he did not literally express this view? Or is the commentator using Aristotle's own doctrines against him in an implicit criticism, implying that Aristotle *should* have recognised that this conclusion follows from his own principles? Whatever the answer to this question may be, both commentators show in their very own way that in the end the concept of the self-moving soul does not conflict with Aristotle's doctrines, thus strongly establishing the authority of the Platonic position.

CHAPTER 10

# Kathēgemōn: *The Importance of the Personal Teacher in Proclus and Later Neoplatonism*[*]

*Christian Tornau*

It is a well-known feature of the later Neoplatonist writings from the fifth century AD onwards that the authors frequently refer to their own philosophical teachers. The standard formula, which is almost invariably used on these occasions, is *ho hēmeteros kathēgemōn* (ὁ ἡμέτερος καθηγεμών, 'our teacher'); it is attested about thirty times in Proclus, ten times in Simplicius and, with a lower frequency, in Damascius and others. The custom is not wholly unprecedented. Philosophers and medical writers from earlier in the Imperial age, such as Plutarch and Galen, sometimes use similar commemorative formulas, and there may even have been precedents in Hellenistic Epicureanism.[1] It is nevertheless remarkable that with the later Neoplatonists its frequency considerably increases and is accompanied by a clear preference for the term *kathēgemōn* (καθηγεμών) as compared with traditional alternatives like *kathēgētēs* (καθηγητής).[2] Although it is fairly obvious, the phenomenon has not received the attention it deserves, and it is my purpose in the present chapter to attempt a rhetorical and philosophical explanation of it that, I hope, will contribute to deepening our understanding of the way in which the Neoplatonists conceived of and construed philosophical authority.[3]

---

[*] I am greatly indebted to Michael McOsker for his careful reading of the English text and his valuable suggestions.

[1] See Section 10.2, 'Leader Gods and Mystagogues'.

[2] For their own teachers, Plutarch and Galen use *kathēgētēs* (Plut. *Adul.* 70E: ὁ δ᾽ ἡμέτερος καθηγητὴς Ἀμμώνιος, 'our teacher Ammonius'; Gal. *Comp. med.* 13.529.5 Kühn: ὁ ἡμέτερος καθηγητὴς Λεύκιος, 'our teacher Lucius'). Galen however prefers ἡμέτερος διδάσκαλος, which he uses (in the singular or plural) ten times.

[3] As far as I can see, Proclus' philosophical pedagogy has hardly been studied. The standard accounts of his philosophy (Beierwaltes 1979; Siorvanes 1996; Chlup 2012) mention his teaching activity only in passing, if at all; so also the new Oxford 'Guide to Proclus' (d'Hoine & Martijn 2016). Radke 2006: 373–6 ('Der Lehrer Sokrates') has some good remarks on Proclus' interpretation of Socrates' teaching methods in the *Alcibiades* commentary. There is a full and apparently exhaustive list of the occurrences of ὁ ἡμέτερος καθηγεμών in Proclus in Luna & Segonds 2007a: LXVI–LXVIII ('Appendice I: Le syntagme ὁ ἡμέτερος καθηγεμών'). According to these scholars, the phrase ὁ

201

## 202 CHRISTIAN TORNAU

That the reference to the speaker's personal teacher primarily works as an argument from authority is indeed unmistakable. More often than not, the *kathēgemōn* is portrayed as an ideal figure. This is particularly obvious in Proclus, who always uses the standard formula to refer to Syrianus, his predecessor as head of the Neoplatonic school at Athens, to whom he, as he rarely fails to mention, owed most of his philosophical knowledge and ability and whom he remembers with almost religious veneration. Syrianus regularly receives praising epithets like 'divine' or 'inspired', and the doxographies in Proclus' exegetical works, e.g. when it comes to determining the *skopos* or guiding issue of a Platonic dialogue, usually end with Syrianus' opinion, which Proclus himself generally follows, sometimes underscoring Syrianus' particular ability to provide orientation in the chaos of conflicting interpretations.[4] Scholars of later Neoplatonism tend to read these passages with a focus on source criticism, hoping to determine the extent of Proclus' philosophical dependence on Syrianus,[5] but the disclosure of his debts to his venerated teacher is certainly not Proclus' most important aim. Rather, the idealizing mention of the *kathēgemōn* on the one hand helps to create a favourable impression of Proclus himself, his modesty and allegiance; on the other, it enhances his authority as a philosopher and head of the school because it establishes him as the pupil and successor of the greatest Platonic philosopher of the time. The legitimizing function is especially obvious when doxographies of the above-mentioned type are extended so as to include founding figures like Plotinus or even Plato himself. For instance, the introduction of Proclus' *Platonic Theology* features Plato as the *kathēgemōn* of a long tradition of philosophical theologians that includes Plotinus, Porphyry and Iamblichus and is crowned with Syrianus – who is not named but described in the familiar manner as Proclus' teacher and benefactor – and, implicitly, with Proclus himself who thus appears as a legitimate member of the diadochy and representative of the Platonic school tradition at its most venerable.[6]

---

ἡμέτερος καθηγεμών was coined by Proclus himself to replace the more traditional ὁ ἡμέτερος διδάσκαλος, which in his work occurs only in the early *Timaeus* commentary (about ten times).

[4] See e.g. Procl. *in Prm.* 640.13–15 Steel (on the *skopos* of the *Parmenides*); ibid. 1061.17–5 (on the number and content of the hypotheses, a hymnic passage); *in Ti.* 3.247.26–8 Diehl; ibid. 3.174.13–15 (Syrianus as the guarantor of safe exegesis, cf. ibid. 3.204.1–3); *in Alc.* 88.10–13 Segonds (combined reference to the *kathēgemōn* and to the 'divine Iamblichus'); *PT* 4.23 p. 70.5 Saffrey & Westerink (Ὁ δὲ πάντα τελεωσάμενος, 'he who brought everything to perfection').

[5] See e.g. d'Ancona & Luna 2000 (on Syrianus as the source of the Proclan principles *peras* and *apeiron*), Sheppard 1980: 39–103 (the chapter entitled 'Proclus' debt to Syrianus'), d'Hoine 2006, and the contributions in Longo 2009. None of these seems to discuss passages that feature the title *kathēgemōn*.

[6] Procl. *PT* 1.1 p. 6.16–7.8 Saffrey & Westerink.

The Personal Teacher in Proclus and Later Neoplatonism    203

Similarly, Simplicius in the *Corollarium de tempore* draws a line from Plotinus to Proclus, 'the *kathēgemōn* of my teachers'.[7] In a tradition that valued orthodoxy as highly as late-antique Platonism did,[8] the importance of such legitimizing practices should not be underrated. It should however be noted that while Proclus happened to be the successor of his *kathēgemōn* in the school, Simplicius had no institutional connection with Ammonius, the teacher he most idealizes in his commentaries, except for his early years in Alexandria. The importance attached to the *kathēgemōn*, the precedence he takes even over such venerable figures of the tradition as Plotinus or Iamblichus ('the divine'), thus does not strictly depend on the diadochy. Rather it seems to reflect an ideal of personal interaction between philosophers at different stages of their respective careers that was deemed indispensable for Neoplatonic pedagogy and teaching. But if this is so, some interesting questions emerge. What are the exact features of this ideal, and what is its Platonic – philosophical and exegetical – foundation? Does the oral instruction by a *kathēgemōn* in any way balance the 'written culture' of the commentaries and the authority of the canonical texts (arguably the most salient feature of late-antique Platonist philosophizing)? And how are we to interpret the religious overtones of the Neoplatonic, especially Proclan, descriptions of the ideal teacher? In pursuing these issues, I shall primarily focus on the work of Proclus, which is especially rewarding in this respect; but I shall also briefly address the *Fortleben* of his ideal in Simplicius and the later tradition.

## 10.1 The Ethics and Metaphysics of Philosophical Instruction: Proclus' *Commentary on the Parmenides*

From tradition Proclus inherits the conviction – prominent in Hellenistic thought, but also implicit in Plato's dialectical method and condensed in the Socratic metaphor of 'maieutics' – that philosophical teaching means not only theoretical instruction but also, and perhaps primarily, moral education. This is often expressed with the vocabulary of rearing and nurture. Proclus says that the teacher, like a father, 'brings to perfection' the pupil he has trained (meaning that he helps him develop his natural talent);[9] in the sixth or seventh century Stephanus of Alexandria takes up

---

[7] Simp. *in Phys.* 790–5 Diels; for the phrase ὁ τῶν ἡμετέρων διδασκάλων καθηγεμών see ibid. 795.4–5.
[8] Athanassiadi 2002 and 2006.
[9] Procl. *in Prm.* 633.22, 24 Steel; ibid. 997.18: τελειοῦσθαι. For the father as the one who 'brings to perfection' his child, whom he 'begot unfinished', see Plot. 5.1(10).3.13–15.

204 CHRISTIAN TORNAU

the ancient metaphor of 'paying one's nursling's dues' (τροφεῖα).[10] Philosophical teaching and learning seems to be conceived of as a kind of spiritual father–son relation, which requires a respectful and responsible behaviour from both sides and, in particular, moral and philosophical allegiance from the pupil. This ideal is beautifully captured by Iamblichus' story that Pythagoras unhesitatingly traveled the long way from Italy to Delos to care for his teacher Pherecydes on his deathbed and, after his demise, to bury him.[11] Proclus repeatedly asserts his allegiance to Syrianus by pointing out, with an etymological wordplay, that he is following the guidance (ὑφήγησις) of his *kathēgemōn*.[12] Usually this disclaimer refers to a concrete exegetical decision, but we may surmise that the willingness to submit to one's teacher's guidance also reflects the moral attitude that is expected from a younger philosopher and a kind of counterpart of the teacher's educational activity.[13] (As we shall see, this does not necessarily entail the pupil's obligation to accept and reproduce his teacher's philosophy *ad verbum* in the manner of Epicurean orthodoxy.)

Let us now move beyond these general observations and look more specifically at late Neoplatonic pedagogy and its philosophical foundations. It may be assumed that for Proclus and his colleagues, an ideal practice of philosophical teaching and spiritual guidance was enacted in Plato's dialogues, where Socrates' interaction with his mostly younger partners is governed by his dialectical method and his pedagogical *erōs*.[14] In some passages of Proclus, *kathēgemōn* actually denotes the leading interlocutor of a Platonic dialogue,[15] and in his comments on the first sentence of the *Alcibiades* he dwells on the importance of 'divine love' for a conversation

---

[10] Steph. ('Philop.') *in de An.* 450.20, 467.4 Hayduck. Cf. Pl. *Rep.* 7.520b.

[11] Iamb. *VP* 30.183–4. The normative value of the story is explicitly pointed out by Iamblichus.

[12] Procl. *in Ti.* 2.221.26–8 Diehl: 'Let us, then, from the beginning, trace back everything that is said to this guidance of my teacher' (Φέρ' οὖν ἀπ' ἀρχῆς ἕκαστα τῶν λεγομένων ἐπὶ ταύτας ἀνενέγκωμεν τὰς τοῦ καθηγεμόνος ἡμῶν ὑφηγήσεις); *in Prm.* 1033.17–18 Steel. Cf. *in Ti.* 3.247.26–8 Diehl, where Proclus states that Syrianus followed the *hyphēgēsis* of 'the theologians', thus employing the idea of guidance in order to establish a diadochy. For (moral) guidance being associated with the term *kathēgemōn*, cf. Plut. *Dion* 1.3 (τῷ καθηγεμόνι τῆς ἀρετῆς, 'their teacher in virtue', on Plato as the teacher of the tyrant slayers Dio and Brutus); *Arat.* 1.4 (τοῦ βίου καθηγεμόνας, 'the founders and directors of their life', an interesting association of guidance and fatherhood).

[13] Porphyry's story about one Diophanes, who shocked Plotinus by claiming that the philosophical pupil ought to yield even to his teacher's sexual desire 'for the sake of virtue' (Porph. *Plot.* 15.6–9), may be read as a caricature of this ideal.

[14] Cf. Radke 2006: 373–6.

[15] Procl. *in R.* 1.123.4 Kroll (Socrates in the *Phaedo*), ibid. 1.270.5 (Parmenides in the *Parmenides*).

## The Personal Teacher in Proclus and Later Neoplatonism 205

aimed at converting the pupil to his true self and to intelligible beauty.[16] His fullest and most profound remarks may however be found in his commentary on the *Parmenides*. As is well known, this dialogue features two ideal philosophers and accomplished dialecticians, Parmenides and Zeno, who are linked by a lifelong erotic relationship;[17] each of them interacts in his own way with the young Socrates, whom Plato characterizes as extraordinarily gifted, but still much in need of perfection. Since according to the late Neoplatonic exegetes the *Parmenides* contained the essence of Plato's theology and had a metaphysical *skopos*, Proclus' comments on the three main interlocutors are especially rich in metaphysical detail and allow a precise reconstruction of what we may call his ethics and metaphysics of philosophical didactics and pedagogy. Let us begin with Proclus' explanation of Parmenides' remarks, in his exchange with Socrates in the first half of the dialogue, on the intellectual and moral standards a philosophical dialectician has to meet.[18] Proclus takes this to refer to the natural ability (εὐφυΐα) which a philosophical learner or 'auditor' (ἀκροατής; the terminology is that of the institutionalized schools) must bring with him and to the specific competence that enables a good instructor (διδάσκαλος or καθηγεμών) to develop his pupil's talents in the best possible way (Procl. *in Prm.* 926.3–928.22 Steel, 924.4–928.27 Luna & Segonds).[19] In addition to εὐφυΐα, 'experience' (ἐμπειρία, in Proclus' opinion, familiarity with the propaedeutic subjects mathematics and logic rather than worldly experience) and enthusiasm (προθυμία) are expected from the pupil. These virtues or rather qualities make a young person suitable for further instruction because they are the seeds of the 'Chaldean virtues' Faith (πίστις), Truth (ἀλήθεια) and Love (ἔρως), a triad of anagogic virtues (originating from the *Chaldean Oracles*) that the post-Iamblichean Neoplatonists deemed indispensable for the attainment of the

---

[16] Procl. *in Alc.* 26.5–13 Segonds (cf. ibid. 30.18–20 with a reference to *Smp.* 202d). See also the subsequent remarks on dialectics (ibid. 27.18–29.7 with a reference to the dialectical ascent to the Good in the *Republic*). For *erōs* as *kathēgemōn*, cf. also Herm. *in Phdr.* 208 p. 218.15–16 Lucarini & Moreschini.

[17] *Prm.* 127b. Cf. Procl. *in Prm.* 684.20–4 Steel: 'As for the fact that he was also Parmenides' beloved, clearly it is because they used the same path of ascent to one and the same god, since this is characteristic of the genuine art of love. So, again, this erotic desire is given a mention because it accords with the purpose to unify plurality about participation in the divine' (Εἰ δὲ καὶ παιδικὰ τοῦ Παρμενίδου γέγονε, δῆλον ὅτι πρὸς ἕνα καὶ τὸν αὐτὸν θεὸν ἀμφοτέροις ἡ ἄνοδος ἦν· τοῦτο γάρ ἐστιν ἴδιον τῆς ὄντως ἐρωτικῆς τέχνης, ὥστε πάλιν καὶ τοῦτο τὸ ἐρωτικὸν μνήμης ἔτυχε, διότι πρὸς τὸν σκοπὸν οἰκείως ἔχει τὸ πλῆθος ἑνίζεσθαι περὶ τὴν τοῦ θείου μετουσίαν).

[18] *Prm.* 133b–c, 135a. The reader of Plato's earlier dialogues is of course aware that Socrates will fully meet these requirements one day.

[19] On this passage, see Luna & Segonds 2013: 430–5; Hoffmann 1998: 225–7.

206      CHRISTIAN TORNAU

highest goal, the Good or the One.[20] The reference to the Chaldean Oracles and the emphasis on *eros* aside, these ideas are largely traditional – already the Middle Platonists and Plato himself had reflected on the qualities that make a good future philosopher.[21] More interestingly, when he reflects on the prerequisites for successful philosophical instruction to be imparted by a teacher,[22] Proclus points out that the latter must have 'journeyed long before on the same path' (*in Prm.* 927.30–1 Steel) before he goes on to discuss the dialectical and didactic methods that a great teacher like Parmenides will use. The first qualification of a teacher, then, is that he has completed the ascent to the intelligible world himself and that his intellect has been filled and, as it were, made pregnant by the transcendent reality he has been contemplating. Proclus does not develop this motif in the present context, but some pages later in his comment on *Prm.* 135a we read (T1):

> And following on this he reminds us again who should be the instructor (ὁ καθηγεμών) in knowledge about this subject, that he should be productive and inventive in respect of his teaching; for some people make sufficient progress so as to be sufficient for themselves, but others are able to stimulate others also to a memory of the truth of things; and for this reason also he has called this person 'still more remarkable' (*Prm.* 135b); such a person is analogous to Resource (Πόρῳ), and the learner to Poverty (Πενίᾳ), and between the two of them is Eros, who joins the less complete to the more complete. (Procl. *in Prm.* 976.12–20 Steel, 14–23 Luna & Segonds; cf. Pl. *Smp.* 203e–204b)[23]

It seems, then, that intense contemplation of intelligible reality is both the necessary and the sufficient condition for good philosophical teaching practice. Not only does a philosopher's teaching activity necessarily result

---

[20] Procl. *in Prm.* 927.15–23 Steel. Cf. Or. Chald. fr. 46 des Places and, for Proclus' interpretation of the triad, *PT* 1.25 p. 109–13 Saffrey & Westerink. For commentary, see Tornau 2006: 218–25 (with further bibliography).

[21] Cf. Alcin. *Did.* 152.8–23 Whittaker & Louis (relying primarily on Pl. *Rep.* 6.485a–486e) with Whittaker's notes. For the distinction between the full-grown virtues and their homonymous εὐφυίαι, cf. ibid. 152.23–9, 183.17–19. Proclus' triad εὐφυΐα, ἐμπειρία, προθυμία (*in Prm.* 927.17 Steel) is inspired by the text of the *Parmenides* (133b, cf. 135a).

[22] Procl. *in Prm.* 927.29–928.22 Steel, 927.34–928.27 Luna & Segonds.

[23] Ἐπὶ δὲ τούτῳ καὶ τίς ὁ καθηγεμὼν τῆς περὶ τούτων ἐπιστήμης, ὑπομιμνήσκει πάλιν, ὅτι γόνιμος καὶ εὑρετικὸς καὶ ὅτι περὶ τὴν διδασκαλίαν· ἔνιοι γὰρ τοσοῦτον προκόπτουσιν, ὅσον αὐτοῖς ἀπόχρη πρὸς ἑαυτούς· ἄλλοι δὲ καὶ ἑτέρους ἀναμιμνήσκειν δύνανται τῆς τῶν πραγμάτων ἀληθείας· διὸ καὶ θαυμαστότερον τοῦτον κέκληκεν· ἀνάλογον ἔστηκεν οὗτος τῷ Πόρῳ, Πενίᾳ δὲ ὁ μανθάνων, μεταξὺ δὲ ἄρα ἀμφοῖν ὁ Ἔρως ὁ τὸν ἀτελέστερον συνάπτων πρὸς τὸν τελειότερον. Cf. Procl. *ET* 131. The *Parmenides* commentary is quoted from Carlos Steel's OCT edition (Steel et al. 2007–2009). The text, translation and notes of the Budé edition (Luna & Segonds 2007–2017) have been used and compared throughout. All translations are adapted from Morrow & Dillon 1987.

## The Personal Teacher in Proclus and Later Neoplatonism    207

from his contemplation, it is also indicative of the latter's degree and intensity. A person who is unable to hand down his or her knowledge and help others with their ascent cannot have attained a particularly deep insight into the intelligible. Conversely, the contemplative philosopher acts as a teacher, as we might say in Proclus' terminology, simply 'because he is what he is' (αὐτῷ τῷ εἶναι).[24] The systematic background for this view is Plotinus' theory of productive contemplation, which he develops especially in *Ennead* 3.8 (περὶ θεωρίας, 'On contemplation') and which remained the backbone of most later Neoplatonic theories of causality. In short, the point of this theory is that natural production and causation, as well as virtuous action, are best explained as immediately and automatically resulting from the productive or active entity's (e.g. the World Soul or Nature, or the individual human soul) contemplation of the higher levels of reality. Through this contemplation it is filled or 'made pregnant' with images or *logoi* of the transcendent level and 'gives birth' to external *logoi*, which may be either lower levels of being or actions that agree with the intelligible standards it contemplates. Plotinus' examples for the ethical side of this theory are, in particular, political (especially legislative) activity and philosophical instruction.[25] Plotinus frames this theory in language of desire and procreation that is inspired by the imagery of Plato's erotic dialogues, especially the *Symposium*,[26] which is also quoted in Proclus' text.

A remarkable element of the passage quoted above (T1) is that Proclus explicitly prefers social interaction through didactic activity to an apparently self-sufficient, isolated life of pure contemplation. Though it is not equally prominent in Plotinus,[27] this idea does not look like Proclus' ad hoc explanation of Plato's term 'still more remarkable' (θαυμαστότερον, *Prm.* 135b). In his mathematical introduction to Plato, the Middle Platonist Theon of Smyrna describes Platonic philosophy as an initiation into the cognition of true being in five successive stages modeled on a (partly fictitious) initiation into the mysteries. These stages are: (1)

---

[24] Procl. *ET* 18 and very frequently.

[25] On Plotinus' theory of contemplation and its ethical and political aspects, see especially O'Meara 2003: 73–6, who cites Plot. 3.8(30).4.31–43, 5.3(49).7.30–4, 6.9(9).7.25–6 (the example of Minos). For the transmission of the contemplative experience cf. esp. 6.9(9).7.21–3: 'and having been in its company and had, so to put it, sufficient converse with it, come and announce, if he could, to another that transcendent union'; trans. Armstrong 1988, slightly modified (κἀκείνῳ συγγενόμενον καὶ ἱκανῶς οἷον ὁμιλήσαντα ἥκειν ἀγγέλλοντα, εἰ δύναιτο, καὶ ἄλλῳ τὴν ἐκεῖ συνουσίαν). On the relation of virtuous action and contemplation, see Wilberding 2008: 375–8.

[26] Cf. e.g. the metaphor of 'travail' (ὠδίς) from *Smp.* 206d–e, quoted in Plot. 3.8(30).7.19.

[27] Plotinus voices understanding for those who, like the philosopher-kings in the *Republic*, would prefer to 'remain above' in eternal contemplation (6.9(9).7.26–8). In 3.8(30).4.31–9, it seems that practice is not indispensable for successful contemplation.

## 208                    CHRISTIAN TORNAU

purification by means of the propaedeutic mathematical sciences; (2) theoretical acquisition of Plato's doctrine; (3) contemplation of the Forms (analogous to the *epopteia* of the mysteries); (4) ability to guide others to the same contemplation (analogous to the function of a priest or hierophant); (5) attainment of the Platonic *telos*, the assimilation to God.[28] Already in this didactic program of Platonic philosophy, those who have the competence to be philosophical instructors and spiritual guides are granted a higher degree of perfection than those whose contemplation remains self-centered and sterile. So apparently Proclus took up a traditional view of philosophical teaching and gave it philosophical depth and some justification by combining it with the Plotinian theory of contemplation. A connection between Proclus and the tradition represented by Theon is also suggested by the mysteries analogy, which, as we shall see in more detail below, is crucial for the religious aspect of Proclus' concept of philosophical instruction.

In a related passage about Syrianus, Proclus alludes to Plotinus' theory of contemplation by borrowing from him the Homeric (and Platonic) example of Minos (T2):

> ... our guide (καθηγεμών) to the truth about the gods [or: our teacher of theology] and, to say it with Homer, Plato's intimate friend (Procl. *PT* 1.10 p. 42.9–10 Saffrey & Westerink; cf. Plot. 6.9(9).7.23–6)[29]

Plotinus had used the famous Homeric verse about the Cretan king and legislator Minos' intimate conversation with Zeus (*Odyssey* 19.179: Minos ... who held converse with Great Zeus)[30] to explain his political activity as the result of his contemplation of true being. Proclus transfers it to Syrianus. His version has a clear religious ring to it: as a guide who reveals the truth about the divine, the *kathēgemōn* is reminiscent of Theon's hierophant in the Platonic mysteries. The most striking feature of the passage is, however, that Homer's (and Plotinus') Zeus is replaced by Plato. This not only means that Plato is deified, which is of course quite common in Neoplatonism, but also that the philosophical teacher no

---

[28] Theon, *Exp.* 14.18–16.2 Hiller. On Theon, see most recently Petrucci 2016. For translation and full discussion of the passage, see Dörrie & Baltes 1996: 36–9, 250–3; Petrucci 2012: 302–5, each with further references and bibliography; Riedweg 1987: 125–7.

[29] ὁ δὲ δὴ τῆς περὶ θεῶν ἡμῖν ἀληθείας καθηγεμὼν καὶ τοῦ Πλάτωνος, ἵνα καθ' Ὅμηρον εἴπωμεν, ὀαριστής.

[30] Μίνως ... Διὸς μεγάλου ὀαριστής. The verse is alluded to in Pl. *Leg.* 1.624a and quoted in [Pl.] *Min.* 319b; it has a subtle erotic colouring (cf. *Il.* 14.216). See also Dio Chrys. *Or.* 4.39–41; Clem. Al. *Protr.* 112.2. It is strikingly applied to the true Christian Gnostic in Clem. Al. *Strom.* 2.104.2 ('Dwelling with the Lord, being his intimate friend and sharing his hearth according to the Spirit'; σύνοικος ὢν τῷ κυρίῳ ὀαριστής τε καὶ συνέστιος κατὰ τὸ πνεῦμα). Cf. O'Meara 2003: 74 with n. 6.

The metaphysical and practical working of this structure is, again, set

longer mediates between the pupil and intelligible or divine reality, as in Plotinus and Theon, but between the pupil and another philosopher (Plato). This latter, however, is entirely situated on the level of the divine and almost a god himself, so that he is not directly accessible; this requires the presence of a more human intermediary, the *kathēgemōn*. The dyad of (human) teacher and pupil has been extended to a triad so as to include the (divine) founder of the philosophical school and author of the inspired texts, whose exegesis will be the main subject of the *kathēgemōn*'s actual teaching practice. No doubt this extension is partly due to the importance of triads and mediation in Proclus' metaphysics – indeed in the passage from the *Parmenides* commentary quoted above (T1), Proclus draws an analogy between teaching and Penia's being 'filled' by Poros through the mediation of Eros, a mythical image that, for Proclus, symbolizes the metaphysical process of matter being filled with images of the Forms contained in Intellect.[31] It is also natural that in a text-based philosophy such as Neoplatonism, the author of the authoritative texts should have his place in a theory of philosophical pedagogy. But it should be noted that personal instruction is nevertheless considered indispensable, and not just for contingent reasons (the author being dead) but for metaphysical ones as well. The relation between the members of Proclus' pedagogical or didactic triad, as we may call it, may be schematized as follows:

| role | pupil | *kathēgemōn* | founder |
| --- | --- | --- | --- |
| *contact* | | personal/direct | remote/mediated |
| *activity* | reader | exegete | author |
| *religious analogy* | worshipper | priest, hierophant | god |
| *metaphysical analogy* | *Penia* | *Erōs* | *Poros* |
| *persons (Pl. Prm.)* | Socrates | Zeno | Parmenides |
| *persons (Platonic tradition)* | Proclus | Syrianus | Plato |

The metaphysical and practical working of this structure is, again, set out most fully in the commentary on the *Parmenides*.[32] Consider the following reconstruction of Zeno's intermediating role (T3), which Proclus finds condensed in the fact that Zeno laughs while Parmenides only smiles (*Prm.* 136d, cf. 130a):[33]

---

[31] Cf. Procl. *in Prm.* 884.17–20 Steel. For the equation of Penia with matter, cf. Plot. 3.5(50).9.49.

[32] There are also some interesting remarks in the *Alcibiades* commentary (see e.g. 30.5–34.10). But as the dialogue is for beginners, has an ethical *skopos* and features only the dyad of Socrates and Alcibiades, they are much less detailed and, with respect to metaphysics, somewhat allusive.

[33] Modern readers often feel that this kind of exegesis is Neoplatonic εἷς σκοπός hermeneutics (exegesis that refers every detail to a single guiding issue) at its worst. As an interpretation of

210                    CHRISTIAN TORNAU

Zeno smiles when he looks at Parmenides (this was stated explicitly earlier), but he laughs when he addresses himself to Socrates. This is because in the divine realm the mediating class (μεσότης)[34] is hidden in so far as it is united with what is above it, but becomes manifest (ἐκφαίνεται) in so far as it consorts with what is below it. So therefore when Zeno laughs, he is manifesting himself to Socrates by ranking him with (συντάττων) himself, through this union calling forth Parmenides' intellection (νόησιν).[35] For he turns Socrates back (ἐπιστρέφει) towards his own teacher and leads everybody[36] towards him as being the primal source of contemplation and generative of all intellection (νοήσεως) he possesses.[37] (Procl. *in Prm.* 1022.24–1023.4 Steel, 1022.29–1023.3 Luna & Segonds)[38]

The backbone of this argumentation is the familiar Neoplatonic pattern of abiding (μονή), procession (πρόοδος) and return (ἐπιστροφή).[39] As usual, Zeno, as the middle term of the triad, connects the lowest term (Socrates) and the highest (Parmenides) by performing a twofold task:[40] on the one hand, he causes Socrates to 'return' (ἐπιστρέφει) towards Parmenides by uniting him with himself and raising him to his own level; on the other, he causes Parmenides, who otherwise would abide entirely with himself, to 'proceed' towards the external and to give his intellectual insight (νόησις) into transcendent being a discursive expression that can be communicated by linguistic

---

Plato's words, it is no doubt artificial, but it may nevertheless contain valuable philosophical material. For a defense, see Radke 2006: 321–9.

[34] For Zeno as μεσότης, cf. e.g. *in Prm.* 700.6–11, 1021.14–17 Steel; Radke 2006: 326 n. 532.

[35] τὴν τοῦ Παρμενίδου προκαλούμενος νόησιν. Cf. *PT* 4.29 p. 84.15–18 Saffrey & Westerink (on number as the mediating entity between the intelligible and the intellective): 'it unfolds the intelligible plurality and calls forth what is hidden and unified in it towards distinction and fecund procreation; and it collects the intellectual into unification and indivisible communion' (ἀνελίσσει μὲν τὸ νοητὸν πλῆθος καὶ προκαλεῖται τὸ κρύφιον αὐτοῦ καὶ ἑνιαῖον εἰς διάκρισιν καὶ γόνιμον ἀπογέννησιν, συνάγει δὲ τὸ νοερὸν εἰς ἕνωσιν καὶ τὴν ἀμέριστον κοινωνίαν). In the dialogic context, the reference is to the exercise of the second half.

[36] πάντας (restored by Steel from Moerbeke's *omnes* against the πάντως of the Greek manuscripts): the other listeners present and, perhaps, also the readers of the dialogue.

[37] παρ' αὐτῷ: referring to Zeno rather than Socrates. It might even refer to Parmenides himself, characterizing him as the embodiment of the self-generating knowledge that is the unity of Being and Intellect in the Neoplatonic νοῦς. (Cf. *in Prm.* 1022.21–2 Steel: 'he [Parmenides] imitates the permanent and quiescent and hidden god' (ὁ μὲν μιμεῖται τὸν μένοντα καὶ ἠρεμοῦντα καὶ κεκρυμμένον θεόν). Cousin's reading παρ' αὐτοῦ, which is rendered in the older translations, has no support in the manuscripts.

[38] ὁ γὰρ Ζήνων μειδιᾷ μὲν πρὸς τὸν Παρμενίδην βλέπων, οὕτω γὰρ εἴρηται πρότερον, γελᾷ δὲ πρὸς τὸν Σωκράτη τὸν λόγον ποιούμενος· καὶ γὰρ ἐν τοῖς θείοις ἡ μεσότης μὲν κρύφιος καθὸ συνήνωται τῷ πρὸ αὐτῆς, ἐκφαίνεται δὲ καθὸ κοινωνεῖ τῷ μετ' αὐτήν· γελᾷ μὲν οὖν διὰ ταῦτα ὁ Ζήνων ἐκφαίνων ἑαυτὸν τῷ Σωκράτει καὶ συντάττων αὐτὸν ἑαυτῷ καὶ διὰ τῆς ἑνώσεως ταύτης τὴν τοῦ Παρμενίδου προκαλούμενος νόησιν· ἐπιστρέφει γὰρ καὶ τοῦτον εἰς τὸν ἑαυτοῦ καθηγεμόνα καὶ πάντας ἀνάγει πρὸς ἐκεῖνον ὡς πρωτουργὸν αἴτιον τῆς θεωρίας καὶ πάσης νοήσεως τῆς παρ' αὐτῷ γεννητικόν. For a German translation and commentary, see Radke 2006: 327.

[39] Cf. Radke 2006: 321–9.     [40] Cf. e.g. *ET* 38, 56.

The Personal Teacher in Proclus and Later Neoplatonism    211

means in the empirical realm. In this sense, Zeno makes 'manifest' the noetic reality that otherwise would remain 'hidden', i.e. intelligible only to an intellect that abides on the same ontological level as itself. This epistemological structure, which explains how suprarational knowledge is accessible to discursive reason and linguistic expression at all, closely corresponds to Proclus' view of the general structure of ontological procession. Proclus' interpretation of the respective roles of Parmenides, Zeno and Socrates thus shows how metaphysical structures are mirrored in, and explanatory of, interpersonal relationships and human interaction. That successful philosophical teaching requires the presence of a mediating figure between an accomplished philosopher and his young pupil (or between Plato's text and its beginning reader) is an empirical fact with obvious bearing on the practicalities and ethics of philosophical didactics. But the fact can be fully grasped and its ethical consequences justified only if we understand it as the outward expression of a deeper metaphysical structure.[41]

The triadic pattern also explains the relation between personal (oral) instruction and canonic texts in Proclus' pedagogy. In the section – briefly touched upon above – on the qualities expected from a philosophical instructor (Procl. *in Prm.* 926.3–928.22 Steel, 924.4–928.27 Luna & Segonds), we learn that the perfect teacher cultivates a peculiar and somewhat paradoxical manner of expressing himself. If he chooses to give verbal utterance to his noetic insight (νόησις), he will avoid lengthy argumentation (πολυλογία), as he is hardly interested in revealing (ἐκφαίνειν) the truth to his pupil step by step in a persuasive way. The focus of his attention is the subject rather than the listener; in order to make his exposition correspond as closely as possible to reality, he will speak allusively, 'say many things with few words' (πολλὰ δι' ὀλίγων)[42] and 'phrase arcane matters in an arcane way' (τὰ μυστικὰ μυστικῶς), thus attempting to bridge the inevitable gap between noetic intuition, which is timeless and holistic, and its discursive representation, which proceeds in a temporal and logical sequence.[43] This manner of speaking is not only

---

[41] I am not sure whether we should (with Radke 2006: 328) go yet one step further and infer from this the personal character of the metaphysical principles themselves.

[42] Amusingly, in his introduction to Porphyry's *Isagoge* Pseudo-Elias says precisely the opposite about Proclus himself: 'For he [Galen] too wrote few things with many words, just as Proclus', Ps.-Elias *in Porph. Isag.* 61.43–62.1 Westerink (καὶ <γὰρ> οὗτος ὀλίγα διὰ πολλῶν συνέγραψεν, ὥσπερ καὶ ὁ Πρόκλος). The point he wants to make is that wordiness may result in obscurity. This would be a rare example of parody in Neoplatonic writings.

[43] Procl. *in Prm.* 927.31–928.8 Steel: 'he will not want to expound divine truth with elaborate verbosity, but rather to reveal much through few words, uttering words of like nature to his intellectual insights ...; nor will he take thought so that he may seem to speak clearly, but he

## 212 CHRISTIAN TORNAU

impressive but also important, because it proves that the teacher's soul has been in direct touch with the intelligible and that the intellectual ascent is, in principle, open to all human souls including the disciple's.[44] It is, however, hardly suitable for the direct instruction of a very young man who, like Socrates in the *Parmenides*, is still at the beginning of his philosophical efforts and who will, more often than not, simply fail to understand his instructor. To bridge the gap, an intermediary is needed, a task that, on Proclus' interpretation, is again undertaken by Zeno. While the poem by the historical Parmenides represents the arcane way of speaking characteristic of the accomplished philosopher, Zeno's treatise – of which the Platonic Socrates somewhat ironically remarks that it offers numerous arguments against the existence of plurality (*Prm.* 128b) – makes Parmenides' vision accessible to discursive reason by adding logical proof and clarifying the sequence of thought (T4):

> (Zeno) moves forward (πρόεισι) into developments of arguments, into combinations and differentiations, expounding and unfolding the unitary and compact insight of his teacher. (Procl. *in Prm.* 705.6–9 Steel, 9–12 Luna & Segonds)[45]

The technical vocabulary of logic and philosophical exegesis marks Zeno's treatise as a commentary on Parmenides' poem. The exegesis of an authoritative but arcane text that would be unintelligible to the reader without assistance is analogous to metaphysical procession (πρόοδος), which brings into existence levels of reality that otherwise would remain hidden in their transcendent source. To put it slightly differently: textual exegesis is as indispensable in philosophical teaching as procession is in the unfolding of reality, even though it remains distinct from and inferior to its source – the commentary can unfold but not replace the text. As we saw in T2 (Procl. *PT* 1.10 p. 42.9–10 Saffrey & Westerink) above, Syrianus – the 'intimate' of Plato and the *kathēgemōn* of Proclus – occupies the middle

---

will content himself with indications; for one should convey mystical truths mystically, and not publicise secret doctrines about the gods' (οὐκ ἐθελήσει διὰ πολυλογίας ἐκφαίνειν τὴν θείαν ἀλήθειαν, ἀλλὰ πολλὰ δι' ὀλίγων ἐνδείκνυσθαι, νοήσεσιν ὅμοια φθεγγόμενος, ... οὐδὲ ποιήσεται λόγον ὅπως ἂν λέγειν δόξῃ σαφῶς, ἀλλὰ καὶ ἀρκεσθήσεται ταῖς ἐνδείξεσι· δεῖ γὰρ τὰ μυστικὰ μυστικῶς παραδιδόναι, καὶ μὴ δημοσιεύειν τὰς ἀπορρήτους περὶ τῶν θεῶν ἐννοίας). The mysteries language in the last sentence is important: see next section below.

[44] Cf. Procl. *in Prm.* 928.3–5 Steel: 'inasmuch as he has separated himself from his immediate surroundings and drawn close to the divine' (ἅτε ἐξιστάμενος τῶν παρόντων καὶ πρὸς τῷ θείῳ γιγνόμενος), quoting Pl. *Phdr.* 249d.

[45] πρόεισι γὰρ εἰς τὰς ἀνελίξεις τῶν λόγων καὶ τὰς συνθέσεις καὶ τὰς διαιρέσεις, ἀναπλῶν καὶ ἀναπτύσσων τὴν ἑνοειδῆ καὶ συνῃρημένην τοῦ καθηγεμόνος ἐπιβολήν. Cf. *in Prm.* 716.1–18 Steel and, immediately before, the comparison of Parmenides with intellect (νοῦς) and Zeno with science (ἐπιστήμη; *in Prm.* 704.24–6).

*The Personal Teacher in Proclus and Later Neoplatonism*    213

position (μεσότης) of a didactic triad that is quite analogous to that of the *Parmenides*: Just as Zeno mediates between the sublime Parmenides and young Socrates, Syrianus is the mediator who discloses to the young Proclus the thought of the remote and (almost) divine Plato. The parallel is further accentuated by a passage of the *Platonic Theology* where Proclus names Syrianus as the source of his *Timaeus* exegesis and applies to him the language of revelation that, in the *Parmenides* commentary, characterizes Zeno (T5):

> Let us follow our teacher (τῷ καθηγεμόνι) while he makes manifest (ἐκφαίνοντι) the ineffable mystagogy about these things. (Procl. *PT* 3.14 p. 52.19–21 Saffrey & Westerink)[46]

It should, however, be noted that just as, in metaphysics, the term *mesotēs* is not tied to a single ontological level, in didactics it is not the privilege of a single person. In Proclus, middle and mediating terms are of course operative on the intelligible as well as on the psychic and even the physical level of reality, and an entity that, from one point of view, is at the top of a triad may, from another, perform a mediating function. By analogy, it is conceivable that the didactic triad moves, as it were, up and down the (chronological and axiological) hierarchy of the Platonic tradition: if a *kathēgemōn* is by definition a mediating guide towards the divine, the term may theoretically, in a differently reconstructed situation or from a different perspective, apply not only to Syrianus (or Zeno) but also to Plato (or Parmenides)[47] or to Proclus (or Socrates). We shall presently encounter texts that suggest as much. The flexibility that Proclus' pedagogical triad inherits from his metaphysical triads and that makes it applicable to various hierarchical levels sometimes results in a curious blending of human and divine attributes in the characterization of his *kathēgemones*, who then appear as gods and priests at one and the same time.[48] For a clearer understanding of this phenomenon, let us now turn to the religious side of the *kathēgemōn* terminology.

## 10.2   Leader Gods and Mystagogues

Religious and initiatory imagery is of course traditional in Platonism and goes back to Plato himself.[49] Systematic comparisons of Platonic philosophy with initiation into mystery cults occur already in Middle Platonism

---

[46] τῷ καθηγεμόνι συνακολουθήσωμεν ἐκφαίνοντι τὴν περὶ αὐτῶν ἡμῖν ἀπόρρητον μυσταγωγίαν.

[47] For Plato, cf. *PT* 1.1 p. 6.18 Saffrey & Westerink; for Parmenides, cf. T4 above and *in Prm.* 633.22 Steel.

[48] Both Plato and Syrianus may be called 'hierophants' (*PT* 1.1 p. 6.6 –7 Saffrey & Westerink, on Plato as the 'hierophant' of the divine mysteries; on Syrianus, cf. *in Prm.* 618.5–6 Steel; *in R.* 1.71.24 Kroll, each quoted below).

[49] See the basic monograph of Riedweg 1987.

214 CHRISTIAN TORNAU

(see the example of Theon of Smyrna discussed above) and become increasingly important in later Neoplatonism. The opening hymn of Proclus' commentary on the *Parmenides* is rich in vocabulary borrowed from the mysteries,[50] and the introductory chapter of the *Platonic Theology* describes Platonism as 'true initiation'[51] and the great thinkers of the Platonic tradition as hierophants. This is because, on Neoplatonic assumptions, philosophy primarily aims at the ascent to the gods who also are the supreme principles of reality; the increased importance of theurgy may also be relevant.[52] The text just quoted (T5 = Procl. *PT* 3.14 p. 52.19–21 Saffrey & Westerink), with its talk of mystagogy and insight into the 'ineffable' (ἀπόρρητον, a notion the mystery cults and Neoplatonic metaphysics have in common), strongly suggests that the metaphysics of philosophical education we found in the *Parmenides* commentary should be seen also in this framework.

The use of initiatory imagery is not confined to the Platonic school but is also found in other philosophical and theological traditions (including Judaism and Christianity) and other educational areas, for instance rhetoric.[53] In some cases, this may be purely metaphorical and simply intended to promote the speaker's subject of study. It is however interesting to note that the Hellenistic school that went furthest in promoting its founder to divine rank and in employing the terminology of the mysteries to this purpose,[54] Epicureanism, is also the first that seems to have consistently given its founder the title of *kathēgemōn* rather than the equally available ones of *didaskalos* or *kathēgētēs*. In the sense of 'philosophical teacher', *kathēgemōn* is first attested in Philodemus,[55] and while it is prominent in Plutarch's anti-Epicurean polemics,[56] it is absent from his references to his own teacher Ammonius, whom he calls

---

[50] E.g. *in Prm.* 618.1–2 Steel (T8): 'this most visionary and mystical contemplation that Plato reveals to us' (τῆς ἐποπτικωτάτης τοῦ Πλάτωνος καὶ μυστικωτάτης θεωρίας).

[51] *PT.* 1.1 p. 6.3 Saffrey & Westerink: τῶν ἀληθινῶν τελετῶν (in a free quotation of *Phdr.* 250b–c).

[52] See most recently van den Berg 2016: 223–4. See also Chlup 2012: 256–65 ('Philosophy and Religion in Late Antiquity').

[53] E.g. Marcellinus, *Vit. Thuc.* 1: 'After having become initiates of the divine words of Demosthenes . . ., it is now time to enter the mystical rituals of Thucydides' (Τῶν Δημοσθένους μύστας γεγενημένους θείων λόγων . . ., ὥρα λοιπὸν καὶ τῶν Θουκυδίδου τελετῶν ἐντὸς καταστῆναι).

[54] Cf. Metrodorus of Lampsacus, fr. 38 Körte *apud* Plut. *Adv. Col.* 1117B: 'the truly divinely revealed mysteries of Epicurus' (τὰ Ἐπικούρου ὡς ἀληθῶς θεόφαντα ὄργια). If Epicurus' name was replaced by that of Plato, exactly the same phrase could appear in Proclus.

[55] Phld. *De pietate* 1 fr. 58.1648 Obbink.

[56] Plut. *Adv. Col.* 1110E, 1118E. But see also *Stoic. rep.* 1048E on the teachers of Chrysippus.

## The Personal Teacher in Proclus and Later Neoplatonism     215

*kathēgētēs*.[57] An anonymous treatise from Herculaneum addresses Epicurus as 'guide [or: teacher] and savior' (τοῦ καθηγεμόνος καὶ σωτῆρος),[58] which demonstrates the association of the title with the Epicurean school's religious veneration for its founder. Jan Erik Heßler has recently related this memorial practice to Hellenistic ruler cult and, in this context, has drawn attention to a cult of 'Dionysus *Kathēgemōn*' that originated in Pergamon but soon spread throughout the Hellenistic world.[59] The preserved cultic inscriptions show that in this cult, the god and the leader of the swarm of ecstatic followers shared the title *kathēgemōn*.[60] Our evidence hardly permits us to construe a historical connection between this Hellenistic cult and Epicurean commemorative practice on the one hand and late Neoplatonic mystery terminology on the other, but the Dionysiac element of enthusiasm is unmistakable in the Platonists' use of initiatory imagery, and the ambiguous character of *kathēgemōn*, which may refer both to a divine and a human figure, is precisely what we expect as a natural consequence of the ontological flexibility of Proclus' didactic triad and what we actually find in his texts. The inherent ambiguity of *kathēgemōn* may even be the reason why the Neoplatonists preferred it to *kathēgētēs*: while *kathēgemōn* is regularly used of god or the gods in Imperial Greek,[61] I know of no comparable use of *kathēgētēs* before the Byzantine age.

An impressive example of the ambiguity of *kathēgemōn* in Proclus is found in the *Platonic Theology*. As usual, Proclus concludes a list of previous exegetes with a mention of Syrianus (T6):

> For why should I mention my own teacher, that true 'Bacchus' whose divine inspiration concerning Plato excelled all and who spread the light of Plato's admirable, stunning vision down to us. (Procl. *PT* 4.23 p. 69.8–12 Saffrey & Westerink)[62]

---

[57] Plut. *Adul.* 70E.     [58] *PHerc.* 346 col. 7.23f–24 Capasso.     [59] Heßler 2018: 420–5.

[60] For the references, see Heßler 2018: 423 n. 121.

[61] Plut. *Thes.* 18.3; *Aud. poet.* 23A: 'certain faculties of which the gods are the givers and guides' (δυνάμεις τινὰς ὧν οἱ θεοὶ δοτῆρές εἰσι καὶ καθηγεμόνες). The same genitive occurs in T2 = Procl. *PT* 1.10 p. 42.9–10 Saffrey & Westerink (τῆς περὶ θεῶν ἡμῖν ἀληθείας καθηγεμών, on Syrianus). One might also speculate that the Neoplatonists tacitly opposed the Christian usage, where καθηγητής (the translation of *rabbi* in the New Testament, *Mt* 23.10) is quite prominent. Porphyry would have been aware of this, but it seems that our evidence allows no more than speculation.

[62] Τί γὰρ δεῖ λέγειν τὸν ἡμέτερον καθηγεμόνα τὸν ὡς ἀληθῶς Βάκχον, ὃς περὶ τὸν Πλάτωνα διαφερόντως ἐνθεάζων καὶ μέχρις ἡμῶν τὸ θαῦμα καὶ τὴν ἔκπληξιν τῆς Πλατωνικῆς θεωρίας ἐξέλαμψεν.

## 216 CHRISTIAN TORNAU

This is of course reminiscent of the Dionysiac hexameter cited in the *Phaedo* (69c–d) according to which there are many narthex-bearers but few 'Bacchi', i.e. truly inspired Bacchants. Proclus invites his readers to imagine Syrianus as the *kathēgemōn* of a mystic swarm of worshippers of Plato and suggests that his leading position is due to the extraordinary degree of his enthusiasm (which, in this exegetic context, is equivalent to a particularly deep understanding of Plato's texts). A few lines later, however, the image has shifted (T7):

> ... he [*sc.* Syrianus] who had intellectual insight into the specific quality of this order [*sc.* of reality] and taught us, his own initiates, the truth about it with exactitude. (ibid. 70.8–11 Saffrey & Westerink)[63]

Here Syrianus is no longer a mere commentator who mediates Plato's ineffable vision to philosophical beginners ('us'). Like Plato himself, he has independent insight into theological reality and transmits it to a swarm of worshippers who are no longer Plato's but his own. After reading this, we will be tempted to reinterpret Βάκχος in the earlier passage (T6) as referring not just to the Bacchic initiate ('Bacchant') but to the god himself. In terms of the 'didactic triad' of the *Parmenides* commentary, we might say that Syrianus has moved from the middle (Zeno) to the top (Parmenides) or, to put it more precisely, that the positions represented by two persons in the *Parmenides* have been fused in the exceptional philosophical personality of Syrianus.

The Platonic text that probably most encouraged the Neoplatonists to exploit the religious overtones of *kathēgemōn* was, I suggest, the myth of the *Phaedrus*, where divine and human souls on their chariots move around the heaven, striving to reach the transcendent 'space beyond heaven' (ὑπερουράνιος τόπος) and the vision of the Forms.[64] The eleven parts of the chorus are each led by a god; the supreme god, Zeus, who is also at the head of the entire procession, is called 'the great leader (μέγας ἡγεμών) in heaven' (*Phdr.* 246e). In his exegesis of the myth, Hermias of Alexandria – whose commentary in fact reproduces the lectures on the *Phaedrus* by Syrianus that Hermias had attended together with Proclus – paraphrases this expression with *kathēgemōn*.[65] Though this usage may just

---

[63] τὴν ἰδιότητα τῆς τάξεως ταύτης νοερῶς ἐθεάσατο καὶ παραδέδωκεν ἡμῖν τοῖς ἑαυτοῦ μύσταις ἀπηκριβωμένην τὴν περὶ αὐτῆς ἀλήθειαν.

[64] *Phdr.* 247c–250c. For Bacchic elements in the *Phaedrus* myth, see ibid. 253a.

[65] Herm. *in Phdr.* 209 p. 218.29–219.1 Lucarini & Moreschini: τοῦ καθηγεμόνος Διός. For a close association of καθηγεμών (the human teacher) and ἡγεμόνες (the beneficiary gods) cf. also Iul. *Or.* 7.23 p. 235a–b Bidez.

## The Personal Teacher in Proclus and Later Neoplatonism    217

reflect traditional religious speech, Hermias certainly had a philosophical reason to blur the distinction between the divine 'leader' (ἡγεμών) and the human 'guide' (καθηγεμών), because in his interpretation of the passage, he first focuses on the anagogic function of the Platonic Zeus and the other gods who, he says, not only govern cosmic movement but also help souls that faithfully give themselves over to them to return to the intelligible.[66] This is quite analogous to what, according to Proclus, Zeno does in the *Parmenides*; like him, they are helpers and mediators of *epistrophē*. This reading was facilitated by the fact that, according to the late Neoplatonic interpretation, the 'leader gods' of the *Phaedrus* were 'intelligible and intellectual gods', i.e. intermediary entities on the metaphysical scale.[67] In particularly solemn passages, e.g. in the prologues of the *Platonic Theology* and the *Parmenides* commentary, when he wants to emphasize Syrianus' (and his own) closeness to divine intellection, he divinizes his teacher by replacing the usual *kathēgemōn* with the *hēgemōn* of the *Phaedrus*. The *Phaedrus* myth is certainly on his mind when he calls Syrianus his 'leader, next to the gods, to everything that is beautiful and good' (*PT* 1.1 p. 7.3–4. Saffrey & Westerink).[68] The prologue of the *Parmenides* commentary blends the language of the *Phaedrus* with that of Bacchic initiation (T8):

> So may all the orders of divine beings help prepare me fully to share this most visionary and mystical contemplation that Plato reveals (ἐκφαίνει) to us in the *Parmenides* with a profundity appropriate to its subject; the one which has been unfolded to us, through his own purified insights, by him [Syrianus] who was in very truth a fellow Bacchant with Plato and with him feasted on the divine truth and who, for us, has become the leader (ἡγεμών)

---

[66] Herm. *in Phdr.* 135 p. 141.20–5 Lucarini & Moreschini: 'Here he wants to disclose the gods that are responsible for the ascent, how they lead the entire cosmos and how they convert everything to the intelligible. When the soul gives herself over to them, then she too governs the universe and ascends to the intelligible and contemplates what is beyond heaven; but when she separates herself from them, she is borne downwards' (βούλεται ἐνταῦθα τοὺς αἰτίους τῆς ἀναγωγῆς παραδοῦναι θεούς, πῶς μὲν ἐξηγοῦνται παντὸς τοῦ κόσμου, πῶς δὲ πάντα ἐπὶ τὸ νοητὸν ἐπιστρέφουσιν· οἷς δὴ καὶ ἡ ψυχὴ ἑαυτὴν ἐπιδοῦσα, τότε καὶ αὐτὴ τὸ πᾶν ἐπιτροπεύει καὶ ἀνάγεται ἐπὶ τὸ νοητὸν καὶ θεωρεῖ τὰ ἔξω τοῦ οὐρανοῦ, ἀφισταμένη δὲ αὐτῶν φέρεται κάτω).

[67] See van den Berg 2016: 229–30, who cites Procl. *PT* 4.5 p. 21.27–22.8 Saffrey & Westerink.

[68] ὁ μετὰ θεοὺς ἡμῖν τῶν καλῶν πάντων καὶ ἀγαθῶν ἡγεμών (for a very similar statement on Plato, see *PT* 1.9 p. 37.13–14 Saffrey & Westerink: τὸν ἡγεμόνα τῆς τῶν ὄντων ἀληθείας, 'the leader to the truth about Being'). In the same context, he talks about the 'divine chorus' that Iamblichus and other great philosophers had followed 'in Bacchic frenzy' (ibid. p. 6.23–7.1 Saffrey & Westerink: Ἰάμβλιχόν τε καὶ Θεόδωρον, καὶ εἰ δή τινες ἄλλοι μετὰ τούτους ἑπόμενοι τῷ θείῳ τούτῳ χορῷ περὶ τῶν τοῦ Πλάτωνος τὴν ἑαυτῶν διάνοιαν ἀνεβάκχευσαν κτλ., 'Iamblichus and Theodorus and all those who after these have followed that divine chorus and who by thinking about Plato's [insights] were moved to Bacchic frenzy').

218 CHRISTIAN TORNAU

to this vision and a true hierophant of these divine doctrines. Of him I would say that he came to humankind as the exact image of philosophy for the benefit of souls here below, in recompense for the statues, the temples, and the whole ritual of worship, and as the chief author of salvation for people who now live and for those to come hereafter. (Procl. *in Prm.* 617.16–618.9 Steel, 617.22–618.13 Luna & Segonds)[69]

Not only does Proclus elevate Syrianus to the level of the gods by terming him *hēgemōn* (the 'leader gods' having been explicitly named a few lines above in the long hymn that opens the proem); he also equates him, by and large, with Plato. The metaphor of the hierophant, which, as we have seen, marks the commentator as an intermediary, is present, but the language of revelation – which is likewise characteristic of the middle figure of the didactic triad whose task it is to 'make manifest what is hidden' (cf. T3 = Procl. *in Prm.* 1022.24–1023.4 Steel) – is now applied to Plato, whereas Syrianus is granted the immediate insight (ἐπιβολή) that, in the body of the commentary, is the privilege of Parmenides (and Plato).[70] Syrianus and Plato are equally Bacchic initiates and guests at the mystic feast of truth. Of course, much of this is rhetorical praise for Syrianus' exegesis, which in Proclus' eulogy seems almost capable of replacing the *Parmenides* itself (a clear hyperbole that, if taken literally, would mean the collapse of the didactic triad). But Proclus also has a philosophical point. If the goal of pedagogical *epistrophē* is taken to be the understanding of an inspired text, it follows that the author and the commentator are on different hierarchical levels and may neatly be assigned to the top and the middle position of the didactic triad. However, if we shift the triad upwards, the goal will be the insight into true being itself. Then the top position will be occupied by the divine, and all philosophers, alive or dead, can be but mediators. But it makes an immense difference, from the point of view of the philosophical learner at the bottom position of the triad, whether his or her *kathēgemōn* and mediator to the divine is a living person

---

[69] πάντα δὲ ἁπλῶς τὰ θεῖα γένη παρασκευὴν ἐνθεῖναί μοι τελέαν εἰς τὴν μετουσίαν τῆς ἐποπτικωτάτης τοῦ Πλάτωνος καὶ μυστικωτάτης θεωρίας, ἣν ἐκφαίνει μὲν ἡμῖν αὐτὸς ἐν τῷ Παρμενίδῃ μετὰ τῆς προσηκούσης τοῖς πράγμασι βαθύτητος, ἀνῆπλωσε δὲ ταῖς ἑαυτοῦ καθαρωτάταις ἐπιβολαῖς ὁ τῷ Πλάτωνι μὲν συμβακχεύσας ὡς ἀληθῶς καὶ ὁμέστιος καταστὰς τῆς θείας ἀληθείας, τῆς δὲ θεωρίας ἡμῖν γενόμενος ταύτης ἡγεμὼν καὶ τῶν θείων τούτων λόγων ὄντως ἱεροφάντης· ὃν ἐγὼ φαίην ἂν φιλοσοφίας τύπον εἰς ἀνθρώπους ἐλθεῖν ἐπ' εὐεργεσίᾳ τῶν τῇδε ψυχῶν, ἀντὶ τῶν ἀγαλμάτων, ἀντὶ τῶν ἱερῶν, ἀντὶ τῆς ὅλης ἁγιστείας αὐτῆς, καὶ σωτηρίας ἀρχηγὸν τοῖς τε νῦν οὖσι ἀνθρώποις καὶ τοῖς εἰσαῦθις γενησομένοις. For a thorough commentarty on this text, see Luna & Segonds 2007b: 169–75.

[70] Cf. T4 = Procl. *in Prm.* 705.6–9 Steel (on Zeno); ibid. 701.24–7. For the analogy between Plato and Parmenides in this respect cf. *in Prm.* 665.8–12 Steel.

## The Personal Teacher in Proclus and Later Neoplatonism 219

and an immediately accessible teacher who works as a personal guide or whether he is the author of an inspired and authoritative but remote and all but incomprehensible text that in turn needs an intermediator, i.e. an exegete. This difference, I suggest, accounts for the exalted praise that Proclus here lavishes on Syrianus and that almost eclipses Plato himself. Proclus wants to thank the gods for the privilege of having met a teacher who, in addition to his deep understanding of Plato, had immediate access to the divine and was able to communicate this knowledge to Proclus himself, in other words, who combined the sublimity of a divine *kathēgemōn* with the accessibility of a human one. For this reason the familiar motif that the gods send philosophical souls to earth not for some defect but as saviors of humankind is, in this particular context, applied to Syrianus rather than to Plato.[71] Read in this way, the text is a striking Neoplatonic variation on the association between philosophical teaching and salvation (καθηγεμών and σωτήρ) that was inaugurated in Hellenistic philosophy and, as we saw above, perhaps even in Epicureanism.

### 10.3 Proclus as a Mediator: The Sixth Essay of the *Republic* Commentary

So far we have only briefly touched upon Proclus' own role as teacher and commentator. Since he clearly subordinates himself to his *kathēgemōn* whenever he mentions him, and since he usually presents Syrianus as a mediator and guide to the texts and thought of Plato, we have assumed so far that in principle Syrianus and Proclus occupy the middle and the bottom positions of the didactic triad, with Plato at the top. However, as we have just seen, the triad is very flexible, and Syrianus may, from a certain perspective, be ranked together with Plato. Does this entail that in such cases Proclus, his disciple, is promoted to the middle position? After all, he is a successful philosophical teacher and the author of commentaries on Plato himself, and his promotion would open a place in the triad for his own pupils and readers, which is certainly an attractive idea. Does Proclus, then, claim the position of a

---

[71] The idea that some people have divine souls that have descended into the realm of becoming, not because of some defect, but as benefactors of humankind, is frequent in Imperial Platonism. Cf. Atticus fr. 1.32–40 des Places, on Plato; Herm. *in Phdr.* 1 p. 1.5–9 Lucarini & Moreschini, on Socrates; see Erler 2008: 202–3. For a general discussion see Iamblichus, *De anima* p. 380 Wachsmuth, chs. 29–30 Finamore & Dillon (I owe this reference to an anonymous reader for Cambridge University Press). For further evidence and commentary, see Staab 2014: 90–3. Staab interprets a funerary epigram about Syrianus in light of this doctrine and convincingly attributes the epigram to Proclus on these grounds.

## 220 CHRISTIAN TORNAU

*kathēgemōn* for himself? For obvious reasons of modesty, he can only do this implicitly, if at all; but at least one text suggests an interpretation along these lines, viz. the sixth essay of the commentary on the *Republic*.

This treatise, which discusses Plato's criticism of Homer and, predictably, attempts to show their harmony on a more elevated level (Procl. *in R.* 1.69–205 Kroll), is of great interest because it offers a rare glimpse into the customs and commemorative practices of the Neoplatonic school at Athens in Proclus' time. It goes back to a speech that Proclus as scholarch had held on Plato's birthday, which in the school of Athens, as in most Platonic schools of Antiquity, was celebrated with a religious ceremony.[72] As Proclus explains in his introduction, his lecture is based on the teaching of Syrianus, on his oral utterances on the issue as well as on some monographic treatises.[73] In the last sentence, Proclus dedicates the text to the memory of his teacher.[74] With Proclus, Syrianus and Plato, we meet the familiar members of the didactic triad in their usual roles. In this text, however, the presence of the listeners – the members of the Athenian school and Proclus' pupils – is more clearly marked than in the majority of Proclus' writings because, in accordance with the generic rules of the commemorative address and of oratory in general, he frequently addresses his audience in the second person. This naturally invites reflection about their role in the didactic and educational process. If I am not mistaken, Proclus in the course of his speech shifts the didactic triad downwards, as it were, so that it includes the listeners. The concluding remark of the proem, which is also the transition to the body of the argument, reads as follows (T9):

> The subject of my speech, then, will be of this sort. But even this speech, as I said, you ought to attribute to Plato and to his emulator[75] and, as I should say, hierophant, and I myself as the speaker ought to do all I can to bring to your mind, exactly and point by point, everything that was said on that occasion and whatever he [Syrianus] deigned to teach us later, when we discussed the same subject. (Procl. *in R.* 1.71.21–7 Kroll)[76]

---

[72] See Sheppard 1980: 30 –1 who refers to Plut. *Quaest conv.* 8.1.717A; Porph. *Plot.* 2.40–2, 15.1–2; Porph. 408F Smith (the fragment about a banquet on Plato's birthday hosted by Longinus with philosophical discussion); Marin. *Procl.* 23.14–17 Saffrey & Segonds (on Proclus' rhetorical abilities): 'if one listened to him when he commented [on texts] and when, at the annual ceremonies for Plato and Socrates, he delivered most beautiful speeches' (εἴ τις … ἐξηγουμένου τε ἤκουσεν καὶ διεξιόντος λόγους παγκάλους, Πλατώνειά τε καὶ Σωκράτεια κατ' ἐνιαυτὸν ἄγοντος). She also points to the parallels in the school of Epicurus (ibid. 31 with n. 27).

[73] Procl. *in R.* 1.69.23–70.7 Kroll. For the genesis and layers of the essay, see Sheppard 1980: 27–34 and, for source-critical inferences, ibid. 39–103.

[74] *In R.* 1.205.21–3 Kroll.    [75] ζηλωτήν. Cf. Procl. *in Ti.* 1.6.21–3 Diehl (quoted in n. 86).

[76] Τὰ μὲν δὴ προκείμενα τοιαῦτα ἄττα ἐστίν, περὶ ὧν ποιήσομαι τοὺς λόγους. δεῖ δὲ ὅπερ ἔφην ὑμᾶς μὲν καὶ τούτων αἰτιᾶσθαι τόν τε Πλάτωνα αὐτὸν καὶ τὸν ἐκείνου ζηλωτὴν καί, ὡς ἂν ἐγὼ φαίην,

## The Personal Teacher in Proclus and Later Neoplatonism    221

Syrianus' role is somewhat ambiguous in this text. On the one hand, the familiar metaphor of the hierophant casts him in the usual function of mediator of Plato's wisdom. On the other, in the binary structure of the text, Plato and Syrianus, the dead and absent persons whom the text celebrates, represent superior and intuitive knowledge,[77] whereas the persons present – Proclus and his audience – are associated with the transposition of this knowledge into a rational and linguistic form, as can be gathered from the word for 'speech' (λόγους), from the prefix δια- in διαμνημονεῦσαι (which for this reason I have rendered as 'point by point'; cf. διάνοια) and probably also from the term 'exactly' (ἀκριβῶς).[78] But while Syrianus, in a manner reminiscent of the prologue of the *Parmenides* commentary (T8 = Procl. *in Prm.* 617.16–618.9 Steel, 617.22–618.13 Luna & Segonds), is virtually fused with Plato, the roles of Proclus and his listeners are kept distinct, with the former mediating Plato's and Syrianus' insights to his audience and the latter receiving them. This structure becomes even more obvious at the end of the speech. Here Plato's name does not appear anymore, so that a formal triad consisting of Syrianus, Proclus and his disciples emerges (T10):

> Let me, dear pupils and friends, dedicate this to the remembrance of the intercourse with my teacher (τῆς τοῦ καθηγεμόνος ἡμῶν συνουσίας). It is expressible for me to you but ineffable for you to the many. (Procl. *in R.* 1.205.21–3 Kroll)[79]

The ambiguous word 'intercourse' (συνουσία) reminds us of the erotic aspect of a philosopher's relationship with his *kathēgemōn*. On Proclus' interpretation, this is perfectly embodied by the couple of Parmenides and

---

ἱεροφάντην· ἐμὲ δὲ τὸν λέγοντα πειρᾶσθαι πάντα ἀκριβῶς ὑμῖν εἰς δύναμιν τὰ τότε ῥηθέντα διαμνημονεῦσαι καὶ ὅσα καὶ ὕστερον ἡμᾶς περὶ τῶν αὐτῶν διασκοπουμένους ἐπεκδιδάσκειν ἐκεῖνος ἠξίωσεν.

[77] On Syrianus' intuitive insight, cf. *in Prm.* 618.2–3. Steel (quoted in T8) and, in the sixth essay of the *Republic* commentary, *in R.* 1.115.27–8 Kroll: ἡ τοῦ καθηγεμόνος ἡμῶν ἐπιβολή ('my teacher's insight').

[78] Cf. *in Prm.* 645.8–12 Steel: Τὰ μὲν [i.e. the transcendent realities discussed in the *Parmenides*] γάρ ἐστι θεῖα καὶ ἐν τῇ ἁπλότητι τοῦ ἑνὸς ἱδρυμένα, τὴν ἀκαλλώπιστον εὐμορφίαν ... προτείνοντα τοῖς εἰς αὐτὰ βλέπειν δυναμένοις· ἡ δὲ [i.e. the discursive procedure of the dialogue] δι᾽ αὐτῶν τῶν ἀκριβεστάτων πρόεισι τοῦ λόγου δυνάμεων ('The subjects are divine beings that have their foundation in the simplicity of the One, who ... extend "unadorned beauty" to those capable of looking at the divine. But the method proceeds by using the most exacting capacities of reason'). Simple noetic intuition corresponds to μονή (cf. ἱδρυμένα), its translation into discursive reasoning to πρόοδος.

[79] ταῦτα, ὦ φίλοι ἑταῖροι, μνήμη κεχαρίσθω τῆς τοῦ καθηγεμόνος ἡμῶν συνουσίας, ἐμοὶ μὲν ὄντα ῥητὰ πρὸς ὑμᾶς, ὑμῖν δὲ ἄρρητα πρὸς τοὺς πολλούς. The phrase μνήμη κεχαρίσθω is a quotation from the *Phaedrus* myth (250c) which, as we have seen, is crucial for the religious overtones of *kathēgemōn*.

## 222 CHRISTIAN TORNAU

Zeno in Plato's *Parmenides*; so we may infer that in our text Proclus discreetly but unmistakably represents himself as a *mesotēs* of Zeno's type, united in mutual philosophical love with his teacher but at the same time directed outwards and downwards and able to communicate the latter's *noēsis* to the discursive reason of his own disciples, thereby assisting their spiritual *epistrophē*. If those at the bottom of the triad attempted to communicate these matters verbally in their turn, they would inevitably fail. By alluding to the secrecy of the mysteries, the last sentence takes up the initiatory language from the beginning and again highlights the religious aspect of philosophical education.[80]

### 10.4  Authority and Orality in Proclus and Simplicius

After Proclus, the formula *ho hēmeteros katēgemōn* remains common among the Neoplatonists, especially in the Athenian school, but it rarely seems to carry the full metaphysical weight it has in Proclus. Ammonius and Damascius mention their teachers (Proclus and Isidorus, respectively) with respect and gratitude,[81] and the hymnic diction of the opening lines of Ammonius' commentary on the *De interpretatione* is reminiscent of Proclus' praise for Syrianus,[82] but neither of them links this to any discernible ethical or metaphysical ideas. In the commentaries by Damascius that were taken down by his pupils at his lectures (ἀπὸ φωνῆς), *ho hēmeteros katēgemōn* is nothing but a polite formula for the professor who is holding the course, i.e. Damascius himself.[83] In Simplicius, however, there are some passages concerning the issues of authority and of orality that are easier understood if the Proclan model is, at least to some extent, presupposed.

So far we have only investigated the ideal relationship between a *kathēgemōn* and his pupil(s), as embodied e.g. by Parmenides and Zeno (and Socrates) or by Proclus and Syrianus (and Plato). But obviously there are also cases in which philosophical, even Platonic, teaching fails. This does not come as a surprise in the case of Epicurus and Democritus,

---

[80] Cf. *in R.* 1.133.5–7 Kroll, where Syrianus is the *mesotēs* (cf. the familiar vocabulary of ἐκφαίνειν): 'our teacher has composed a special treatise on this myth as a whole, revealing his ineffable insight in a divinely inspired way' (ὁ μὲν οὖν ἡμέτερος καθηγεμὼν προηγουμένην καταβαλλόμενος πραγματείαν εἰς τοῦτον ἅπαντα τὸν μῦθον ἐνθεαστικώτατα τὴν ἀπόρρητον αὐτοῦ θεωρίαν ἐξέφηνεν).

[81] Ammon. *in Int.* 181.30–2 Busse (thanking Proclus for providing handy tables for those who wish to learn Aristotelian logic); Dam. *Princ.* 3.111.12–14 Westerink & Combès (remembering an oral discussion, probably with Isidorus); *in Prm.* 3.4.22–3. Westerink & Combès.

[82] Ammon. *in Int.* 1.3–11 Busse.      [83] Dam. *in Phd.* 1.207 tit.; *in Phlb.* 6 etc.

## The Personal Teacher in Proclus and Later Neoplatonism    223

neither of whom has the philosophical standing that is necessary for a successful return to true being.[84] The case of Aristotle is more complex. As is well known, Proclus does believe in the general harmony of Plato and Aristotle but is very critical especially of the latter's natural philosophy, which he rejects as Aristotle's deviation from his *kathēgemōn* Plato.[85] The way in which he formulates this criticism is telling. Proclus enlists Aristotle as an 'emulator' of Plato (ζηλώσας, a phrase elsewhere applied to Syrianus),[86] but, he adds, the fact that in explaining nature, Aristotle usually does not go beyond matter and immanent form betrays 'how much he lags behind the guidance (ὑφήγησις) of his *kathēgemōn*'.[87] Aristotle is blamed for his lack of philosophical allegiance, not because he sometimes contradicts Plato, but because he was unable or unwilling to submit to the quasi-divine guidance of his *kathēgemōn*, which resulted in his failure to return to the intelligible and in his developing a metaphysics that falls short of the ontological level that Plato had reached. Conversely, as long as he philosophizes on Plato's ontological level, a thinker qualifies as a true Platonist even if on some points he deviates from him: according to Proclus, Plotinus was 'endowed with a nature similar to that of his own *kathēgemōn* [*sc.* Plato]' and was himself able to offer theological guidance (ὑφήγησις) to others, even though Proclus rejects his theory of the undescended soul.[88] Neoplatonic orthodoxy, if we may call it thus, seems to admit of a certain pluralism.

Simplicius, who, of course, went further than Proclus and most other Platonists in claiming the agreement of Plato and Aristotle,[89] takes up this basic view while at the same time opposing Proclus' verdict (just paraphrased). In his commentary on the *Physics*, he repeatedly says that

---

[84] Cf. Procl. *in R.* 2.113.6–13 Kroll, accusing the Epicurean Colotes of not knowing the doctrine of his teacher's *kathēgemōn* (perhaps with an allusion to Epicurus' well-known habit of minimizing his debts to Democritus, cf. Plut. *Non posse* 1100A). Should this be a kind of caricature of the 'pedagogic triad'?

[85] See esp. Procl. *in Ti.* 1.6.21–7.16 Diehl and Steel 2003.

[86] Procl. *in Ti.* 1.6.22–3 Diehl: τὴν τοῦ Πλάτωνος διδασκαλίαν κατὰ δύναμιν ζηλώσας ('the ingenious Aristotle who emulated Plato's teaching with all his energy'). For Syrianus cf. *in R.* 1.71.24 Kroll (T9 above). I doubt that ζηλώσας in the *Timaeus* commentary means that Aristotle attempted to surpass Plato (thus Steel 2003: 177).

[87] Procl. *in Ti.* 1.7.13–16 Diehl: 'For in most cases he stops at the point of matter, and by pinning his explanations of physical things on this he demonstrates to us just how far he falls short of the guidance of his teacher', trans. adapted from Baltzly 2007 (τὰ πολλὰ γὰρ ἄχρι τῆς ὕλης ἵσταται καὶ τὰς ἀποδόσεις ἀπὸ ταύτης τῶν φυσικῶν ποιούμενος δείκνυσιν ἡμῖν, ὅσον ἀπολείπεται τῆς τοῦ καθηγεμόνος ὑφηγήσεως).

[88] Procl. *PT* 1.1 p. 6.16–20 Saffrey & Westerink. For Proclus' rejection of the theory of the undescended soul, cf. e.g. *ET* 211.

[89] See e.g. Baltussen 2008: 9–10; Perkams 2006; Golitsis 2018.

224    CHRISTIAN TORNAU

Aristotle 'is not in disharmony with his *kathēgemōn*',[90] implying – and sometimes stating – that philosophical allegiance is not a matter of verbal agreement. This occurs especially in discussions of points on which Aristotle was notoriously critical of Plato, e.g. whether movement (κίνησις) and change (μεταβολή) were to be distinguished or were one and the same thing (which has some bearing on the difficult issue of the movement of the soul, on which Aristotle explicitly contradicted Plato).[91] Naturally, Simplicius does not deny the difference in terminology, but he does deny that it shows Aristotle's inability or unwillingness to reach the more sublime regions of Plato's thought (T11):

> It is important to note that here again Aristotle has expressed the same ideas (ἐννοίας) as his teacher with different words. (Simp. *in Phys.* 1336.25–6 Diels, introducing a long comparison of the accounts of the First Principle in *Physics* 8 and the *Timaeus*)[92]

When he reports especially impressive cases of the agreement of the two philosophers, Simplicius likes to employ the vocabulary of 'willing' or 'striving' in order to highlight the ethical aspect of the issue (T12):

> In the *Categories*, Aristotle emulated even this terminology of his teacher, that he calls all natural changes movements. (Simp. *in Phys.* 824.20–2 Diels)[93]

> On this, too, Aristotle wants (βούλεται) to be in harmony with his teacher. (Simp. *in Phys.* 1267.19 Diels)[94]

Simplicius agrees with Proclus that Aristotle was an emulator of Plato; against Proclus, he insists that this emulating was successful, and he seems to do so on Proclus' own assumption that philosophical allegiance is primarily a moral decision. Simplicius' use of *kathēgemōn* may not have the philosophical depth of Proclus', but it is, as it were, metaphysically pregnant and strengthens Aristotle's authority as a Platonist and helps to ward off the charge of anti-Platonism.

---

[90] Simp. *in Phys.* 451.1–7 Diels; cf. ibid. 761.5–9, 824.17–25, 1077.3–5, 1267.20–8, 1336.25–6, 1360.24–31.

[91] Arist. *DA* 1.3.405b31–406a2. For an overview of the commentary tradition from Alexander of Aphrodisias, see Sorabji 2004: 217–20.

[92] Ἐπιστῆσαι δὲ ἄξιον, ὅτι κἀνταῦθα πάλιν ὁ Ἀριστοτέλης ἐν διαφόροις ὀνόμασι τὰς αὐτὰς ἐννοίας τῷ σφετέρῳ καθηγεμόνι προύβάλετο.

[93] ὁ δὲ Ἀριστοτέλης καὶ τοῦτο μέν, τὸ τὰς φυσικὰς πάσας μεταβολὰς κινήσεις καλεῖν, ἐζήλωσε τοῦ καθηγεμόνος ἐν ταῖς Κατηγορίαις. The allusion is to Arist. *Cat.* 14.15a13–14.

[94] κἀνταῦθα δὲ ὁ Ἀριστοτέλης συμφωνεῖν βούλεται τῷ ἑαυτοῦ καθηγεμόνι.

## The Personal Teacher in Proclus and Later Neoplatonism 225

Concerning orality, we have seen that for Proclus the inspired texts of Plato and others have their full impact on the philosophical learner only if they are unfolded to her or him personally by an experienced exegete. For this reason in the prologue of the *Parmenides* commentary, Syrianus, not Plato, is the savior of humankind, and in the commentary on the *Republic*, Proclus himself re-transfers a written text by Syrianus into orality. Later Neoplatonists remain alive to the importance of personal instruction; several of them record oral discussions with their *kathēgemones*. Simplicius is no exception, though he more often cites Ammonius' lectures or written treatises.[95] However, there seems to be an important difference. Commenting on the problem of squaring the circle, Simplicius recalls a scene between himself and Ammonius in Alexandria (T13):

> My teacher Ammonius used to say that it was perhaps not necessary that, if this [*sc.* a square of the same size as a circle] had been found in the case of numbers, it should also be found in the case of magnitudes. For the line and the circumference were magnitudes of a different kind. 'It is', he said, 'no wonder that a circle of the same size as a polygon has not been found, seeing that we find this in the case of angles too. . . .' I replied to my teacher that if the lune over the side of a square could be squared (and this was proven beyond doubt) and if the lune, which consisted of circumferences, was of the same kind as the circle, there was, on this assumption, no reason why the circle could not be squared. (Simp. *in Phys.* 59.23–60.1 Diels)[96]

Simplicius surely tells this story not just in order to voice his disagreement with Ammonius but also to commemorate him honorifically, as he usually does.[97] We should therefore read the passage as an example of successful philosophical didactics. As an experienced teacher and versed dialectician, Ammonius challenges his promising pupil with an agnostic argument on a thorny mathematical problem, and Simplicius meets the

---

[95] Oral discussion: Simp. *in Cael.* 462.20 Heiberg; *in Phys.* 183.18 Diels. Quotations or paraphrases: *in Phys.* 192.14, 198.17–18, 1363.8–10. Cf. Baltussen 2008: 163. For Damascius, see n. 81. For an early parallel, see Alex. Aphr. *De an. mant.* 110.4. Interestingly, in both Alexander and Damascius, the discussion reported is controversial, as in Simp. *in Phys.* 59.23–60.1 Diels (see below).

[96] Ἔλεγε δὲ ὁ ἡμέτερος καθηγεμὼν Ἀμμώνιος ὡς οὐκ ἀναγκαῖον ἴσως, εἰ ἐπ' ἀριθμῶν εὑρέθη τοῦτο, καὶ ἐπὶ μεγεθῶν εὑρίσκεσθαι. ἀνομογενῆ γὰρ μεγέθη ἐστὶν εὐθεῖα καὶ περιφέρεια. 'καὶ οὐδέν, φησί, θαυμαστόν, μὴ εὑρεθῆναι κύκλον εὐθυγράμμῳ ἴσον, εἴπερ καὶ ἐπὶ τῶν γωνιῶν εὑρίσκομεν τοῦτο. . . .' ἔλεγον δὲ ἐγὼ πρὸς τὸν καθηγεμόνα ὡς εἴπερ μηνίσκος τετραγωνίζοιτο ὁ ἀπὸ τῆς τοῦ τετραγώνου πλευρᾶς (τοῦτο γὰρ ἀνεξαπατήτως συνῆκται), ὁμογενὴς δὲ ὁ μηνίσκος τῷ κύκλῳ ἐκ περιφερειῶν συγκείμενος, τί κωλύει καὶ τὸν κύκλον, ὅσον ἐπὶ τούτῳ, τετραγωνίζεσθαι; Simplicius is referring to the so-called lunes of Hippocrates of Chios, of which the subsequent fragment of Eudemus gives a fuller account.

[97] There is apparently no other passage in which Simplicius contradicts Ammonius. Contrast *in Phys.* 774.28–9 Diels on Damascius: παραιτοῦμαι δὲ ἐνταῦθα τὸν ἐμαυτοῦ καθηγεμόνα Δαμάσκιον ('At this point I respectfully disagree with my own teacher Damascius').

226                          CHRISTIAN TORNAU

challenge and succeeds in developing a convincing counterargument. He then goes on to explain why he will stick to the argument he devised ad hoc in his dialectical exchange with Ammonius long ago.[98] Rather than taking the form of a dialectical argument, however, his justification consists of extensive quotations from Iamblichus and, in particular, from the *History of Geometry* by Aristotle's disciple Eudemus (fr. 140 Wehrli). Elsewhere, Simplicius implies that Eudemus' authority as an exegete is enhanced by the fact that Aristotle was his immediate *kathēgemōn*.[99] So it seems that although Simplicius remains grateful to Ammonius for having prompted him to tackle a difficult mathematical problem and its solution, now that he has reached the status of a mature philosopher, it is no longer a personal *kathēgemōn* who mediates the correct understanding of the authoritative texts to him but the exegetes who were closest to the author himself. The authority of these is no doubt due to their personal acquaintance with the inspired author; Proclus' views on mediation are still operative on this score. But from the point of view of Simplicius as a philosopher of the present time, the mediators are texts, just as Plato and Aristotle themselves are texts. Philosophy has become much more bookish in Simplicius than it had ever been in Proclus.

---

[98] Cf. *in Phys.* 60.6 Diels: οἶμαι.

[99] Simp. *in Phys.* 517.15–16 Diels: κάλλιον γὰρ οἶμαι τὸ ἔξω τοῦ ἄστεος οὕτως ἀκούειν, ὡς ὁ Εὔδημος ἐνόησε τὰ τοῦ καθηγεμόνος ('I think it is better to read "outside the city" in the way Eudemus understood what his teacher said'; on Eudemus fr. 70 Wehrli). For the importance of the early Peripatetics in Simplicius, see Baltussen 2008: 91–106 (on Eudemus: ibid. 99–104). Contrast Procl. *in Ti.* 1.310.4–7 Diehl, where it is Syrianus whose understanding comes closest to Plato's meaning – obviously not for temporal reasons but because, like Plato, he has ascended to the highest ranks of the intelligible (T8 = Procl. *in Prm.* 617.16–618.9 Steel).

CHAPTER 11

# 'In Plato we can see the bad characters being changed by the good and instructed and purified.'
## Attitudes to Platonic Dialogue in Later Neoplatonism[*]

### Anne Sheppard

The quotation in my title is taken from the *Anonymous Prolegomena to Platonic Philosophy*, a work probably originating from the Neoplatonist school of Alexandria in the sixth century AD, which exhibits many parallels with the commentaries of Olympiodorus and which, like the work of Olympiodorus and the other Alexandrian commentators of the fifth and sixth centuries, is strongly influenced by Proclus.[1] The author of the *Prolegomena* is concerned by the implications of Plato's use of dialogue form; in particular he is worried that Plato's use of a variety of characters lays him open to the same charges which he himself makes against drama:[2]

> It is worth enquiring why Plato, who elsewhere criticizes variegated things –
> for example, he criticizes pipe-playing because it uses variegated instruments with many openings, playing the cithara because it uses a number of different strings, comedy because of the variety of its characters and tragedy for the same reason – why does Plato, who criticizes all these things for this reason, himself use the literary form of the dialogue which involves a variety of characters? We should reply that the variety of characters in tragedy and comedy is not of the same kind as in Plato. In drama there are good and bad characters and they remain as they are, whereas in Plato, although we find good and bad characters there too, we can see the bad characters being changed by the good and instructed and purified; they always disengage themselves from their materialistic way of life. So the variety in drama is different from the variety in Plato; therefore Plato has not fallen into any contradiction here. (*Anon. Prol.* 14.9–23 Westerink, my translation)[3]

---

[*] I am grateful to Federico Petrucci for helpful comments and especially for drawing my attention to some Middle Platonic texts.

[1] See Westerink 1990: vii–lxxxix.

[2] Presumably the author has primarily in mind *Republic* 3.394–9 where, after criticizing the mimetic presentation of characters in tragedy and comedy, Socrates goes on to discuss musical modes and musical instruments. Cf. also *Grg.* 501d–502d.

[3] Ἄξιον δ' ἐστὶν ζητῆσαι διὰ τί, ἀλλαχοῦ τοῦ Πλάτωνος διαβάλλοντος τὰ ποικίλα τῶν πραγμάτων – ἀμέλει τὴν αὐλητικὴν διαβάλλει ὡς ποικίλοις καὶ πολυτρήτοις ὀργάνοις χρωμένην, καὶ τὴν

227

228                           ANNE SHEPPARD

As we shall see in the course of this chapter, a similar approach to Plato's use of characters in his dialogues can be found in Proclus, Olympiodorus and elsewhere.[4] Twenty-first century readers of Plato, conscious of the need to appreciate Plato's dialogues as works of literature as well as philosophy, may well be struck by remarks like these,[5] and may wonder how the Neoplatonists of late antiquity reconciled their awareness of Plato's skill in characterization with treating Plato as a philosophical authority. That will be my topic in this chapter. I begin with a brief discussion of some modern interpreters who emphasize Plato's use of dialogue form, from which we shall see that even in our postmodern age such an emphasis can still be combined with a belief that Plato is a dogmatic philosopher. I will then turn to fuller examination of the interpretation of Plato's characters by Proclus and Olympiodorus, including how this relates to their acceptance of Plato's authority.

## 11.1   Modern Approaches to Plato's Use of Dialogue Form

It has become increasingly common for interpreters of Plato to take seriously the implications of Plato's use of dialogue form, whether they are writing about Plato in general or about particular Platonic dialogues. Notoriously, Plato never appears in his dialogues himself but presents us in each dialogue with a group of characters holding different views, with Socrates usually, but not always, playing the dominant role and leading the conversation. The more seriously we take the variety of characters and views presented, the less likely we are to accept that there are specific Platonic doctrines for which the dialogues are arguing. However, consideration of some representative samples of scholarly works which explicitly

---

κιθαριστικὴν ὡς διαφόροις χορδαῖς, καὶ τὴν κωμικὴν διὰ τὸ διάφορον τῶν προσώπων, ὁμοίως δὲ καὶ τὴν τραγικήν – ταῦτα οὖν διὰ τοῦτο διαβάλλων διὰ τί αὐτὸς ἐκ ποικίλων προσώπων συγκειμένου τοῦ διαλόγου κέχρηται τῇ τοιαύτῃ συγγραφικῇ ἰδέᾳ. ἢ ἐκεῖνο δεῖ λέγειν ὡς οὐκ ἔστιν τοιοῦτον τὸ ποικίλον τῶν προσώπων τῶν παρὰ κωμῳδοῖς καὶ τραγῳδοῖς οἷόν ἐστιν τὸ παρὰ Πλάτωνι. ἐν ἐκείνοις γὰρ ἀγαθῶν καὶ κακῶν ὄντων προσώπων ἐπὶ ταὐτῷ μένειν συμβαίνει τὰ πρόσωπα, παρὰ Πλάτωνι δέ, εἰ καὶ ἔστιν τοῦτο εὑρεῖν, ἀγαθὰ λέγω καὶ κακὰ πρόσωπα, ἀλλ' ἔστιν ἰδεῖν ἀμειβόμενα τὰ κακὰ ὑπὸ τῶν ἀγαθῶν καὶ διδασκόμενα καὶ καθαιρόμενα καὶ τῆς ἐνύλου ζωῆς ἀπαναχωροῦντα πάντως. ὥστε ἄλλο ἐστὶν τὸ παρ' ἐκείνοις ποικίλον καὶ ἄλλο τὸ παρὰ τούτῳ· οὐκ ἄρα τοῖς ἐναντίοις ὑπέπεσεν.

[4] Cf. Layne 2014. Layne focuses particularly on the *Anon. Prol.* and on Proclus' *Commentary on the First Alcibiades*, developing the parallel between a Platonic dialogue and the cosmos found in *Anon. Prol.* 17.33–9 and offering only a few pages (86–8) on the Neoplatonic treatment of Plato's characters.

[5] For example, Blondell 2002 includes ten references to the *Anon. Prol.*, mainly in footnotes. She cites 14.9–23 at 88 n. 175, and at 47 somewhat rashly describes 15.7–13 as 'foreshadowing modern reception-theory'.

take account of Plato's use of dialogue form will show that, while there is some common ground, modern interpreters differ considerably from one another both in their approach to this topic and in their conclusions. I have deliberately selected only a small number from a potentially very large list of modern scholarly works on Plato; my aim is not to provide any kind of survey but to bring out some key features of the chosen works in order to compare and contrast their approach with that of the Neoplatonists.

I begin with Ruby Blondell's book, *The Play of Character in Plato's Dialogues*. Blondell focuses on the dramatic presentation of characters in the dialogues and starts with an assumption of 'the primacy of the individual dialogue' as the object of interpretation although she recognizes shared themes and 'apparent ties' between dialogues.[6] This emphasis on the individual dialogue as primary is accompanied by considerable scepticism about the possibility of placing the dialogues in a chronological order, although she does recognize the existence of a late group of dialogues. Blondell argues that the use of dialogue form implies the avoidance of dogmatism: 'The avoidance of dogmatism is a simple formal fact, one that accords with the definition of dramatic form as the absence of an authorial or narrative voice. Since Plato never speaks in his own voice, he never adopts a dogmatic or authoritative pedagogical stance towards his audience or readership.'[7]

Blondell's desire to start by considering each dialogue individually is shared by many modern interpreters of Plato. Similar views to hers are expressed, for example, by Richard Rutherford in *The Art of Plato*. Rutherford writes: 'the best approach to Plato is to treat each dialogue as essentially self-contained, an independent literary artefact which does not build on its predecessors or form part of a larger structure or "course" in philosophy'. Like Blondell, Rutherford does not have much interest in a chronological approach, although he describes his position on the chronology of the dialogues as 'agnosticism' rather than scepticism.[8] Rutherford too stresses the importance of Plato's presentation of characters, noting that 'the dialogues present different people expressing different views, and often these views clash and conflict'. However he is more cautious than Blondell about just what this variety implies. In Rutherford's view, 'the dialogue form enables Plato to avoid the *appearance* of dogmatism and to encourage independent thinking'.[9]

---

[6] Blondell 2002: 8.    [7] Blondell 2002: 39.    [8] See Rutherford 1995: 3.

[9] Both quotations come from Rutherford 1995: 9. The italics in the second one are mine.

Similar characteristics of the dialogue form are highlighted by Charles Kahn in *Plato and the Socratic Dialogue*. For Kahn, Plato's use of this form is philosophically problematic. He writes, 'Since we never hear Plato's own voice, how can we know where, and to what extent, what Socrates says represents what Plato thinks? The problem is made more acute both by the formal independence of the dialogues from one another, and by the discrepancy between the positions attributed to Socrates in different contexts.'[10] Kahn has his own, distinctive solution to this problem, arguing that the dialogues commonly regarded as early present 'not the development of Plato's thought, but the gradual unfolding of a literary plan for presenting his philosophical views to the general public'.[11] Central to those philosophical views, according to Kahn, is a 'metaphysical vision' which he at one point describes as 'recognizably that of Plotinus and the Neoplatonists'.[12] Kahn places less emphasis than either Blondell or Rutherford on the variety of characters in the dialogues, although he notes that 'the philosophical content of each dialogue is adapted to the personality and understanding of the interlocutors'.[13]

All three of these modern interpreters feel obliged to take up a position on the chronology of Plato's dialogues, although none of them offers a conventional developmentalist account of Plato's thought. In this respect their positions are quite different from that of the Neoplatonists of late antiquity who simply assume that Plato's thought is a consistent whole and know nothing of arguments over the development of either his thought or his style.[14] Both Blondell and Rutherford wish to start by treating each dialogue on its own, as an independent literary work, rather than discussing themes and topics across dialogues. Kahn, however, despite his awareness that the literary form of the dialogues pulls interpreters in this direction and despite the subtlety and complexity of his discussion of individual dialogues, does not want to go down this road and in the end offers his readers not just a dogmatic Plato but a broadly Neoplatonist one. Of the three modern interpreters, Blondell has the clearest focus on Plato's presentation of his characters; that is why, despite her insistence on an

[10] Kahn 1996: 36–7.    [11] Kahn 1996: xv.
[12] Kahn 1996: 66. Kahn does not pursue the connection of his interpretation of Plato with that of the Neoplatonists in any detail, either in this book or in his 2013 subsequent work on the later dialogues, *Plato and the Post-Socratic Dialogue*.
[13] Kahn 1996: 381.
[14] Cf. Annas 1999: 3–4. Note also Annas' comments on the connection between the skeptical Academy's approach to Plato and Plato's use of dialogue form (9–10) and her discussion in Chapter 1 of the interpretative assumptions underlying Middle Platonic treatments of Plato's ethics.

*Platonic Dialogue in Later Neoplatonism*  231

undogmatic Plato, her book includes some references to the remarks about Platonic characterization found in the *Anonymous Prolegomena*.[15]

Comparing the Neoplatonists with these modern interpreters brings out some significant features of the ancient commentators' approach to Plato's texts. All three of the modern interpreters I have discussed emphasize, each in their own way, the protreptic element of Platonic dialogue, i.e. the way in which the dialogues encourage engagement by the reader.[16] The Neoplatonic commentators do that too, but with a difference, because they not only believe in the consistency of Plato's views across dialogues but also hold that those views express the truth. This means that the reader is being encouraged not so much to work things out for him or herself as to develop an understanding of ultimate truths. Like the modern interpreters, the Neoplatonists recognize the affinities of Platonic dialogue to drama but their belief in the consistency of Plato's views means that this recognition troubles them: well aware of Plato's own hostility to drama, they seek to interpret the dramatic elements of Platonic dialogue and particularly the presentation of the characters in a way which distinguishes between the two literary forms.

Despite their conviction that Plato's views are ultimately consistent across dialogues, the Neoplatonist commentators of late antiquity resemble Blondell and Rutherford in treating each dialogue as an independent literary work. We shall see in the next section that there was a standard set of questions to be considered when beginning the study of an individual dialogue. The comments in the *Anonymous Prolegomena* with which I began need to be set against this background, as do the discussions of some individual characters in particular dialogues which will follow.

## 11.2  Neoplatonic Preliminary Questions

Jaap Mansfeld has shown that by late antiquity there was a standard set of preliminary questions to be considered before reading a Platonic dialogue with a teacher; these included discussion of the *skopos* or 'aim' of the work as well as of the dialogue form and of the characters. Often a *Life* of Plato would be included too. These questions appear in various forms and in various different orders in the *Anonymous Prolegomena* and in the Plato commentaries by Proclus and Olympiodorus. Similar questions were

---

[15] See n. 5.
[16] See, for example, Blondell 2002: 46–8, 99–103; Rutherford 1995: 9, 99–100, 116; Kahn 1996: xiv–xv, 136–7, 381.

considered before reading a work of Aristotle, as we can see from the introductions to the ancient commentaries on the *Categories*. Some of these questions were already being asked by much earlier teachers and commentators: brief remarks on the dialogue as a literary genre and its inclusion of πρεπούση ἠθοποιία, 'appropriate presentation of character', can already be found in Diogenes Laertius' *Life* of Plato 3.48.[17] It is well known that the later commentators' concern with the *skopos* of a Platonic dialogue and the stipulation that each dialogue has a single *skopos* derive from Iamblichus.[18] More broadly, Mansfeld emphasizes the wide range of precedents for considering preliminary questions in commenting on texts of all kinds – literary, medical and mathematical as well as philosophical – but suggests that 'a systematic codification of the introductory questions to the study' of both Aristotle and Plato 'may have been Proclus' contribution'.[19]

Proclus and his successors were not only systematic in their method as commentators; they were also methodologically self-aware and so we can learn a good deal about their approach from looking at the introductions to their commentaries as well as from examining how they put some of their principles into practice in commenting on particular Platonic passages. They do not share our modern scepticism about the biographical information provided by ancient *Lives* of philosophers, nor do they have any qualms about associating an author's biography with literary and philosophical discussion of his work. For them 'the divine Plato' is an authoritative teacher and the stories told about his life serve only to confirm that.[20] They do consider each dialogue as an independent literary work. The principle that each dialogue has only one *skopos* demands that each one should be interpreted as a unity, concerned with one topic; parts of a dialogue that appear to be on another topic must be read in such a way that they can be shown to reflect the main theme. Allegorical interpretation offers a powerful tool with which to achieve such unified interpretation.[21] But of course the Neoplatonists are not primarily literary

---

[17] Mansfeld 1994: ch. 1, esp. 28–37, and, on Diogenes Laertius, 106.

[18] Larsen 1972: 435–42; Dillon 1973: 56 and 264–5; Westerink 1990: lxvi.

[19] Mansfeld 1994: 55.

[20] See Riginos 1976: 212. Griffin 2015b: 43–6 argues that the structure of Olympiodorus' *Life* of Plato reflects the Neoplatonic curriculum and scale of virtues. The tradition of prefacing an account of Plato's doctrines with a biography of the philosopher goes back at least to Apuleius' *De Platone*. On the wider background to the ancient interest in relating the biographies of philosophers to their works, see Mansfeld 1994: 179–91.

[21] For a brief account of how such allegory is used at the beginning of Proclus' *Commentary on the Parmenides*, together with a fuller treatment of how Proclus applies his view about the *skopos* of the

## Platonic Dialogue in Later Neoplatonism

interpreters and they also read Plato's dialogues as expositions of a unified and consistent doctrine; here, too, allegory is enormously helpful to them as a way of resolving apparent inconsistencies between dialogues. In their curriculum, as laid down by Iamblichus, a total of twelve dialogues were read in a specific order, starting with the *First Alcibiades* and the *Gorgias* and concluding with the *Timaeus* and the *Parmenides*. This was an order established with the progression of their students in mind, rather than one that made any claims to reflect Plato's philosophical intentions.[22] The *Republic* did not form part of this curriculum, but Proclus' interpretative essays on that dialogue reflect study and teaching of it within his school.[23]

The first of those essays apparently formed the beginning of a course of lectures on the *Republic*, continued in essays 2–5, 7, 8, 10–12, 14 and 15. In it, Proclus lists seven issues which should be considered before studying the dialogue: the aim (σκοπός); the genre (εἶδος); the matter (ὕλη); the different types of constitution (πολιτεία) according to Plato; the nature of the constitution which conforms to reason, whether one or more than one; how Plato wants us to regard the chosen constitution and whether he has given a complete account of it; and, finally, the consistency of the work as a whole. The characters and the setting of the dialogue in place and time (πρόσωπα, τόποι, καιροί) are specifically mentioned as points to be considered under the heading of matter.[24] The latter part of this essay is lost; frustratingly, the text breaks off at the point where Proclus is about to discuss the characters of the dialogue, having dealt with *topoi* and *kairoi*, i.e. the setting in the Piraeus on the day of the festival of Bendis. However, the part of the essay that we have includes Proclus' discussion of the dialogue's genre. Proclus begins that discussion by making use of Plato's own classification of literary forms into three – mimetic, narrative and a mixture of the first two – at *Republic* 3.392d–394c and argues that Platonic dialogue (like the poetry of Homer) belongs to the mixed kind, not the mimetic kind to which tragedy and comedy belong. This passage does contain some rather general comments on Plato's presentation of characters, mentioning its 'clarity' (εὐκρίνεια) and Plato's skill in making different characters speak appropriately.[25]

---

*Timaeus* in his *Commentary* on that dialogue, see the general introduction by Dirk Baltzly and Harold Tarrant in Baltzly & Tarrant 2007: 17–20.

[22] See *Anon. Prol.* ch. 26 with Westerink 1990: lxvii–lxxiii. Cf. also Siorvanes 1996: 114–16.

[23] See Sheppard 2013. Cf. also Annas 1999: 5, on how, from 'the ancient perspective', 'the *Republic* . . . is not privileged as the central, most important dialogue'.

[24] See Proclus, *In R.* 1.5.28–7.4 and Mansfeld 1994: 22–3 and 30–3.

[25] See *In R.* 1.14.15–15.19.

It is clear that Proclus' interest in what we might regard as literary features of the *Republic*, such as genre and character presentation, is subordinate to his interest in its philosophical content: his discussion of the *skopos* occupies over seven pages of Teubner text (1.7.5–14.14), while his treatment of the genre occupies less than three pages in all (1.14.15–16.25); his treatment of the 'matter' of the dialogue appears to have been a bit longer, but not perhaps much longer since, when it breaks off at 1.19.25, after three pages, the setting of the dialogue in place and time has already been covered and only the characters remain to be dealt with. The remaining four of the seven issues listed at the start of the essay are all concerned with content, and we may note that the issue of consistency, apparently the last to be covered, is described at 1.6.24–5 as 'the consistency *of doctrine* running through the whole work' (τὴν δι' ὅλου τοῦ συγγράμματος διήκουσαν τῶν δογμάτων ἀκολουθίαν).

Other surviving Platonic commentaries by Proclus begin with similar 'preliminary questions', but there is considerable variation in the number and order of the questions as well as in the depth of discussion. The *skopos* is always examined, but the amount of attention paid to the genre, characters and setting differs from one commentary to another.[26] Although such topics are most often considered in the introductions to Proclus' commentaries, remarks on the presentation of the characters can also be found within the main text. In the next section of this chapter I shall turn to Proclus' treatment of Alcibiades in his *Commentary on the First Alcibiades*. We shall see that, for Proclus, at one level Alcibiades is precisely the kind of character alluded to in *Anon. Prol.* ch. 14, a bad character who is instructed and purified in the course of the dialogue, but that there is also a further, allegorical level of interpretation to be taken into account.

## 11.3  Alcibiades: The Bad Pupil Reformed

From the beginning, Alcibiades presented a problem for the defenders of Socrates as a hugely talented pupil who turned out very badly.[27] The

---

[26] Sometimes the term πρόθεσις (theme) is used instead of σκοπός. Mansfeld 1994: 33–7 offers a helpful summary of the topics covered in the introductions to Proclus' other commentaries on Platonic dialogues as well as some brief remarks about introductions by Olympiodorus and Damascius.

[27] For a convenient summary of the problem and of the responses given by Plato and other followers of Socrates, see Denyer 2001: 1–5; note also Xenophon, *Memorabilia* 1.2.24–5, which is alluded to by Proclus and Olympiodorus in the passages referred to in n. 29.

## Platonic Dialogue in Later Neoplatonism

Neoplatonists had no doubts about the authenticity of the *First Alcibiades* and, as mentioned above, the dialogue was the first one to be read in the curriculum prescribed by Iamblichus.[28] They read the dialogue as offering a model of progress in philosophy, although they were well aware that Socrates' attempt to reform Alcibiades was not finally successful.[29] Proclus' introduction to his commentary on the dialogue mentions that characters, time and 'what some people call the setting' (τὰ πρόσωπα καὶ ὁ καιρὸς καὶ ἡ καλουμένη παρά τισιν ὑπόθεσις)[30] fall under the heading of 'matter' (*in Alc.* 10.13–14 Westerink) but offers no discussion of these. As part of his lengthy treatment of the opening words of the dialogue in 103a, he offers an allegorical interpretation of Alcibiades, Socrates and the lovers of Alcibiades, according to which Alcibiades represents the rational soul (ψυχὴ λογική), Socrates represents intellect (νοῦς), and the lovers of Alcibiades, whom Proclus compares both to the 'many-headed beast' of *Republic* 9.588c and to the Titans who dismembered Dionysus, represent the lowest part of the soul which constantly tries to drag the rational soul down into the divided material world (*in Alc.* 43.4–44.1). In Proclus' view, in showing us the reform of Alcibiades the dialogue shows us the purification of the rational soul.

According to *Anon. Prol.* 23.16–18, some earlier commentators described the *First Alcibiades* as *peri philotimias* ('On ambition').[31] The author of the *Anon. Prol.* regards these interpreters as wrongly inferring the *skopos*

---

[28] Albinus, *Isagoge* §5.149.35–7 Hermann provides evidence that already in the second century AD the *First Alcibiades* was recommended as the first dialogue that students of Plato should read. I am grateful to one of the anonymous readers for the Press for drawing my attention to this passage.

[29] See Proclus, *in Alc.* 85.17–92.2 on the problem of why Socrates' δαιμόνιον allowed him to encounter Alcibiades when Alcibiades was not going to be benefited by this. Proclus mentions Xenophon's discussion of the problem at *Memorabilia* 1.2.24–5, the portrayal of Alcibiades in Plato's *Symposium* and the reference at *Rep.*6.498c–d to the possibility that even the intractable Thrasymachus might benefit from his discussion with Socrates at some time in the future. Olympiodorus offers a much shorter discussion along the same lines as Proclus at *in Alc.* 26.22–27.16; cf. also Olympiodorus, *in Grg.* §41.3, Proclus, *in Ti.* 1.61.12–15. Note also Proclus, *in Alc.* 154.13–14 and Olympiodorus, *in Alc.* 54.9–10, where the two Neoplatonist commentators recognize that it would be possible to read *Alc.* 105c–d less positively than they do.

[30] For the use of ὑπόθεσις to mean 'setting' cf., with Segonds 1985: 131 n. 7, Proclus, *in Ti.* 1.8.30–9.13.

[31] Renaud & Tarrant 2015: 14 n. 26 express some scepticism about how commonplace such an interpretation was. Whether this was a common title for the dialogue or not, my argument in this chapter is that in regarding Alcibiades as a type of *philotimia* Proclus and his successors are drawing on a pre-Neoplatonic tradition of interpretation. Plutarch's references to Alcibiades' *philotimia* in his *Life of Alcibiades* 6.4, 7.5 and 34.3 are worth noting (cf. also 39.7), as is the description of Alexander as *philotimotatos* in Dio Chrys. *Or.* 4.4, a passage which arguably echoes *Alc.* 105a–c (see Trapp 2000: 226).

236 ANNE SHEPPARD

of the dialogue from its matter, by which in this case he must mean from the nature of the characters. In an earlier part of his discussion of *Alc.* 103a, before he comes to the allegorical interpretation of the characters, Proclus notes that Alcibiades is ambitious (φιλότιμος),[32] and although at *in Alc.* 7.18–8.1 he argues against referring the theme (πρόθεσις) of the dialogue to Alcibiades alone, he uses the adjective *philotimos* of Alcibiades at a number of other points in his commentary; it is clear that he regards the turning of Alcibiades' *philotimia* in the right direction as part of his education by Socrates.[33]

An interesting passage from Proclus' commentary on Socrates' words at *Alc.* 106c4–9 shows us Proclus combining the interpretation of Alcibiades as *philotimos* with comment on literary features of the text and with his Neoplatonist allegorical interpretation of the characters.[34] *In Alc.* 185.18–186.10 runs as follows:

> The handling of the discussion is also worthy of admiration, so great is its vividness, forcefulness and knowledgeability . . . To bring before his eyes, in the assembly, as if on a stage, the people and the speaker's platform itself with Alcibiades hastening to seize the position of counsellor and himself taking hold of him and as it were applying reason as a bridle to his impulse, presents a very vivid picture and at the same time makes it clear that one should do nothing without examination, nor before enquiring into one's own knowledge rush to correct that of others. (*in Alc.* 185.18–186.10 Segonds, trans. O'Neill, modified)[35]

In praising the vividness (ἐνάργεια) of Plato's presentation here and in talking of Socrates bringing a hypothetical situation before his eyes (ὑπ' ὀφθαλμοῖς ἀγαγεῖν) Proclus is using language with a long history in the ancient literary critical tradition, language particularly associated with literary *mimēsis*.[36] It is also worth noting that, encouraged by the allusion

---

[32] See *in Alc.* 24.12, and cf. 23.13–21.

[33] See *in Alc.* 133.17–139.10, 154.2–155.12 and 243.6–13. Note also the use of *philotimos* in 146.19 and 148.3 as well as the references in 137.4–139.10 to the Myth of Er in *Republic* 10 and the different types of constitution in *Republic* 8 and 9. On the Neoplatonist view of *philotimia* more generally, see van den Berg 2017.

[34] I am grateful to R.M. van den Berg for drawing my attention to this passage; see van den Berg forthcoming.

[35] Ἄξιον δὲ θαυμάσαι καὶ τὴν μεταχείρισιν τῶν λόγων, ὅσον μὲν ἔχει τὸ ἐναργές, ὅσον δὲ τὸ πληκτικόν, ὅσον δὲ τὸ ἐπιστημονικόν . . . Τὸ δὲ ὥσπερ ἐν σκηνῇ τῇ ἐκκλησίᾳ αὐτῷ τὸν δῆμον ὑπ' ὀφθαλμοῖς ἀγαγεῖν καὶ αὐτὸ τὸ βῆμα, καὶ τὸν μὲν σπεύδοντα τὴν τοῦ συμβούλου χώραν καταλαβεῖν, τὸν δὲ λαμβανόμενον αὐτοῦ καὶ οἷον χαλινὸν ἐπάγοντα τῇ ὁρμῇ τὸν λόγον, πολλὴν παρέχεται τὴν ἐνάργειαν, ἅμα δὲ κἀκεῖνο ποιεῖ δῆλον ὡς οὐδὲν ἀνεξετάστως προσήκει πράττειν οὐδὲ πρὸ τοῦ τὴν ἑαυτοῦ γνῶσιν ἀνακρῖναι πρὸς τὴν τῶν ἄλλων ἄττειν ἐπανόρθωσιν.

[36] See Sheppard 2014: 19–34 and 41–3.

## Platonic Dialogue in Later Neoplatonism 237

in Plato's text to the speaker's platform in the assembly, the *bēma*, Proclus compares the vividness of Socrates' words with dramaturgy (ὥσπερ ἐν σκηνῇ, 'as if on a stage'). Taken by itself, this passage looks like purely literary comment on Plato's own dramatic skill. However the lines which follow draw out what for Proclus was the deeper meaning of the passage:

> Let reason, then, be the guide of our actions and moderate the ambitious disposition, and may it lead unreflecting impulse to testing and judgment; saying farewell to the speaker's platform and the people let us set in order the populace within us: cutting out the tumult of the emotions let us listen to the counsels of the intellect (for it is the true counsellor of souls), and reverting to that, let us search out the Good. (*in Alc.* 186.10–16 Segonds, trans. O'Neill, modified)[37]

Here we can see the allegorical interpretation of the characters being put to work, alongside the characterization of Alcibiades as *philotimos*: as the ambitious Alcibiades was urged to listen to Socrates before he ascended the speaker's platform, so we should make our ambitious disposition (τὴν φιλότιμον ἕξιν) more sensible and listen to the advice of the intellect (νοῦς). Olympiodorus' comments on this passage (*in Alc.* 67.14–19) preserve the reference to the theatre, but do not include either the detailed comment on literary aspects that we find in Proclus or the allegorical interpretation of the characters. Although Olympiodorus says nothing about Alcibiades' *philotimia* here either, there are plenty of other references to that elsewhere in his commentary.[38]

If for the moment we leave aside Proclus' allegorical interpretation of Alcibiades as the rational soul and consider only his characterization as *philotimos*, found in both Proclus and Olympiodorus, we can see that Alcibiades, the bad pupil who is reformed by Socrates (at least to some degree), offers something like an *exemplum* of a bad character who is changed, instructed and purified by his good teacher, along the lines suggested in the passage of the *Anon. Prol.* which I quoted at the start of this chapter. The use of the word 'purified' (καθαιρόμενα) there is an indication that the author of the *Anon. Prol.* did indeed have Alcibiades in

---

[37] λόγος οὖν ἡγεμὼν ἔστω τῶν πράξεων καὶ τὴν μὲν φιλότιμον ἕξιν σωφρονεστέραν ποιείτω, τὴν δὲ ἀνυπεύθυνον ὁρμὴν εἰς βάσανον ἀγέτω καὶ κρίσιν, καὶ χαίρειν εἰπόντες τῷ βήματι καὶ τῷ δήμῳ τὸν ἐν ἡμῖν δῆμον καταστησόμεθα καὶ τὸν θόρυβον τῶν παθῶν ἐκκόψαντες ἀκούσωμεν τῶν τοῦ νοῦ συμβουλῶν (αὐτὸς γάρ ἐστιν ὁ τῶν ψυχῶν σύμβουλος ἀληθής) καὶ πρὸς τοῦτον ἐπιστρέψαντες τὸ ἀγαθὸν ἀνερευνήσωμεν.

[38] Specific references to Alcibiades as *philotimos* occur at 24.1 and 15, 31.3, 33.5, 45.18–21, 50.20, 98.14–16, 101.1–7, 102.23–4, 115.4, 119.13, 125.16, 133.7–8, 143.2, 144.4, 146.2 and 24, 175.24. *to philotimon* is associated with the intermediate, spirited part of the soul, the *thymos*, at 10.13 and 33.8–10. Cf. also 38.3–16, 42.10–43.3, 50.25–51.12, 84.1.

238  ANNE SHEPPARD

mind, an indication which is confirmed by two further passages.[39] In *Anon. Prol.* 15.21–9, the author is still trying to answer the question why Plato used the dialogue form and writes as follows:

> Plato used this form of writing so as not to present us with facts in isolation and bare of characters. For example, when he discusses friendship, he does not want to tell us about friendship in isolation but about friendship as it appears in a particular person, and likewise when he discusses ambition not by itself but as it appears in a particular person. In that way our soul, seeing others refuted, for example, or praised, is more effectively compelled to agree with the refutations or to emulate those who are praised. This is like what happens to the souls in the Underworld who see others punished for their sins and become better through fear of the punishments that are imposed on others. (*Anon Prol.* 15.21–9 Westerink, my translation)[40]

It might not be immediately obvious that in referring to an example of *philotimia* 'as it appears in a particular person' the author has Alcibiades in mind, but the point becomes clear later in the text, in ch. 23. Here, as noted earlier, the author argues against inferring the *skopos* of a dialogue from the *hylē*, that is, from the characters (πρόσωπα). His criticism of the suggestion that the *First Alcibiades* is *peri philotimias* and concerned only with exposing the ambition in the soul of Alcibiades is presented as an illustration of this point. Instead:

> It is better to say in general that the dialogue has the aim of exposing the ambition in every individual soul. For in each of us lives ambition like that of Alcibiades which must be trained and ordered for the better. (*Anon Prol.* 23.22–4 Westerink, my translation)[41]

### 11.4 Callicles, Polus and Thrasymachus

When the author of the *Anon. Prol.* defended Plato's use of variety and his presentation of dramatic characters by appealing to the moral outcomes for

---

[39] Here again I am indebted to the paper by R.M. van den Berg referred to in n.34 for drawing to my attention the connections between the passages of Proclus, *in Alc.* and the *Anon. Prol.*

[40] ὅτι διὰ τοῦτο τοιοῦτον εἶδος συγγραφῆς ἐπετήδευσεν, ἵνα μὴ ψιλὰ τὰ πράγματα καὶ γυμνὰ προσώπων παραδῷ ἡμῖν· οἷον περὶ φιλίας διαλεγόμενος, ἵνα μὴ αὐτῆς ψιλῆς μνημονεύσῃ ἀλλὰ τῆς ἐν τῷδε γενομένης, καὶ περὶ φιλοτιμίας οὐκ αὐτῆς καθ᾽ ἑαυτὴν ἀλλὰ τῆς ἐν τῷδε. οὕτως γὰρ μᾶλλον ἡ ἡμετέρα ψυχὴ ὁρῶσα ἄλλους οἷον ἐλεγχομένους ἢ ἐπαινουμένους ἀναγκάζεται συγκατατίθεσθαι τοῖς ἐλέγχοις ἢ ζηλοῦν τοὺς ἐπαινουμένους· καὶ ἔοικεν τοῦτο ταῖς ὁρώσαις ψυχαῖς ἐν ᾅδου ἄλλας ἁμαρτήμασι τιμωρουμένας καὶ σωφρονούσαις τῷ φόβῳ τῶν τιμωριῶν τῶν ἐν ἐκείναις γινομένων. This looks like an allusion to the Myth of Er in *Republic* 10 and also to *Grg.* 525b1–c8. Cf. Westerink 1990: 64 n. 146 and also n. 45.

[41] ἄμεινον οὖν καθόλου λέγειν ὅτι περὶ τῆς ἐν ἑκάστῃ ψυχῇ φιλοτιμίας σκοπὸν ἔχει τοῦ ἐλέγξαι. ἔστιν γὰρ ἑκάστῳ ἡμῶν οἷον Ἀλκιβιάδειος φιλοτιμία, ἣν δεῖ ῥυθμίζειν καὶ κοσμεῖν ἐπὶ τὸ βέλτιον.

## Platonic Dialogue in Later Neoplatonism 239

those characters, he will have had in mind a tradition which ultimately goes back to Plato's own argument in the *Republic* about the moral effects of imitation.[42] Olympiodorus' commentary on the *Gorgias* offers a very similar approach to the characters of that dialogue which makes the link with the *Republic* more explicit. Olympiodorus begins the proem to his commentary by tackling the issue head-on:

> Note that a dialogue contains characters in conversation, and it is for this reason, because they have characters, that Plato's works are called dialogues. In his *Republic* he criticizes those who produce comedy and tragedy and banishes them, because tragedians encourage our inclination towards grief and comedians our inclination towards pleasure-seeking. So it is worth inquiring why he himself follows their practice and introduces characters. We reply that if we were following the constitution of Plato, those who introduced decadent characters would actually have to be beaten. But since that is not the way we live, characters are introduced – not untested ones as in drama, but characters subject to scrutiny and chastisement. He criticizes Gorgias, you see, and Polus, Callicles and Thrasymachus, too, as shameless and never given to blushing, whereas he praises upright men who live a philosophic life. (*in Grg.* §0.1 Westerink, trans. Jackson, Lycos & Tarrant)[43]

Later in the proem, in §0.8, Olympiodorus considers the characters in the *Gorgias* a little more fully, this time offering an allegorical interpretation according to which Socrates, Chaerephon, Gorgias, Polus and Callicles all correspond to different parts of the soul with different moral characteristics. He puts this allegory to work in the main body of the commentary: Callicles, for example, is said in §0.8 to correspond to the 'swinish and pleasure-loving' part of the soul (τῷ ὑώδει καὶ φιληδόνῳ),[44] and

---

[42] See *Republic* 3.394b–398b and 10.604e–606d and cf. n. 2. Sedley 1999 argues that the interpretation of Platonic dialogues, especially the proems, as teaching practical ethics by presenting exemplary individuals goes back to the Early Academy and specifically to Polemo. In his final paragraph, Sedley makes the connection both with Platonic psychological theory and with Plato's remarks in the *Republic* about the imitation of role models. Cf. Proclus, *in Prm.* 658.23–659.17 Steel and *in Ti.* 1.16.6–12. I owe the reference to Sedley to R.M. van den Berg (cf. n. 34).

[43] Ἰστέον ὅτι ὁ διάλογος περιέχει διαλεγόμενα πρόσωπα, καὶ διὰ τοῦτο καὶ οἱ λόγοι Πλάτωνος διάλογοι προσαγορεύονται ὡς ἔχοντες πρόσωπα. καὶ ἄξιον ζητῆσαι διὰ ποίαν αἰτίαν, μεμφόμενος ἐν τῇ Πολιτείᾳ τοὺς κωμῳδίαν ἐπαγγελλομένους καὶ τραγῳδίαν καὶ ἐκβάλλων αὐτοὺς διὰ τὸ τοὺς μὲν τραγικοὺς αὔξειν τὸ ἐν ἡμῖν λυπηρόν, τοὺς δὲ κωμῳδιοποιοὺς τὸ ἐν ἡμῖν φιλήδονον, αὐτὸς μιμεῖται αὐτοὺς καὶ εἰσφέρει πρόσωπα. φαμὲν ὅτι εἰ τὴν πολιτείαν Πλάτωνος ἐδιώκομεν, εἶχον ἂν καὶ πληγαῖς ὁμιλεῖν οἱ κακοὺς εἰσηγούμενοι λόγους· ἐπειδὴ δὲ οὐχ οὕτως ζῶμεν, εἰσφέρονται μὲν πρόσωπα, οὐκ ἀνέλεγκτα δὲ ὡς παρ' ἐκείνοις ἀλλ' ἐλεγχόμενα καὶ ἐπιρραπιζόμενα. Μέμφεται γὰρ τῷ Γοργίᾳ καὶ τῷ Πώλῳ καὶ τῷ Καλλικλεῖ καὶ τῷ Θρασυμάχῳ ὡς ἀναιδεῖ καὶ μηδέποτε ἐρυθριῶντι, ἐπαινεῖ δὲ τοὺς χρηστοὺς καὶ ἐμφιλοσόφως ζῶντας.

[44] Jackson, Lycos & Tarrant 1998: 61 translate the allegory of the characters as referring to types of soul rather than parts of the soul, although they recognize in n. 38 that a complex division of the

## 240 ANNE SHEPPARD

subsequent passages of the commentary draw attention to the way in which his love of pleasure is exhibited in the dialogue.[45]

In the passage quoted above from the proem to the *Gorgias* commentary, Olympiodorus mentions not only Polus and Callicles but also Thrasymachus from *Republic* 1. Thrasymachus is mentioned again as a type of shamelessness (ἀναίδεια) at §1.1 and §18.1. He reappears in a similar context, again alongside Polus and Callicles, in Olympiodorus' *Commentary on the First Alcibiades*:

> This is also the case in the *Gorgias* – for there, through Socrates' cross-examination of the spirited emotion of Thrasymachus, we learn how to put a stop to the Thrasymachus in us. And likewise, by studying Callicles' love for pleasure and Polus' ambition. (*in Alc.* 61.8–11 Westerink, trans. Griffin, modified)[46]

Olympiodorus has carelessly conflated the *Gorgias* and *Republic* 1 here, and Thrasymachus is treated, rather surprisingly, as a character dominated by *thymos*, the intermediate, spirited part of the soul, while Callicles and Polus are characterized much as in §0.8 of the *Gorgias* commentary, as pleasure-loving and ambitious respectively. In Proclus' *Alcibiades* commentary (218.13–219.1) Thrasymachus is again described as shameless (οὐκ ἐπῃσχύνετο) and is treated as corresponding to the desiring part of the soul, while Alcibiades, who recognizes that injustice is base (αἰσχρόν), is in an intermediate position between desire on the one hand and reason, in the person of Socrates, on the other.

If we put all these passages together, it becomes evident that we are dealing with a stock typology of a number of the characters in Plato's dialogues. Alcibiades, Callicles, Polus and Thrasymachus all have places within this interpretative structure. The association of these *prosōpa* with particular characteristics – Alcibiades and Polus with ambition, Callicles

---

soul, using both the tripartition of *Republic* 4 and the list of five types of constitution in *Republic* 8–9, is involved. The parallel with Proclus' allegory of the characters in the *First Alcibiades* suggests that Olympiodorus has parts of the soul in mind throughout, although, as in the *Republic*, a pleasure-loving type of soul will no doubt be one dominated by its pleasure-loving part; in §18.1 Olympiodorus explicitly treats the characters as paradigms of people who live certain types of life, with Callicles as an example of someone who lives by pleasure.

[45] See §1.1, §1.2, §8.11, §10.11, §11.3, §25.2. Westerink 1970: 7 on §0.8, points out that the association of Callicles with *philēdonia* recurs in Proclus, *in R.* 2.176.4–9, in Proclus' commentary on the Myth of Er. Thrasymachus is mentioned there alongside Callicles, as in the passages discussed in the next paragraph, although in the *in R.* Thrasymachus appears to be an *exemplum* of love of money (φιλοχρηματία) rather than shamelessness.

[46] καθάπερ ἐν Γοργίᾳ· καὶ γὰρ ἐκεῖ διὰ τοῦ Θρασυμάχου τὸν θυμὸν ἐλέγχοντος τοῦ Σωκράτους ἡμεῖς ἐννοοῦμεν καταπαῦσαι τὸν ἐν ἡμῖν Θρασύμαχον. καὶ πάλιν διὰ μὲν τοῦ Καλλικλέους τὸ φιλήδονον, διὰ δὲ τοῦ Πώλου τὸ φιλότιμον.

## Platonic Dialogue in Later Neoplatonism

with the love of pleasure, Thrasymachus with shamelessness – is likely to be something which the Neoplatonists inherited from earlier interpreters.[47] It is one form of interpretation *ek prosōpou* ('from the person'), applied originally to the text of Homer and subsequently to other texts, both pagan and Christian, including the text of Plato.[48]

Much of our evidence for Middle Platonic interpretation *ek prosōpou* justifies apparent inconsistencies in the views attributed to different characters in Plato's dialogues by interpreting these in such a way as to preserve Plato's consistency overall.[49] By contrast, treating the characters as moral *exempla* applies interpretation *ek prosōpou* not primarily to resolve doctrinal contradictions but so that, in Olympiodorus' words, 'we learn how to put a stop to the Thrasymachus in us'. The association of individual *prosōpa* with particular characteristics has an evident foundation in Plato's own texts; the clearest example is the way in which Socrates in the *Gorgias* treats Callicles as someone who pursues pleasure, exposing hedonism as the basis on which his arguments rest. It may well have been the later Neoplatonists who linked a moral typology of Socrates and his interlocutors to systematic allegorical interpretation of all these characters as representing different parts of the soul. Although the details of the correspondences vary a little between different commentators, there is a remarkable similarity in the interpretations offered by Proclus, Olympiodorus and the *Anon. Prol.*[50] For Proclus and his successors, we will learn all the better 'how to put a stop to the Thrasymachus in us' if we understand the different parts of the soul and their place in the larger structure of the Neoplatonic system. Although their curriculum led them to comment on dialogues individually, they also saw the similarities between characters in different dialogues and the typology I have been uncovering runs across dialogues rather than being confined to just one; that explains Olympiodorus' momentary carelessness in slotting Thrasymachus into the *Gorgias*.

---

[47] See Sedley 1999, as cited in n. 42.

[48] Mansfeld 1994: 12 n. 7 offers a brief account of interpretation ἐκ προσώπου or ἀπὸ προσώπου which stresses the connections with Homeric exegesis and gives further references; however, he does not distinguish between the different types of interpretation which fall under this heading.

[49] See, for example, Diogenes Laertius 3.51–2, claiming that the views of characters such as Thrasymachus, Callicles and Polus are simply shown to be false (with the comments in Mansfeld 1994: 80 and n. 134); Aulus Gellius 10.22.1–24 (whose source might be Taurus of Beirut: see Petrucci 2018: 17–18 and 199–201), suggesting that Callicles' derogatory comments about philosophy in *Grg.* 484c–e are directed only at the wrong kind of philosophy; Stobaeus 2.7.3f (2.49.25–50.1) and 2.7.4a (2.55.5–6), declaring that Plato is πολύφωνος but not πολύδοξος.

[50] Cf. also Asclepius, *in Metaph.* 138.7–9.

242 ANNE SHEPPARD

We are now a long way from Blondell's Plato, who 'never adopts a dogmatic or authoritative pedagogical stance'. For the Neoplatonists, behind the variegated literary surface of the dialogues discussed so far stands Plato as an author with lessons to teach, setting up characters who, for all their clarity and vividness, are ultimately exempla intended to show us what kind of behaviour to pursue and what to avoid.

## 11.5 Platonic Characters as Metaphysical Abstractions

This is not the whole story. When we turn to Proclus' commentary on the *Parmenides*, we again find that the characters are interpreted allegorically but this time the characters correspond not to parts of the soul but to metaphysical entities. Parmenides, we are told, may be treated as 'an analogue to the unparticipated and divine Intellect' (ἀνάλογον ... τῷ ἀμεθέκτῳ καὶ θείῳ νῷ), Zeno as an analogue 'to the Intellect which is participated in by the divine Soul' (τῷ μετεχομένῳ ὑπὸ τῆς θείας ψυχῆς νῷ), and Socrates 'could be compared to the particular intellect' (ἐοίκοι ἂν τῷ μερικῷ νῷ). From another point of view, Socrates corresponds 'to Intellect without qualification' (ἁπλῶς τῷ νῷ), while Parmenides corresponds to Being (τὸ ὄν, οὐσία) and Zeno to Life (ἡ ζωή). The narrators of the conversation between these three key characters are also interpreted allegorically, as entities at lower levels in Proclus' metaphysical system: Pythodorus corresponds to 'the divine Soul' (ἡ θεία ψυχή) and perhaps also to 'the angelic order' (ἡ ἀγγελικὴ τάξις), Antiphon to 'the daemonic soul' (ψυχὴ δαιμονία) and Cephalus and the philosophers from Clazomenae to partial souls which live in the realm of Nature (αἱ μερικαὶ ψυχαὶ καὶ τῇ φύσει συμπολιτευόμεναι).[51]

At this point we might be tempted to echo a famous sentence by E.R. Dodds and to complain that Plato's characters are being placed 'on the dusty shelves of [a] museum of metaphysical abstractions'.[52] However, it is worth considering why it is these characters from the *Parmenides* who end up on the shelves of the museum while Alcibiades and Polus, Callicles and Thrasymachus are treated primarily as moral exempla. We might also wonder how the allegory of the characters of the *Parmenides* relates to the allegories of other Platonic characters discussed above. The answer to the first question, in my view, is that these characters appear in different

---

[51] See Proclus, *in Prm.* 628.1–630.10. Translations in quotation marks are taken from Morrow & Dillon 1987.
[52] See Dodds 1963: 260.

*Platonic Dialogue in Later Neoplatonism* 243

kinds of dialogue, read at different stages in the Neoplatonic curriculum. The *First Alcibiades* and the *Gorgias* were read at the beginning of the sequence, when it would be appropriate to focus on the moral improvement of the students; the *Republic* fell outside the standard curriculum, but the parallels between Thrasymachus in *Republic* 1 and Callicles in the *Gorgias* are easily discerned by both ancient and modern readers, as is the similarity between the kind of conversation Socrates conducts with Thrasymachus and the kind of conversation conducted in what we are accustomed to think of as 'early' or 'Socratic' dialogues such as the *Gorgias.* The *Parmenides,* on the other hand, was one of the two dialogues read right at the end of the sequence, when students would be equipped to understand the complexities of Neoplatonic metaphysics. Modern readers have tended to see the *Parmenides* as moving away from the dialogue form, ignoring the presentation of characters and setting with which it opens.[53] The Neoplatonist reading of the dialogues, and of the characters, offers an explanation of the difference between the *Parmenides* and the *Gorgias*, not in terms of the chronology of the dialogues but in terms of their subject matter: the *Parmenides* is, precisely, a dialogue about 'metaphysical abstractions' and so offers us characters who are to be understood in a different way from the characters in the *Gorgias* or the *First Alcibiades.*

However, we should note that Socrates appears in both kinds of dialogue – and is allegorized in the same terms.[54] In the *First Alcibiades*, according to Proclus, Socrates corresponds to intellect within the human soul; in the *Parmenides* he corresponds to the particular intellect. As the dominant character who appears in the majority of Plato's dialogues, it is Socrates who links together what appear at first sight to be two different kinds of allegory. Just as in the interpretation of Homer, Proclus, following his master Syrianus, transposed earlier allegories to offer a complex interpretation of a whole range of characters and episodes,[55] so too in interpreting Plato, Proclus reworked earlier interpretations of characters in the dialogues as moral exempla in such a way that these interpretations fit within a broader allegory which ranges over all levels of the Neoplatonic

---

[53] See, for example, Rutherford 1995: 276 and 280. The damning judgement of Cornford 1939: 64 ('The subject of the dialogue is, to last degree, prosaic; and it is written throughout in the plainest, conversational style') is more about prose style (χαρακτήρ in Neoplatonist terms) than about characters or setting. McCabe 1996: 16 is more nuanced, referring to 'the richly personal characterizations of the first part' of the dialogue.

[54] On the Neoplatonic allegory of Socrates in particular, cf. Griffin 2014. Griffin's conclusions complement my own.

[55] See Sheppard 1980: 39–85 and Sheppard forthcoming.

system and accords with the reading order of dialogues which he has inherited from Iamblichus. This kind of reworking is unlikely to have originated with Proclus,[56] but the system of interpretation he used was inherited by subsequent Neoplatonic commentators on Plato. Just as Proclus' allegorical interpretation of Homer provided him with a way of defending the authority of Homer within the Greek cultural tradition, so too his allegorical interpretation of the characters in Plato's dialogues offered a way of preserving Plato's philosophical authority while recognizing the variety of characters presented in his work.

I noted at the beginning of this chapter how modern interpreters' approaches to Plato's dramatic skill in portraying a range of characters are underpinned by their assumptions about how readers should approach the dialogues. This is equally true of ancient approaches to the depiction of Platonic characters. Whereas Middle Platonic interpreters used interpretation *ek prosōpou* to remove contradictions within and between dialogues,[57] Proclus and his successors, engaged in large-scale commentary on Platonic dialogues, were concerned not only to expound what they took to be Plato's philosophical system but also to transform the moral outlook of their students by changing their understanding of the world. For them, appreciation of Plato's dialogues as carefully constructed literary texts was one of the tools to be used in that endeavour. The order in which the dialogues were read in the Neoplatonic curriculum offered a framework within which individual dialogues were placed, both as part of the larger literary structure formed by Plato's oeuvre as a whole and as part of the philosophical structure which, for the Neoplatonists, informed all the dialogues. I have argued that the order in which the dialogues were read explains differences in the way the characters are interpreted; moral and psychological allegory was appropriate to dialogues concerned with moral and educational issues such as the *First Alcibiades* and the *Gorgias*, while metaphysical allegory was appropriate for a dialogue with the metaphysical content of the *Parmenides*. As Proclus' pupils progressed through the curriculum, they would come to appreciate their teacher's understanding of Plato as not just an author who teaches moral lessons but also a philosopher who reveals ultimate truths.

---

[56] Allegorical interpretation of the πρόσωπα of the *Song of Songs* in terms of (Christian) Platonist metaphysics was already present in Origen's minor commentary on that work: see Mansfeld 1994: 12 and Hadot 1990: 36–7.

[57] See n. 49 and cf. Annas 1999: 13 ff.

# References

Adamson, P. (2007). '*Porphyrius Arabus* on Nature and Art: 463F Smith in Context'. In: G. Karamanolis & A. Sheppard (eds.) *Studies on Porphyry*. London: 141–63.

Adamson, P., Baltussen, H. & Stone, M.W.F. (eds.) (2004). *Philosophy, Science and Exegesis in Greek, Arabic and Latin Commentaries*, Vol. I. London.

Aerts, S. (2019). 'Historical Approaches to Epistemic Authority: The Case of Neoplatonism'. *Journal of the History of Ideas* 80: 343–63.

Aerts, S. & Opsomer, J. (2017). 'Teksten bekleed met autoriteit: Een model voor de analyse van epistemische autoriteit in commentaartradities'. *Tijdschrift voor Filosofie* 79: 277–94.

Algra, K. (2001). 'Comments or Commentary? Zeno of Citium and Hesiod's *Theogonia*'. *Mnemosyne* 54: 562–81.

  (2017). 'The Academic Origins of Stoic Cosmo-Theology and the Physics of Antiochus of Ascalon – Some Notes on the Evidence'. In: Y. Liebersohn & I. Ludlam (eds.) *For a Skeptical Peripatetic: Festschrift in Honour of John Glucker*. Sankt Augustin: 158–76.

  (2018). 'Arius Didymus as a Doxographer of Stoicism: Some Observations'. In: J. Mansfeld & D.T. Runia (eds.) *Aëtiana IV: Papers of the Melbourne Colloquium on Ancient Doxography*. Leiden: 53–102.

Algra, K., Barnes, J., Mansfeld, J. & Schofield, M. (eds.) (1999). *The Cambridge History of Hellenistic Philosophy*. Cambridge.

Alline, H. (1915). *Histoire du texte de Platon*. Paris.

Annas, J. (1999). *Platonic Ethics Old and New*. Ithaca.

Armstrong, A.H. (ed.) (1980). *Plotinus*, Vol. III. Cambridge, MA & London.

  (ed.) (1988). *Plotinus*, Vol. VI. Cambridge, MA & London.

Arnott, W.G. (ed.) (1996). *Alexis: The Fragments*. Cambridge.

Arruzza, C. (2011). 'Passive Potentiality in the Physical Realm: Plotinus' Critique of Aristotle in *Enneads* II 5 [25]'. *Archiv für Geschichte der Philosophie* 93: 24–57.

  (ed.) (2015). *Plotinus. Ennead II.5: On What Is Potentially and What Actually*. Las Vegas, Zurich & Athens.

Athanassiadi, P. (2002). 'The Creation of Orthodoxy in Neoplatonism'. In: G. Clark & T. Rajak (eds.) *Philosophy and Power in the Graeco-Roman World*. Oxford: 271–91.

(2006). *La lutte pour l'orthodoxie dans le platonisme tardif: de Numénius à Damascius*. Paris.

(2018). 'Numenius: Portrait of a Platonicus'. In: Tarrant et al. 2018: 183–205.

Babbitt, F.C. (ed.) (1936). *Plutarch's Moralia*, Vol. V. Cambridge, MA & London.

Babut, D. (1969). *Plutarque et le Stoïcisme*. Paris.

(1994). 'Du scepticisme au dépassement de la raison: philosophie et foi religieuse chez Plutarque'. In: *Parerga. Choix d'articles de D. Babut (1974–1994)*. Lyon: 549–81.

Baghdassarian, F. & Guyomarc'h, G. (eds.) (2017). *Réceptions de la théologie aristotélicienne. D'Aristote à Michel d'Ephèse*. Leuven.

Baldassarri, M. (1993). 'Ein kleiner Traktat Plutarchs über stoische Logik'. In: K. Döring & T. Ebert (eds.) *Dialektiker und Stoiker. Zur Logik der Stoa und ihrer Vorläufer*. Stuttgart: 33–45.

Baltes, M. (ed.) (1972). *Timaios Lokros. Über die Natur des Kosmos und der Seele*. Leiden.

Baltussen, H. (2008). *Philosophy and Exegesis in Simplicius. The Methodology of a Commentator*. London.

Baltzly, D. & Share, M. (eds.) (2018). *Hermias. On Plato's Phaedrus 227A–245E*. London.

Baltzly, D. & Tarrant, H. (eds.) (2007). *Proclus. Commentary on Plato's Timaeus. Vol. I: Book 1. Proclus on the Socratic State and Atlantis*. Cambridge.

Barnes, J. (ed.) (1984). *The Complete Works of Aristotle*. The Revised Oxford Translation, Vol. I. Princeton.

(1989). 'Antiochus of Ascalon'. In: Griffin & Barnes 1989: 51–96.

Bastianini, G. & Sedley, D. (1995). *Commentarium in Platonis Theaetetum*. In: *Corpus dei papiri filosofici greci e latini III*. Florence: 227–562.

Beierwaltes, W. (1979). *Proklos. Grundzüge seiner Metaphysik*. Frankfurt (1st ed. 1965).

Berman, K. & Losada, L.A. (1975). 'The Mysterious E at Delphi'. *Zeitschrift für Papyrologie und Epigraphik* 17: 115–17.

Berryman, S. (2003). 'Ancient Automata and Mechanical Explanation'. *Phronesis* 48: 344–69.

(2009). *The Mechanical Hypothesis in Ancient Greek Natural Philosophy*. Cambridge.

Berti, E. (2012). *Sumphilosophein: la vita nell'Accademia di Platone*. Rome & Bari.

Birt, T. (1907). *Der Buchrolle in der Kunst*. Leipzig.

Blank, D. (2012). 'Varro and Antiochus'. In: Sedley 2012a: 251–89.

Blondell, R. (2002). *The Play of Character in Plato's Dialogues*. Cambridge.

Bodnár, I., Chase, M. & Share, M. (eds.) (2012). *Simplicius. On Aristotle Physics 8.1–5*. London.

Bonazzi, M. (2003). *Academici e Platonici. Il dibattito antico sullo scetticismo di Platone*. Milan.

(2004). 'Un lettore antico della *Repubblica*, Numenio di Apamea'. *Méthexis* 17: 71–84.

(2005). 'Eudoro di Alessandria alle origini del Platonismo Imperiale'. In M. Bonazzi & V. Celluprica (eds.) *L'eredità Platonica. Studi sul Platonismo da Arcesilao a Proclo*. Naples: 115–60.

(2006). 'Continuité et rupture entre l'Académie et le platonisme'. *Études Platoniciennes* 3: 231–44.

(2007). 'Eudorus' Psychology and Stoic Ethics'. In: Bonazzi & Helmig 2007: 109–32.

(2008). 'L'offerta di Plutarco. Teologia e filosofia nel *De E apud Delphos* (capitoli 1–2)'. *Philologus* 152: 205–11.

(2012). 'Antiochus and Platonism'. In: Sedley 2012a: 307–33.

(2013). 'Pythagoreanising Aristotle: Eudorus and the Systematisation of Platonism'. In: Schofield 2013: 160–86.

(2015). *À la Recherche des Idées. Platonisme et Philosophie Hellénistique d'Antiochus à Plotin*. Paris.

(2017–2018). 'Le Bien selon Numénius et la *République* de Platon'. *Chôra* 15–16: 127–38.

(2018). 'Héraclite, l'Académie et le platonisme: Une confrontation entre Cicéron et Plutarque'. In: S. Franchet & C. d'Espèrey-Lévy (eds.) *Les présocratiques à Rome*. Paris: 129–42.

Bonazzi, M. & Helmig, Ch. (eds.) (2007). *Platonic Stoicism, Stoic Platonism. The Dialogue between Platonism and Stoicism in Antiquity*. Leuven.

Bonazzi, M. & Opsomer, J. (eds.) (2009). *The Origins of the Platonic System. Platonisms of the Early Empire and their Philosophical Contexts*. Leuven.

Bonitz, H. (1870). *Index Aristotelicus*. Berlin.

Boulogne, J., Broze, M. & Couloubaritsis, L. (eds.) (2006). *Les Platonismes des premiers siècles de notre ère. Plutarque, E de Delphes*. Brussels.

Boys-Stones, G. (2001). *Post-Hellenistic Philosophy. A Study of Its Development from the Stoics to Origen*. Oxford.

(2007). '"Middle" Platonists on Fate and Human Autonomy'. In: Sharples & Sorabji 2007: Vol. II, 431–47.

(2011). 'Time, Creation and the Mind of God: The Afterlife of a Platonist Theory in Origen'. *Oxford Studies in Ancient Philosophy* 40: 319–37.

(2012). 'Antiochus' Metaphysics'. In Sedley 2012a: 220–6.

(2016). 'Are We Nearly There Yet? Eudorus on Aristotle's *Categories*'. In: T. Engberg-Pedersen (ed.) *From Stoicism to Platonism. The Development of Philosophy 100 BCE–100 CE*. Cambridge: 67–79.

(2018a). *Platonist Philosophy 80 BC to 250 AD. A Study and Collection of Sources in Translation*. Cambridge.

(2018b). 'Numenius on Intellect, Soul, and the Authority of Plato'. In: Bryan et al. 2018: 184–201.

Brisson, L. (1974). *Le Même et l'Autre dans la structure ontologique du Timée*. Sankt Augustin.

Brittain, Ch. (2001). *Philo of Larissa. The Last Academic Sceptic*. Oxford.

(2005). 'Common Sense: Concepts, Definitions and Meaning in and out of Stoa'. In: Frede & Inwood 2005: 164–209.

(2012). 'Antiochus' Epistemology'. In: Sedley 2012a: 104–30.

Brittain, Ch. & Palmer, J. (2001). 'The New Academy's Appeal to the Presocratics'. *Phronesis* 46: 38–72.

248                                    *References*

Broadie, S. (2007). 'Why No Platonistic Forms of Artefacts?' In: D. Scott (ed.) *Maieusis. Essays in Ancient Philosophy in Honour of Myles Burnyeat*. Oxford: 232–53.

Brouillette, X. & Giavatto, A. (eds.) (2010). *Les dialogues Platoniciens chez Plutarque. Stratégies et méthodes exégétiques*. Leuven.

Bryan, J., Wardy, R. & Warren, J. (eds.) (2018). *Authors and Authorities in Ancient Philosophy*. Cambridge.

Burkert, W. (1961). 'Hellenistische Pseudopythagorica'. *Philologus* 105: 16–43, 226–46.

(1971). 'Zur geistesgeschichtlichen Einordnung einiger Pseudopythagorica'. In: K. von Fritz (ed.) *Pseudepigrapha I*. Vandœuvres & Geneva: 25–55.

(1972). *Lore and Science in Ancient Pythagoreanism*. Cambridge, MA.

Burnyeat, M. (1997). 'Antipater and Self-Refutation: Elusive Arguments in Cicero's *Academica*'. In: Inwood & Mansfeld 1997: 277–310.

(2005). 'Archytas and Optics'. *Science in Context* 18: 35–53.

Calabi, F. (2017). 'L'agricoltura divina in Filone di Alessandria e in Numenio'. *Études platoniciennes* [online] 13.

Carlini, A. (1972). *Studi sulla tradizione antica e medievale del Fedone*. Rome.

Caruso, A. (2013). *Akademia: Archeologia di una scuola filosofica ad Atene da Platone a Proclo (387 a.C.–485 d.C.)*. Studi di Archeologia e di Topografia di Atene e dell'Attica 6. Athens & Paestum.

(2014). 'Il "giardino di Teofrasto". Inquadramento topografico della scuola peripatetica di Atene tra il IV e il III sec. a.C.'. In: L. Caliò & V. Parisi (eds.) *Gli Ateniesi e il loro modello di città*. Rome: 197–216.

Caston, V. (1999). 'Something and Nothing: The Stoics on Concepts and Universals'. *Oxford Studies in Ancient Philosophy* 17: 145–213.

Catana, L. (2013). 'The Origin of the Division Between Middle Platonism and Neoplatonism'. *Apeiron* 46: 166–200.

Centrone, B. (ed.) (1990). *Pseudopythagorica ethica. I trattati morali di Archita, Metopo, Teage, Eurifamo. Introduzione, edizione, traduzione e commento*. Naples.

(1992). 'L' VIII libro delle Vite di Diogene Laerzio'. In: *Aufstieg und Niedergang der römischen Welt, Band II.36.6*. Berlin & New York: 4183–217.

(2000a). 'Che cosa significa essere pitagorico in età imperiale. Per una riconsiderazione della categoria storiografica di neopitagorismo'. In: A. Brancacci (ed.) *La filosofia in età imperiale*. Naples: 139–68.

(2000b). 'La letteratura pseudopitagorica. Origini, diffusione, finalità'. In: G. Cerri (ed.) *La letteratura pseudepigrafa antica*. AION, sez. filol.-lett. 22: 429–52.

(2000c). 'Platonism and Pythagoreanism in the Early Empire'. In: Ch. Rowe & M. Schofield (eds.) *The Cambridge History of Greek and Roman Political Thought*. Cambridge: 559–84.

(2005). 'Myia'. In: R. Goulet (ed.) *Dictionnaire des Philosophes Antiques*, Vol. IV. Paris: 573–4.

(2014). 'The Pseudo-Pythagorean Writings'. In: Huffman 2014b: 315–40.

Chase, M. (2012). 'Porphyre de Tyr (P263): Commentaires sur des traités aristotéliciens'. In: R. Goulet (ed.) *Dictionnaire des philosophes antiques*, Vol. Vb. Paris: 1350–7.

Cherniss, H. (1945). *The Riddle of the Early Academy*. Berkeley.

Chiaradonna, R. (2009). 'Autour d'Eudore: les debuts de l'exégèse des *Catégories* dans le Moyen Platonisme'. In Bonazzi & Opsomer 2009: 89–112.

(2011). 'Interpretazione filosofica e ricezione del *corpus*: Il caso di Aristotele (100 a.C.–200 d.C.)'. *Quaestio* 11: 83–114.

(2013). 'Platonist Approaches to Aristotle: From Antiochus of Ascalon to Eudorus of Alexandria (and beyond)'. In: Schofield 2013: 28–52.

(2014a). 'Plotinus' Metaphorical Reading of the *Timaeus*: Soul, Mathematics, Providence'. In: P. d'Hoine & G. Van Riel (eds.) *Fate, Providence and Moral Responsibility in Ancient, Medieval and Early Modern Thought. Studies in Honour of Carlos Steel*. Leuven: 187–210.

(2014b). 'Substance'. In: Remes & Slaveva-Griffin 2014b: 216–30.

(2016). 'Porphyry and the Aristotelian Tradition'. In: A. Falcon (ed.) *The Brill's Companion to the Reception of Aristotle in Antiquity*. Leiden & Boston: 321–40.

(2017). 'Théologie et époptique aristotéliciennes dans le médioplatonisme: La réception de *Métaphysique* Λ'. In: Baghdassarian & Guyomarc'h 2017: 143–57.

Chiaradonna, R. & Rashed, M. (eds.) (2020). *Boéthos de Sidon: Exégète d'Aristote et philosophe*. Berlin.

Chlup, R. (2012). *Proclus. An Introduction*. Cambridge.

Colvin, M. (2005). 'Heraclitus and Material Flux in Stoic Psychology'. *Oxford Studies in Ancient Philosophy* 28: 257–72.

Cornford, F.M. (1939). *Plato and Parmenides*. London.

Corssen, P. (1912). 'Die Sprengung des pythagoreischen Bundes'. *Philologus* 71: 332–52.

Corti, A. (2014). *L'Adversus Colotem di Plutarco. Storia di una polemica filosofica*. Leuven.

Dancy, R. (1999). 'The Categories of Being in Plato's *Sophist* 255c–e'. *Ancient Philosophy* 19: 45–72.

(2003). 'Xenocrates'. In: *The Stanford Encyclopedia of Philosophy*. https://plato.stanford.edu/entries/xenocrates/.

D'Ancona, C. & Luna, C. (2000). 'La doctrine des principes: Syrianus comme source textuelle et doctrinale de Proclus'. In: A.Ph. Segonds & C. Steel (eds.) *Proclus et la théologie platonicienne. Actes du Colloque International de Louvain (13–16 mai 1998)*. Leuven & Paris: 189–278.

de Haas, F.A.J. & Fleet. B. (eds.) (2001). *Simplicius. On Aristotle Categories 5–6*. London.

Denyer, N. (ed.) (2001). *Plato. Alcibiades*. Cambridge.

des Places, É. (ed.) (1973). *Numénius. Fragments*. Paris.

(ed.) (1977). *Atticus. Fragments*. Paris.

d'Hoine, P. (2006). 'Proclus and Syrianus on Ideas of Artefacts. A Test Case for Neoplatonic Hermeneutics'. In: Perkams & Piccione 2006: 279–302.

250 References

d'Hoine, P., & Martijn, M. (eds.) (2016). *All from One. A Guide to Proclus.* Oxford.

Dillon, J.M. (ed.) (1973). *Iamblichi Chalcidensis in Platonis dialogos commentariorum fragmenta.* Leiden.

(1977). *The Middle Platonists: 80 BC to AD 220.* Ithaca & London (rev. ed. 1996).

(1991). *The Golden Chain: Studies in the Development of Platonism and Christianity.* London.

(ed.) (1993). *Alcinous: The Handbook of Platonism.* Oxford.

(2003). *The Heirs of Plato.* Oxford.

(2007). 'The Origins of Platonists' Dogmatism'. ΣΧΟΛΗ 1: 25–37.

(2014). 'Pythagoreanism in the Academic Tradition'. In: Huffman 2014b: 250–73.

Dodds, E.R. (ed.) (1963). *Proclus. The Elements of Theology.* Oxford.

Donini, P. (1974). *Tre studi sull'aristotelismo nel II secolo d.C.* Turin.

(1982). *Le scuole, l'anima, l'impero: la filosofia antica da Antioco a Plotino.* Turin.

(1990). 'Medioplatonismo e filosofi medioplatonici. Una raccolta di studi'. *Elenchos* 11: 79–93 = Donini 2011: 283–96.

(1992). 'Plutarco e i metodi dell'esegesi filosofica'. In: I. Gallo & R. Laurenti (eds.) *I moralia di Plutarco tra filologia e filosofia.* Naples: 79–96.

(1999). 'Platone e Aristotele nella tradizione pitagorica secondo Plutarco'. In: A. Pérez Jiménez, J. García López, R. Mᵃ Aguilar (eds.) *Plutarco, Platón y Aristóteles.* Madrid: 9–24 = Donini 2011: 359–73.

(2002). 'L'eredità academica e i fondamenti del platonismo in Plutarco'. In: M. Barbanti, G. Giardina & P. Manganaro (eds.) *Henosis kai philia: Unione e amicizia. Omaggio a Francesco Romano.* Catania: 247–73 = Donini 2011: 375–402.

(2003). 'Socrate pitagorico e medioplatonico'. *Elenchos* 24: 333–59.

(2011). *Commentary and Tradition. Aristotelianism, Platonism and Post-Hellenistic Philosophy*, ed. M. Bonazzi. Berlin & New York.

(2012). 'Review of Sedley 2012a'. *Méthexis* 25: 151–63.

(ed.) (2017). *Plutarco. Il demone di Socrate.* Rome.

Dorandi, T. (1982). 'Filodemo. *Gli Stoici* (PHerc. 135 e 339)'. *Cronache Ercolanesi* 12: 91–133.

(2016). 'Potamone di Alessandria'. *Zeitschrift für Papyrologie und Epigraphik* 199: 33–5.

Dörrie, H. & Baltes, M. (1993). *Der Platonismus in der Antike III: Der Platonismus im 2. und 3. Jahrhundert nach Christus.* Bausteine 73–100. Stuttgart & Bad-Cannstatt.

(1996). *Der Platonismus in der Antike IV: Die philosophische Lehre des Platonismus. Einige grundlegende Axiome / Platonische Physik (im antiken Verständnis) I.* Bausteine 101–24. Stuttgart & Bad Cannstatt.

Erler, M. (1992). 'Orthodoxie und Anpassung: Philodem, ein Panaïtios des Kepos?' *Museum Helveticum* 49: 171–200.

## References

(2008). 'Die helfende Hand Gottes. Augustins Gnadenlehre im Kontext des kaiserzeitlichen Platonismus'. In: Th. Fuhrer (ed.) *Die christlich-philosophischen Diskurse der Spätantike: Texte, Personen, Institutionen.* Stuttgart: 189–204.

(2018). '"Mulier tam imperiosae auctoritatis" (Boeth., *Cons.* 1,1,13): *Auctoritas* und *philosophia* in römischer und griechischer Philosophie'. In: J. Müller & Ch. Rode (eds.) *Freiheit und Geschichte: Festschrift für Theo Kobusch zum 70. Geburtstag.* Münster: 39–57. English version: '"Mulier tam imperiosae auctoritatis" (Boeth., *Cons.* 1.1.13): On the relationship between *auctoritas* and *philosophia* in Greek and Roman philosophy'. *Politeia. International Interdisciplinary Philosophical Review* 1 (2019): 195–210.

Falcon, A. (2013). 'Aristotelianism in the I century BC. Xenarchus of Seleucia'. In: Schofield 2013: 78–94.

Ferrari, F. (1995). *Dio, idee e materia. La struttura del cosmos in Plutarco di Cheronea.* Naples.

(2001). 'Struttura e funzione dell'esegesi testuale nel medioplatonismo: il caso del *Timeo*'. *Athenaeum* 89: 525–74.

(2010). 'La costruzione del Platonismo nel *de E apud Delphos* di Plutarco'. *Athenaeum* 98: 71–87. French version: 'La construction du Platonisme dans le *de E apud Delphos* de Plutarque'. In: Brouillette & Giavatto 2010: 47–62.

(2014). 'Gott als Vater und Schöpfer. Zur Rezeption von *Timaios* 28c3–5 bei einigen Platonikern'. In F. Albrecht & R. Feldmeier (eds.) *The Divine Father: Religious and Philosophical Concepts of Divine Parenthood in Antiquity.* Leiden & Boston: 57–69.

(2018). 'Harpokration von Argos'. In: Ch. Riedweg, Ch. Horn & D. Wyrwa (eds.) *Philosophie der Kaiserzeit und der Spätantike, Band 5-1 von Grundriss der Geschichte der Philosophie, begründet von F. Ueberweg, völlig neu bearbeitete Ausgabe von H. Holzhey.* Basel: 601–4.

Festa, N. (ed.) (1935). *I frammenti degli Stoici antichi*, Vol. II: *Aristone, Apollofane, Erillo, Dionigi di Eraclea, Perseo, Cleante, Sfero.* Bari.

Festugière A.J. (1954). *La Révélation d'Hermès Trismégiste IV. Le dieu inconnu et la gnose.* Paris.

Flamand, J.-M. (1992). '*Deus otiosus*, Recherches lexicales pour servir à la critique religieuse d'Épicure'. In: ΣΟΦΙΗΣ ΜΑΙΗΤΟΡΕΣ, *Chercheurs de Sagesse, Hommage à Jean Pépin.* Paris: 147–66.

Fleischer, K. (2015). 'Der Stoiker Mnesarch als Lehrer des Antiochos im *Index Academicorum*'. *Mnemosyne* 68: 413–23.

(2016). 'New Readings in Philodemus' *Historia Academicorum*: Dio of Alexandria (PHerc 1021, col. XXXV 17–19)'. In: T. Derda et al. (eds.) *Proceedings of the 27th Congress of Papyrology.* Warsaw: 459–70.

Frede, D. (2018). 'A Superannuated Student: Aristotle and Authority in the Academy'. In: Bryan et al. 2018: 78–101.

Frede, D., & Inwood, B. (eds.) (2005). *Language and Learning. Philosophy of Language in the Hellenistic Age.* Cambridge.

252           *References*

Frede, M. (1987). 'Numenius'. In: *Aufstieg und Niedergang der römischen Welt, Band II.36.2.* Berlin & New York: 1034–75.

(1999). 'Epilogue'. In: Algra et al. 1999: 771–97.

Fronterotta, F. (ed.) (2013). *Eraclito. Frammenti.* Milan.

Gaiser, K. (1980). *Das Philosophenmosaik in Neapel. Eine Darstellung der platonischen Akademie.* Abhandlungen der Heidelberger Akademie der Wissenschaften, Phil.-hist. Klasse, Heidelberg.

Gallo, I. (1981). *Teatro ellenistico minore.* Rome.

Gerson, L. (2005). *Aristotle and Other Platonists.* Ithaca & London.

(ed.) (2013). *The Cambridge History of Philosophy in Late Antiquity.* Cambridge.

Gertz, S. (2010). 'Do Plato and Aristotle Agree on Self-Motion in Souls?' In: J.F. Finamore & R.M. Berchman (eds.) *Conversations Platonic and Neoplatonic: Intellect, Soul, and Nature.* Sankt Augustin: 73–85.

Gill, M.L. (1994). 'Aristotle on Self-Motion'. In: Gill & Lennox 1994: 15–34.

Gill, M.L. & Lennox, J.G. (1994). *Self-motion: From Aristotle to Newton.* Princeton.

Gioè, A. (ed.) (2002). *Filosofi medioplatonici del II secolo d.C. Testimonianze e frammenti: Gaio, Albino, Lucio, Nicostrato, Tauro, Severo, Arpocrazione.* Naples.

Glucker, J. (1978). *Antiochus and the Late Academy.* Göttingen.

Golitsis, P. (2015). 'On Simplicius' Life and Works: A Response to Hadot'. *Aestimatio* 12: 56–82.

(2018). 'Simplicius, Syrianus and the Harmony of Ancient Philosophers'. In: B. Strobel (ed.) *Die Kunst der philosophischen Exegese bei den spätantiken Platon- und Aristoteles-Kommentatoren. Akten der Tagung der Karl und Gertrud Abel-Stiftung vom 4. bis 6. Oktober 2012 in Trier.* Berlin & New York: 69–99.

Görler, W. (1990). 'Antiochos von Askalon über die "Alten" und über Die Stoa'. In: P. Steinmetz (ed.) *Beiträge zur hellenistischen Literatur und ihrer Rezeption in Rom.* Stuttgart: 123–39 = Görler 2004: 87–104.

(1997). 'Cicero's Philosophical Stance in the *Lucullus*'. In: Inwood & Mansfeld 1997: 36–57.

(2004). *Kleine Schriften zur hellenistisch-römischen Philosophie.* Leiden.

Graham, D.W. 2003, 'Does Nature Love to Hide? Heraclitus B123 DK'. *Classical Philology* 98: 175–9.

(2013). 'Once More unto the Stream'. In: Sider & Obbink 2013: 303–20.

Graßhoff, G., & Meyer, M. (eds.) (2016). *Representing Authority in Ancient Knowledge Texts.* Special issue of eTopoi Journal of Ancient Studies, 6.

Griffin, Michael (2014). 'Hypostasizing Socrates'. In: Layne & Tarrant 2014: 97–108.

(2015a). *Aristotle's "Categories" in the Early Roman Empire.* Oxford.

(ed.) (2015b). *Olympiodorus. Life of Plato and On Plato First Alcibiades 1–9.* London.

Griffin, Miriam (1997). 'The Composition of the *Academica*: Motives and Versions'. In: Inwood & Mansfeld 1997: 3–32.

## References

Griffin, Miriam & Barnes, J. (eds.) (1989). *Philosophia Togata I*. Oxford.
(eds.) (1997). *Philosophia Togata II*. Oxford.

Griffiths, A. (2016). 'Navel-Gazing in Naples? The Painting Behind the "Pompeii Philosophers"'. *Syllecta Classica* 27: 151–66.

Hadot, I. (ed.) (1990). *Simplicius. Commentaire sur les catégories*, Vol. 1. Leiden.

Hadot, I. (ed.) (2015). *Athenian and Alexandrian Neoplatonism and the Harmonization of Aristotle and Plato*. Leiden.

Hadot, P. (1981). 'Ouranos, Kronos and Zeus in Plotinus' Treatise against the Gnostics'. In: H. J. Blumenthal & R.A. Markus (eds.) *Neoplatonism and Early Christian Thought. Essays in Honour of A.H. Armstrong*. London: 124–38.

Hahm, D.E. (1977). *The Origin of Stoic Cosmology*. Columbus.
(2007). 'Critolaus and Late Hellenistic Peripatetic Philosophy'. In: Ioppolo & Sedley 2007: 47–101.

Hankinson, R.J. (1985). *The Skeptics*. London.

Hatzimichali, M. (2011). *Potamo of Alexandria and the Emergence of Eclecticism*. Oxford.
(2013). 'The Texts of Plato and Aristotle in the I century BC'. In: Schofield 2013: 1–27.

Helmig, Ch. (2009). 'The Truth Can Never Be Refuted: Syrianus' Views on Aristotle Reconsidered'. In: A. Longo (ed.) *Syrianus et la métaphysique de l'antiquité tardive*. Naples: 347–80.

Henry, P. & Schwyzer, H.-R. (eds.) (1983). *Plotini opera,* Vol. III (*editio minor*). Oxford.

Heßler, J.E. (2018). 'Plato, Hyperides, and Hellenistic Cult Practice. On the Commemoration of the Dead in the School of Epicurus'. *Mnemosyne* 71: 408–33.

Hicks, R.D. (ed.) (1925). *Diogenes Laertius. Lives of Eminent Philosophers*. Cambridge, MA & London.

Hoffmann, Ph. (1998). 'La fonction des prologues exégétiques dans la pensée pédagogique néoplatonicienne'. In: J.-D. Dubois & B. Roussel (eds.) *Entrer en matière: Les prologues*. Paris: 209–45.

Horky, Ph. (2013). 'Theophrastus on Platonic and "Pythagorean" imitation'. *Classical Quarterly* 63: 686–712.

Huffman, C. (2005). *Archytas of Tarentum*. Cambridge.
(2014a). 'The Peripatetics on the Pythagoreans'. In: Huffman 2014b: 274–95.
(ed.) (2014b). *A History of Pythagoreanism*. Cambridge.

Inwood, B. (2007). *Seneca: Selected Philosophical Letters*. Oxford.
(2012). 'Antiochus' Physics'. In: Sedley 2012a: 188–219.

Inwood, B. & Mansfeld, J. (eds.) (1997). *Assent and Argument: Studies in Cicero's 'Academic Books'*. Leiden.

Ioppolo, A.M. (1980). *Aristone di Chio e lo Stoicismo antico*. Naples.
(1986). *Opinione e scienza. Il dibattito tra Stoici e Accademici nel terzo e secondo secolo a.C.* Naples.

(1990). 'Presentation and Assent: a Physical and Cognitive Problem in Early Stoicism'. *Classical Quarterly* 40: 433–49 = Ioppolo 2013: 137–58.

(1995). 'Socrate nelle tradizioni accademico-scettica e pirroniana'. In G. Giannantoni et al. (eds.) *La tradizione socratica.* Naples: 89–123 = Ioppolo 2009: 209–40.

(1997). 'Fidelity to Zeno's Theory'. In: E.A. Moutsopoulos (ed.) *Chypre et les origines du stoïcisme.* Diotima 25: 62–73 = Ioppolo 2013: 181–92.

(2000). 'Su alcune recenti interpretazioni dello scetticismo dell'Accademia. Plutarch *Adv. Col.* 26.1121F–1122F: una testimonianza su Arcesilao'. *Elenchos* 21: 333–60.

(2004). 'La posizione di Plutarco nei confronti dello scetticismo'. In I. Gallo (ed.) *La biblioteca di Plutarco.* Naples: 289–310.

(2008). 'Arcésilas dans le *Lucullus* de Cicéron'. *Revue de Métaphysique et de Morale* 1: 21–44 = Ioppolo 2013: 251–70.

(2009). *La testimonianza di Sesto Empirico sull'Accademia scettica.* Naples.

(2013). *Dibattiti filosofici ellenistici. Dottrina delle cause, Stoicismo, Accademia scettica.* ed. B. Centrone, R. Chiaradonna, D. Quarantotto, E. Spinelli. Sankt Augustin.

(2018). 'Arcesilaus'. In D. Machuca & B. Reed (eds.) *Skepticism from Antiquity to the Present.* New York: 36–50.

Ioppolo, A.M. & Sedley, D. (eds.) (2007). *Pyrrhonists, Patricians, Platonizers: Hellenistic Philosophy in the Period 155–86 BC.* Naples.

Irwin, Th. (2012). 'Antiochus, Aristotle and the Stoics on Degrees of Happiness'. In: Sedley 2012a: 151–72.

Isnardi Parente, M. (ed.) (1980). *Speusippo. Frammenti.* Naples.

(ed.) (2012). *Senocrate e Ermodoro. Testimonianze e frammenti,* 2nd ed., ed. T. Dorandi. Pisa.

Jackson, R., Lycos, K. & Tarrant, H. (eds.) (1998). *Olympiodorus: Commentary on Plato's Gorgias.* Leiden.

Jourdan, F. (2015). 'Eusèbe de Césarée et les extraits de Numénius dans la *Préparation Évangélique*'. In: S. Morlet (ed.) *Lire en extraits, Lecture et production des textes de l'Antiquité à la fin du Moyen-Âge.* Paris: 107–48.

(2017–2018). 'Sur le Bien de Numénius: L'enseignement oral de Platon comme occasion de rechercher son pythagorisme dans ses écrits'. *Chôra* 15–16: 139–65.

Kahn, Ch. (1979). *The Art and Thought of Heraclitus.* Cambridge.

(1996). *Plato and the Socratic Dialogue.* Cambridge.

(2001). *Pythagoras and the Pythagoreans. A Brief History.* Indianapolis & Cambridge.

Karamanolis, G. (2004). 'Porphyry: The First Platonist Commentator on Aristotle'. In: Adamson et al. 2004: 97–120.

(2006). *Plato and Aristotle in Agreement? Platonists on Aristotle from Antiochus to Porphyry.* Oxford.

(2013). 'Numenius'. In: *The Stanford Encyclopedia of Philosophy.* https://plato.stanford.edu/entries/numenius/.

(2014). 'The Platonism of Eusebius of Caesarea'. In: R. Fowler (ed.) *Plato in the Third Sophistic*. Berlin & New York: 171–91.

Kirk, G.S., Raven, J. & Schofield, M. (eds.) (1983). *The Presocratic Philosophers*. Cambridge.

König, J., & Woolf, G. (eds.) (2017). *Authority and Expertise in Ancient Scientific Culture*, Cambridge.

Lakmann, M.-L. (ed.) (2017). *Platonici minores, 1. Jh.v.Chr. - 2. Jh.n.Chr. Prosopographie, Fragmente und Testimonien, mit deutscher Übersetzung*. Leiden.

Laks, A. (2010). 'Éclairer l'obscurité. Brucker et le syncrétisme platonicien'. In: A. Neschke (ed.) *Argumenta in dialogos Platonis*, Vol. I. Basel: 352–69.

Larsen, B.D. (ed.) (1972). *Jamblique de Chalcis: exégète et philosophe*. Aarhus.

Layne, D. (2014). 'The Character of Socrates and the Good of Dialogue Form'. In: Layne & Tarrant 2014: 80–96.

Layne, D. & Tarrant, H. (2014). *The Neoplatonic Socrates*. Philadelphia.

Lernould, A. (2001). *Physique et Théologie. Lecture du Timée de Platon par Proclus*. Villeneuve d'Ascq.

(2006). 'Sur la composition de l'*E de Delphes* de Plutarque'. In: Boulogne et al. 2006: 17–29.

Lévy, C. (2001). 'Pyrrhon, Enésidème et Sextus Empiricus: la question de la légitimation historique dans le scepticisme'. In A. Brancacci (ed.) *Antichi e moderni nella filosofia di età imperiale*. Naples: 299–329.

(ed.) (2014). *Présocratiques Latines. Traductions. Introductions et commentaires*. Paris.

Linguiti, A. (2014). 'Physics and Metaphysics'. In: Remes & Slaveva-Griffin 2014b: 343–55.

Long, A.A. (1975–1976). 'Heraclitus and the Stoics'. *Philosophia* 5–6: 133–56 = Long 1996: 35–57.

(1986). 'Diogenes Laertius, Life of Arcesilaus'. *Elenchos* 7: 429–50 = 'Arcesilaus in His Time and Place' in Long 2006: 96–113.

(1996). *Stoic Studies*. Berkeley, Los Angeles & London.

(1999). 'Stoic Psychology'. In: Algra et al. 1999: 560–84.

(2006). *From Epicurus to Epictetus*. Oxford & New York.

(2013). 'Heraclitus on Measure and the Explicit Emergence of Rationality'. In Sider & Obbink 2013: 201–23.

Longo, A. (ed.) (2009). *Syrianus et la métaphysique de l'Antiquité tardive. Actes du colloque international, Université de Genève, 29 septembre – 1er octobre 2006*. Naples.

(2017). 'Numénius d'Apamée précurseur de Plotin dans l'allégorèse de la théogonie d'Hésiode: le mythe de Kronos, Ouranos et Zeus'. In: M.-A. Gavray & A. Michalewski (eds.) *Les principes cosmologiques du platonisme: Origines, influences et systématisation*. Turnhout: 167–85.

(2020). 'What is the Principle of Movement, the Self-moved (Plato) or the Unmoved (Aristotle)? The Exegetic Strategies of Hermias of Alexandria and Simplicius in Late Antiquity'. In: J.F. Finamore, C.-P. Manolea & S. Klitenic Wear (eds.) *Studies in Hermias' Commentary on Plato's* Phaedrus. Leiden & Boston: 115–41.

Lucarini, C.M. & Moreschini, C. (eds.) (2012). *Hermias Alexandrinus. In Platonis Phaedrum Scholia*. Berlin.

Luna, C. (ed.) (2001). *Simplicius. Commentaire sur les Catégories d'Aristote. Chapitres 2–4*. Paris.

Luna, C. & Segonds, A.Ph. (eds.) (2007–2017). *Proclus. Commentaire sur le Parménide de Platon. Texte établi, traduit et annoté*. 6 vols. Paris.

    (eds.) (2007a). *Proclus. Commentaire sur le Parménide de Platon*, Vol. 1.1: *Introduction générale*. Paris.

    (eds.) (2007b). *Proclus. Commentaire sur le Parménide de Platon*, Vol. 1.2: *Livre I*. Paris.

    (eds.) (2013). *Proclus. Commentaire sur le Parmánide de Platon*, Vol. 4.2: *Notes complémentaires et index du livre IV*. Paris.

Mansfeld, J. (1992). *Heresiography in Context. Hippolytus' Elenchos as a Source for Greek Philosophy*. Leiden.

    (1994). *Prolegomena. Questions to Be Settled Before the Study of an Author, Or a Text*. Leiden.

    (2010). 'Plato, Pythagoras, Aristotle, the Peripatetics, the Stoics, and Thales and His Followers "On Causes"'. In J. Mansfeld & D.T. Runia (eds.). *Aëtiana*, Vol. III: *Studies in the Doxographical Traditions of Ancient Philosophy*. Leiden & Boston: 377–413 (previosuly published in A. Brancacci (ed.) *Antichi e moderni nella filosofia di età imperiale*. Naples 2001: 17–68).

Marcovich, M. (ed.) (2001). *Heraclitus: Greek Text with a Short Commentary*. Sankt Augustin.

Marg, W. (ed.) (1972). *Timaeus Locrus, De Natura Mundi et Animae. Überlieferung, Testimonia, Text und Übersetzung*. Leiden.

Mathieu, J.-M. (2007). 'La connaissance de Dieu comme navigation en haute mer: en remontant de Grégoire de Nazianze vers Platon'. In: J. Laurent (ed.) *Les dieux de Platon*. Caen: 251–61.

Mattusch, C. (2008.) *Pompeii and the Roman Villa*. London.

Mayhew, R. (ed.) (2008). *Plato. Laws 10*. Oxford.

Mayor, A. (2018). *Gods and Robots: Myths, Machines, and Ancient Dreams of Technology*. Princeton.

McCabe, M.M. (1996). 'Unity in the *Parmenides*: The Unity of the *Parmenides*'. In: Gill, C. & McCabe, M.M. (eds.) *Form and Argument in Late Plato*. Oxford: 5–47.

McDowell, J. (ed.) (1973). *Plato. Theaetetus*. Oxford.

Meerwaldt, J.D. (1951). 'Cleanthea I'. *Mnemosyne* 4: 40–69.

Menn, S. (2002). 'Aristotle's Definition of Soul and the Programme of the *De Anima*'. *Oxford Studies in Ancient Philosophy* 22: 83–139.

    (2012). 'Self-Motion and Reflection: Hermias and Proclus on the Harmony of Plato and Aristotle on the Soul'. In: Wilberding & Horn 2012: 44–67.

    (2013). 'Avicenna's Metaphysics'. In: P. Adamson (ed.) *Interpreting Avicenna: Critical Essays*. Cambridge: 143–69.

# References

257

Michalewski, A. (2012). 'Le Premier de Numénius et l'Un de Plotin'. *Archives de Philosophie*, 75: 29–48.

(2014). *La puissance de l'intelligible. La théorie plotinienne des Formes au miroir de l'héritage médioplatonicien.* Leuven.

(2017). 'Faut-il préférer Epicure à Aristote ? Quelques réflexions sur la providence'. In: Baghdassarian & Guyomarc'h 2017: 123–42.

Moraux, P. (1984). *Der Aristotelismus bei den Griechen von Andronikos bis Alexander von Aphrodisias, II. Der Aristotelismus im I. und II. Jh.n.Ch.* Berlin & New York.

(1985). 'Porphyre, commentateur de la *Physique* d'Aristote'. In: Ch. Rutten & A. Motte (eds.) *Aristotelica: Mélanges offerts à Marcel de Corte*. Brussels: 227–39.

Moreschini, C. (ed.) (1997). *Plutarco: L'E di Delfi*. Naples.

Morlet, S. (2015). '"Extraire" dans la littérature antique'. In: S. Morlet (ed.) *Lire en extraits: Lecture et production des textes de l'Antiquité à la fin du Moyen-Âge.* Paris: 29–52.

Morrow, G.R. & Dillon, J.M. (eds.) (1987). *Proclus' Commentary on Plato's Parmenides*. Princeton.

Noble, Ch. (2013). 'Plotinus' Unaffectable Matter'. *Oxford Studies in Ancient Philosophy* 44: 233–77.

(2016). 'Plotinus' Unaffectable Soul'. *Oxford Studies in Ancient Philosophy* 51: 231-81.

O'Brien, C.S. (2015). *The Demiurge in Ancient Thought*. Cambridge.

O'Brien, D. (1996). 'Plotinus on Matter and Evil'. In: L.P. Gerson (ed.) *The Cambridge Companion to Plotinus*. Cambridge: 171–95.

O'Meara, D.J. (1989). *Pythagoras Revived: Mathematics and Philosophy in Late Antiquity*. Oxford.

(2003). *Platonopolis. Platonic Political Philosophy in Late Antiquity*. Oxford.

O'Neill, W. (ed.) (1965). *Proclus: Alcibiades 1. A Translation and Commentary*. The Hague.

Obsieger, H. (ed.) (2013). *Plutarch. De E apud Delphos*. Stuttgart.

Opsomer, J. (1998). *In Search of the Truth. Academic Tendencies in Middle Platonism*. Brussel.

(2005a). 'Demiurges in Early Imperial Platonism'. In: R. Hirsch-Luipold (ed.) *Gott und die Götter bei Plutarch*. Berlin: 51–99.

(2005b). '*A Craftsman and His Handmaiden. Demiurgy According to Plotinus*'. In: T. Leinkauf & C. Steel (eds.) *Plato's Timaeus and the Foundations of Cosmology in Late Antiquity, the Middle Ages and Renaissance*. Leuven: 67–102.

(2006a): 'To Find the Maker and Father. Proclus' Exegesis of *Tim.* 28C3–5'. *Études Platoniciennes* 2: 261–83.

(2006b). 'Éléments stoïciens dans le *De E apud Delphos* de Plutarque'. In Boulogne et al. 2006: 148–70.

(2009a). 'M. Annius Ammonius, A Philosophical Profile'. In: Bonazzi & Opsomer 2009: 123–86.

(2009b). 'The Integration of Aristotelian Physics in a Neoplatonic Context: Proclus on Movers and Divisibility'. In: R. Chiaradonna & F. Trabattoni (eds.) *Physics and Philosophy of Nature in Greek Neoplatonism*. Leiden & Boston: 189–229.

(2010). 'Arguments non-linéaires et pensées en cercles. Forme et argumentation dans les *Questions Platoniciennes* de Plutarque'. In Brouillette & Giavatto 2010: 93–116.

(2012). 'Self-Motion According to Iamblichus'. *Elenchos* 33: 259–90.

(2015). 'A Much Misread Proposition from Proclus' *Elements of Theology* (prop. 28)'. *Classical Quarterly* 65: 433–8.

Opsomer, J. & Ulacco, A. (2016). 'What is Epistemic Authority? A Model and Some Examples from Ancient Philosophy'. In: J. Leemans, B. Meijns, S. Boodts (eds.) *Proceedings of the Leuven Conference 'Shaping Authority'*. Turnhout: 21–46.

Pearson, A.C. (1891). *The Fragments of Zeno and Cleanthes*. London.

Pépin, J. (1995). 'Plotin et les mythes'. *Revue Philosophique de Louvain* 37: 5–27.

Perkams, M. (2006). 'Das Prinzip der Harmonisierung verschiedener Traditionen in den neuplatonischen Kommentaren zu Platon und Aristoteles'. In: M. van Ackeren & J. Müller (eds.) *Antike Philosophie verstehen – Understanding Ancient Philosophy*. Darmstadt: 332–47.

Perkams, M. & Piccione, R.M. (eds.) (2006). *Proklos: Methode, Seelenlehre, Metaphysik. Akten der Konferenz in Jena am 18.–20. September 2003*. Leiden.

Petrucci, F.M. (ed.) (2012). *Teone di Smirne. Expositio rerum mathematicarum ad legendum Platonem utilium. Introduzione, traduzione, commento*. Sankt Augustin.

(2014). 'Le témoignage du deuxième livre du *Commentaire au Timée* de Proclus sur la forme des arguments médioplatoniciens au sujet de la genèse du monde'. *Revue des Études Grecques* 127: 331–75.

(2016). 'Théon de Smyrne'. In: R. Goulet (ed.) *Dictionnaire des Philosophes Antiques*, Vol. VI. Paris: 1016–29.

(2018). *Taurus of Beirut: The Other Side of Middle Platonism*. London & New York.

Planeaux, C. (2001). 'Socrates, an Unreliable Narrator? The Dramatic Setting of the *Lysis*'. *Classical Philology* 96: 60–8.

Polanski, R.M. (1992). *Philosophy and Knowledge: A Commentary on Plato's Theaetetus*. London & Toronto.

Pradeau, J.-F. (ed.) (2002). *Héraclite. Fragments. [Citations et Témoignages]*. Paris.

Rackham, H. (ed.) (1931). *Cicero: De finibus bonorum et malorum*. Cambridge, MA & London.

(ed.) (1967). *Cicero: De natura deorum, Academica*. Cambridge, MA & London.

Radke, G. (2006). *Das Lächeln des Parmenides. Proklos' Interpretationen zur Platonischen Dialogform*. Berlin & New York.

Rapp, Ch. (2017). 'His Dearest Enemy. Heraclitus in the Aristotelian Oeuvre'. In: E. Fantino et al. (eds.) *Heraklit im Kontext. Studia praesocratica*, 8. Berlin & Boston: 415–38.

Rashed, M. (ed.) (2011). *Alexandre d'Aphrodise, Commentaire perdu à la Physique d'Aristote: Livres IV–VIII. Les scholies byzantines.* Berlin & Boston.

(2013a). 'La mosaïque des philosophes de Naples: une représentation de l'académie platonicienne et son commanditaire'. In: C. Noirot & N. Ondine (eds.) *Omnia in uno: Hommage à Alain Segonds.* Paris, 27–49.

(2013b). 'Boethus' Aristotelian Ontology'. In: Schofield 2013: 53–77. Reprinted with changes in R. Sorabji (ed.) (2016). *Aristotle Re-Interpreted: New Findings on Seven Hundred Years of the Ancient Commentators.* London: 103–23.

(2016). 'Proclus, commentaire perdu sur la Palinodie du *Phèdre*: vestiges byzantins'. In: *L'héritage aristotélicien. Textes inédits de l'Antiquité. Nouvelle édition revue et augmentée.* Paris: 473–561.

(2018). *La jeune fille et la sphère: études sur Empédocle.* Paris.

Rashed, M. & Auffret, Th. (2014). 'Aristote, *Métaphysique* A 6, 988a 7–14, Eudore d'Alexandrie et l'histoire ancienne du texte de la *Métaphysique*'. In: Ch. Brockmann, D. Deckers, L. Koch & S. Valente (eds.) *Handschriften- und Textforschung heute. Zur Überlieferung der griechischen Literatur: Festschrift für Dieter Harlfinger aus Anlass seines 70. Geburtstages.* Wiesbaden: 55–84.

Reid, J. (1885). *M. Tulli Ciceronis Academica: The Text Revised and Explained.* London.

Remes, P. & Slaveva-Griffin, S. (2014a). 'Introduction: Neoplatonism Today'. In: Remes & Slaveva-Griffin 2014b: 1–10.

(eds.) (2014b). *The Routledge Handbook of Neoplatonism.* London & New York.

Renaud, F. & Tarrant, H. (eds.) (2015). *The Platonic Alcibiades I: The Dialogue and Its Ancient Reception.* Cambridge.

Reydams-Schils, G. (1999). *Demiurge and Providence. Stoic and Platonist Readings of Plato's Timaeus.* Turnhout.

(2007). 'Calcidius on God'. In: Bonazzi & Helmig 2007: 243–58.

Reydams-Schils, G. & Ferrari, F. (2014). 'Middle Platonism and Its Relation to Stoicism and the Peripatetic Tradition'. In: Remes & Slaveva-Griffin 2014b: 40–51.

Richards, H. (1901). 'On a Greek Adverb of Place'. *Classical Review* 15: 442–5.

Richter, G.M.A. (1965). *The Portraits of the Greeks.* London.

Riedweg, Ch. (1987). *Mysterienterminologie bei Platon, Philon und Klemens von Alexandrien.* Berlin & New York.

(1997). '"Pythagoras hinterliess keine einzige Schrift". Ein Irrtum?' *Museum Helveticum* 54: 65–92.

Riginos, A.S. (1976). *Platonica: The Anecdotes Concerning the Life and Writings of Plato.* Leiden.

Rohde, E. (1872). 'Die Quellen des Jamblichus in seiner Biographie des Pythagoras'. *Rheinisches Museum für Philologie* 27: 23–62.

Romano, F. (1985). *Porfirio e la fisica aristotelica*. Catania.

Runia, D.T. (1986). *Philo of Alexandria and the Timaeus of Plato*. Leiden & New York & Cologne.

   (2001). *Philo of Alexandria. On the Creation of the Cosmos According to Moses*. Leiden, New York & Cologne.

Runia, D.T. & Share, M. (eds.) (2008). *Proclus. Commentary on Plato's Timaeus*, Vol. II.2, *Proclus on the Causes of the Cosmos and its Creation*. Cambridge.

Rutherford, R.B. (1995). *The Art of Plato*. London.

Sambursky, S. (1959). *Physics of the Stoics*. London.

Schibli, H. (1993). 'Xenocrates' Daimons and the Irrational Soul'. *Classical Quarterly* 43: 143–67.

Schofield, M. (2012). 'Antiochus on Social Virtue'. In: Sedley 2012a: 173–87.

   (ed.) (2013). *Aristotle, Plato and Pythagoreanism in the I century* BC. *New Directions for Philosophy*. Cambridge.

   (2014). 'Archytas'. In: Huffman 2014b: 69–87.

Schoppe, C. (1994). *Plutarchs Interpretation der Ideenlehre Platons*. Münster & Hamburg.

Sedley, D. (1981). 'The End of the Academy'. *Phronesis* 26: 67–75.

   (1982). 'The Stoic Criterion of Identity'. *Phronesis* 27: 259–75.

   (1985). 'The Stoic Theory of Universals'. In: R.H. Epp (ed.) *Recovering the Stoics. The Southern Journal of Philosophy* 23, Supplement: 87–92.

   (1989). 'Philosophical Allegiance in the Greco-Roman World'. In: Griffin & Barnes 1989: 97–119.

   (1992). 'Sextus Empiricus and the Atomist Criteria of Truth'. *Elenchos* 13: 19–56.

   (1997). 'Plato's *Auctoritas* and the Rebirth of the Commentary Tradition'. In: Griffin & Barnes 1997: 110–29.

   (1999). 'The Stoic-Platonist Debate on *Kathēkonta*'. In K. Ierodiakonou (ed.) *Topics in Stoic Philosophy*. Oxford: 128–52.

   (2002a). 'The Origins of Stoic God'. In: D. Frede & A. Laks (eds.) *Traditions of Theology*. Leiden: 41–83.

   (2002b). *The Midwife of Platonism. Text and Subtext in Plato's Theaetetus*, Oxford.

   (2003a). *Plato's Cratylus*. Cambridge.

   (2003b). 'The School, from Zeno to Arius Didymus'. In: B. Inwood (ed.) *The Cambridge Companion to the Stoics*. Cambridge: 7–32.

   (2003c). 'Philodemus and the Decentralisation of Philosophy'. *Cronache Ercolanesi* 33: 31–41.

   (ed.) (2012a). *The Philosophy of Antiochus*. Cambridge.

   (2012b). 'Antiochus as Historian of Philosophy'. In: Sedley 2012a: 80–103.

   (2017). 'Divinization'. In: P. Destrée & Z. Giannopoulou (eds.) *Plato's Symposium: A Critical Guide*. Cambridge: 66–107.

(2019). 'The *Timaeus* as Vehicle for Platonic Doctrine'. *Oxford Studies in Ancient Philosophy* 56: 45–71.

Segonds, A.Ph. (ed.) (1985). *Proclus. Sur le premier Alcibiade de Platon*, Vol. 1. Paris.

Sharples R.W. & Sorabji, R. (eds.) (2007). *Greek and Roman Philosophy 100 BC–200 AD*. London.

Sheppard, A. (1980). *Studies on the 5th and 6th Essays of Proclus' Commentary on the Republic*. Göttingen.

(2013). 'Proclus' Place in the Reception of Plato's *Republic*'. In: A. Sheppard (ed.) *Ancient Approaches to Plato's Republic*. London: 107–15.

(2014). *The Poetics of Phantasia*. London.

(Forthcoming). 'Allegory, Metaphysics, Theology: Homeric Reception in Athenian Neoplatonism'. In: C.-P. Manolea (ed.) *The Brill's Companion to the Reception of Homer from the Hellenistic Age to Late Antiquity*. Leiden.

Sider, D. & Obbink, D. (eds.) (2013). *Doctrine and Doxography: Studies on Heraclitus and Pythagoras*. Berlin & Boston.

Simonetti, E.G. (2017). *A Perfect Medium? Oracular Divination in the Thought of Plutarch*. Leuven.

Siorvanes, L. (1996). *Proclus: Neoplatonic Philosophy and Science*. Edinburgh.

Smith, A. (ed.) (1992). *Porphyrii Philosophi fragmenta: Fragmenta Arabica David Wasserstein interpretante*. Stuttgart & Leipzig.

(2012). 'The Significance of "Physics" in Porphyry: The Problem of Body and Matter'. In: Wilberding & Horn 2012: 30–43.

Sorabji, R. (ed.) (2004). *The Philosophy of the Commentators 200–600 AD. A Sourcebook,* Vol. 1: *Psychology*. London.

(2014). 'The Alexandrian Classrooms Excavated and Sixth-Century Philosophy Teaching'. In: Remes & Slaveva-Griffin 2014b: 30–9.

Spinelli, E. (2010). 'Presocratici scettici? Assunti genealogici nel *Varro* di Cicerone'. In: S. Giombini & F. Marcacci (eds.) *Il quinto secolo. Studi di filosofia antica in onore di Livio Rossetti*. Passignano sul Trasimeno: 235–46.

Staab, G. (2009). 'Das Kennzeichen des Neuen Pythagoreismus innerhalb der kaiserzeitlichen Platoninterpretation: "Pythagoreischer" Dualismus und Einprinzipienlehre im Einklang'. In: Bonazzi & Opsomer 2009: 55–88.

(2014). 'Der hymnische Nachruf des Proklos auf seinen Lehrer Syrianos (IG II/III² 13451) im Lichte des Athener Neuplatonismus'. *Zeitschrift für Papyrologie und Epigraphik* 190: 81–96.

Steel, C. (2003). 'Why Should We Prefer Plato's *Timaeus* to Aristotle's *Physics*? Proclus' Critique of Aristotle's Causal Explanation of the World'. In: R.W. Sharples & A. Sheppard (eds.) *Ancient Approaches to Plato's Timaeus*. London: 175–87.

Steel, C. et al. (eds.) (2007–2009). *Proclus: In Platonis Parmenidem commentaria*. 3 vols. Oxford.

Syme, R. (1972). 'Fraud and Imposture'. In: K. von Fritz (ed.) *Pseudepigrapha I*. Vandœuvres & Geneva: 1–17.

Szlezàk, Th.A. (1972). *Pseudo-Archytas über Die Kategorien*. Berlin & New York.

Tarán, L. (ed.) (1981). *Speusippus of Athens: A Critical Study with a Collection of the Related Texts and Commentary*. Leiden.

(1999). 'Heraclitus: The River-fragments and Their Implications'. *Elenchos* 20: 9–52 = in *Collected Papers (1962–1999)*. Leiden 2001: 126–67.

Tarrant, H. (1985). *Scepticism or Platonism? The Philosophy of the Fourth Academy*. Cambridge.

(2000). *Plato's First Interpreters*. Ithaca.

(2004). 'Must Commentators Know Their Sources? Proclus *In Timaeum* and Numenius'. In: Adamson et al. 2004: 175–90.

(2007). 'Antiochus: A New Beginning?' In: Sharples & Sorabji 2007: Vol. II, 317–32.

Tarrant, H. et al. (eds.) (2018). *The Brill's Companion to the Reception of Plato*. Leiden, Boston & Cologne.

Thesleff, H. (1961). *An Introduction to the Pythagorean Writings of the Hellenistic Period*. Åbo.

(1962). 'Okkelos, Archytas and Plato'. *Eranos* 60: 8–36.

(ed.) (1965). *The Pythagorean Texts of the Hellenistic Period*. Åbo.

Thompson, D'Arcy W. (1895). *A Glossary of Greek Birds*. Oxford.

Tieleman, T. (2007). 'Panaetius' Place in the History of Stoicism with Special Reference to his Moral Psychology'. In: Ioppolo & Sedley 2007: 103–41.

Tornau, Ch. (2006). 'Der Eros und das Gute bei Plotin und Proklos'. In: Perkams & Piccione 2006: 201–29.

Trapp, M. (2000). 'Plato in Dio'. In: S. Swain (ed.) *Dio Chrysostom. Politics, Letters, and Philosophy*. Oxford: 213–39.

Trouillard J. (1958). 'Agir par son être même, la causalité selon Proclus'. *Revue des sciences religieuses* 118: 347–57.

Tsouni, G. (2018). 'The Emergence of Platonic and Aristotelian Authority in the First Century BCE'. In: Bryan et al. 2018: 263–77.

(2019). *Antiochus of Ascalon and Peripatetic Ethics*. Cambridge.

Ulacco, A. (2017). *Pseudopythagorica Dorica. I trattati di argomento metafisico, logico ed epistemologico attribuiti ad Archita e a Brontino*. Berlin & New York.

Ulacco, A. & Opsomer, J. (2014). 'Elements and Elemental Properties in Timaeus Locrus'. *Rheinisches Museum für Philologie* 157: 154–206.

Van den Berg, R.M. (2016). 'Theurgy in the Context of Proclus' Philosophy'. In: d'Hoine & Martijn 2016: 223–39.

(2017). 'Proclus and Damascius on φιλοτιμία: The Neoplatonic Psychology of a Political Emotion'. *Philosophie antique* 17: 149–65.

(Forthcoming). 'Imitation and Self-examination: The Later Neoplatonists on the Platonic Dialogue as Moral Education through Visualisation'. In: S. Xenophontos & A. Marmodoro (eds.) *The Reception of Greek Ethics in Late Antiquity and Byzantium*. Cambridge.

Vander Waerdt P. (1989). 'Colotes and the Epicurean Refutation of Skepticism'. *Greek, Roman, and Byzantine Studies* 30: 225–67.

# References

263

Van Nuffelen P. (2011). *Rethinking the Gods. Philosophical Readings of Religion in the Post-Hellenistic Period*. Cambridge.

Warren, J. (2002). 'Socratic Scepticism in Plutarch's *Adversus Colotem*'. *Elenchos* 23: 333–56.

Westerink, L.G. (ed.) (1966). *Olympiodorus. Commentary on the First Alcibiades of Plato*. Amsterdam.

(ed.) (1970). *Olympiodori in Platonis Gorgiam commentaria*. Leipzig.

(ed.) (1990). *Prolégomènes à la philosophie de Platon*. Paris.

Whittaker, J. (1969). 'Ammonius on the Delphic E', *Classical Quarterly* 19: 185–92.

(1984). *Studies in Platonism and Patristic Thought*. London.

(ed.) (1990). *Alcinoos: Enseignement des doctrines de Platon*. Paris.

(2000). 'Harpocration d'Argos'. In: R. Goulet (ed.) *Dictionnaire des philosophes antiques* Vol. III. Paris: 503–4.

Wilberding, J. (2008). 'Automatic Action in Plotinus'. *Oxford Studies in Ancient Philosophy* 34: 373–407.

Wilberding, J. & Horn, Ch. (eds.) (2012). *Neoplatonism and the Philosophy of Nature*. Oxford.

Wilson, R.J. (2006). 'Aspects of Iconography in Romano-British Mosaics: The Rudston "Aquatic" Scene and the Brading Astronomer Revisited'. *Britannia* 37: 295–336.

Wycherley, R.E. (1962). 'Peripatos: The Athenian Philosophical Scene-II'. *Greece & Rome* 9: 2–21.

Zambon M. (2002). *Porphyre et le moyen platonisme*. Paris.

Zanker, P. (1995). *The Mask of Socrates* (English translation). Berkeley.

Zhmud, L. (2012). *Pythagoras and the Early Pythagoreans*. Oxford.

(2019). 'What Is Pythagorean in the Pseudo-Pythagorean Literature?'. *Philologus* 163: 72–94.

# Index Locorum[1]

### Aelian

#### Various histories

3.19  44n21

### Aetius

#### Opinions of the philosophers

1.7.30  16n11, 36n69
1.11.4  165

### Albinus

#### Isagoge

5.149.35–37  235n28

### Alcinous

#### Didaskalikos

1.152.8–23  206n21
1.152.23–29  206n21
6  155n17
8.163.8–10  167
10  152n12
10.164.18–27  166n15
13.169.4–5  165n9
30.183.17–19  206n21

### Alexander of Aphrodisias

#### Commentary on Aristotle's Metaphysics

58.25–59.8  163
82.11–83.26  30n58

#### Mantissa

110.4  225n95

### Alexis

#### Fragments

99  59n58

### Ammonius

#### Commentary on Aristotle's On Interpretation

1.3–11  222n82
181.30–32  222n81

### Anonymous

#### Commentary on Plato's Theaetetus

3.7–12  82n67
11.27–31  76n47
71.12–35  80n57

### Anonymous

#### PHerc. 346 (Capasso)

col. 7.23f–24  215n58

### Anonymous

#### Prolegomena to Platonic philosophy

14  234
14.9–23  227, 228n5

---

[1] We indicate editions and original (or Latin) titles only in the case ambiguities may occur.

# Index Locorum

15.7–13  228n5
15.21–29  238
17.33–39  228n4
23  238
23.16–18  235
23.22–24  238
26  233n22

## Antiochus of Ascalon

### Testimonies (Sedley)

8  101n35

## Apollinaris Sidonius

### Letters

1.6.3  49n33
4.8.5  49n33
9.9  48–50

## Apuleius

### On Plato and his doctrine

1.3  123n23

### On Socrates' God

20  133n8

## Archytas (DK)

A7  44n19
A10a  54n44

## [Archytas] (Thesleff)

### On first principles

19.5–20.17  127

### On the whole system

22.29  122

## Aristophanes

### Clouds

1005  41n10

## Aristotle

### Categories

14.15a13–14  224n93

## Metaphysics

A6.987a29–b7  80n60
A6.988a10–11  163
A9.991b6–7  33n63
A9.992a20–22  19n22
Γ5.1010a10–15  82n66
Δ1.1013a16–17  172n27
E1  173
Z2.1028b21–24  28n50
Z2.1028b24–27  22n31
Z7.1032a25  188n41
Z8.1033b32  188n41
Θ8.1049b25–26  188n41
Λ  166, 175
Λ3.1070a8  188n41
Λ7  36
Λ7.1072b30–1073a1  32n61
Λ8  36, 62–63
Λ8.1073b32–38  62
Λ8.1073b32–1074a17  62n62
Λ9  189n43
Λ10.1075b37–1076a4  28n50
N5.1092a16  188n41

## Nicomachean ethics

7.13.1153b1–7  44n19

## On the heavens

1  42n13
1.9  24n35
1.9.279a17–30  25n38
1.10  21
1.10–12  188n42

## On the soul

1.2.405a24  72n27
1.3  178, 182–183, 185, 191, 199
1.3.405b31–406a2  224n91
3.4–5  189n43

## Physics

1.9  170, 175
1.9.192a35–36  175
2.2.194b9–15  175
2.2.194b13  188n41
2.7.198a22–31  175
3.2  198–199
3.2.201a10–11  198n70
3.2.201b31–33  169
4.2.209b11–12  167
4.11  168
4.11.219a8–14  169n22
4.12.220b32–221a1  169
5.1  190n47

## 266 Index Locorum

5.3.227a7–226b32 (transp. Ross) 187n34
8  181, 224
8.2.252b21–23  182n15
8.4.255b30–31  196n65
8.5  178, 181–182, 189, 198
8.5.256a13–21  186n30
8.5.256a19–21  181n10
8.5.257a12–14  181n13
8.5.257a28–30  190n45
8.5.257b2–6  181n11
8.5.257b6–12  181n12
8.5.257b8–9  198n70
8.5.257b12–13  182n14
8.5.257b13–26  186n31
8.5.258a1–8  182n14
8.6.259b1–19  182n15
8.6.259b20–28  183n21
8.10.267b2–6  183n22

### Fragments (Rose)

1  85n75
192  117n7

### Aristoxenus

#### Fragments (Wehrli)

43  117n7
47–50  123n26

### Arius Didymus

#### Fragments (Diels)

39  72

### Asclepius

#### Commentary on Aristotle's Metaphysics

138.7–9  241n50
377.22–24  23n33

### Athenaeus

#### Deipnosophistae

163F–164A  125n31
279E–F  43n17
546D  43n17

### Atticus

#### Fragments (des Places)

1  1, 113
1.32–40  219n71

5.39–41  165n9
8  166

### Augustine

#### Against the Academics

3.41  92n17

#### City of God

19.3  92n17

### Aulus Gellius

#### Attic nights

10.12.8–10  54n44
10.22.1–24  241n49

### Boethus of Sidon

#### Fragments (Rashed)

18  174n34

### Calcidius

#### Commentary on Plato's Timaeus

295–297  134n12

### [Callicratidas]

#### On the felicity of families (Thesleff)

103.20–23  121n16

### Cicero

#### On the ends of goods and evils

2.2  71n25
2.15  88n91
4.3  99
5  92
5.1–3  95n24
5.2  40n7, 101–102
5.3  101n34
5.4  40n7
5.7  95, 97, 100–101
5.7–8  95n24
5.12–14  101n36
5.13–14  95–96, 99,
   105–106
5.14  98
5.74  97, 104

## Index Locorum

5.87 58n57, 123n23
5.87–88 100, 110

### On the nature of the Gods

1.10 94
1.11 71n25
1.19–24 108
1.73 17n15

### On the orator

3.67 71n25, 105n44

### Posterior Academics (Varro)

5–8 106n45
17 100–101
19 18n18, 100
26–28 20
27–28 20
30–32 114n63
33 99n27, 101, 103
33–35 92, 111
34 60n59, 101–103
35 104–105, 104n42
44 67, 70n19, 87n86–87
44–45 70
45 71n25, 85n79

### Prior Academics (Lucullus)

13 67n6, 69n16
13–15 70n19
14 67n7
15 67n8, 69n13, 100, 104–105, 105n44
16 87n89
19–20 106n45
32 87n86
46 105n44
72–74 70n19
75 70n19, 87n88
79 106n45
115 103
118 68n10
137 94n22

### Republic

1.16 58n57, 123n23

## Clemens of Alexandria

### Protrepticus

112.2 208n30

### Stromata

2.22.133 44n19
2.104.2 208n30

## Crantor

### Testimonies (Mette)

10 20n25

## Damascius

### Commentary on Plato's Parmenides

3.4.22–3 222n81

### Commentary on Plato's Phaedo

1.207 222n83

### Commentary on Plato's Philebus

6 222n83

### On first principles

3.111.12–14 222n81

## [Damippus]

### On prudence and happiness (Thesleff)

68.21–25 128

## Democritus (DK)

A135 76n47

## Dio Chrysostom

### Orations

4.4 235n31
4.39–41 208n30

## Diogenes Laertius

### Lives of the philosophers

1.16 116
1.21 90n9
3.2 13n3
3.38 22n29
3.48 232
3.51–52 241n49
4.1 15n7, 43n16–17, 44n19, 60n59
4.2 43n18, 44n20

# Index Locorum

4.12 32n60
4.19 40n7
4.22 105n44
4.29 82n66
4.32 105n44
5.2 48n29
5.52 48n29
5.54 48n29
5.68 48n29
7.2 71n24
7.31 71n24
7.39–41 95n23
7.45 76n47
7.71 156n19
7.157 72n29
7.163 116
7.174 68n12
7.175 73n35
7.177 68n12
8.6 116n2, 117n8
8.15 117n7
8.55 118n9
8.79–80 123
9.5 68n12
9.6 88n91

## [Elias]

### Commentary on Porphyry's Isagoge

61.43-62.1 211n42

## Epicrates

### Fragments (Kassel-Austin)

10 12n1

## Epiphanius

### Against Heresies

3.29 86n82

## Eudemus

### Fragments (Wehrli)

70 226n99
140 226

## Eudorus

### Testimonies and fragments (Mazzarelli)

T1 107
T3–5 110

## Eusebius

### Preparation for the Gospel

11.22 141, 144n54
14.4 131
14.5.1 60n59
14.5.12 68n12
15.12.2–4 166
15.20.2–3 71–72, 74n38,
    76n45

## Favorinus

### Fragments (Barigazzi)

93 54n44

## Galen

### Introduction to logic

3.4 156n19

### On the composition of drugs (Kühn)

13.529.5 201n2

### On the doctrines of Hippocrates and Plato (De Lacy)

2.8.48 (166.12–14) 73n34,
    75n44
5.6.43 (334.30–34) 116n2

## [Galen]

### Philosophical history

3 15n6

## Heraclitus (DK)

B12 71–73, 72n28, 73n32, 81n61
B93 85n80
B101 85n74
B123 87n86

## Hermias

### Commentary on Plato's Phaedrus (Lucarini & Moreschini)

1.5–9 219n71
108.13–14 184n23

# Index Locorum

108.21–109.29  184n24
109.22–24  184n25
109.25–28  184n26
109.30-110.9  184
110.10–21  185n29
110.17–18  186n30
110.21–111.3  186–187
111.1–2  188n37
111.6–29  188n39
112.1–7  196n64
112.7–14  196n63
112.22–113.8  197n66
113.5–8  195n58
114.13–17  184n25
115.2–8  195n59
115.28–116.12  196n62
115.31–33  188n37
118.31–119.4  195n58
119.16–34  194
121.22–23  188n40
141.20–25  217n66
141.25–30  35n67
218.15–16  205n16
218.29–219.1  216n65
272.2–7  61
273.11–14  61

### Hermodorus

#### Testimonies and fragments (IP²)

F5  29n55

### Homer

#### Ilias

14.216  208n30

#### Odyssey

19.179  208

### Iamblichus

#### On the Soul (Wachsmuth)

380  219n71

#### The Pythagorean Life

31  117n7
183–184  204n11
250–267  122–127
265–266  6
267  122

### [Iamblichus]

#### Arithmetical Theology (De Falco)

82.12–15  15n5

### Isocrates

#### Ad Demonicum

22  43n18
25  43n18

### John Philoponus

#### On the eternity of the world

148.7-149.16  193n54

### John Stobaeus

#### Anthology

1.13.1b  165
2.7.3f  107, 241n49
2.7.4a  107, 241n49

### Julian

#### Orations

7.23  216n65

### Marcellinus

#### Life of Thucydides

1  214n53

### Marinus

#### Life of Proclus

23.14–17  220n72

### Metrodorus of Lampsacus

#### Fragments (Körte)

38  214n54

### Neanthes

#### Fragments (FGrHist)

F26  118n9

## Numenius

### Fragments (des Places)

1a 150n5
8.13 131n2
11 130, 147
11.11–14 137
12.2–4 138n29
12.13 138n26
13 138n27
16 147n61
16.8–10 141
20.4–7 144n54
22 138n27
23 135
23.12–14 135n16
23.15 135n17
24 60n59, 127n35
24.52–56 133
24.57–59 133
24.67–73 134
24.73–79 136
25 68n12
28 92n17
52 134n12

## Olympiodorus

### Commentary on Plato's Alcibiades

10.13 237n38
24.1 237n38
24.15 237n38
31.3 237n38
33.5 237n38
33.8–10 237n38
38.3–16 237n38
42.10–43.3 237n38
45.18–21 237n38
50.20 237n38
50.25–51.12 237n38
54.9–10 235n29
61.8–11 240
67.14–19 237
84.1 237n38
98.14–16 237n38
101.1–7 237n38
102.23–24 237n38
115.4 237n38
119.13 237n38
125.16 237n38
133.7–8 237n38
143.2 237n38

144.4 237n38
146.2 237n38
146.24 237n38
175.24 237n38

### Commentary on Plato's Gorgias

0.1 239
0.8 239, 240n45, 240
1.1 240n45, 240
1.2 240n45
8.11 240n45
10.11 240n45
11.3 240n45
18.1 240n44, 240
25.2 240n45
41.3 235n29

## [Onatas]

### On Gods (Thesleff)

139.11–140.5 128

## Oracles, Chaldean

### Fragments (des Places)

46 206n20

## Origen

### Against Celsus

1.9 150n3
3.14 150n3
3.18 150n3
3.38 150n3

## Panaetius

### Testimonies (Alesse)

1 89n1
120 89n1
130–4 90n10
160–3 89n1

## Pausanias

### Description of Greece

1.30.2 41n10

# Index Locorum

### Philo of Alexandria

#### On the eternity of the world

14–17  108

### Philodemus

#### On piety (Obbink)

I fr. 58.1648  214n55

#### On the Stoics (Dorandi)

col. 13  71n24

#### History of the Academy (Dorandi)

col. 7  43n16
col. 15  105n44

### Philolaus (DK)

A8  119n11

### Photius

#### Library

249.438b  123, 123n23

### Plato

#### Alcibiades I

103a  236
105a–c  235n31
105c–d  235n29
106c  236

#### Apology

20e–23b  84n71
21b  85n80
21d  70n17
23a  86n81

#### Charmides

164c–165a  160

#### Cratylus

389a–390b  33n64
395e–396c  144
402a  72n28, 81n61

405b–e  161n26
409a  159n23

#### [Epinomis]

985a  26n43

#### Gorgias

484c–e  241n49
501d–502d  227n2
525b–c  238n40

#### Laws

1.624a  208n30
6  42
6.769a–c  63
6.769b–770b  41
9.875c–d  121
10  28n48, 134, 185, 191, 195–196,
    199
10.894b  195n58
10.894b–896c  180–181
10.894e–895a  181, 186n30
10.895a–b  181
10.895b  190n45
10.895c  181n9
10.896b  181n8
10.897a–c  134n13

#### Lysis

203a–b  45

#### [Minos]

319b  208n30

#### Parmenides

127b  205n17
128b  212
130a  209
133b  206n21
133b–c  205n18
135a  205n18, 206,
    206n21
135b  206–207
136d  209

#### Phaedo

62b  30n58
69c–d  216
78d–e  30n58

# Index Locorum

### Phaedrus

229a–230b 58
229e–230a 85n76
245c 27–28, 183n19, 190n45
245c–d 180, 183
245c–246a 21n26
245c–249d 23
246a 26
246b–c 21n27
246e 26n42, 36n69, 216
246e–247a 34
247a 26, 36n68
247a–c 26
247c–250c 216n64
247e 25
248b 25n37, 25
248e 31
249a–b 31
249d 212n44
250b–c 214n51
250c 221n79
253a 216n64
254b 27n46
275d 60

### Philebus

23c–e 159n23

### Politicus

301a–e 121
302e 121

### Republic

1 240, 243
3.392d–394c 233
3.394–399 227n2
3.394b–398b 239n42
4 240n44
6 24
6.485a–486e 206n21
6.498c–d 235n29
6.506d–507a 142
6.509d–513e 152
6.509e 155
6.510a 154
6.510c 155
6.510d 156
6.511a 156
6.511b 157
6.511b–c 157
6–7 32
7 24, 156

7.520b 204n10
8 236n33
8–9 239n44
9 236n33
9.588c 235
9.592b 24n36
10 236n33, 238n40
10.596a–597b 33
10.604e–606d 239n42
10.617c–d 31
10.620d–e 31

### Sophist

254b 159n23
255c 29
255c–d 109

### Symposium

202d 205n16
202d–204b 26
203d–e 26n41
203e–204b 206
206d–e 207n26
211c 152

### Theaetetus

151–187 82n67
152e 80n57, 81n61
153a 81
156a 81n62
156e–160a 81
159b–e 81n63
160d 80n60
173e 30n57
174b 85n76
183a–b 82n64
191c 76n47, 77
192a–b 77

### Timaeus

20a 56
27a 56
27d–28a 114n63
27d–28c 22n30
28a–29b 32
28b 144n52, 193n54
28c 139–140, 139n34, 145
31a 159n23
33b–40d 34
34b–36b 28
37b 25, 28n48, 30
38c–d 154n14

40d  34
41b  108
46e–47c  24
51b–52a  22n30
52a–d  24n35
53d  19
69c–71a  27n44
70a–c  44n19
90a  56
90b–c  27
92c  140n36

## Pliny

### Natural history

12.1.5  41n10

## Plotinus

### Enneads

1.8(51)  173–174
2.4(12).16.3–16  170
2.5(25).5.10–13  171
3.5(50).9.49  209n31
3.7(45)  169
3.7(45).9.10–12  170
3.7(45).11  170
3.8(30)  207
3.8(30).4.31–39  207n27
3.8(30).4.31–43  207n25
3.8(30).7.19  207n26
4.4(28).10.1  145
5.1(10).3.13–15  203n9
5.1(10).8.4  145n56
5.3(49).7.30–34  207n25
6.1(42)  168
6.1(42).3.13–16  168
6.1(42).3.19–22  168
6.1(42).16.4–8  169
6.1–3(42–44)  169
6.3(44)  168
6.3(44).15.24–38  168
6.3(44).23.21  169
6.9(9).7.21–23  207n25
6.9(9).7.23–26  208
6.9(9).7.25–26  207n25
6.9(9).7.26–28  207n27

## Plutarch

### Alcibiades

6.4  235n31
7.5  235n31

34.3  235n31
39.7  235n31

### Alexander

7  48n29
7.9  164

### Aratus

1.4  204n12

### Brutus

2.2–3  101n35

### Cicero

4  92n17

### Cimon

13.7  47n27

### Dion

1.3  204n12

### Numa

22.3  116n2

### Theseus

18.3  215n61

### How to study poetry

23A  215n61

### How to tell a flatterer from a friend

53C  41n9, 55n48
70E  201n2, 215n57

### On Isis and Osiris

369A–370C  107
370E–F  113
382D  164

### On the E at Delphi

384E  151
386A  154
386B  154

274        *Index Locorum*

386C  154
386E  155, 159
386E–387F  155
386F–387A  155
387B  155
387D  156n19
387E  155n18, 156, 156n19, 158
387E–F  156
387F  153
389F  159n23, 159
391A  159n23, 159
391B  156n21, 159n23, 159
391B–C  159n23, 159
391C  159
391E  156
391F  153n13
392A  160
393C  160, 161n26
394A–B  160
394C  161

### Abandoned oracles

416C–D  26n39

### Table talk

3.5  106n45
7.2.2  86n83
8.1.1.717A  220n72

### Platonic questions

2.1001A–B  141n38
3.1001E–F  156n20
3.1002E  152n12

### On the procreation of the soul in the Timaeus

1012D–F  108
1013B  108
1014A  150n5
1016A  21n28
1026B–D  107

### Stoic self-contradictions

1034D  72n28
1035A  95n23
1048E  241n56

### On common concepts

1059B  79
1078B–C  80n57

1083A–1084A  80n57
1083B–C  80n57
1084F–1085A  74–75
1085A  73n33, 77n50

### One can't live pleasurably

1100A  223n84

### Against Colotes

1108D–F  106n45
1110E  214n56
1116E–F  84n72
1117B  214n54
1118A  84n70
1118C  84n73, 85n75, 86n84
1118E  214n56
1120C  65n2
1121E–F  65n3
1121F  64
1121F–1122A  65
1122A–B  84
1122B  66n5
1122E–F  84n70
1124D–E  69n13

### Fragments (Sandbach)

85  59n58

## Porphyry

### Commentary on Aristotle's Categories

95.17–20  174n34

### Life of Plotinus

2.40–42  220n72
15.1–2  220n72
15.6–9  204n13
17.1–3  132n5

### Life of Pythagoras

19  117
57  116

### Fragments (Smith)

58F  174
119F  173
120F  165, 172
148aF  174
152F  174

# Index Locorum

159F 176
163F–164F 175n36
236F 176
408F 220n72
118T–162T 172n28

## Posidonius

### *Fragments* (Edelstein & Kidd)

88 95n23
186–187 89n1
190 89n1
194–195 89n1
197–214 89n1
266 89n1

## Proclus

### *Commentary on Plato's Alcibiades*

7.18–8.1 236
10.13–14 235
23.13–21 236n32
24.12 236n32
26.5–13 205n16
26.22–27.16 235n29
27.18–29.7 205n16
30.5–34.10 209n32
30.18–20 205n16
43.4–44.1 235
85.17–92.2 235n29
88.10–13 202n4
133.17–139.10 236n33
137.4–139.10 236n33
146.19 236n33
148.3 236n33
154.2–155.12 236n33
154.13–14 235n29
185.18–186.10 236
186.10–16 237
218.13–219.1 240
225.12–15 190n46
243.6–13 236n33

### *Commentary on Plato's Parmenides* (Steel)

501.4–11 17n12
617.16–618.9 217–218, 221, 226n99
618.1–2 214n50
618.2–3 221n77
618.5–6 213n48
628.1–630.10 242n51

633.22 203n9, 213n47
633.24 203n9
640.13–15 202n4
645.8–12 221n78
658.23–659.17 239n42
665.8–12 218n70
684.20–24 205n17
700.6–11 210n34
701.24–27 218n70
704.24–26 212n45
705.6–9 212, 218n70
716.1–18 212n45
884.17–20 209n31
926.3–928.22 205, 211
927.15–23 206n20
927.17 206n21
927.29–928.22 206n22
927.30–31 206
927.31–928.8 211n43
928.3–5 212n44
976.12–20 206
997.18 203n9
1021.14–17 210n34
1022.21–22 210n37
1022.24–1023.4 210, 218
1033.17–18 204n12
1061.17–25 202n4

### *Commentary on Plato's Republic*

1.5.28–7.4 233n24
1.6.24–25 234
1.7.5–14.14 234
1.14.15–15.19 233n25
1.14.15–16.25 234
1.19.25 234
1.69.23–70.7 220n73
1.69–205 220
1.71.21–27 220
1.71.24 223n86
1.115.27–28 221n77
1.123.4 204n15
1.133.5–7 222n80
1.205.21–23 220n74, 221
1.270.5 204n15
2.10.6 144n52
2.113.6–13 223n84
2.176.4–9 240n45

### *Commentary on Plato's Timaeus*

1.6.21–23 220n75
1.6.21–7.16 223n85
1.6.22–23 223n86
1.7.13–16 223n87

# 276         *Index Locorum*

1.8.30–9.13 235n30
1.16.6–12 239n42
1.61.12–15 235n29
1.279.30–280.8 193n54
1.300.8–13 139n34
1.303.27–304.3 140
1.303.27–305.16 147
1.303.27–306.15 138–139
1.304.3–5 142
1.304.13–22 141n42
1.304.25–26 142
1.304.28 142
1.305.11–16 144n51
1.305.17 145n57
1.310.4–7 226n99
1.392.28–30 143
1.393.1 143
1.439.29–440.7 175
2.221.26–28 204n12
3.174.13–15 202n4
3.204.1–3 202n4
3.247.26–28 202n4, 204n12

## *Elements of theology*

7 186n31
14 186n32, 188n38,
    196n65
14–24 186n32
18 207n24
20 188n38
28 187n36
38 210n40
56 210n40
131 206n23
211 223n88

## *Platonic theology*

1.1 202n6, 213n47–48, 217,
    223n88
1.9 217n68
1.10 208, 212, 215n61
1.14 196n65
1.25 206n20
3.14 213–214
4.5 217n67
4.23 202n4, 215–216
4.29 210n35

# Quintilian

## *Institutes of oratory*

12.10 62n61

# Scriptures

## *Matthew*

23.10 215n61

# Seneca

## *Letters*

65 171
65.4–7 165

# Sextus Empiricus

## *Against the Professors*

7.16 18n18
7.19 95n23
7.141–260 114n63
7.147–149 23
7.149 31n59
7.151–154 83n69
7.228 76n48, 77n50
7.229 77n49, 79n53
7.230 75n40
7.230–231 78
7.236 75n40
7.372–375 77n49
7.373 76n47, 79n53,
    79
7.377–380 79n54
8.400 76n48, 77n50

## *Outlines of Pyrrhonism*

1.235 92n17
2.70 77n49–50

# Simplicius

## *Commentary on Aristotle's Categories*

2.15–25 178n1
7.27–29 161
78.20–24 174

## *Commentary on Aristotle's On the heavens*

92.33–97.17 193n54
377.29–34 162
462.20 225n95

# Index Locorum

### *Commentary on Aristotle's Physics*

9.11–12  173
10.25–11.3  165, 172
10.30–31  173
11.4–5  171n27
59.23–60.1  225, 225n95
60.6  226n98
151.6–11  15n8
181.7–30  163
183.18  225n95
192.14  225n95
198.17–18  225n95
230.34–231.24  176
277.24–27  174
320.20–32  171
406.31–32  174
451.1–7  224n90
517.15–16  226n99
761.5–9  224n90
774.28–29  225n97
790–795  203n7
795.4–5  203n7
802.7–13  176
824.17–25  224n90
824.20–22  224
1077.3–5  224n90
1247.27–1250.31  189n44
1247.29–1248.3  190n45
1248.3–21  190n46
1248.21–1249.6  190
1249.6–8  191n48
1249.8–12  191n49
1249.12–13  191n50
1249.13–17  192n51
1249.32–1250.4  197
1250.5–16  198n67
1250.19–22  198n69
1250.22–31  198n71
1267.19  224
1267.20–28  224n90
1336.25–26  224n90, 224
1359.30–1360.23  192n52
1359.38–40  192n53
1359.40–1360.6  193n55
1360.24–31  224n90
1363.8–10  225n95

### Sosicrates

### *Fragments* (FHG)

fr. 20  125n31

### Speusippus

### *Testimonies and fragments* (Tarán)

T1 (2 IP)  43n16–17
T2 (1 IP)  43n16–17
T3 (3 IP)  43n16–17
T12 (19 IP)  15n6
T39a (7 IP)  43n17
T39b  43n17
F1a (147 IP)  13n3
F28 (122 IP)  15n5
F42a (53 IP)  32n61
F48 (62 IP)  17n12
F77 (101 IP)  44n19
F80a (108 IP)  44n19

### Stephanus ('Philoponus')

### *Commentary on Aristotle's On the soul*

450.20  204n10
467.4  204n10

### *Suidas*

s.v. Σπεύσιππος  43n16–17

### *SVF*

1.1  71n24
1.6  71n24
1.58  75n40
1.135  72n29
1.135–138  75n41
1.140  73n34, 75n44
1.141  72, 76n45
1.481  68n12, 73n35
1.484  76n48, 77n50
1.518  75n41
1.519  72, 76n45
1.521  73n34, 75n41
1.525  75n41
1.620  68n12
2.42  95n23
2.53  76n47
2.56  76n47, 78, 79n53
2.783  76n46
2.847  75

### Synesius

### *Letters*

154  59n58

## 278 — Index Locorum

### Taurus of Beirut

#### Texts (Petrucci)

14.7 113
24.1 113

### Theon of Smyrna

#### Mathematics Useful for Reading Plato

14.18–16.2 208n28
16.24–18.2 156n20

### Theophrastus

#### History of plants

1.7.1.8–14 58n56

#### Metaphysics

6b6–9 22

### Timaeus (historian)

#### Fragments (FGrHist)

F16 (=T9) 125

### [Timaeus of Locri]

#### On the nature of the world and the soul

206.5–7 165

### Timon of Phlius

#### Fragments (Diels)

54 119n11

### Vitruvius

#### On architecture

9.8.1 41n11

### Xenocrates

#### Testimonies and fragments (IP$^2$)

T1 32n60
T2 59n58
T46 59n58
T78 59n58
T79 59n58
F1 18n18
F2 23
F14 27n46, 32n62
F15 29n54
F16 23n33
F18 15n8
F21–22 16n10
F37 15n9
F44–71 19n21
F73–77 19n19
F85–119 27n47
F108 28n51
F126 27n44
F131 27n45
F133 16n10–11, 36n69
F138–139 30n58
F142 26n39
F143 30n55
F143–146 26n39
F154–158 27n45

### Xenophon

#### Memorabilia

1.2.24–25 234n27, 235n29

# General Index

Academic Sceptics 64, 67, 70–1, 74, 77, 87–8, 93, 105–6, 131, 135, *See also* Academy, sceptical
Academics 1, 4, 33, 87, 95, 97–101, 103, 105, 135
Academy 1, 3, 6, 11–14, 17, 23, 29, 33, 38–40, 42, 44–5, 47–9, 55–6, 59, 61–2, 82, 88–9, 91, 93, 97, 100–12, 134, 164
  Early 1–2, 4, 12, 20, 34, 91, 93, 97–8, 102–3, 106–10, 112, 128, 130, 239
  exedra 39, 42, 55–6
  Fourth 93
  gateway 50–2, 54
  grove 12, 41, 47
  Old (i.e., Antiochus') 93, 95, 97–8, 100, 102, 106, *See also* Antiochus of Ascalon
  plane tree 41, 58
  sceptical 2, 7, 66, 68–9, 84, 87–9, 91, 93, 95, 98, 100, 103, 105–7, 112, 131, 135, 230
Aenesidemus 77
*akatalēpsia* 65–6
Alcibiades (Platonic character) 209, 234–8, 240, 242
Alcinous 155, 166–7
Alexander of Aphrodisias 14, 99, 162–3, 171, 173–4, 224–5
Alexandria 107, 118, 203, 227
Alexinus 70
Allegiance 14, 202, 204, 223–4
Amelius 137
Ammonius (Plutarch's teacher) 201, 214
Ammonius (Plutarch's character) 151–62
Ammonius (Neoplatonist) 203, 222, 225–6
Anaxagoras 67, 70
*Anonymous Prolegomena to Platonic Philosophy* 10, 227, 231, 235, 237–8, 241
Antiochus of Ascalon 5–6, 18, 20, 22–3, 60, 89–114, 135
Antiphon (Platonic character) 242
Apollinaris Sidonius 48–50, 61
Apollo 84, 86, 152–3, 160–2

Apollonius of Tyana 124–5
Apuleius 90, 133, 232
*arachnē* sundial 41–2, 56, 59
Aratus 49, 56
Arcesilaus 5, 10, 62, 64–72, 76–7, 79–88, 91, 93, 103, 105–6, 133
Archytas 6, 15, 17, 43–4, 50–5, 59, 115, 119, 122–6, 128, 178, *See also* Ps.-Archytas
Aresas Lucanus 124–5
Arian controversy 138
Aristaeus (Pythagorean) 124–5
Aristo of Ceus 116
Aristo of Chios 68, 79, 99, 116
Aristombrotos (Pythagorean) 122
Aristotle 4, 8, 10, 12, 14, 17, 19–23, 25, 28–30, 33, 36–7, 42, 44–50, 59–63, 72–3, 82, 85, 89, 91, 93, 95–9, 101–4, 107–11, 114, 117, 123, 127–8, 134–5, 155, 161–77, 223–4, 226, 232
  *Categories* 163–4, 174, 178, 224, 232
  *Metaphysics* 163–4, 166, 175
  *On the Heavens* 164
  *On the Soul* 190
  *Physics* 8, 164–72, 175–6, 179, 182, 187, 189–90, 192
  *Posterior Analytics* 173
  [*De mundo*] 166
Aristoxenus 123–6
Arius Didymus 72, 75, 165, 171–2, 177
Aspasius 90
Athens 12, 38, 46, 48, 59, 61, 151, 202, 220
Atticus (Middle Platonist) 113, 132, 136, 139–40, 143–4, 146, 165–6, 170, 219
Aulus Gellius 54

Bacchus 215
Boethus of Sidon 174
Boulagoras (Pythagorean) 124
Brontinus (Pythagorean) 118, 123
Bryson (Pythagorean) 123
Butherus (Pythagorean) 123

279

## 280            *General Index*

Callicles (Platonic character) 239–43
Callicratidas (Pythagorean) 119, 121
Callippus 62
Carneades 40, 79
Categories 28–30, 109, 111, 127
   dual categorial scheme 29
Celsus 150, 161
Cephalus (Platonic character) 242
Chaerephon (Platonic character) 239
Chaeronea 151
Chaldean Oracles 132, 162, 205
Charondas (Pythagorean) 123
Christians 150, 161, 215
   Christianity 131, 214
Chrysippus 48–9, 70, 74, 77–9, 99, 121, 156, 214
Cicero 20, 64–71, 87–8, 94–5, 99–100, 106, 110, 123, 152
Cimon (Athenian politician) 47
Cleanthes 48–9, 64, 68, 71–82, 99
Clinias (Pythagorean) 119, 123–5
Colotes 64–6, 69, 84, 86, 223
consistency 4, 99, 121, 231, 233–4, 241
Crantor 20, 82, 95, 97, 101–2, 108
Crates 101
Cratylus 80
Critias (character in Plato's *Charmides*) 160
Criton (Pythagorean) 123
Ctesibius 54
Cyrenaics 65

daimons 25–7, 34
Damascius 201, 222, 225, 234
Delphi 85–6, 149, 152
demiurge 7, 32, 34, 128, 132, 137–48
Democritus 49, 65, 67, 70, 87, 222–3
Demosthenes 214
*diadochē* 6, 99, 125–6, 128, 203–4
   *diadochoi* 6, 41–2, 124, 133, 147
*diaphōnia* 102–3, 107
Dicaearchus 117
Diocles (Pythagorean) 124
Diodorus Cronus 70
Diodorus of Aspendus 124–6
Diogenes Laertius 117, 119, 123, 232
Diophanes 204
Dios (Pythagorean) 123
Diotima (Platonic character) 26
Diotogenes (Pythagorean) 122
Dipylon Gate 45
dogmatism 5, 7, 89–90, 98–9, 102, 106, 133, 229
   dogmatic authority 5, 11, 91
   dogmatics 93, 103, 114
   Heraclitus as a dogmatic philosopher 68

Plato as a dogmatic philosopher 4, 7, 89, 112, 114, 228, 230
Socrates as a dogmatic philosopher 67, 132–7
Dyad (of Plato's unwritten doctrines) 15, 17, 28–9, 32, 134

Eccelus (Pythagorean) 123
Echecrates (Pythagorean) 124
Ecphantus (Pythagorean) 122–3
Empedocles 65, 67, 70, 118
Epicharmus 80–1, 126
Epicureanism 106, 201, 204, 214, 219
Epicurean Garden 89, 100–1
Epicrates 12
Epicureans 100, 106
Epicurus 17, 49, 64, 100–1, 106, 214–15, 220, 222–3
epistemology 22, 24, 26, 30–1, 80, 82–3, 87, 90, 92, 104, 111
*epochē* 65–6, 132
ethics 18, 33, 80, 92, 95–6, 103–4, 109, 112, 127–8, 137, 203, 205, 211, 230, 239
Euclides (Megaric) 49–50
Eudemus 226
Eudorus 6, 90–1, 107–14, 128, 163–4
Eudoxus 13, 34, 36, 41–2, 49, 56, 58–9, 62
Euripides 160
Euryphamus (Pythagorean) 123
Eurytus (Pythagorean) 123–5
Eusebius 72, 75, 130–1, 133, 136–8, 141, 146
Eustrophus (Plutarch's character) 153, 155–6
Euthyphro (Platonic character) 135
exegesis 58, 91, 108, 112, 114, 140, 143–5, 148, 150, 159–60, 171, 174, 176, 202, 209, 212–13, 216, 218, 241
   allegorical 142, 232, 236–7, 240–4
   exegete 1, 20, 130, 132, 134, 137, 140, 143–5, 147, 205, 209, 215, 219, 225–6
   exegetical authority 132, 147
   exegetical method 92, 179
   exegetical strategy 9, 135, 187
   exegetical work 164, 171, 176, 202
   textual 113, 212

Favorinus 54
flux 74–5, 77–8, 80–3
Forms 13, 15–16, 18, 22, 24, 28, 32–3, 92, 99, 101–4, 111–12, 128, 130, 134, 146, 155–6, 173, 175, 197, 208–9, 216
   of artefacts 33
   founder 4–6, 12, 14–15, 20–1, 44, 50, 94, 97–104, 112–13, 115, 130, 149, 162, 204, 209, 214

## General Index

Galen 15, 76, 116, 156, 201, 211
Gartydas (Pythagorean) 124
god 1, 16, 19, 23, 25–7, 34, 36, 63, 86, 128, 130–1, 133–47, 153, 157, 160–1, 166, 205, 208–10, 213–19
Gorgias (Platonic character) 239
Growing Argument 80

Hadrian (Emperor) 47
Harpocration (Middle Platonist) 139–40, 142–6
*hēgemonikon* 74, 76, 78
Heraclea 124
Heraclides Lembus 117
Heraclides Ponticus 39, 122
Heraclitus 5, 11, 49, 64–88, 160
Herculaneum 215
Herillus 99
Hermias of Alexandria 9, 36, 60, 62, 179–80, 183–91, 194–7, 199–200, 216
Hermodorus 29
Hesiod 142
Hieronymus (Peripatetic) 96, 101, 106
Hippasus 118
Hippocrates of Chios 225
Hippothales (Platonic character) 45
Homer 80–1, 160, 208, 220, 233, 241, 243
hylomorphism 128, 164–5, 170–1, 173–4, 177

Iamblichus 6, 122–3, 125–6, 137, 178–9, 182, 202–4, 217, 226, 232–3, 235, 244
Isidorus (Damascius' teacher) 222
Isocrates 43

*kathēgemōn* 9, 11, 100, 201–26
*kathēgētēs* 201, 214–15
Kronos 142

Lamprias (Plutarch's brother and character) 152–4, 157
logic 18, 127, 154, 158, 205, 212, 222
Longinus 220
Lucania 123
Lucullus (Cicero's character) 67, 69, 106
Lyceum 13, 33, 42–8, 58, 62

Marcus Aurelius 68
mathematics 24, 32, 54–5, 153, 156, 158, 205, 208
  arithmetic 14, 24, 28, 34, 153, 156
  astronomical calculations 36
  astronomical doctrines 61
  astronomical lesson 39
  astronomy 23–4, 27, 30–1, 34, 56, 153
  celestial 34, 58
  geometry 14, 24, 153, 155–6, 173

harmonics 24
  mathematical intermediates 24, 34
  mathematical terms 16
  mathematicals 22, 24
  music 90, 156
  stereometry 156
Melissus 65
metaphysics 8–9, 14, 17–18, 32–4, 144, 173, 175, 203, 205, 209, 213–14, 223, 243–4
Metapontum 124
Metopus (Pythagorean) 119, 123
Metrodorus of Lampsacus 214
Middle Platonism 1–2, 7–9, 63, 90–1, 111–14, 128, 132, 163, 166, 179, 219, 230, 241, 244
Minos 208
Mnemarchus (Pythagorean) 124
Moderatus 176
Mosaic of the Philosophers 33, 35–6, 38–63
Moses 131
mover
  celestial 33, 36, 62–3
  divine 58, 61, 128
  first 176, 180–1, 183, 186
  unmoved 36, 62, 181–3, 186, 188–9, 195–6
Myia (Pythagorean) 122
mystagogy 213–14

Neanthes of Cyzicus 117
Neoplatonism 1–2, 8–10, 137, 163, 179, 202, 208–9, 214
Nicander (Plutarch's character) 153–4
Numenius 7, 60, 68, 113, 127, 130–48, 150

Ocellus (Pythagorean) 123
Olympeion 47
Olympiodorus 10, 227–8, 231–2, 234, 237, 239–41
Onatas (Pythagorean) 123
One
  Neoplatonic principle 132, 141, 144–6, 188, 206, 221
  Plato's unwritten doctrines 15, 17–18, 28–9, 32, 134
optics 173
Origen 244
orthodoxy 100, 203–4, 223
Ouranos 142–3

Pamphilus (Epicurus' teacher) 17
Panaetius 116
Parmenides 17, 64–6, 69–70, 81, 212
Parmenides (Platonic character) 17, 205–6, 209–11, 213, 216, 218, 221, 242
Pempelus (Pythagorean) 122

## 282           *General Index*

Pentheus 134
Pergamon 215
Peripatetics 14, 95, 97–8, 100, 103
Peripatos 14, 82, 89, 98–9, 104, 106
Phanto (Pythagorean) 124
Pherecydes 204
Philip of Opus 39, 56
Philo of Alexandria 108
Philo of Larissa 89, 98, 100, 105–6, 108, 112
Philodemus 43, 89–90, 107, 214
Philolaus 15, 17, 119–20, 123–5
Phyntis (Pythagorean) 122
physics 8, 18, 20, 68, 71, 80, 90, 101, 165,
    171–7
Pindar 160
Pisistratus 47
Piso (Cicero's character) 92, 95–7, 100–1
Platonic dialogues 4–5, 9–11, 13, 20, 41, 114,
    230, 244
   *Alcibiades I* 201, 204, 209, 233, 235, 238,
     240, 243–4
   *Apology of Socrates* 84–6
   *Charmides* 160–1
   *Cratylus* 33, 159
   *[Epinomis]* 56
   *Euthyphro* 135–6
   *Gorgias* 233, 239–44
   *Laws* 42, 56, 190
   *Lysis* 46
   *Parmenides* 11, 17, 132, 141, 145–7, 202,
    205, 209, 212–14, 216–17, 221–2, 225,
    233, 242–4
   *Phaedo* 30, 180, 204
   *Phaedrus* 4, 10, 21–37, 42, 58, 60–2, 142,
    179, 183, 190, 216–17
   *Philebus* 17, 159
   *Republic* 24, 30–3, 142, 150, 205, 207, 219,
    225, 233–4, 239–40, 243
   *[Second Letter]* 135
   *Sophist* 29, 153, 159
   *Symposium* 30, 152, 154, 207, 235
   *Theaetetus* 5, 11, 30, 64, 68, 76–7, 79–87
   *Timaeus* 4, 8, 10, 16, 18–37, 42, 119, 132,
    136, 140, 142, 159–60, 165, 175–7, 185,
    192, 213, 223–4, 233
Plotinus 8, 99, 132, 137, 139, 144–7, 163–74,
    177, 182, 202–4, 207–8, 223, 230
Plutarch 7, 11, 59, 64–6, 69–80, 82–7, 90, 101,
    103, 106–8, 113, 116, 133, 136, 138, 141,
    149–62, 164, 183, 201, 214, 235
   Younger (character of the *De E*) 153–61
*pneuma* 74–80
Polemo 20, 40, 61, 95–6, 101–6, 239
Polus (Platonic character) 239–42
Polymnastus (Pythagorean) 124

Pomponius (Cicero's character) 101
Porphyry 8–9, 29, 117, 139–40, 143, 164–5,
    169, 171–7, 179, 182, 193, 202, 204, 211,
    215
Posidonius 95, 116
post-Hellenistic Platonism *See* Middle Platonism
Potamo of Alexandria 90
Presocratics 65, 68–70, 87, 115
Proclus 7, 9, 17, 119, 130, 132, 137–47, 186–8,
    190, 193, 195–6, 201–26
Protagoras 85
Ps.-Archytas 118–27
Ps.-Elias 211
Ps.-Timaeus 119, 165
Psellus 142
psychology 18, 180 *See also* Soul
Pyrrhonists 106
Pythagoras 6–7, 94, 110, 115–20, 123–4, 126,
    131–6, 147, 204
Pythagoreanism 15, 17, 43, 60, 110, 116, 121,
    123, 126–8, 134, 136
   Platonist-Pythagorean tradition 129, 133
   Pseudo-Pythagorean corpus 6, 110, 115,
    117–21, 123–4, 126–8, 164
   Pythagorean doctrine 123–4, 126, 129, 134
   Pythagorean leanings 17, 164
   Pythagorean scholarchs 124–6
   Pythagorean source 58, 134
   Pythagorean tradition 115, 126
   Pythagorean women 122
   Pythagoreans 6, 15, 17, 94, 110, 115, 118,
    120, 123–8, 133–4, 163
Pythodorus (Platonic character) 242

Quintilian 62

Rhegium 124
Rome 118

Sarapion 151
Sarsina mosaic 38, 50, 52–5
scepticism 54, 69, 87–9, 93, 103, 105, 108, 112,
    114, 131, 150
   sceptical shift 5
   sceptical source 85–6
   sceptical tradition 5
scholarch 4, 40, 123, 161, 220
Seneca 165, 172
Serenus 142
Sextus Empiricus 22, 24, 30–1, 92
Sicily 123
Siminius Stephanus 38
Simplicius 9, 15, 29, 161–2, 171–2, 178–80,
    182, 189–95, 198–200, 222–6
*skopos* 202, 205, 209, 231–5, 238

# General Index

Socrates 5, 7, 48, 61, 64–7, 69, 71, 83–6, 100, 110, 123, 131–3, 135–6, 147, 203, 219–20, 234
  Socratism 135
Socrates (Platonic character) 17, 33, 45, 68, 84, 86, 135, 142, 160, 201, 204–5, 209–13, 222, 227–8, 230, 234–7, 239–43
Solon 39
Sophocles 160
Sophocles of Sunium 59
Sosicrates 116, 125
Sotion 117
soul 16, 21, 24, 26–7, 30–1, 36, 38, 61, 68, 71, 80, 82–3, 86, 142, 212, 216–19, 224, 235, 237–43
  as a daimon 27
  as a self-moving number 27–8
  disembodied 23
  self-moving 9, 28, 178–200
  Stoic theory of 71–9
  tripartite 18, 26–7, 44, 237, 239
  undescended 223
  world soul 16, 21, 24–5, 30, 134, 140, 145, 166, 170, 207
  Xenocrates' theory of 25–8
Speusippus 4, 10, 13–15, 17, 19, 22–3, 28–9, 32, 39, 42–4, 48–51, 55, 58–62, 95, 97, 100–3, 106, 111
Sphaerus 68
Stephanus of Alexandria 203
Stesichorus 160
Sthenidas (Pythagorean) 122–3
Stilpo 65, 70
Stobaeus 107, 241
Stoics 5–6, 10, 14, 64, 66, 68, 71, 74–7, 79–82, 90, 93–5, 97–9, 103–4, 109, 111, 156
Strato 95–6, 99, 101
Synesius 59
Syracuse 126
Syrianus 132, 139, 145–7, 202, 204, 208–9, 212–13, 215–23, 225–6, 243
system 4–6, 10, 13, 18, 20, 28, 30, 34, 36, 38, 60–3, 68, 80, 90–114, 120–1, 127–8, 147, 241–2, 244

Tarentum 122, 124
Taurus of Beirut 113, 136, 166, 193, 241
teacher 8–9, 11, 17, 46, 54, 102, 131–2, 135–6, 139, 144, 150–2, 158, 201–4, 206–8, 210–26, 231–2, 237, 244
Telauges (Pythagorean) 118
Thales 39
Theages (Pythagorean) 119
Theano (Pythagorean) 124
Thearides (Pythagorean) 124
Theodorus 217
theology 7, 128, 130–3, 135–7, 139, 147, 205, 208
Theon (Plutarch's character) 153–6, 159, 208
Theon of Smyrna 156, 207–8, 214
Theophrastus 13–14, 22–5, 47, 82, 95–104
Thrasymachus (Platonic character) 235, 238–42
Thucydides 214
Tiberius Gracchus 67
Timaeus of Tauromenium 125
Timaeus (Platonic character) 18, 21, 24, 30, 34, 48, 56, 58–9

Varro (Cicero's character) 70, 100, 105
Varro (historical figure) 100

William of Moerbeke 17, 210

Xenocrates 4–6, 9–11, 12–37, 59–61, 91, 95, 101–3, 106, 108, 111
Xenophanes 67
Xenophilus (Pythagorean) 124
Xenophon 235

Zaleucus (Pythagorean) 123
Zeno (Platonic character) 205, 209–11, 213, 216–18, 222, 242
Zeno of Citium 49, 64, 66–8, 70–6, 79–80, 82, 87, 91, 99, 102–4, 134
Zeno of Elea 212
Zeus 15–16, 26, 36, 47, 142, 208, 216

Printed in the United States
By Bookmasters